From Trent to Vatican II

Historical and Theological Investigations

RAYMOND F. BULMAN and
FREDERICK J. PARRELLA, editors

Foreword by JILL RAITT

OXFORD
UNIVERSITY PRESS

2006

OXFORD
UNIVERSITY PRESS

Oxford University Press, Inc., publishes works that further
Oxford University's objective of excellence
in research, scholarship, and education.

Oxford   New York
Auckland   Cape Town   Dar es Salaam   Hong Kong   Karachi
Kuala Lumpur   Madrid   Melbourne   Mexico City   Nairobi
New Delhi   Shanghai   Taipei   Toronto

With offices in
Argentina   Austria   Brazil   Chile   Czech Republic   France   Greece
Guatemala   Hungary   Italy   Japan   Poland   Portugal   Singapore
South Korea   Switzerland   Thailand   Turkey   Ukraine   Vietnam

Published by Oxford University Press, Inc.
198 Madison Avenue, New York, New York 10016

www.oup.com

Oxford is a registered trademark of Oxford University Press

Library of Congress Cataloging-in-Publication Data
From Trent to Vatican II : historical and theological investigations /
    Raymond F. Bulman and Frederick J. Parrella, editors; foreword by
    Jill Raitt.
        p. cm.
    Includes index.
    ISBN-13 978-0-19-517806-7; 978-0-19-517807-4 (pbk.)
    ISBN 0-19-517806-8; 0-19-517807-6 (pbk.)
        1. Catholic Church—Doctrines—History—Modern period, 1500–2.
    Vatican Council (2nd : 1962–1965) 3. Council of Trent (1545–1563)
        I. Bulman, Raymond F., 1933–   II. Parrella, Frederick J.
    BX8301962 .T74 2006
    262'.52—dc22   2005017167

9 8 7 6 5 4 3 2 1

Printed in the United States of America
on acid-free paper

To John Macquarrie and Ewert Cousins
Mentors extraordinaires

Foreword

A creative and healthy tension between conservatives and progressives serves to keep both secular and ecclesiastical governments strong and viable. This tension, however, becomes unhealthy when either side hardens its views into absolutes that prevent the give-and-take of dialogue. Since the Second Vatican Council, the debate concerning its meaning and mandate threatens at times to become shrill and to lack a constructive and necessary civility. To keep different interpretations in not only a civil but also a productive exchange with regard to the two great councils, Trent (between 1545 and 1563) and Vatican II (1962–1965), few things serve better than balanced historical analyses that answer critical questions such as these: What happened before and after Trent? What was Trent's primary purpose? How well did it succeed? The same inquiries need to be made of Vatican II, with the addition of one other fundamental and multifaceted question: In what ways did Vatican II build on Trent, and in what ways did it extend or change Trent's direction?

The essays in this volume attempt to address these basic questions as well as concentrate on specific aspects of Catholic life affected by both councils, including the Eucharist, liturgical music, the laity, marriage, confession, and devotion to the Virgin Mary. The authors accept both councils as legitimate ecumenical councils duly convoked by a reigning Roman Pontiff and attended by a majority— in the case of Vatican II, an overwhelming majority—of active bishops. The contributors understand that their task is to strictly adhere to scholarly standards that preclude special pleading for either conservatives or progressives. Their hope is to facilitate discussion about the direction of the post–Vatican II Church. None of these scholars thinks that either reversion or aversion to Trent will help the Roman Catholic Church as it moves into the twenty-first century.

Each of the authors in this volume has established a record of scholarship in the particular issues he or she engages; not a few are renowned experts on their subjects. They have consulted primary documents and other respected historians and theologians. Some summarize current scholarship; others break new ground—for example, John W. O'Malley and Anthony M. Stevens-Arroyo. John O'Malley's work on Roman rhetoric and on the Roman Catholic Church in the sixteenth century allows him to see the different styles of Trent and Vatican II as part of the different goals and methods of the two councils. Trent's object was reform, and its language was primarily legislative and juridical. Vatican II's object was renewal, and its language was primarily poetic, working through image and metaphor, and almost sacramental in character.

Using documents only recently made available, Stevens-Arroyo brings material theology to bear on the often facile judgments of some historians and commentators concerning the situation in the Americas at the time of the Council of Trent and during the following century. By "material theology," Stevens-Arroyo means a theology based on what people were actually doing rather than what theologians were thinking at the time. While some readers may want to question several of his more controversial positions, I am certain that no one will argue with the fresh portrait of the contributions of the dynamic mixture of indigenous and Spanish peoples and cultures that made the baroque era in the Americas so different from its European counterpart.

The most visible, audible, and therefore neuralgic changes of Vatican II occurred in the liturgy, its language, its music, and the degree of participation by laity. Sonorous Latin, often supported by the remarkably apt Gregorian chant, united text and music in a meditative flow that may never be equaled. Nevertheless, to move laypeople from passive observers of a distant liturgical drama in a language they could not understand to vibrant participants in the liturgy required the use of the vernacular. Gerard S. Sloyan's account of the use and the demise of Latin in the West may help those who miss the "old" Mass to understand why the change was necessary and inevitable. Liturgists have spoken of the need for the Church to subsidize qualified musicians to assure that the Church's music goes beyond the adaptation of nineteenth-century Protestant hymns. The creativity of folk and spiritual music has added to the post–Vatican II repertoire, but one hopes for continuing musical inspiration to accompany a more participatory liturgy.

In one of the more provocative essays, Robert J. Daly combs through the language and context of the two councils on the Mass as a sacrifice. He focuses on the role of the priest and his position with regard to the risen Christ and the Church as the Body of Christ on Earth. Emblematic of the priest's role is the location of the altar. When the priest's back was turned to the congregation, his position was clearly that of a mediator between the people and God; he was a second Christ (*alter Christus*), standing in the person of Christ (*in persona Christi*) by virtue of his ordination and liturgical function. The language of the Council of Trent reinforces this view of the priest. In stipulating that celebrants face the people, Vatican II required that altars be moved out from the back wall of the sanctuary, toward the congregation. The altar now reflects its character not only as a place of sacrifice but also as a table around which God's children gather for the Supper of the Lord. The place of the priest, who leads the people through the liturgy of the Mass, is to stand also as the leader of the Church (*in persona Christi capitis ecclesiae*). Daly finds that this "consensus position of contemporary liturgical theology" of the priest's role during Mass has not been maintained in later papal documents. After analyzing the major theologies of the sacrifice of the Mass between Trent and Vatican II, he indicts the present magisterium of the Church on four points stressed by Vatican II: (1) Trinitarian perspective, (2) ecclesiological perspective, (3) the role of the participating faithful, and (4) the eschatological goal of the Eucharist.

In short prefatory remarks such as these, it is neither possible nor necessary to comment further on the individual contributions of each of the book's authors. I hope that the sampling provided above will encourage the reader to proceed further into the volume. However, I would like to quote directly from one of the remaining authors, Joseph A. Komonchak, who in his comprehensive study of the continuity between the two councils illustrates the objective balance and fairness that characterize the entire collection. He concludes his own study as follows: "There is no point at which Vatican II departs from any dogmatic teaching of the Council of Trent, but at Vatican II, Trent and its problematic ceased to serve as the supreme touchstone of faith. The tradition was no longer read in the light of Trent; Trent was read in the light of the tradition."

Together the various contributors offer a veritable banquet of essays that are scholarly and objective, yet understandable by theologians and non-theologians alike. This collection will be of special interest to all readers who seek a better understanding of the continuities and discontinuities between the Council of Trent and the Second Vatican Council and a clearer picture of the new style, the new vision, that Vatican II presented to the faithful—a vision that continues to carry them into the third millennium.

Jill Raitt
Professor Emerita of Religious Studies
University of Missouri–Columbia

Acknowledgments

The editors wish to express their special appreciation:

To the University Seminars at Columbia University for their assistance in the preparation of the manuscript for publication and for providing opportunities in the University Seminar on Studies in Religion for airing some of the ideas presented in this book. To Professor Robert Belknap, director of the Seminars, for his confidence in the outcome of the enterprise.

To Cynthia Read, Executive Editor of Oxford University Press, for her support, her patience, her guidance, and her gracious professional advice.

To St. John's University for providing both time and support for the project. In particular, to Sister Mary Ann Spanjers and to Carla Funk for their skillful and enthusiastic help in research.

To Gabriella Coccia Roy and Emily Michelson for their painstaking and expert work on translation and to Frances Fico of St. John's University and Victoria Gonzalez of Santa Clara University for their cheerful and reliable assistance in communicating with contributors and in the timely circulation of documents.

To Rev. Gerard S. Sloyan for his warm encouragement of the project from the beginning and to Rev. Frederick Cwiekowski, Rev. Thomas A. Lynch, and Rev. Michael Fahey for both their helpful suggestions and their strong commendation of the volume.

To Professor Jill Raitt of the University of Missouri for gracing the book with her Foreword and for the many valuable suggestions she made to the editors.

To John Macquarrie and Ewert Cousins, our former mentors, in grateful appreciation of the rich theological legacy they have given us. To them we also gladly dedicate this volume.

Finally, to our loved ones, friends, and colleagues who have provided continuous support and helpful advice throughout the long process of publication.

Contents

Contributors

Raymond F. Bulman is professor of Systematic Theology and Religious Studies at Saint John's University, Jamaica, New York. He holds a graduate degree in theology from the Gregorian University and earned his Ph.D. at Columbia University in 1973. He is the author of *A Blueprint for Humanity: Paul Tillich's Theology of Culture*, winner of the Choice Award as best academic book in religion for 1981 (Bucknell University Press, 1981), and *The Lure of the Millennium: The Year 2000 and Beyond* (Orbis, 1999). He has published widely in scholarly journals, such as *Journal of Church and State*, *Dialog*, and *Theology Today*. Since 1993, he has chaired the Columbia University Seminar on Studies in Religion.

Frederick J. Parrella, Associate Professor of Theology in the Religious Studies Department at Santa Clara University, Santa Clara, California, received his doctorate from Fordham University in 1974. He has published in *Lumen Vitae, Communio, Spirituality Today, Proceedings of the Catholic Theological Society of America, Dialog*, and *Lectionary Homiletics*. He has also contributed chapters to the three volumes in the series Tillich Studien from the International Symposium on Paul Tillich, held biannually in Frankfurt, Germany, and is the editor of *Paul Tillich's Theological Legacy: Spirit and Community* (Walter de Gruyter, 1995).

Professors Bulman and Parrella have previously co-edited two scholarly volumes: *Paul Tillich: A New Catholic Assessment* (Liturgical Press, 1994) and *Religion in the New Millennium: Theology in the Spirit of Paul Tillich* (Mercer University Press, 2001).

Giuseppe Alberigo is Professor Emeritus of Church History at the University of Bologna. He is director of the Institute for the Religious Sciences at Bologna, where he is also the principal investigator for various research projects on the history of Vatican Council II and the issue of conciliarity in the Christian churches. He is the editor of the quarterly journal *Cristianesimo nella Storia* and has published widely on Church councils and ecumenism. His most recent book, *Dalla Laguna al Tevere: Angelo Giuseppe Roncalli da San Marco a San Pietro* (Il Mulino, 2000), is a study of the papacy of Pope John XXIII. His other publications examine the conciliarist movement, the history of Vatican II, and doctrinal developments on Church authority.

James J. Boyce, O. Carm., received his Ph.D. in historical musicology from New York University in 1984 and is currently Assistant Professor of Music at Fordham University. He has published extensively on the medieval chant tradition of the Carmelite Order and the medieval choir books of the cathedral of Salamanca, Spain, besides giving numerous conference papers and publishing articles in the area of chant scholarship. In addition to his academic work, Fr. Boyce has served in Carmelite parishes for many years, including nine years as pastor of St. Therese of Lisieux Church in Cresskill, New Jersey.

Robert J. Brancatelli is an Assistant Professor in the Religious Studies Department and the Graduate School of Counseling Psychology, Education, and Pastoral Ministries at Santa Clara University, Santa Clara, California, where he teaches courses in catechesis, liturgy, and the catechumenate. He holds a Ph.D. from The Catholic University of America. He has published articles on Hispanic popular religion in *Worship* and *Pastoral Music*, and on transformative catechesis in *Horizons*, the annual volume of the College Theology Society (2003). He has been awarded several grants for research on catechesis and liturgical enculturation in El Salvador and Guatemala.

Lawrence S. Cunningham is John A. O'Brien Professor of Theology at the University of Notre Dame. Honored by the university three times for teaching, he is the author or editor of twenty books and is a frequent lecturer in the United States and abroad. A longtime contributor to journals of opinion, he also sits on a number of editorial boards of scholarly presses and journals. His most recent book is *A Brief History of Saints* (Blackwell, 2004).

Robert J. Daly, S.J., is Professor Emeritus of Theology at Boston College. He received the D.Theol. degree from the Julius Maximilians Universität, Würzburg, in 1972. He has served for many years as chairperson of the Theology Department at Boston College, as well as shorter terms as director of the Jesuit Institute there and as editor of *Theological Studies*. His research foci have been in systematic and fundamental theology and, more recently, in liturgical theology. He has been the author, editor, or translator of fifteen scholarly books and several dozen research articles. Recently, he has published three articles in *Theological Studies*: "Robert Bellarmine and Post-Tridentine Eucharistic Theology" (2000), "Sacrifice Unveiled or Sacrifice Revisited" (2003), and "Eucharistic Origins: From the New Testament to the Liturgies of the Golden Age"

(2005). At present, he is preparing a book on Christian sacrifice based on the liturgical theology of Edward Kilmartin, S.J.

Jeannine Hill Fletcher is an Assistant Professor of Theology at Fordham University. She received her Th.D. from Harvard Divinity School in 2001 and wrote her dissertation on theologies of religious pluralism, assessing the projects of Karl Rahner and George Lindbeck through the lens of feminist and postcolonial theory. Her most recent work, *Monopoly on Salvation? A Feminist Response to Religious Pluralism* (Continuum, 2005), reclaims Rahner's theology of God's incomprehensibility in a feminist theology of religious pluralism. Her published articles include "Shifting Identity: The Contribution of Feminist Thought to Theologies of Religious Pluralism," *Journal of Feminist Studies in Religion* (2003); and "Karl Rahner's Principles of Ecumenism as Resources for Contemporary Religious Pluralism," in *Horizons*, the annual publication of the College Theology Society (2001).

Doris Gottemoeller, R.S.M., holds a Ph.D. in theology from Fordham University and is the Senior Vice President for Mission and Values Integration of Catholic Healthcare Partners. She served as chair of the Board of Trustees of the Catholic Health Association. Her leadership experiences in religious life include serving as president of the Sisters of Mercy of the Americas, as president of the Leadership Conference of Women Religious, as an auditor at the 1994 Synod on Consecrated Life, and as a U.S. delegate to the International Union of Superiors General. She has lectured and published extensively on questions of ecclesiology, ministry, health care, and religious life in the United States and abroad.

James F. Keenan, S.J., Professor of Theological Ethics at Boston College, received his doctorate from the Gregorian University (1988). His newest book is *The Works of Mercy: The Heart of Catholicism* (Rowman & Littlefield, 2005). Earlier works include *Goodness and Rightness in Thomas Aquinas's Summa Theologiae* (Georgetown University Press, 1992); *Virtues for Ordinary Christians* (Sheed & Ward, 1996); *Commandments of Compassion* (Sheed & Ward, 1999); *Jesus and Virtue Ethics*, with Dan Harrington (Sheed & Ward, 2002); and, more recently, *Moral Wisdom: Lessons and Texts from the Catholic Tradition* (Rowman & Littlefield, 2004). He edited *Practice What You Preach: Virtues, Ethics and Power in the Lives of Pastoral Ministers and Their Congregations* (Marquette University Press, 2000) and *Catholic Ethicists on HIV/AIDS Prevention* (Continuum, 2000). He has published more than 200 essays, articles, and reviews in over twenty-five international journals. He is the editor of the series Moral Traditions, published by Georgetown University Press.

Joseph A. Komonchak is a priest of the Archdiocese of New York and holds the John and Gertrude Hubbard Chair in Religious Studies at The Catholic University of America. Ordained in 1963, he received his Licentiate in Sacred Theology at the Gregorian University, Rome, in 1964 and his Ph.D. at Union Theological Seminary, New York, in 1976. He taught theology at St. Joseph's

Seminary, Dunwoodie, New York, from 1967 to 1977, when he joined the faculty of the Department of Religion and Religious Education at The Catholic University of America, where he teaches courses on ecclesiology, modern theology, the thought of John Courtney Murray, and the history and theology of Vatican II. He was the principal editor of the *New Dictionary of Theology* (Michael Glazier, 1987) and is the editor of the English-language edition of the *History of Vatican II* (Orbis, 1995–2003), of which four of the five volumes have appeared. A collection of his essays was published as *Foundations in Ecclesiology* (Boston College, 1995).

Paul Lakeland teaches at Fairfield University in Fairfield, Connecticut, where he holds the Aloysius P. Kelley, S.J., Chair of Catholic Studies. He is the author of six books, the latest of which is *The Liberation of the Laity: In Search of an Accountable Church* (Continuum, 2003), which won the Catholic Press Association 2004 Award for the Best Book in Theology, and of over fifty articles on ecclesiology, religion and politics, and the intersections of theology with cultural and critical theory. He currently serves as chairperson of the Theology and Religious Reflection Section of the American Academy of Religion, and is co-convener of the Work Group for Constructive Theology, an independent ecumenical association of systematic and constructive theologians.

W. David Myers, Associate Professor of History at Fordham University, received his Ph.D. in religious studies from Yale University. His work ranges widely, from religion in the Reformation and Catholic Reformation to the history of crime and women in early modern Europe. He has published *"Poor, Sinning Folk": Confession and Conscience in Counter-Reformation Germany* (Cornell University Press, 1996). Currently he is completing a historical account of infanticide, torture, and injustice in seventeenth-century Germany, *Death and a Maiden: The Tragical Tale of Margarethe Schmidt, Infanticide*. Myers has been awarded fellowships by the National Endowment for the Humanities, the Herzog August Bibliothek, and the German Academic Exchange Service.

John W. O'Malley, S.J., is Distinguished Professor of Church History at the Weston Jesuit School of Theology in Cambridge, Massachusetts. He received his doctorate in history in 1966 from Harvard University and he has written extensively on various aspects of the religious culture of early modern Europe, especially Italy. His best-known book is *The First Jesuits*, published in 1993 by Harvard University Press and translated into six languages; his most recent is *Four Cultures of the West*, published by Harvard in 2004. He is a Fellow of the American Academy in Rome (Prix de Rome); Fellow of Villa I Tatti, Florence; Fellow of the American Academy of Arts and Sciences (elected 1995); member of the American Philosophical Society (elected 1997); and member of the Accademia di San Carlo, Milan (elected 2002). He has received a number of awards for his books and his scholarship, including the Paul Oskar Kristeller Prize for Lifetime Achievement, bestowed in 2005 by the Renaissance Society of America.

Kenan B. Osborne, O.F.M., is Professor Emeritus of Systematic Theology at the Franciscan School of Theology, Graduate Theological Union, Berkeley, California. He received his D.Theol. from Ludwig Maximilians Universität, Munich, Germany, and has taught at the Graduate Theological Union since 1968. He is past President of the Catholic Theological Society of America and is an associate editor of *Journal of Ecumenical Studies*; he has written extensively on the sacraments, the priesthood, and lay ministry.

William P. Roberts received his Licentiate in Theology from the Weston School of Theology, and his doctorate in theology from Marquette University. He is Professor of Theology at the University of Dayton, and the author/editor of fourteen books, including *Marriage: Sacrament of Hope and Challenge* (St. Anthony Messenger Press, 1983); *Partners in Intimacy: Living Christian Marriage Today*, written with his wife, Challon (Paulist Press, 1988); *Thorny Issues: Theological and Pastoral Reflections* (Nova Science, 2000); and *Prayers for Reflective Christians* (University of Dayton, 2003). He has lectured widely on topics relating to marriage and family and to spousal and parental spirituality.

Gerard S. Sloyan is a priest of the Diocese of Trenton and Professor Emeritus of Religion at Temple University. He is currently teaching at The Catholic University of America and Georgetown University. He is the author of many books and articles, the most recent book being *Preaching from the Lectionary: An Exegetical Commentary* (Fortress, 2004).

Anthony M. Stevens-Arroyo is Professor of Puerto Rican and Latino Studies at Brooklyn College and Distinguished Scholar of the City University of New York. Widely published in both English and Spanish, he has written more than forty scholarly articles and nine books, including the four-volume PARAL series on religion among Latinos/as. His book *Prophets Denied Honor: An Anthology on the Hispano Church of the United States*, ed. with María E. Sánchez (Orbis, 1980), is considered a "landmark of Catholic literature." With his spouse, Ana María Díaz-Stevens, he wrote *Recognizing the Latino Religious Resurgence in U.S. Religion* (Westview Press, 1998), which was named an Outstanding Academic Book for 1998 by *Choice* magazine. A spokesperson for civil and human rights, he has testified before the U.S. Congress and the United Nations, and was named by President Jimmy Carter to the Advisory Board of the U.S. Commission on Civil Rights for two terms. Presently, he directs the Research Center for Religion in Society and Culture (RISC).

From Trent to Vatican II

under way, the Protestant/Catholic divide had hardened through the development of more radical theological differences and the proliferation of mutual condemnations from both sides. For this reason, Pope Paul III did not look to Trent as a council of union. His more modest and probably more realistic goal in convoking the Council was to clarify the doctrines that "defined the boundaries between Catholic and Protestant thought" and to work toward the reform of those many abuses which damaged the Catholic Church from within and provided the Reformers with grounds for grievance from without.[2]

While historians still differ as to what extent the reforms and decrees of Trent were a direct response to the challenges of the Protestant Reformation, there can be no doubt that a genuine and powerful movement toward reform had been active within the Catholic Church, especially throughout the fifteenth century. This ongoing and persistent effort without doubt provided much of the background for the reforms that were actually proposed or legislated at the Council of Trent.

Certainly, a significant reform of the religious orders in both Italy and Spain had been well under way since the middle of the fifteenth century. A good example of such reform was the work of a Dominican, Antonino Pierozzi, in Florence, who even as a young friar had been a powerful force in rebuilding the strict observance of the Dominican way of life. In 1436, he established the famous convent of San Marco, which later in the century would become the main center for Savonarola's reform efforts. It was on the basis of his reputation for monastic reform that Pierozzi was appointed Archbishop of Florence by Eugenius IV in 1444. This trust placed in him had not been in vain, for in the exercise of his office he distinguished himself in untiring pastoral care for his people, especially for the poor. This outstanding pastoral commitment was perhaps most conspicuously expressed through his persistent residence in his diocese—a sharp contrast to the widespread abuse of episcopal absenteeism, a practice that would remain the most controversial and hotly disputed focus of the Church reforms of the Council of Trent.[3] In addition to the far-reaching Dominican reforms, similar renewals were taking place among the Camaldolese monks, the Benedictines, and the Observant Franciscans. It was the Camaldolese order, for example, that provided Pope Leo X with the strongest support for his efforts at reform during the Lateran Council in 1516.

Apart from these significant monastic efforts at renewal, the Catholic reform movement was very much influenced and inspired by growing schools of spirituality also with roots in the fifteenth century. Most notable among these was the *devotio moderna*, a highly influential movement of Flemish and Netherlandish spirituality, which emphasized the discipline of contemplative prayer and which also had a deep impact on the piety of the southern Catholic countries, especially Italy and Spain. This northern school of devotion was joined by an even older monastic tradition of meditation and mysticism coming especially from the Franciscan and Carthusian traditions. Together they helped

form a very powerful backdrop to the spiritual foundations of Tridentine reform and the inner renewal that quickly followed in its wake. The culmination
of this pre-Reformation religious renewal probably found its clearest expression in the *Spiritual Exercises* of St. Ignatius of Loyola, though Ignatius was
inclined to put much less stress on the mystical or contemplative tradition than
he did on conversion and the active life.[4]

The pre-Tridentine reform movement, however, was not limited to the
devotional and spiritual areas of Catholic life. Far more dramatic and controversial attempts at reform occurred at the institutional level, with attempts to
correct rampant abuses among the hierarchy, with special attention to the papal
court. The leaders of Catholic reform were convinced that true reform could
not succeed if it did not include the papacy. The battle cry, as it were, was
reformatio in capite et in membris. The principal abuses among the higher clergy
had to do with regular appointments of unworthy bishops or priests for the
sake of gaining lucrative benefices from established churches or accumulating
revenues (prebends) from cathedrals or monasteries. The papacy was often in
indirect complicity with these abuses through its own array of nepotistic practices. No doubt the most flagrant and spiritually harmful practice of the higher
clergy was the failure of bishops to maintain actual residence in their dioceses
and to neglect pastoral responsibility for the dioceses or churches from which
they were drawing substantial income. In the decades preceding Trent, there
were any number of local attempts to bring about reform of both upper and
lower clergy as well as broad efforts to rein in papal power by making the
papacy responsible to the authority of an ecumenical council.

Diocesan reform regulations for the clergy had been quite intense and
extensive in both pre-Reformation England and Spain. John Fisher, Bishop of
Rochester until his execution by Henry VIII in 1535, provided thirty years of
exemplary pastoral commitment to the priests of the diocese. In a diocese beset
by extreme poverty, his own life of self-denial and moderation gave him the
moral authority he needed to demand simplicity of life and material detach-
ment from his priests. In his zeal for reform of abuses and pastoral dedication,
Fisher did not hesitate to remove unworthy priests from their posts. As Michael
Mullett points out, Fisher's policy was an obvious anticipation of Trent, which
went a step further by ordering bishops to deprive unworthy priests of their
benefices.[5] In Spain, Cardinal Francisco Ximenes de Cisneros led the diocesan
reform. A Franciscan friar of the strict observance and Archbishop of Toledo,
Spain's primatial see, he strongly encouraged his clergy to improve their ministry by pursuing theological and biblical studies, and through his own pastoral
example he inspired a movement of Spanish bishops whose dedication to episcopal reform would exert significant influence on the disciplinary decisions at
Trent.[6] Cardinal Reginald Pole of England, one of the most influential reform
leaders at Trent, had previously set up in his home country a very comprehensive system of clerical and seminary reform that would directly affect the Coun-

cil's legislation on the establishment and management of seminaries. As a more direct preparation for the Council, Pole, in conjunction with the Italian reformers Gasparo Contarini and Giacomo Sadoleto, had also drawn up a comprehensive list of urgent ecclesiastical reforms for presentation at the papal court and later at the Council itself.[7]

As a result of the Council of Constance, which in effect arranged for the abdication of the three "competing" Popes, finally ending the Great Schism of 1378–1417, a growing conviction was emerging, especially among a significant number of non-Italian reformers, that the ecumenical council must have final authority—even over the Pope. This theory, which historians dubbed "conciliarism," was based, at least in part, on the belief that Constance had actually deposed the real Pope together with the two pretenders. But although Constance had been approved by Pope Martin V, he had excluded from this endorsement all those decrees which had favored the conciliarist doctrine.

Following the recommendation of Constance for frequent ecumenical councils, the bishops gathered once again at Basel in 1431, only to have the Council dissolved by Eugenius IV. In frustration and defiance, the Council fathers reissued the conciliarist teachings of Constance. Well before the beginnings of the Protestant Reformation, then, the Council of Basel had once again raised the banner of conciliarism, and in this way challenged the singular authority of the Pope. The conciliar movement would continue to surface periodically, especially in response to the ongoing scandals associated with the corruption and abuses of the papal court.

According to Hubert Jedin, the renowned historian of Trent, while the decrees of Constance and Basel were "intended to counter the papal policy in the sphere of prebends and finances," their conciliarist underpinnings represented a continuous challenge to papal primacy. The very mention of calling a council, therefore, soon became a thinly veiled threat, often used by secular powers, to try to win concessions from the Roman Curia.[8] As a result, therefore, despite the rapid spread of Lutheranism after 1520, Rome's reluctance to call a council was due in very large part to the memory of Constance and Basel, which continued to hover ominously over the world of papal politics.[9] In a word, it was the fifteenth-century challenges to papal authority that made the calling of an ecumenical council a very difficult choice for a sixteenth-century Pope. In fact, even with the final convocation of the Council of Trent in 1536, Pope Paul III felt compelled to employ a variety of very effective stalling tactics to delay the opening date of the Council,[10] with the result that Trent was not actually convened until 1545.

There can be little doubt, therefore, that a combination of theological concerns and ecclesiastical politics delayed the opening of the Council. These same concerns would also continue to dominate and complicate the deliberations of the participating fathers to the point that on several occasions the Council came very close to being aborted. On the other hand, inner Church politics were not the only source of interference with the workings of the Council.

In sixteenth-century Europe, the Church's hegemony was vigorously challenged by a fast emerging nationalism and the resulting competition and conflict it created among the aggressive secular states. Accordingly, the delay of Trent was occasioned not only by papal fear of conciliarism, but also by successive wars waged by France against the Holy Roman Empire and Spain.[11] The Council itself would be moved from Trent to Bologna and finally back to Trent as a result of the military threats and political interventions of secular monarchs. Trent had originally been chosen (1545) as the Council's site in response to the wishes of Emperor Charles V, precisely because it belonged to the Holy Roman Empire, and therefore was more likely to be swayed by the wishes of Charles. The Emperor was deeply committed to Church reform, in the hope that this would help mend the Protestant split within his empire. Paul III, on the other hand, sought from Trent primarily clarity of doctrine, so as to provide definite guidelines for distinguishing Catholic doctrine from "heresy." While Pope Paul and his worldly court had little reason to welcome ecclesiastical reform, their resistance was further intensified by their conviction that the call for reform was nothing but a push for conciliarism under a new guise, and thus a new threat to papal authority.[12]

After a year the Council, begun in 1545, was transferred from Trent to Bologna (within papal territory), this time at the urging of the Pope, who wanted to stay clear of imperial influence. Pressure from the Spanish government and Neapolitan prelates eventually brought the Council back to Trent for a second period in 1551–1552. By 1560, however, the European situation had changed dramatically as the Calvinist branch of the Reformation began to make serious advances in France. The monarchy was strongly tempted to convene a local French council to deal with the nationally divisive situation. To convene such a council, however, in the view of Pius IV, would be tantamount to calling for a Gallican or conciliarist assembly. Accordingly, backed by Philip II of Spain, the Pope hastily decided to reconvene the suspended council at Trent and to bring it to a successful conclusion in 1562–1563. In all, due to both ecclesiastical infighting and interference from the secular powers, the Council of Trent lasted, on and off, for a total of eighteen years.[13]

When we turn our attention to the Second Vatican Council (1962–1965), it is immediately apparent that this other landmark ecclesial event took place before a vastly different historical backdrop. The world of Vatican II was certainly much more similar to our present situation in the twenty-first century. It was a world that was already undergoing radical change, "marked by the end of colonialism, the rapid spread of industrialization and major advances in communications,"[14] especially through jet travel and the global expansion of television.

Pope Paul III (1534–1549) convoked the Council of Trent in 1536.
Titian (Tiziano Vecelli), Pope Paul III Farnese (1468–1549), painted after 1546. Erich
Lessing/Art Resource, NY ART209022

The fact that about 300 Latin American bishops attended the Council—compared with a total of about 200 bishops altogether at Trent—illustrates quite strikingly how significant the end of colonialism was for the business of the Council and how far apart were the historical settings of the two councils. Hubert Jedin, while serving as *peritus* (theological adviser) at Vatican II, could not but reflect on the sharp contrasts in the physical settings alone, as he watched bishops address their audience by means of microphones and loudspeakers.[15]

The rapid spread of industrialization, especially in formerly primarily agricultural countries, such as Italy, Spain, and Mexico, brought about not only a striking economic transformation and population shift, but also helped create a new "more dynamic, often restless" mentality, "more open to innovation, as linked to an industrial economy." As a result, on the eve of the Council, the Church found itself "on the defensive, immobile, in the face of a rapidly changing world."[16]

While courier messages from Trent to Rome during the proceedings of the earlier council had required a journey of at least three months, at the start of Vatican II jet travel had enabled bishops and their advisers to commute easily to the Council from far removed corners of the globe. As the industrial world was reaching a new peak in political, economic, and transportation progress, the rapid global spread of television had the effect of both amplifying and accelerating the profound psychological changes affecting most of humanity in the mid-twentieth century.[17]

It was in response to this new and unsettling world situation that the newly elected Pope John XXIII convoked the Second Council of the Vatican, the twenty-first ecumenical council of the Catholic Church, on January 25, 1959. This was a courageous act, indeed, for not all Catholic leaders favored any change of course, preferring that the Church continue its role of a strong and safe bastion against the inroads of modernity and secularization. The affable and jovial Pope, so popular with the media, was unremittingly serious when it came to his decision for Church renewal and modernization. He well knew that calling a council to help the Church face the new challenges and to achieve a healthy relationship to the modern world was risky and controversial, but necessary all the same. He was well aware that the Council represented an epochal moment in Church history and that it was far from just another stage in the evolution of the post-Tridentine Church. In his allocution of January 6, 1962, he did not hesitate to refer to the coming council as a "new epiphany."[18]

Pope John's many years of experience as a papal diplomat gave him a deep sense of this new world situation, and his unswerving pastoral commitment fired his desire for both updating the Church and reaching out to other Christian communities. At the same time, he was thoroughly convinced that both a genuine *aggiornamento* and an effective ecumenism would be impossible without a profound renewal of Church life from within. Just as the fathers at Trent

knew that true Church reform had to begin with an authentic spiritual transformation, so also did John and the bishops at Vatican II understand the need
for spiritual renewal in areas such as liturgical development, priestly formation,
and revitalization of both the religious and lay vocations. On the other hand,
while the focus of Trent was on reform, that of Vatican II was on renewal.

Given the marked differences of historical contexts separating the two
councils, it is not surprising that scholars have raised questions about the
legitimacy of comparing the two events. This was exactly the dilemma facing
the historian Hubert Jedin while observing the deliberations at Vatican II. Yet,
Jedin could not resist the comparison and supported this decision on the
grounds that a scholarly, historical comparison was both possible and valuable:
possible because scholarship was quite capable of restricting itself to written
texts and historically secure facts, while leaving aside all untested polemics;
valuable because both Councils, despite their separation in time, represent
genuine and careful attempts to express the essential self-understanding of the
same Catholic Church, albeit in different times and settings. In this sense, he
argued, the councils share the same subject matter.[19] Finally, both councils
represent turning points and defining moments in Church history, so that the
perceptive historian is bound to recognize a "before" and an "after" period both
for Trent and for Vatican II.

Even some of the apparently superficial comparisons between the councils
can be telling. While, for example, the fathers at Trent were singing the last *Te
Deum* to mark the close of the Council, the foundations of Michelangelo's
dome were being laid for the new basilica of St. Peter. The bishops at Vatican
II were to meet under that very dome some four centuries later. The makeup
of attending bishops at both councils, however, was strikingly different. Leibniz
had not been altogether wrong when he contemptuously described Trent to
Bossuet as "a synod of the Italian nation." There were never more than 237
voters at Trent, and the vast majority of these were Italian. Other nationalities,
such as the French, German, English, Dutch, and Polish, were often represented by a single bishop, if any at all. As Jean Delumeau puts it, "The council
was ecumenical in theory but not in fact. It represented mainly southern Europe."[20] By way of contrast, Vatican II was attended by "over two thousand
Catholic bishops and approximately eighty non-Catholic observers from the
major Christian denominations." The bishops came from 134 countries, including many from Africa, Asia, and Central and South America. The Catholic
bishops represented an unprecedented number of both industrial and developing nations. Compared to Trent's small circle of theologians in attendance,
Vatican II had as many as 480 *periti* (theological advisers). Furthermore, as a
further reflection of the realities of modern times, there were about a thousand
members of the press at the Vatican Council, all recipients of special courtesy
by the Council organizers.[21]

At a much deeper level, however, Trent and Vatican II differed quite dramatically in attitude and approach (what John O'Malley will describe as difference in *style*). The differences, no doubt, were to a great extent the result of the very different purposes for which each council was called. Since Pope Paul III saw no possibility of reconciliation with the Protestant churches in convoking the Council of Trent, he was committed to generating a clear formulation of Catholic doctrine on all issues where it was understood to be challenged by the Protestant Reformers. In contrast, the Pope and his delegates only reluctantly conceded the agenda of the Catholic reform party, and even then tried very hard to limit its pursuit by insisting that in the Council's deliberations, reform issues be alternated with doctrinal teachings.

The doctrinal decrees of Trent were intended to set up what Jedin calls "boundary stones" between the Catholic and Protestant positions. These, however, were not intended to "obstruct all free movement,"[22] but rather to overcome the widespread theological uncertainty that characterized the Church's intellectual life at the beginning of the sixteenth century.[23] In order to handle the need for doctrinal clarity, Trent relied on the ancient methodology of expressing its decrees in the form of canons, intended to expose and condemn (*anathema sit*) the opposing teaching. At least the papal party—which ultimately had its way—felt its primary obligation to be the need to defend the fundamental teachings of faith on justification, the sacraments, the sacrifice of the Mass, and the Real Eucharistic Presence. While for a contemporary reader Trent's methodology might well appear harsh and authoritarian, it is important to bear in mind the cultural situation of the time, exacerbated further by the shock of the Reformation and the long delay in the Church's response. All this had pressured the Council to emphasize the differences rather than the common features of Catholic and Protestant faith positions.

The contextual situation at Vatican II was almost a polar opposite in this regard. Pope John XXIII was convinced that the *aggiornamento* so badly needed in the Church was impossible without profound spiritual renewal—a renewal that included a reaching out to the churches separated from Rome. For this reason, Pope John strongly urged the Council fathers to prefer the "medicine of compassion" to the "weapon of strictness," and made it very clear that "the Council was to be pastoral rather than dogmatic." Rather than proclaiming new dogmas, the task of the Council was to "find new ways of expressing the old."[24] As a result, the Council was able to bring about a series of progressive liturgical, pastoral, ecumenical, institutional, and cultural changes in the spirit of renewal, without any sense of diverging from the ancient tradition of the Church. Certainly, the fathers of Vatican II had no intention of undermining the decrees of Trent nor of breaking continuity with that earlier landmark council of the modern Church. Nevertheless, the innovations of Vatican II were so profound as to constitute an epochal event and a "point of no return" in the history of the Church.[25]

While these considerations certainly point to the difficulty of comparing the two councils, they also suggest both the possibility and the importance of attempting such a comparison. Yves Congar, one of the most influential theologians at Vatican II, gives us further reason for examining the theological and historical connections between the two councils. It was Congar's claim that one of the greatest benefits of the Second Vatican Council was the demise of "Tridentinism," which he described as "an all embracing system of theology, ethics, Christian behavior, religious practice, liturgy, organization and Roman centralization"[26] that developed in the aftermath of the Council of Trent. In distinguishing Trent from *Tridentinism,* Congar was indebted to the work of the conciliar historian Giuseppe Alberigo, who restates his case in chapter 2 of this volume. This distinction is obviously an important one theologically, because it leaves open the possibility of departing from post-Tridentine practices and religious attitudes without in any way breaking from the teachings and guidelines of the Council itself.

There can be little doubt that the years, even centuries, following Trent saw the gradual development of a more tightly structured and highly uniform organization of Catholic practice and thought. The Counter-Reformation period began to produce a growing rigidity and defensiveness in Catholic outlook. These changes were accompanied by an increasing centralization of Church authority, which, at least to a great extent, resulted from the Council's decision, in its final days, to cede to the newly established Curial Congregation of the Council the implementation of the conciliar decisions. This papal Congregation in the years following Trent very quickly and efficiently saw to the promulgation of the *Professio Fidei Tridentina*, as well as a new Roman missal and breviary. It also established an Index of Forbidden Books, reinforced the authority of the Roman Inquisition, and further enhanced the power of Roman authority through the strategic employment of papal nuncios throughout the Catholic world. This path to a successful implementation of the Council tended to produce a certain doctrinal inflexibility as well as a fearful "vigilance against heterodoxy" that characterized Catholicism until Vatican Council II.[27] Reflecting on these results, Jedin suggests that despite the obvious downside of these developments, the Church at the time of Trent had little choice but to take this course, if it were successfully "to overcome the great crisis of the sixteenth century."[28] Historical events, he argues, have to be judged in the context of their times.

It is noteworthy, nonetheless, that even conservative historians, such as Jedin, do recognize the adverse side effects of the ecclesial developments that took place in the wake of Trent. On the other hand, despite a number of clearly unfortunate outcomes, an objective overview of the Council's aftermath does not justify an unequivocally negative judgment.[29] For example, the new diocesan seminary system created at Trent has been hailed as the greatest single accomplishment of the Council.[30] The Tridentine seminaries certainly turned out far better educated and spiritually trained priests in the centuries that followed, notwithstanding the fact that the same system, in the long run, tended to encourage a more authoritarian, segregated, and secretive clergy. Similarly, the imposing movement of Catholic spirituality, with its firm roots in the pre-Tridentine Church reform movement, would, in the aftermath of Trent, undergo a new transformation both among members of religious orders and among the laity. Yet, this same revival of spirituality, grounded as it was in meditation and asceticism, has been blamed for encouraging an excess of individual piety at the expense of genuine "communal or liturgical values."[31]

In the cultural realm, the dramatic and vibrant style of baroque art and architecture is widely viewed as an outcome and expression of the newly revitalized and self-confident Catholicism of the post-Tridentine era. Yet despite the greatness of its monuments and productions, the baroque has also been persistently criticized by art critics for its excess and "reckless extravagance."[32] In similar fashion, many other post-Tridentine developments, such as the struggle against superstition, the new and dynamic interest in theology, the evangelization of the New World, and the flourishing of new religious orders, especially of teaching congregations of both men and women, had their successes and failures, their assets and liabilities. Overall, sociohistorical studies of the period differ as to the degree to which the dynamism of the post-Tridentine Church was driven by popular enthusiasm or simply by effective ecclesiastical disciplining of both clergy and laity.[33] What is beyond question, however, is that the impact of the Council of Trent on the development of early modern Catholicism was both pervasive and profound, and that its reforms, despite their frequent one-sidedness,[34] did, on a broad scale, bring about a general improvement in the life of the Church. The power of this influence, for both good and ill, would persist well into the middle of the twentieth century.

In view of the long-term effects of Trent on Church life, it becomes all the more historically legitimate to compare Trent and Vatican II, despite the wide chronological gap that separates them. What Church historians, however, might still seriously question about the book's project is the acceptability of bypassing Vatican I, the nineteenth-century ecumenical council, in the attempt to explore connections between Trent and Vatican II. Answering his own objection on this score, Jedin, in his reflection on Trent and Vatican II, observed that the First Vatican Council, with its declaration of papal primacy and infallibility, was for all practical purposes a reinforcement and formalization of the Roman centralization that characterized the post-Tridentine Church."[35] In fact, outside the Catholic world, and often within as well, Vatican I is still widely criticized for having canonized an absolutist "Roman system," established during the decades following Trent, and historians have cited Pius IX's fear of Gallicanism and conciliarism as a primary motive in his promotion of the "Vatican dogmas."[36] What seems clear is that the nineteenth-century Council, for all its intrinsic importance, served as a further intensification of the

Counter-Reformation, as well as a Catholic critical response to the Enlightenment. From the perspective of the present volume, then, the First Vatican
Council is linked with the post-Tridentine tradition, and for this reason it does
not require a separate, independent treatment. To be sure, the relationship
between the two Vatican Councils also remains a very important and much
discussed theological concern today, but that question will have to be left to
other scholars and another book.[37]

The collection of essays that follows focuses rather on the far-reaching
changes of Vatican Council II and their possible connections with the Council
of Trent. With this in view, the authors examine a broad range of doctrinal and
disciplinary developments emerging from Trent and compare them with corresponding changes in Church life and thought occurring at Vatican Council
II and its aftermath. The goal is to provide a more historically informed and
theologically accurate understanding of the origin and nature of change in the
twentieth-century Catholic Church. While the individual contributors are not
required to directly address this guiding concern, they are well aware, nevertheless, that their collective efforts will likely cast some light on the status of
Congar's thesis that the innovations of Vatican Council II are best understood
as an outcome of the collapse or demise of the Tridentine system.

There is evidently no way of testing Congar's thesis short of a careful and
detailed historical investigation of the post-Tridentine era, as well as by an
accurate account of the key ecclesial changes initiated by the Second Vatican
Council. Since the individual scholar could spend a lifetime investigating these
details and searching for connections between these two great councils, the
editors have chosen a shortcut by assembling a team of scholars to work in a
collaborative effort to achieve the same goal.

These researchers were selected on the basis of reputation and scholarly
expertise in their field, without any consideration of religious affiliation, national origin, gender, or ethnicity. They selected their topics of investigation
from a list of issues that the editors judged to be likely important links between
the Councils. While no one volume can expect to cover all areas of connection
between Trent and Vatican II, both the range and the significance of the selected topics should serve well to illuminate the trail that links the two Councils.

In chapter 1, Giuseppe Alberigo attempts to show the emergence, following the Council of Trent, of the organized system he calls "Tridentinism." This
is followed by a study of the impact of this system in Latin America, and a
review of the use of Trent by Vatican II. These foundational chapters set the
historical and theological stage for the studies that follow. The latter cover a
spectrum of topics broad enough to provide a good sampling of interconciliar
connections, such as post-Tridentine eucharistic theology, priestly formation,
the demise of liturgical Latin, developments in church music, Marian doctrine,
religious pluralism, moral theology, the changing role of the laity, Christian

marriage, the status of women religious, and the role of the universal cate-chism. In chapter 17, "From Trent to Vatican II: Reformation or Stylistic Change," John O'Malley brings the reader full circle by once again addressing the underlying question of the volume.

The contributions in this volume are intended to bring an objective, schol-arly, historical methodology to the sensitive and controversial issue of ecclesial change. For this reason, the individual authors were asked to avoid, as much as possible, any unduly polemical stance on disputed theological issues. As editors, we do include a brief summary and some final reflections on the contributions. This is more of an attempt to help tie the chapters together and to understand their overall impact. In so doing, we make no pretense of saying the last word on the Trent connection with Vatican Council II or of deciding the validity of Congar's thesis. Those crucial and definitive tasks we are happy to leave to the honest assessment and critical judgment of our readers.

NOTES

1. Christopher M. Bellitto, "Councils and Reform: Challenging the Misconcep-tions," paper presented to the American Catholic Historical Association, Scranton University, March 2003, 2.

2. Jean Delumeau, *Catholicism Between Luther and Voltaire*, trans. Jeremy Moiser (London: Burns & Oates, 1977), 6. See also Hubert Jedin, *Crisis and Closure of the Council of Trent: A Retrospective View from the Second Vatican Council*, trans. N. D. Smith (London and Melbourne: Sheed and Ward Stagbooks, 1967), 165.

3. Michael A. Mullett, *The Catholic Reformation* (London and New York: Rout-ledge, 1999), 17–18.

4. See H. Outram Evennett, *The Spirit of the Counter-Reformation* (Cambridge: Cambridge University Press, 1968), 32–36, 43ff.

5. Mullett, *The Catholic Reformation*, 20.

6. Ibid., 22.

7. Ibid., 34. The report, which was presented to Pope Paul III in 1537, was titled *Consilium Delectorum Cardinalium et Aliorum Praelatorum de Emendanda Ecclesia.* The report drew heavily on an earlier document produced by the Diocese of Cologne, which had detailed a series of serious reforms focusing on the duties of bishops and the standards to be used in the ordination of priests.

8. Hubert Jedin, *A History of the Council of Trent*, vol. 1, trans. Ernest Graf (Lon-don: Thomas Nelson and Sons, 1957), 48–49.

9. See John L. Murphy, *The General Councils of the Church* (Milwaukee, Wis.: Bruce Publishing, 1960), 137, 139.

10. Delumeau, *Catholicism*, 5–6.

11. Ibid., 6.

12. R. Po-Chia Hsia, *The World of Catholic Renewal 1540–1770* (Cambridge: Cam-bridge University Press, 1998), 14.

13. For the translation of the Council from Trent to Bologna, see ibid., 14–16,

and for a clear overview of the Council's meanderings and achievements during this long span, see Murphy, *The General Councils*, 164–169.

14. Raymond F. Bulman, "Vatican Council II (1962–1965)," in *Encyclopedia of the Vatican and Papacy*, ed. Frank J. Coppa (Westport, Conn.: Greenwood Press, 1999), 429.

15. Jedin, *Crisis and Closure*, 17.

16. Giacomo Martina, "The Historical Context in Which the Idea of a New Ecumenical Council Was Born," in *Vatican II: Assessment and Perspectives*, ed. René Latourelle (New York: Paulist Press, 1988–1989), 10, 13.

17. Ibid., 12.

18. Ibid., 4.

19. Hubert Jedin, *Vaticanum II und Tridentinum: Tradition und Fortschritt in der Kirchengeschichte* (Cologne and Opladen: Westdeutscher Verlag, 1968), 8.

20. Delumeau, *Catholicism*, 7.

21. Michael J. Walsh, "The History of the Council," in *Modern Catholicism: Vatican II and After*, ed. Adrian Hastings (New York: Oxford University Press, 1991), 36.

22. Jedin, *Crisis and Closure*, 164.

23. Jedin, *Vaticanum II und Tridentinum*, 10. See also A. D. Wright, "The Significance of the Council of Trent," *Journal of Ecclesiastical History* 26, 4 (1975): 354, who claims that even at the Council of Trent, certain leading fathers had "individual sympathies" for the Protestant position.

24. Jedin, *Vaticanum II und Tridentinum*, cites John's opening address to the Council in which he calls for "misericordiae medicinam, potius quam severitatis arma," 9. See also Walsh, "The History of the Council," 36.

25. Giuseppe Alberigo, "Il Vaticano II nella Storia della Chiesa," *Cristianesimo nella Storia* 6 (1985): 444.

26. Yves Congar, *Fifty Years of Catholic Theology*, ed. Bernard Lauret (Philadelphia: Fortress Press, 1988), 3–4.

27. Wright, "The Significance of the Council of Trent," 355.

28. Jedin, *Crisis and Closure*, 187.

29. Hsia, *The World of Catholic Renewal*, 194.

30. Wright, "The Significance of the Council of Trent," 357. See also James A. O'Donohoe, "The Seminary Legislation of the Council of Trent," in *Il Concilio di Trento e la Riforma Tridentina* (Rome and Vienna: Herder, 1965), 157.

31. Evennett, *The Spirit of the Counter-Reformation*, 36.

32. Mullett, *The Catholic Reformation*, 196.

33. John W. O'Malley, *Trent and All That: Renaming Catholicism in the Early Modern Era* (Cambridge, Mass.: Harvard University Press, 2000), 64. O'Malley makes the point that while this imposed discipline effectively created uniformity, it often also produced deep resentments.

34. In Hans Küng's critique of Trent's accomplishments, he points out that despite the wide range of ecclesial reforms introduced in the wake of the Council, none of them addressed a genuine reform of the papacy—the much needed *reformatio in capite*. See Hans Küng, *Christianity: Essence, History and Future* (New York: Continuum, 1995), 483.

35. Jedin, *Crisis and Closure*, 90.

36. See Georges Dejaifve's *Pape et evêques au Premier Concile du Vatican* (Brussels: Desclée de Brouwer, 1961), 7 and 57, for a clear analysis of the Orthodox critique of Vatican I along these lines.

37. Important aspects of this relationship between the Councils, such as collegiality and membership in the Church, are discussed in Georges Dejaifve's *Un tournant décisif de l'écclésiologie à Vatican II* (Paris: Éditions Beauchesne, 1978).

2

From the Council of Trent to "Tridentinism"

Giuseppe Alberigo
Translated by Emily Michelson

The Battle for Interpretation

On December 4, 1563, the papal legates presiding over the Council of Trent asked the collected Council fathers, "Do you think it fitting that this sacred ecumenical council be concluded, with praise to God Almighty, and that the overseers and legates of the apostolic see, in the name of this sacred council, ask the blessed Roman pontiff to confirm each of the items established and defined by the Roman pontiffs Paul III and Julius III of blessed memory, and by our own most holy Pius IV?"[1] The affirmative response concluded a council that had mesmerized all of Western Christendom for nearly twenty years, and that would dominate Christian life for centuries to come. The conclusion of one of Christianity's most complicated and significant councils initiated a period thick with uncertainty and rife with problems.

The Council closed in a context very different from the one in which it had opened in December 1545. Western Christendom had long since lost its unity, and any hopes that the Council could restore it had vanished. Regions loyal to Rome had trusted the Council to halt the process of fragmentation that the Reformation had started. By the end of the Council, however, other vast and well-established areas had built up their own autonomous and alternative ecclesiastical traditions. The general political, cultural, economic, and geographical situations had changed no less.

Perhaps none of those present at Trent could be certain that the decisions made there would produce consistent results, given such a compromised situation. The most astute members of the Council admitted that they risked replicating the unfortunate situation that had followed the Fifth Lateran Council, whose decrees had remained a dead letter. Furthermore, it was hard to believe that the decrees of Trent would contribute meaningfully to any revival of Roman Catholicism, given the diffidence with which the papacy had always treated the Council. Finally, they recalled the negative experiences which had ensured that the decisions of the Council's earlier sessions of 1545–1547 and 1551–1552, too, remained dormant.

To request that Pius IV confirm all the decisions of the Council as quickly as possible, and thereby give them canonical validation, was therefore more than mere protocol. The leader of the assembly, Cardinal Morone, accompanied by many of the most authoritative Council fathers, promptly moved to Rome, where he could directly oversee the papal confirmation. This act was as much political as bureaucratic. Both at the Council and in Rome, many wanted the Pope to submit the Tridentine decisions to a meticulous review, to confirm only a few of them, or to impose modifications, as some medieval Popes had chosen to do.[2] Those who opposed a global and unconditional confirmation also had never fully accepted the Council's technique of alternating discussions of doctrine with discussions of institutional reform. They now suggested to the Medici Pope that he confirm, without delay, only the doctrinal decrees. A tense conflict followed in Rome, beginning in the last days of 1563 and lasting until the first half of 1564. In many important ways, these months constitute the "prehistory" of the long journey Roman Catholicism would take after Trent.

The principal issues at stake were essentially these: the Pope's decision whether to accept the Council's decrees; the conditions of such an acceptance; and the fulfillment in Rome of a series of important mandates that the Council had entrusted to the papacy. Pius IV's hesitancy was short-lived. By January 26, 1564, he had verbally approved the decrees, universally and without reservations. The authority that Morone enjoyed at the Vatican; the pressure from his nephew, Cardinal Charles Borromeo; and, finally, the belief that the papacy had everything to gain and nothing to lose by supporting the Council had helped him to overcome all uncertainties.

Nonetheless, the bull of confirmation, *Benedictus Deus*, was not published until June 30, still bearing the date of January 26.[3] This long and poorly hidden gestation period was due not only to the unceasing pressure on the Pope to change his position but also to the laborious rewordings of the bull. The campaign against the Council turned into a battle to control its implementation, as opponents sought to insert the various criteria for interpretation into the bull itself. For their part, the Council fathers had already predicted problems regarding interpretation. They had above all exhorted "that the princes should assist in protecting its decrees from being corrupted and violated by heretics, ensuring that these and all others accept them with devotion and observe them loyally."

That same decree of session XXV of the Council had proceeded to affirm:

> If some difficulty should arise in the reception of the decrees or if something should escape us that requires further declaration or definition, the council believes that, beyond the measures at the disposition of this sacred council, the most holy Roman Pontiff should concern himself with providing for the needs of the provinces, by calling whomever he considers necessary for treating the problem (especially if they come from the region in question), or by celebrating a general council, if he deems it necessary, or in any other way that seems fit to him, for the glory of God and the tranquility of the Church.[4]

It is noteworthy that the bull *Benedictus Deus* addressed this same problem in a notably different manner. It gave the Apostolic See exclusive jurisdiction over any kind of problem of interpretation, without mentioning collegial or conciliar options, as the Tridentine fathers had done explicitly.[5] Granting this authority to Rome alone fulfilled two different functions. It showed loyalty to the Council by ensuring that a proliferation of interpretations could not delay or hamper its implementation. At the same time, it isolated those decrees from the rest of the acts of the Council, and thereby increased the possibility of their becoming too rigid. Indeed, even as the first printed edition of the acts of the Council was completed in March 1564, publication of the rich surrounding material was forbidden, and those texts would remain buried in Roman archives until the early twentieth century.[6]

Without delay, a Roman congregation for the interpretation of the Council began its work on December 30, 1563. The following August 2, the *motu proprio, Alias nos nonnullas*, institutionalized what would later become the Congregation for the Council. By centralizing control over its interpretation, Rome soon became the sole and indispensable channel for the implementation of the Council, or so it hoped.[7] The tasks that the Council had assigned to the Holy See—publishing an index of prohibited books, a profession of faith, a catechism, a breviary, and a missal—lent considerable weight to Rome's position. The bishops and theologians previously employed at Trent carried out this mandate with enthusiasm. March 24, 1564, saw the publication of the *Index librorum prohibitorum*.[8] The *Professio fidei*[9] followed on November 13, and the *Catechismus romanus* in September 1566.[10] The new breviary followed later that same year, and before 1570, the new missal had appeared.[11] These publications helped to standardize certain key aspects of Catholic life, and gave the impression that Tridentine theology was far more systematic than the conciliar decrees had suggested.

The conclusion of the Council had also prompted commitments and initiatives, as well as resistance, far beyond the microcosm of Rome, important though it was. Many bishops had returned to their dioceses determined to faithfully apply the decisions that they had helped to formulate. Others, even if they had not attended the Council, planned to introduce its decrees. In addition, many sovereigns were interested in seeing a resurgence of the Church, even while protecting their own political prerogatives.[12] In short, the faithful, who for decades had endured the hardships of ecclesiastical corruption, showed a hopeful and eager spirit.

At the same time, opposition to the Council was widespread. Its most insidious and formidable opponents were not the Protestants, who rejected it outright in harsh and ironic tones, but those Catholics, both lay and clerical, who wanted to avoid any restoration of Church discipline. Both in Rome and in outlying regions, among both high and low clergy, abuses persisted, alongside a tenacious attachment to what had been the status quo. This mind-set strongly fostered a rejection of the conciliar renewal, using every strategy available. Passive resistance, intentional and organized inertia, arrogant and stubborn defiance all constituted—though in different ways and in different places—one of the principal challenges to the campaign for the reception of the Council. Scholars must have a thorough appreciation of this challenge. It will keep them from depicting the reception as straightforward and idyllic, and will make it clear how much assertiveness, even aggressiveness, the protagonists of the post-Council period would need in order to prevent a substantial disregard for Tridentine reform.

We must also mention that the disappointments it had produced brought about a certain lack of enthusiasm for the Council. To have sanctioned the division, not the reunification, of the Church and to have omitted the long-desired *reformatio in capite* led some to believe that the Council had failed completely. Cardinal Pole's decision to abandon his work at the Council, despite his having been one of its papal legates, symbolizes this frustration.[13]

Toward an Implementation

The first phase of implementation thus got under way in a context of uncertainty and contradiction. It would last for twenty intense years, between the end of the Council and the passing of the generation that had lived through it. Implementation during this period was polycentric. In Rome, the papacy committed itself strongly to ensuring that conciliar decrees were accepted and put into practice throughout the Church's many territories; the Society of Jesus provided highly qualified personnel for this task.[14] Papal nuncios, their network expanded and reinforced, increasingly supplemented their diplomatic work with missions representing the Holy See to local churches and bishoprics.[15]

While in Rome the diocesan application of Trent was difficult and any-thing but exemplary,[16] bishops elsewhere took up the task of reforming their churches with great zeal, and often with inspired creativity. Not only Borromeo in Milan and Martyribus in Braga, but, Pedro Guerrero, Gabriele Paleotti, Sci-pione Burali, and many others considered themselves leaders of "Catholic re-form." For them, the Council was an event in which they had participated in various ways, and which had attracted, involved, and changed them. From this point of view, their commitment was not only unequivocal but also sponta-neous, original, and creative. Making the Council into a reality was *rem pro-priam agere,* and they were prepared to risk their lives for it. For these men, reestablishing discipline coincided with their dedication to the *salus animarum,* and was indistinguishable from their personal pursuit of holiness.[17]

The devotion and independence with which they sought to implement the Council explain why the men of this generation, starting with Charles Borro-meo, were shocked to learn that Rome was more suspicious than supportive of their efforts—despite the fact that none of these men were suspect regarding their absolute loyalty to the Pope, their full doctrinal orthodoxy, or, even less so, their strict adherence to the Council.[18] The conflict, which would become increasingly evident, was essentially pastoral in nature. Would post-Tridentine Catholicism find itself capable of accepting more than one pastoral model?

The Strengths and Limits of Pluralism

Upon further investigation, the dispute suggested that more than one eccle-siology existed, but this would become clear only at the end of the sixteenth century. In the period immediately following the end of the Council, only one ecclesiology was in fact at work in Roman Catholicism. As we know, the Council fathers unanimously chose parishes and dioceses as the central and primary locus of reform.[19] This does not mean, however, that the Council ever debated the question of choosing between a universal and a local ecclesiology. Luther had not raised such a problem, and the Council did not even broach the topic.

In reality, Church reform was defined entirely as the revitalization of local churches. It was in response to the Protestants that the Council had empha-sized the sacramental grounding of the ministerial priesthood and had reaf-firmed the legitimacy of an ecclesiastical hierarchy, which resulted in a heavily sacralized theology of priesthood. This theology was a direct counterpoint to the Protestant "spiritualization" of the priesthood of all believers, a concept that was gradually stripped of any concrete meaning.[20] During this stage of implementation, the Council's doctrinal decisions were never at stake; these were administered exclusively by the Inquisition.[21] The efficacy of the Council was judged entirely by its implementation of the disciplinary decrees and by its management of the tensions between different, though not opposing, pastoral models.

Reception of the conciliar decrees met its limits on two fronts. On the one hand, the defenders of the status quo disagreed with those who championed a renewal of discipline. On the other hand, there was a tension between those who advocated a pluralist model of implementation—calling for a galvanization of the energies residing in the authentic traditions of the churches—and those who firmly supported a unified and centralized strategy, relying on one exclusive pastoral model. The pluralist model drew upon the vitality of the various local church traditions, while the centralized model promoted a single pastoral mode. For the former, implementation meant combining the actual event of the Council with local zeal for renewal, and emphasizing the best aspects of each. "Reception" in this case meant a dynamic process of active assimilation, in which the Council and the churches were both actors. The latter group saw the Council as definitively concluded. For them, all that remained was to follow its decisions as though they were stone tablets containing blueprints for the reestablishment of Catholicism. The papacy, like Moses, had control of the tablets, and the right and duty to impose obedience to them on the Church. The Council itself, dominated as it was by the conflict with the Protestants, had not been able to resolve these differences, leaving room for the disputes that followed in its wake.

Nonetheless, the Council had repeatedly reaffirmed its promise not to intervene in unresolved questions of faith among loyal Catholics. It thus displayed a pluralism that now seemed destined to disappear together with the generation that had lived through the Council and all its accompanying troubles. In the final moments of the sixteenth century, pressure from the Protestants, incipient stirrings of a non-Christian culture, and ultimately drastic social changes aroused sentiments of fear, defensiveness, and arrogant superiority in various Catholic circles. In the end, the discomfort of living in a society in which the Church was no longer the "soul" would have an unforeseen impact on Catholic theology.

In Catholic regions, the *cura animarum* inspired a phase of intense reform. Its leaders were well-known bishops who, despite their cultural and generational differences, all considered the parish to be the fulcrum of Catholic renewal. More than ever, the word "parish" signified the parochial clergy, just as "diocese" had come to mean "bishop." Thus, reform leaders revived earlier practices such as pastoral visits and diocesan synods,[22] paid great attention to the selection and education of their clerics, and subjected the latter to moralizing efforts against concubinage, gaming, hunting, and other vices.

Such a complex and difficult reform operation compelled the zealous bishops to safeguard the reform itself against a variety of dangers. These came both from nearby churches that still maintained a lax attitude toward abuses and from the Roman Curia, which was reluctant to give up the prestige and capital it earned from authorizing those abuses. Such pressures made the bishops acutely aware that the decisions of Trent would require an essentially pastoral application focused on local communities.[23] For their part, the faithful agreed with and adhered to this model of reform and pastoral commitment.[24]

Even decisions that abolished community privileges, such as excluding the community from the selection and education of its clergy, or establishing episcopal control over confraternities, were accepted with goodwill, inasmuch as they were motivated by the urgent need for reform. The strategy for Catholic renewal compelled the most perceptive bishops to defend local liturgies and to attempt to create stable ties among parishes, especially in the countryside.[25] The often active and dynamic presence of religious orders, such as the Capuchins and the Jesuits, complicated the matter. In areas where parish organization was slow to revive, the work of religious orders was critical; often the orders themselves came to govern the parishes. Even where the bishop's efforts were effective, his success often sparked friction or even conflict with the religious orders, which could barely tolerate episcopal authority. Nonetheless, the bishops needed their collaboration, especially for preaching and for directing the newly founded seminaries.[26]

Implementation and/or Reception

A few months after the death of Charles Borromeo, Sixtus V was elected Pope. His pontificate would signal a turning point in the post-Tridentine era. Among other things, the conclusion of the Council and the beginning of its reception had restored the centrality of Rome as a symbol of Catholic renewal and a locus for promoting or overseeing myriad initiatives.

Many of the tools of reform first conceived at Trent were brought to life in Rome, in particular a renewed role for bishops that applied the arrangement of a monarchical structure and the standard of obedience to the Church at large.[27] The resulting Church organization was neither horizontal nor polycentric, but hierarchical and centralized. Such a strategy became systematically organized with the ecclesiology of Robert Bellarmine, but was already clearly pursued as early as the 1570s. In this model of application, bishops remained central, but were subject to Roman guidance and control. In the five years of his reign (1585–1590), Sixtus V launched an array of institutional changes that would have ramifications for centuries to come. Not all of these initiatives directly concerned the implementation of the Council, but each one strongly influenced the way the Council was received, sometimes far more than many official decisions about interpretation.

Some of these changes related directly to the Council, such as the formalization of the obligation of all bishops to make a visit *ad limina apostolorum* (i.e., to Rome) every five years. Another was the centralization, again in Rome, of the process for nominating bishops.[28] The reports of nuncios, rather than those of city or provincial councils, came to govern these nominations.[29] A third was the production of an official edition of the "Sistine" Vulgate (1590) as an instrument for controlling the use of the Bible.[30] Other changes concerned the *reformatio in capite,* which the Popes had vigorously opposed at the Council. These included the bull *Immensa aeterni Dei* (1587), which instituted Roman congregations as regular and standard tools of government; these congregations were committees of cardinals, each assigned to a particular sphere of competence.[31] Such innovations signaled the inexorable decline of the Consistory as an entity for governing the Universal Church and, at the same time, paved the way for Rome to intervene much more frequently and thoroughly in individual dioceses.[32] Even the decisions of diocesan and provincial synods came under centralized, lengthy, and sometimes financial scrutiny.

The bishops' obedience to Rome, not the effectiveness of their pastoral work, often determined whether they were considered loyal to the Council.[33] They therefore risked finding themselves "with the miter, but without the crosier," as Paleotti would observe many years after the end of the Council. What caused such great novelty? Undoubtedly the sluggish and unsatisfying process of implementing the Council played a considerable part.

It is interesting, in this regard, to review some of the "memoranda" that Cardinal Robert Bellarmine published more than once between 1600 and 1612 for the Popes of those years.[34] The esteemed Jesuit vigorously emphasized the precarious state of the Council's implementation. For example, he notified Clement VIII of six deficiencies in the reform process: (1) too many dioceses were still vacant; (2) many appointments were second-rate, and seemed prompted by the desire to place particular people in good churches, and not the reverse; (3) many bishops still did not live in residence; (4) many in fact still held more than one diocese; (5) too many bishops were too frequently transferred; (6) resignations due to personal interests were routinely accepted. It is a disconcerting picture: the implementation of Trent had not failed, but everything implied that failure was still possible. Bellarmine, for that matter, had proposed in 1600–1601 the convocation of a new General Council.[35]

Popes thus had good reason to worry, and it is logical that they tried to improve results, as Sixtus V did, by taking measures that may have been motivated by the search for efficiency but that were destined to have lasting ecclesiological effects. One could also argue that the Holy See now felt pressed to take primary responsibility for the implementation of the Council. The era of great political, religious, cultural, and economic changes, which had altered the face of the West, had by now ended. Confessional conflict had stabilized, and by now, Catholicism and Protestantism faced one another in trench warfare.

The effort to re-Catholicize Protestant territories was failing. The rule of "cuius regio, eius et religio" increasingly held sway, paving the way for the double concept of throne and altar that would come to typify the *ancien régime*. The Catholic churches of Europe entered a stage where they were strictly controlled by the political forces of Gallicanism and jurisdictionalism. Despite their vast differences, all these forces demonstrate how sovereigns attempted to manipulate the Church in their regions.

These tendencies visibly affected local Christian communities. Political authorities unanimously favored the regional and communal aspects of the Church. They increasingly assigned to parishes social functions such as schools, civic records, and social control, and thereby earned the strict loyalty of the clergy. They disparaged the centralization and uniformity of Rome and tended to intervene in every interaction between local churches and the papacy and Curia. In various ways, the great political centers of Madrid, Paris, and later, Vienna each tried to control how conciliar reforms were introduced. Rome, in turn, took the opportunity to present itself as the champion of the Council and the defender of Church liberty.[36]

The Ideology of "Tridentinism"

From the end of the sixteenth century, the papacy encouraged the Church to view the Council as the last word in matters of faith and discipline. The Council had incorporated, redefined, and updated the norms of the previous centuries to such an extent that it became sufficient, and preferable, to know these norms only through the lens of the Council's decrees. The body of Tridentine decrees increasingly edged all previous sources out of ecclesiastical use.[37] Therefore, it became obligatory to refer to Trent for solutions to every problem that arose, doctrinal or institutional. As a result, post-Tridentine Catholicism gradually took on a uniformity that nobody would have dared to think possible in the acute phase of the Protestant schism. In fact, this "Tridentinism" even managed to penetrate, in important ways, into certain parts of the Protestant world.

As an event, the Council was concluded and entered into history. Rather than being absorbed into ecclesiastical tradition, however, the Council's decrees were elevated until they were considered equal to the rest of tradition. All influence and contact between ecclesiastical tradition and the realities of the Church were filtered through the Council. The corpus of Tridentine decisions *regulated* the new ecclesiastical system that the end of the medieval status quo and the growth of new social needs had made necessary. These decisions were granted so much authority that basic elements of the new system were judged positive or negative on the basis of how closely they conformed to the Council's decrees.

During this ambiguous phase, local churches were bounced back and forth, sometimes violently, between the poles of political "protection" and Roman "guardianship." Compared with the Europe of the Peace of Westphalia, concluded in 1648, a map of the areas where the disciplinary decisions of the Council were introduced is notably fragmented and discontinuous. The governments both of great nation-states and of small territorial polities followed their own strategies in favoring, delaying, or preventing the publication of the decrees and their de facto observance. For their part, the clergy, especially the high clergy, were completely unpredictable as they decided whether to conform to the new discipline. Direct challenges to the Council were rare, but evasions, often buttressed by appeals to Rome, persisted—the cathedral chapters of Spain are a case in point.[38] The Roman attempt to win obedience through bureaucracy, even to the point of sending apostolic visitors, exerted an undeniable pressure, but in the end achieved only uncertain and superficial results.

The models provided by the great bishops, Charles Borromeo above all, undoubtedly had a much greater effect on the implementation of the Council, and for this reason the papacy wanted to stake its own claim to these models. In fact, Rome canonized Borromeo very quickly (1610), even if it publicized an image of him that highlighted his private virtues while leaving in shadow the exceptional importance of his pastoral example. Knowledge of the latter would take the publication of his biographies and, above all, the incredible circulation of the *Acta ecclesiae mediolanensis*, which documented his pastoral activities.[39]

Borromeo was very soon touted as the model of the post-Tridentine Church, and the champion of the Council's implementation.[40] By associating the prestige of the Council with the celebrity of one of its most tireless executors, the Church created a cornerstone of Tridentinism, but one that used both Council and saint to advance an ecclesiastical outlook that was, in fact, foreign to both. In reality, Charles Borromeo had devoted all his energies to implementing the Council, which he saw as the guideline and inspiration for all his pastoral efforts. For him personally, this meant not only respecting conciliar decisions but also, above all, believing in the broad ecclesiological vision implicit in much of the doctrinal and reforming work of the Council. As a result of effective ecclesiastical marketing, the image of Borromeo as a pastoral prototype appeared rather colorless, but all the same continued to play a decisive role in the reception of the Council.

The Tridentine system, as described above, comprised not only the decisions themselves but also, above all, the ideas, concepts, mental habits, institutional realities, and practical organization equated with them between 1564 and the first decades of the seventeenth century. They include a certain number of defining features and, above all, a static ecclesiology—a defensive attitude that favored the Church's social dimensions over the interior dimensions that addressed the mysteries of faith. From this perspective, organizational needs and the defense of traditional faith mattered tremendously, and led the Church to resort to controversy and repression.

The Church's uncertainty about the place of Scripture in Christian life would also play a decisive role. It is true that the decree of the Council's fourth session (1546) left many possibilities open. But the procedure that gained strength after the Council, and the spirit behind it, led to an increasingly limited and suspicious treatment of the two Testaments, particularly the Old Testament.[41] This attitude strongly affected both liturgy and preaching. Liturgy, no longer sustained by a dynamic sense of Christian mystery and deprived of all scriptural sustenance, focused ever more closely on the Eucharist alone.[42] But the imbalance between the sacrificial and the communal values of the Mass forced eucharistic piety out of its natural context in the liturgy and gave it an unduly individualistic meaning. At the same time, sermons came under the massive influence of the literary baroque, except when they sought refuge in a catechetical style that, while responding to the need for religious instruction, was far less effective than it would have been if it had not relied so heavily on stereotypical formulas.

A little less than a century following the end of the Council, what was the fate of its doctrinal decrees? Certainly the conflict with the Protestants influenced Catholic theology far more than did the Tridentine decrees themselves. Scholasticism, which had dominated discussions of theology in Roman Catholicism, was pressed into service to respond above all to Protestant reformulations of Catholic dogma.[43] The theology that resulted was primarily apologetic, not constructive, and was far too easily satisfied with repeating arguments that made for good polemics. In this way, post-Tridentine scholasticism absorbed the Council's formulas into its own late medieval system. The Council had never attempted to reformulate all of Catholic doctrine, but only claimed to "take special care to condemn and anathematize the principal errors of the heretics of our day and to present and teach true Catholic doctrine, as in fact it has condemned, anathematized, and defined" (session XXV). Even so, it had made an enormous effort to offer an adequate explanation of the Catholic faith.

Theologians in the postconciliar period rejected the option of rethinking their own "system" in light of the Council's doctrinal decrees. Instead, they resolved to absorb the Council's formulations into the preexisting system, which they felt the need to reaffirm precisely because of Protestant criticism. As a result, they suppressed the most innovative element of those formulations—that is, justification—while at the same time they amplified any element that sharply contrasted with the Protestant position, such as the sevenfold nature of the sacraments; the ministry of the priesthood; and the sacrificial element of the Mass.[44] Consequently, the reception of the Council's theology was both widespread and distorted. A crucial moment in this process is evident in the *De fide* (1610/1620) of Suárez, in which the illustrious theologian proposes that revelation be seen not as an event but as a collection of doctrines.[45]

The intransigent threads of "Roman" theology increasingly fostered an ecclesiology so elaborate that it compromised its connection to the mystical and sacramental elements vital to Tridentine theology. A Church-centric outlook entirely unknown at Trent emerged. This deepening gulf between a "teaching" church (*docens*) and a "learning" church (*discens*) is evident in the semantic transition from "*magisterium*," understood as doctrinal instruction, to "*magisterium*," as teaching authority.[46] This transgression of Tridentine values in the name of Trent itself reached its peak at Vatican I. That Council formulated papal prerogatives that the fathers at Trent had firmly refused to endorse.[47] It also promoted a juridical code for the Latin Church that sanctioned ecclesiastical unity, debilitating local churches in a manner wholly foreign to Tridentine reception.

Finally, "Tridentinism" meant a particular way of interacting with the larger world. Resistance, then refusal, characterized these relations, and threatened to reduce the borders of the Church to strictly clerical circles. Even the great missionary impulse, full of energy and frequently capable of heroism, failed to expand the Church's primarily European horizons in these centuries. Any attempt to broaden the Church's vision, such as the controversies over Chinese rites or the state of Christianity in South America, was seen as a threat to the status quo.

The Council of Trent underwent a transformation. It came to be seen less and less as a significant event and more and more as a cogent but lifeless corpus of doctrinal and disciplinary norms. The decision, mentioned above, not to publish the acts of the Council is largely to blame for this fossilization. The acts were suppressed out of fear that the Protestants might mine them for polemical arguments. As a result, the Council's decisions were isolated from their surrounding context, dehistoricized, and viewed without the rich surrounding material and the pathos in which the Council had labored. When the Servite Paolo Sarpi published his *Istoria del concilio tridentino* in 1619, and the Jesuit Pallavicino put out his response in 1656–1657, it was clear that the Council was the object of more controversy than comprehension. The fear of Protestant attacks led the Council to be embalmed and turned into myth. Anything Catholic that received approval from the Apostolic See was labeled "Tridentine." Thus, the Council became the primary source of legitimacy for modern Catholicism.

A thorough rediscovery of the Council as an event and not a body of doctrinal and disciplinary norms could yield considerable fruit if conducted carefully. This certainly would not mean erasing or diminishing the impressive impact exerted by the Tridentine decisions over at least three centuries. Nor does it mean condemning the complex system of "Tridentinism" that has shaped the face of modern Catholicism, granted that it often did so by way of basking in the prestige of the Council itself. A rediscovery of the Tridentine context in all its richness, its contradictions, its unceasing dynamism would be revealing in itself, but important also for grasping the full dimensions of the time period in which the Council's decrees were implemented.[48]

In this way, a better awareness of the Council as an event would allow us to situate it more accurately in the historical context—social, cultural, as well as ecclesiastical—in which it has been celebrated. From this point of departure we can better trace the Council's decisions in their development, avoiding the temptation of a simple hermeneutic that has too often read them as sterile formulas removed from time and space. Above all, it would enable us to recover that "something more" which the mere words of the decisions cannot express and which cannot be grasped by analysis alone—which nonetheless constitute a real element of the *humus* and spirit of the Council. Separating the Council's identity from its decisions, and recognizing that it was richer and more expressive than the texts it approved, would be an important step forward. Such a development was made possible by the publication of new sources by the Görresgesellschaft[49] and the unsurpassed historical reconstruction of Hubert Jedin. Younger generations of historians can show their gratitude by taking the next step forward.

Tridentinism up to Vatican II

In the last few centuries, it has been easy to believe that one or another of the columns of the Tridentine system would crumble, but the system as a whole has always overcome its various crises. These crises, for that matter, never did more than denounce particular failings. Only in 1958–1959—under pressure from a complex of spiritual and historical factors, and thanks, no doubt, to inspiration of the Holy Spirit—did the Catholic Church, and the Christian world at large, finally abandon all of the fundamental features of Tridentinism. The intervening half-century leaves no doubt about the global reach and definitive significance of that departure.

The new council, Vatican II, took a step forward, prompted by the new historicization of the Council of Trent. Even the different uses of the nouns "implementation" and "reception" reflect this step. When on December 4, 1564, the Tridentine fathers approved the decree *De recipiendis et observandis decretis concilii*, they spoke of "reception." Later, in a transparent semantic evolution, "application" or "implementation" replaced the original term. "Reception" implies an active subject, which upon reflection could be none other than the entire *congregatio fidelium*—according to an ascending rhythm from the outside in and from the bottom up. "Application" and "implementation," however, connote a process in which the *congregatio fidelium* would become a passive recipient of centralized and authoritarian initiatives—and this is exactly what occurred. The transition from one term to the other gives a privileged status to the corpus of decisions rather than to the conciliar event in all its complexity.

In comparison with other councils, the Council of Trent enjoyed great liberty. It was not beholden to schemata arranged beforehand with the presumed approval of the Pope. The influence of Rome and of the secular political powers was relatively modest. On the other hand, the influence "from within," coming from late medieval scholasticism, was very significant—all the more so because it had been ostracized and demonized by Luther. The Council of Trent played a key role in history in that it reversed a tendency toward disintegration that, between Protestant threats and internal friction, was in the process of destroying Roman Catholicism. It is quite possible, however, that had there been a clearer understanding by the conciliar leaders of the complexity of the issues at stake, the Council's historical role might actually have been weakened.

It is obvious that a brief synthesis such as this can offer only an incomplete picture; it has done little more than reveal the limits of the system. This is not to deny that Tridentinism also had undeniable and authentic merits, if for no other reason than that it nurtured the seeds of a revival for the Church.

The successive years of implementation, with the exaggeration of some elements and the marginalization of others, created a rigid and intransigent image of the Council. Given that Vatican II defused the conflicts addressed at Trent, the provocative question remaining today is whether the Council's anathemas—intended as they were to keep a check on dissent from the magisterium, rather than from the faith itself—have become historically obsolete.[50] The Tridentine formulations, which the Council fathers had always understood as specific responses to problems raised by the Protestants, had come to be understood as absolute and final definitions only after the Council. Does not the very courage displayed at Trent in allowing the Church to be divided in view of very painful historical circumstances, today—in totally changed circumstances—call for a move toward unity and convergence? In other words, would it not allow us to revisit and reexamine these formulations in the same spirit that had originally inspired them: the pursuit of the *bonum animarum*?[51]

The Council of Trent, when seen separately from the imposing but suffocating ideology of Roman Tridentinism, bears witness to a commitment of sixteenth-century Catholicism to genuine theological and disciplinary research, of a sort that later centuries would avoid and repress even to the point of considering it destructive.

NOTES

1. G. Alberigo et al., eds., *Conciliorum oecumenicorum decreta*, 3rd ed. (COD) (Bologna: Istituto per le Scienze Religiose, 1973), 799. This initiative of the Council was due to the fact that the Popes had never participated in the assembly but had always remained in Rome.

2. Cf. G. Alberigo, "Una cum patribus. La formula conclusiva delle decisioni del Vaticano II," in *Ecclesia a Spiritu Sancto edocta: Mélanges philosophiques, hommages à Mgr. Gérard Philips* (Gembloux: J. Duculot, 1970), 291–319, esp. 300–319.

3. Görres-Gesellschaft, ed., *Concilium tridentinum* (CT), 3rd ed., vol. 9 (Freiberg im Breisgau: Herder), 1152–1156.

4. COD, 798, 5–29.

5. P. Prodi offers an enlightening comparison between the two texts in "Note sulla genesi del diritto nella chiesa post-tridentina," in *Legge e vangelo. Discussione su una legge fondamentale per la chiesa* (Brescia: Paideia, 1972), 191–223, esp. 197–198.

6. Cf. H. Jedin, *Das Konzil von Trient: Ein Überblick über die Erforschung seiner Geschichte* (Rome: Storia e Letteratura, 1948); and P. Prodi, "Le prime riflessioni storiografiche sul Tridentino negli Acta di Gabriele Paleotti," in *Reformata reformanda. Festgabe für Hubert Jedin*, vol. 1, ed. E. Iserloh and K. Repgen (Münster: Aschendorff Verlag, 1965), 701–730.

7. Cf. *La S. Congregazione del Concilio. Quarto centenario dalla fondazione (1564–1964)* (Vatican City: Libreria Editrice Vaticana, 1964).

8. Cf. H. Jedin, *Storia del concilio di Trento*, vol. 4, pt. 2 (Brescia: Morcelliana, 1978), 334–338. More recently, V. Frajese, "La politica dell'Indice dal Tridentino al Clementino (1571–1596)," in *Archivio italiano per la storia della pietà* 11 (1998): 269–356; and E. Brambilla, *Alle origini del Sant'Uffizio* (Bologna: Il Mulino, 2000), 590.

9. Cf. G. Alberigo, "Profession de foi et doxologie dans le catholicisme de XV et XVI siècles," *Irénikon* 47 (1974): 14–16; and H. Jedin, "Zur Entstehung der Professio fidei Tridentina," *Annuarium historiae conciliorum* 6 (1974): 169–175.

10. On the preparation of the catechism, see P. Rodriguez and R. Lanzetti, *El catecismo romano: Fuentes e historia del texto y de la redacción. Bases críticas para el estudio teológico del catecismo del concilio de Trento (1566)* (Pamplona: Ediciones Universidad de Navarra, 1985), and *El manuscrito original del catecismo romano* (Pamplona: Ediciones Universidad de Navarra, 1985); P. Rodriguez, *El catecismo romano ante Felipe II y la inquisición española: Los problemas de la introducción en España del catecismo del concilio de Trento* (Madrid: RIALP, 1998).

11. H. Jedin, "Il concilio di Trento e la riforma dei libri liturgici," in *Chiesa della fede, chiesa della storia*, ed. G. Alberigo (Brescia: Morcelliana, 1972), 391–425; J. M. Pommares, *Trente et le missel: L'Évolution de la question de l'autorité compétente en matière des missels* (Rome: Liturgiche, 1997). To understand how the conciliar spirit became hardened and rigid in the postconciliar period, it is very helpful to examine the papal bulls promulgating the breviary and the missal. *Quod a nobis*, of July 6, 1568, heartily deplores "dissimilitudo" and "varietas," and makes the Roman breviary obligatory for everyone. *Quo primum*, of July 14, 1570, asserts that "cum unum in ecclesia Dei psallendi modum, unum Missae celebrandae ritum esse maxime deceat."

12. For the case of France, see A. Tallon, *La France et le concile de Trente (1518–1963)* (Rome: École Française de Rome, 1997).

13. Pole himself, at the opening of the Council on January 7, 1546, had exhorted the Council fathers, in the name of the papal legates, to recognize the limits and, above all, the responsibilities of Rome during that dramatic juncture in the history of the Church, when it was torn apart by the conflict between "Romans" and Lutherans.

14. For the Jesuits, see M. Scaduto, *Storia della Compagnia di Gesù in Italia*, vol. 4, *L'epoca di Giacomo Lainez* (Rome: Civiltà Cattolica, 1970–1974), and vol. 5, *L'opera di Francesco Borgia* (Rome: Civiltà Cattolica, 1992).

15. Cf. H. Jedin, "Nunziaturberichte und Durchführung des Konzils von Trient," *Quellen und Forschungen aus Italienischen Archiven und Bibliotheken* 53 (1973): 180–213.

16. See A. Monticone, "L'applicazione del concilio di Trento a Roma," *Rivista di storia della chiesa in Italia* 8 (1954): 23–48.

17. Cf. G. Alberigo, "Carlo Borromeo come modello di vescovo nella chiesa post-tridentina," *Rivista storica italiana* 79 (1967): 1031–1052; and G. Panzeri, "Carlo Borromeo e la figura ideale del vescovo della chiesa tridentina," *Scuola cattolica* 124 (1996): 685–731.

18. Cf. Paolo Prodi, "Charles Borromé, archevêque de Milan et la papautée," *Revue d'histoire ecclésiastique* 62 (1967): 379–411, and *Il cardinale Gabriele Paleotti (1522–1597)*, 2 vols. (Rome: Storia e Letteratura, 1959–1967), 2: 233, 623.

19. Cf. G. Alberigo, *Lo sviluppo della dottrina sui poteri nella chiesa universale: Momenti essenziali tra il XVI e il XIX secolo* (Rome: Herder, 1964), 103–106.

20. Cf. Session XXI de ref. can. IV; Session XXII, *Decretum de observandis et vitandis in celebratione missarum* and de ref. can. I; Session XXIII, *Vera et catholica doctrina de sacramento ordinis ad condemnandos errores nostri temporis*, chs. I and IV; Session XXIV de ref. can. XIII and XVIII (COD 737–738); Session XXII Decretum de observandis et vitandis in celebratione missarum (COD 736–737) and de ref. can. I (COD 737–738); Session XXIII Vera et catholica doctrina de sacramento ordinis ad condemnandos errors nostri temporis chs. I and IV (COD 742–743); Sessio XXIV de ref. can XIII and XVIII (COD 770–772). Cf. A. Duval, *Des Sacrements au concile de Trente* (Paris: Éditions du Cerf, 1985); and P. Telch, "La teologia del presbiterato e la formazione dei preti al concilio di Trento e nell'epoca post-tridentina," *Studia patavina* 18 (1971): 343–389.

21. Cf. H. Maisonneuve, *Études sur les origines de l'inquisition* (Paris: Vrin, 1942); K. Pennington, " 'Pro peccatis patrum puniri'? A Moral and Legal Problem of the Inquisition," *Church History* 47 (1978): 137–154; see also E. van der Vekene, *Bibliotheca bibliographica historiae sanctae inquisitionis/Bibliographisches Verzeichnis des gedrückten Schrifttums zur Geschichte und Literatur der Inquisition*, 3 vols. (Vaduz: Topos Verlag, 1983).

22. There are many editions of these sources, and their value for social history has been recently recognized. More rare are comparative studies bringing into focus the significance and the effects of these pastoral tools.

23. According to the Council, "Praecepto divino mandatum est omnibus, quibus animarum cura commissa est, oves suas agnoscere, pro his sacrificium offerre, verbique divini praedicatione, sacramentorum administratione ac bonorum omnium operum exemplo pascere. . . ." Session XXIII de ref. can. I (COD 744, 24–27).

24. Cf. A. Lottin, "Contre-Réforme et religion populaire: Un Mariage difficile mais réussi aux XVI et XVII siècles en Flandre et en Hainaut?" in *Religion populaire: Aspects du christianisme populaire à travers l'histoire*, comp. Y.-M. Hilaire (Lille: Centre Interdisciplinaire d'Études des Religions de l'Université de Lille II, 1981), 43–57.

25. The debate over whether to abolish local rites after the Council of Trent was particularly lively and significant. Cf. G. Alberigo, "Dalla uniformità liturgica del concilio di Trento al pluralismo del Vaticano II," *Rivista liturgica* 69 (1982): 604–619, esp. 608–609.

26. The experience of Charles Borromeo in Milan is typical for this subject as

well. A few interesting features appear in *San Carlo e il suo tempo. Atti del Convegno Internazionale nel IV centenario della morte* (Milan: May 21–26, 1984), 2 vols. (Rome: Storia e Letteratura, 1986); and *San Carlo Borromeo and Ecclesiastical Politics in the Second Half of the XVI Century*, ed. J. M. Headley and J. B. Tomaro (Washington, D.C.: Folger Shakespeare Library, 1988).

27. Cf. Paolo Prodi, ed., *Disciplina dell'anima, disciplina del corpo e disciplina della società tra medioevo ed età moderna* (Bologna: Il Mulino, 1994).

28. Cf. R. Robres and V. Castell, "La visita ad limina durante el pontificado de Sisto V (1585–1590)," *Anthologica annua* 7 (1959): 147–213.

29. Cf. H. Jedin, "La riforma del processo informativo per la nomina dei vescovi al concilio di Trento," in *Chiesa della fede, chiesa della storia*, ed. G. Alberigo (Brescia: Morcelliana, 1972), 316–319. After Trent, the choice of bishops, based on the information provided by nuncios, fell to the Curia. The participation of provincial councils, as established in chapter 1 of the reforming decree of session XXIV of Trent, never came to pass. In 1591, Gregory XIV also excluded metropolitans from the procedure; cf. M. Faggioli, "Problemi relativi alle nomine episcopali dal concilio di Trento al pontificato di Urbano VIII," *Cristianesimo nella storia* 21 (2000): 531–564, and "Urbano VIII e la riforma del procedimento di nomina dei vescovi," *Cristianesimo nella storia* 23 (2002): 79–121.

30. Cf. G. Fragnito, *La bibbia al rogo* (Bologna: Il Mulino, 1997).

31. Cf. G. Alberigo, "Servire la comunione delle chiese," *Concilium* 15 (1979): 1137–1164, esp. 1140–1143.

32. Cf. M.-T. Fattori, "Appunti sulla crisi del sacro Collegio durante il pontificato di Gregorio XIV," *Cristianesimo nella storia* (2004), and *Clemente VIII e il Sacro Collegio 1592–1605: Meccanismi istituzionali e accentramento di governo* (Stuttgart: A. Hiersemann, 2004).

33. A Congregation on Residence was instituted in Rome, authorized to supervise bishops and make sure that they resided in their own dioceses. Cf. A. Lauro, "La curia romana e la residenza dei vescovi," in *Società religiosa nell'età moderna*. Atti del Convegno di studi di storia sociale e religiosa, Cappacio–Paestum, May 18–21, 1972, gen. ed. F. Malgeri (Naples: Ed. Guida, 1973), 869–883.

34. These have been edited by X.-M. Le Bachelet, *Auctarium Bellarminianum* (Paris: Beauchesne, 1913), 513–518, 518–520, 533–535. I summarize the memorandum submitted to Clement VIII in 1600–1601. A few years later, in the draft of a note to Paul V in October 1612, Bellarmine writes, "Reformatio Ecclesiae omni tempore necessaria est, quia fragilitas et imbecillitas humana semper labitur in deterius. Sed hoc tempore facile obtineri posset absque novis constitutionibus et decretis, si concilium Tridentinum diligenter observaretur."

35. Ibid., 518, n. 1; cited by L. Orabona, *Chiesa e società moderna* (Rome and Naples: L.E.R, 1995), 39.

36. Cf. V. Martin, *Le Gallicanisme et la réforme catholique: Essai historique sur l'introduction en France des décrets du concile de Trente 1563–1615* (Geneva: Slatkine-Megariotis Reprints, 1975); and P. Blet, *Le Clergé de France et la monarchie: Étude sur les assemblées générales du clergé de 1615 à 1666* (Rome: Librairie de l'Université Grégorienne, 1959). For the Low Countries, see the classic work of F. Willocx, *L'Introduction des décrets du concile de Trente dans les Pays-Bas et dans la principauté de Liège* (Louvain:

Librairie Universitaire, 1929); for Spain, B. Llorca, "Aceptación en España de los de-
cretos del concilio de Trento," *Estudios eclesiásticos* 39 (1964): 341–360, 459–482.

37. Cf. J. W. O'Malley, *Trent and All That: Renaming Catholicism in the Early Modern Era* (Cambridge, Mass.: Harvard University Press, 2000), 219.

38. J. Goñi Gaztambide, "Los cabildos españoles y la confirmación del concilio
de Trento," *Annuarium historiae conciliorum* 7 (1975): 425–458.

39. E. Cattaneo, "La singolare fortuna degli 'Acta ecclesiae mediolanensis,' " *Scuola cattolica* III (1983): 191–217. Like Borromeo, Cardinal G. Paleotti collected the acts
of his own episcopal ministry in Bologna in *Archiepiscopale bononiense* (Rome: A. Zan-
netus, 1594).

40. Many of his contemporaries, from G. Paleotti to D. Bollani, considered Borromeo's severe asceticism and government to be excessive and counterproductive.
Some historians have mechanically subscribed to these evaluations, endorsing them
as critically researched conclusions. It seems to me that, instead, it is absolutely necessary to study in greater depth the reasons behind the choices of Borromeo, bearing
in mind not only his personality traits but also, above all, his experience in Rome and
later in Milan with church corruption. Faced with a real system of abuses and immorality, Borromeo felt that the only appropriate course was an intransigent style of reform that avoided any compromise toward any circles of decadence. A. G. Roncalli's
perception of this situation is interesting; cf. A. Melloni, "Il modello di Carlo Borromeo nell'esperienza e negli studi di A. G. Roncalli," *Rivista di storia e letteratura religiosa* 22 (1986): 68–114.

41. Cf. C. Wackenheim, "Écriture et tradition depuis le concile de Trente: Histoire d'un faux problème," *Revue des sciences religieuses* 55 (1981): 237–252.

42. On the doctrine of transubstantiation, cf. J. Wohlmuth, *Realpräsenz und
Transsubstantiation im Konzil von Trient. Eine historisch-kritische Analyse der Canones 1–
4 der sessio XIII*, 2 vols. (Bern: Lang, 1975).

43. Cf. O. H. Pesch, "La Réponse du concile de Trente (1545–1563): Les Décisions
doctrinales contre la réforme et ses conséquences," *Irénikon* 73 (2000): 5–38.

44. Robert Bellarmine expanded his ecclesiology after 1570, and between 1586
and 1593 published the *Disputationes de controversiis* . . . , G. Galeota TRE 5 (1980),
coll. 525–531. Cf. P. Eyt, "L'Ordre du discours et l'ordre de l'église: Hypothèse sur les
structures profondes d'un texte des Controverses de Bellarmin," *Bulletin de littérature
ecclésiastique* 73 (1972): 229–249.

45. G. Ruggieri, "Per una storia dell'apologia cristiana nell'epoca moderna. Note
bibliografiche e metodologiche," *Cristianesimo nella storia* 4 (1983): 33–58.

46. Cf. Y. Congar, "Pour une histoire sémantique du terme 'magisterium,' " *Revue des sciences philosophiques et théologiques* 60 (1976): 85–98, and "Bref historique
des formes du 'magistère' et de ses relations avec les docteurs," ibid., 99–112.

47. I have analyzed the sources dealing with Trent's refusal, in 1563, to approve
a Roman project on the person and authority of the Pope in "L'Unité de l'église dans
le service de l'église romaine et de la papauté (XIe–XXe siècle)," *Irénikon* 51 (1978): 46–
72, esp. 58–63.

48. Cf. G. Fransen, "L'Application des décrets du concile de Trente. Les Débuts
d'un nominalisme canonique," *L'Année canonique* 27 (1983): 5–16.

49. The final volume (XIII/2) of the series Concilium Tridentinum, dedicated to

the *Tractate nach der XXII. Session (September 17, 1562) bis zum Schluss des Konzils*, ed. and rev. K. Ganzer (Freiburg im Breisgau: Herder, 2001), was published exactly a century after the publication of the first volume, edited by S. Merkle.

50. As Jedin has observed in his *Storia*, vol. 2, 441.

51. Cf. G. Alberigo and I. Rogger, eds., *Il concilio di Trento nella prospettiva del terzo millennio* (Brescia: Morcelliana, 1997).

3

A Marriage Made in America: Trent and the Baroque

Anthony M. Stevens-Arroyo

A familiar debate asks whether the principal purpose of the Council of Trent was to launch a Counter-Reformation aimed at combating Protestantism or to coordinate a Catholic Reformation that restructured the Church. From the perspective of the Americas, however, neither of these views tells the whole story. Across the Atlantic in Spanish America,[1] there were no Protestants to combat and virtually no preexisting Church structures to reform. Trent's decrees assumed a new function as the blueprints for Christianity in the Americas, linking Church order in Spain's colonies with the institutionalization of the faith for millions of believers. Trent became a constituent element of Latin America's sociohistorical identity. If a military simile were to be used, the Counter-Reformation was like taking the battlefield against the enemy, the Catholic Reformation represented the reinforcement of battle stations, and Trent in America became an exercise in nation-building. Although the American results of Trent may not be as familiar to scholars as its European effects, we are blessed with a growing literature on the ecclesiastical history of the Americas that documents religious concerns within the social setting of the period.[2]

Intergenerational and Interracial Catholic Identities

The Council of Trent began in 1545, scarcely fifty years after Columbus had erected the first stone government building in Santo Domingo. Cortés had marched into the Aztec capital of Tenochtitlán only twenty years before the council's opening, and a scant ten years had passed since the conquistadores had subjugated Incan Peru. By the time the Council had closed in 1563, however, serious epidemics had greatly reduced the native population and the majority of the population living under the shadow of colonial power had been born after the Spanish arrival.[3] Even among the pure-blooded native population, leadership often fell to the ladinos who had learned to speak Spanish. Hence, the emergence of a Tridentine Catholicism in Latin America coincided with the accession of a new population that was in the process of shaping a distinctly hybrid culture.

In order to understand more fully the intergenerational and interracial character of the colonial population beginning in the last quarter of the sixteenth century in Spanish America, it may be useful to indicate the social and cultural importance of the mestizos and mestizas.[4] These mixed-race peoples were less affected by devastating epidemics than the natives were because they had acquired immunities to many imported diseases from their European parent. Their social importance was also greater than that of most pure-blooded natives because they bridged the gap between two cultures. Additionally, the mestizos and mestizas were not criollos or criollas, who had two European parents. Although racially distinguishable, both of these groups had been born in the colonies and shared common interests in limiting European control over American social and political institutions. They became the twin pillars of the Spanish colonial identity after Trent.

While it is essential to recognize the distinctly American character of such categories of generation, race, and racial mixture, it should not be forgotten that they echoed medieval Spain. For at least 700 years, Iberian Catholicism had accommodated itself to sharing social space with Muslims, Jews, and the offspring of intermarriage across such boundaries. The centuries of military *reconquista* were partnered with longer periods of *convivencia* in which racial and religious toleration and cooperation were common.[5] Hence, unlike most of Europe's Catholic countries, Spain was equipped with established legal constructs to incorporate non-Christians and to oblige large numbers of converts. In fact, the laws that had applied to "new Christians" in Spain were applied to native converts in the colonies in the series of earliest diocesan synods and councils that preceded Trent.[6] As will be described below, these matters focused on theological discussion of evangelization. After Trent, however, the significant demographic diversity of the colonies required a theology that went beyond issues of first encounter and addressed the integration of diverse groups within a new hybrid society.

Race and racial mixture were not the only factors for cultural diversity in Spanish America of the sixteenth century. The predominant language in colonial Latin America was not Spanish. Castilian, distinguished from other languages of the Iberian kingdoms, was mainly used for writing official documents and in the domestic conversations of sheltered urban elites, while Latin remained the ecclesiastical language of theology and liturgy. The majority of the colonial population, however, spoke native tongues because the small number of Spanish settlers made it virtually impossible to force a European language upon the new American colonies. In Mexico, for instance, Nahuatl speakers limited their use of Spanish to imported nouns until the 1660s, when Spanish verbs begin to appear in common discourse.[7] It took another century before use of Nahuatl eroded in urban Mexico, while in other places, the native language lasted into the nineteenth century.[8]

This mixture of languages is a metaphor for similar exchanges in other social commodities. The food, dress, tools, and transportation in the Americas copied the most useful objects from two worlds. Spaniards came to rely on potatoes, tomatoes, and corn, and the Americans incorporated coffee, sugar, rum, chicken, and pork into their diet. European clothing was made with local materials, and the music of the Spanish guitar was accompanied by native instruments such as the maraca. In sum, the material elements of life in colonial society served mostly to connect the diverse cultures of the racial/ethnic groups rather than to divide them. The cultural mixing was perhaps even more influential than biological intermarriage, or *mestizaje*, in shaping both secular and religious facets of society. Moreover, the church was an important ladder for social mobility, as is indicated by the number of American-born clerics, nuns, and professors of theology entering positions of social leadership.

Standard secular history texts do not always reflect the sophistication of ecclesiastical discourse beginning in the late sixteenth century, preferring to state only *that* the emerging colonial elites wrote, without analyzing *what* they wrote. While students of Church history may be inclined to pardon a professional reluctance to wander outside of one's expertise, secular history is reproachable when it confuses the initial stages of evangelization before Trent with the institutionalization of a vital Catholicism after it. Condemnation of Catholicism for attacking the shamans of native religions in the early sixteenth century does not absolve the historian of a need to study the Church's contribution to a new hybrid society in the seventeenth century. Without trivializing the mistakes and errors of the evangelizers and conquistadores, competent historians ought to examine the assessment of those mistakes from within the Church once Trent had taken place. Hence, study of the first generation of criollo and mestizo literature is also a study of Tridentine Catholicism.

Another scholarly misstep is located in an overly rigorous distinction between a "high" Catholicism of clerical orthodoxy and a "low" or "popular" religion. Dichotomous views of social class may have an analytical utility, but they run the danger of failing to recognize that Catholicism includes both its clerical leaders and the mass of believers.[9] In fact, defense of the interests of the intergenerational and interracial population of Spanish America during the sixteenth and seventeenth centuries generally came from within the Church, and it distorts colonial history to omit this self-critical facet of Catholicism.

The frequent fusion of civic and religious spheres in Spanish America can be understood with the interpretative tool of "material theology."[10] As I have argued in other places, material theology allows the ideational creations of faith to be observed in terms of frequency and distribution within the social and civic polity. Consideration of materiality allows the importance of any theological pronouncement to be measured by its empirically verifiable effects on the practice of religion. Thus, for instance, the importance of Trent's decree for seminaries can be measured by assessing how many eventual priests attended such seminaries, what they studied, what books they published, and what posts they occupied after ordination. Empirical evaluation of material effects, I submit, is preferable to classifying decrees as to their theological orthodoxy.

Pre-Tridentine Theologies of Evangelization in the Americas

Trent did not encounter a backwater, a disorganized and neglected American Catholicism. The first fifty years of Iberian presence after Columbus's second voyage of 1493 had provoked intensive theological, philosophical, and legal debates concerning the conflicts about evangelization by incorporation into feudalism and respect for the rights of non-Christian peoples. Such debates in Spain represented the most advanced stage of Europe's understanding of the natural law as the basis for the relationships among nations.[11] Theologians of the caliber of Bartolomé de Las Casas and Francisco de Vitoria of the sixteenth-century University of Salamanca were architects of the pre-Tridentine strategies of evangelization. These debates explored whether the existing Iberian pastoral legislation for converts from non-Christian religions could be applied to the Native Americans. Iberian proximity to Islam had created a tradition of preaching in native languages[12] and of writing catechisms that used non-Christian images. As Robert Ricard points out in his classic work, the material theology of grassroots missionaries to New Spain (Mexico) was a signal glory for Catholicism and one that presaged current missiological emphasis upon the enculturation of the faith.[13]

The evangelization of the Americas was not an *ex nihilo* creation. The earliest Franciscans had brought to the Americas a pre-Tridentine theology of conversion that employed feudal conceptions of authority. Conversion of a ruler was expected to be followed by the mass conversion of all "vassals" within the dominions of the lord.[14] The Dominicans, on the other hand, intended a greater emphasis upon individual conversions and set a higher bar for baptism and reception of the other sacraments. To allow time for individual conversions, Las Casas proposed that each native people erect a *res publica de los indios* to function with its own inherited laws within a polity under the Spanish crown. The Dominican friar sought to explain religious practices not as culpable idolatry but as reformable customs that could be accommodated by Catholic belief.[15] The two approaches were not completely resolved when the Council opened. Moreover, the tension was exacerbated by the theological underpinning of much of Franciscan missiology.

Several Franciscan chroniclers reflect a millennial view of the American Church. Casting the Indians as the lost tribes of Israel, some Franciscans utilized Joachimite rhetoric to state that the souls of the natives would replace the Europeans lost to Lutheranism.[16] They argued that America would become the most faithful reflection of Catholicism in the New World because Europe had been irretrievably corrupted by heresy and laxity.[17] This millennial language fit better with late medieval Catholicism than with Trent's decrees. By 1563, when the Council of Trent closed, the Franciscan hold over the colonial Spanish American policy had been weakened largely because the conversion of Native Americans was no longer the chief pastoral concern. The Spanish monarchy began to shrink the privileges and exemptions that had been provided to the regular clergy and the evangelizing bishops drawn from their ranks in addressing the religious education of those Americans born into the faith. Trent's emphasis upon pastoral care from the secular clergy also pushed the missionary Franciscans in the Americas to an ever expanding and continually dangerous frontier populated by natives increasingly hostile to European intentions.

However, the Franciscan chiliastic view of Christianity in Spanish America never completely disappeared, and was to be recast later as writers born in the colonies looked to legitimize the distinctly American contours of their Catholicism. Ironically, Trent produced a theology in the Americas that both accepted institutional hierarchies and attacked policies that identified the faith with Spanish imperial interests. The millennial vision of the Franciscans has been embedded into Latin American self-vision, and one can discover its basic tenets within the twentieth-century theology of liberation.[18]

The Arrival of Tridentine Reforms in the Americas

The call of the Council for reforms that focused on diocesan policies was welcomed in the Americas, largely because the bishops were already convinced of such an emphasis. Mexico, to provide just one example, already had held about seventeen episcopal meetings, beginning in 1524, scarcely three years after Cortés had "pacified" the Aztecs. Both Mexico City and Lima, Peru's archdiocese, had given major attention to the drafting of catechisms, usually in the native languages.[19] This task was intensified after 1537 with the proclamation by Paul III of *Sublimis Deus*,[20] and again in 1542 with the New Laws of Burgos that attacked many of the exploitative institutions of colonization.[21] During Trent's intersession, Lima (1551–1552) and Mexico (1555) held episcopal councils to formalize the pastoral policies that had emerged as those most effective and theologically sound. In 1553, both jurisdictions founded pontifical universities.

At the Council's close, Phillip II gave the papal decree *Benedictus Deus* of Paul IV the force of royal law with his own proclamation on July 12, 1564.[22] Additionally, Philip proposed that a Catholic Patriarch be named to oversee the conciliar implementation in the Americas.[23] Rome, however, responded with the institution of a Vatican congregation that was to become *De Propaganda Fide*. This congregation, originally intended to focus on the Americas, developed a concern for missions everywhere. However, its origins lie in Tridentine concern for the Americas.

In response to conciliar directives, Mexico held its second episcopal council in 1565, and a third in 1585. Lima's second such council took place during 1567–1568, and a third in 1581–1583 under the direction of Bishop Toribio de Mogrovejo. Quito, Ecuador, held its first council in 1570, a second in 1594, and a third in 1596. The substance of each of these post-Tridentine councils is analyzed in detail by Saranyana and his collaborators. I suggest, however, that the swift response and substantial attention from the American bishops indicates the genuine fervor with which they embraced the Council of Trent.

The issues addressed by these post-Tridentine councils of sixteenth-century America can be summarized as follows: (1) the continued revision of catechisms in native languages, now to be restructured in accordance with the decrees of Trent; (2) the development of confessionaries to guide pastors on how to deal with common doctrinal errors and questionable behavior, such as polygamy for native caciques; (3) policies to "extirpate idolatries." This last concern was reflected in the unanticipated resurgence of native religions in bloody revolts against missions thought to be safely established.[24] While the effort to stamp out the recrudescence of native religions had its reactionary face, the dictates of Trent also empowered a more liberal pastoral view. Some argued that the extirpation should be focused not on attacks against native religious practices but upon better education of these new Catholics. Such was the policy explained by the Cuzco-born cleric Francisco Dávila (c. 1573–1647) in his treatise outlining sermon topics on the Gospels for each Sunday of the year.[25]

Jesuit influence in the Americas was a collateral result of the Council, although not without criticism and jealousy from both secular and ecclesiastical sources. Animated by the confidence that nature would not contradict faith, Jesuit education explored new issues, often blurring the boundaries of religion and culture. Among the first Jesuits arriving in the Americas after 1570 was José de Acosta, a descendant of a family of Jewish conversos. He introduced a new genre of theology that relied upon considerable data taken from observing native cultures.[26] There is a similarity between such theological treatises and the encyclopedias that foreshadowed the rational learning of the Enlightenment. Thus, Jesuit influence exceeded mere ecclesiastical matters and shaped the thinking of a new generation of native-born leaders. Equipped with concepts from European science and theology, the post-Tridentine American writers produced a body of knowledge that bridged ecclesiastical concern and secular curiosity.

Post-Tridentine Thinking about American Catholicism

Native-born and American-educated clerics emerged as scholars who not only participated in the theological discussions of Europe but also fashioned new arguments that focused upon uniquely American issues. Thus, for instance, one can view the *Symbolo catholico indiano* of the Peruvian-born Franciscan Jerónimo Oré (1554–1630), who eventually was named a bishop in Chile's diocese of La Imperial. This work interprets Incan prayers to the earth mother, Pachacamac, as an inchoate monotheism and includes Christian hymns in the native Quechua language, each of which is explained in Castilian. Although the respect that Oré shows the native Incan religion carries vestiges of the medieval Franciscan Joachimite rhetoric, his theology of symbols moves beyond that of Saints Augustine, Thomas, and even Bonaventure. Echoing ideas from the Neoplatonism of Richard of St. Victor, Oré argues that mysteries such as the Trinity and the Resurrection are symbolized in native religion. While extolling the pre-Christian value of Peru's Incans, he criticizes Church and civic policies that he considers to have ignored the richness of native beliefs.[27]

Oré was not the only the post-Tridentine cleric born in the Americas to be both erudite in European theology and attuned to an anthropology of the native religion. His theology is faithful to Tridentine Catholicism and critical of hispanizing tendencies that stigmatized his own people's expression of the faith. In Peru, other writers such as the mestizo cleric Gracilaso de la Vega (1539–1616) and Felipe Guamán Poma de Ayala (c. 1538–c. 1620) criticized Spanish civil and ecclesiastical policies. While more of a historian than a theologian, de la Vega wrote in the spirit of Trent, defending the Church but simultaneously praising the native culture of Peru. Poma de Ayala, or Wuaman Puma, was an indigenous ladino, conversant in the Castilian language, who became a government official. He completed his *Nueva crónica y buen gobierno,* to be sent to King Philip III, in 1615. Although his narrative was a detailed list of abuses committed against the natives in the name of religion, it was written by a believer. The contrasts he drew between words and deeds provided a telling assessment of the positive impact of sermons and catechisms upon Peru's faithful, while offering an unflattering portrait of a lax ecclesiastical culture. His work was replete with graphic depictions of offending clerics along with his listing of dos and don'ts for pastoral care. It evaluated the Council's reforms in the Americas from the perspective of a native believer in the Gospel who was unafraid to denounce the shortcomings of ecclesiastics.[28]

In Mexico, the curriculum of the pontifical university reflected the work of the Dominican Pedro de Pravia (1525–1590), who came to the Americas early and developed a textbook synthesizing the *Summa* of St. Thomas Aquinas. This text was repeatedly revised by Jesuit professors at the university long after Pravia had died.[29] Examination of this theological textbook provides a window into the sophistication of theological education in the Americas during the first century after the Council of Trent. Like that of others in the Americas, Pravia's theology was never so speculative as to neglect social issues. The Dominican friar had sent King Philip II an important denunciation of abuses against the Indians. His polemics against colonial administrators was endorsed by the Third Episcopal Council of Mexico, indicating that his advocacy of social justice was widely shared.

American Tridentine theology also took on the issues of European theology. Juan Díaz de Arce (1594–1653) was a secular priest, born in Mexico City, who rose to occupy the chair of biblical studies at the pontifical university. His major work focused on the biblical bases for the Immaculate Conception,[30] thus broaching the centuries-old debate between Dominicans and Franciscans.[31] His biblical justification for the Immaculate Conception of Mary contributed to the theology of Our Lady of Guadalupe in Mexico.

Tridentine theology in the Americas also enhanced the newly emerging cultural identity of the criollos and criollas. A preeminent contributor to this commingling of religion and culture was Carlos Singüenza y Góngora (1645–1700), a native of Mexico City. He was a secular priest without a parish assignment who simultaneously held the chair of mathematics at the University of Mexico and was chief geographer of New Spain, chaplain of a hospital, examiner of artillery, and accountant for the university. His writings on topics ranging from archaeology and history to theology and science were surpassed in quality only by a contemporary, the Jeronymite nun Sor Juana Inés de la Cruz (1651–1695). Considered together, their works are regarded as important contributions to seventeenth-century Spanish literature, and rival literary production in Europe.[32]

Tridentine Catholicism and the American Baroque

Material theology measures the impact of formal theology by its empirical effects on society. For the post-Tridentine period, material results were shaped by the style and fashions of the baroque period, and it is difficult to separate the impact of Trent from its cultural milieu. Traditionally, the Catholic baroque is considered to have begun during the reign of the Hapsburg Philip II and to have ended with the Bourbon reforms after 1750.[33] I see the baroque as different from the Renaissance and the Enlightenment, and not merely their "darker side."[34] We are fortunate that as a mentality, which embraces far more than merely an artistic style, the baroque has received considerable scholarly attention since the 1970s.[35] However, we should not presume that the baroque in the Americas was the same as in Europe.[36] In seeking the effects upon religion, several traits merit special attention, even while recognizing that no mentality ever totally consumes a society.

The Baroque and Medieval Piety

As a conservative age, the baroque looked to the past rather than the future for its inspiration. The pre-Reformation era of a unified Christendom was viewed as a happier time than a fragmented future with competing Christian religions and warring states. The idealized picture of the medieval world was an argument that a return to the past would undo the evils brought by rationalism, individualism, and greed in a postfeudal economy. Cervantes's gaunt figure of Don Quixote challenges readers to decide who is really mad: those who live by the values of nobility and honor or those who believe such things are only fables. Rather than present itself as a new era, baroque Catholicism preferred to "recycle" these values of the Middle Ages whenever possible, sometimes leaving the impression that it contributed nothing new to culture or religion.

In fact, Trent subtly accepted elements of the Reformers' criticism of the accretions of superstition in popular religion. Conciliar reforms expunged magical elements from existing devotions, denounced commercialism, and reconstructed devotions to conform to theological orthodoxy.[37] Thus recast, baroque Catholicism undertook a Tridentine preservation of the acceptable pious traditions of medieval Christendom while rejecting objectionable elements.

The new Catholicism of Spanish America, however, had a past that included indigenous religious customs. Most of these employed rituals using water, fire, images, processions, music, and the like in ways that were not very different from rituals of medieval Europe. Often connected to planting, harvest, and social rites of passage, these events were "baptized" as local American variants of hallowed European traditions. Tridentine theology in the Americas used Trent's purification technique of medieval European Catholicism in asserting that indigenous religion predisposed the natives in favor of the Catholic religion. Thus, while Trent's European effect was to extol medieval Catholic practice, in the Americas the Council engendered a form of enculturation.

The Catholic Baroque and the Marvelous

Since the Reformation had disparaged clergy, sacraments, and devotions to Mary, Trent emphasized them. The reception of the sacraments or devotion to Mary was cast by baroque exuberance as an invitation for contact with heaven that Protestants could not duplicate. As Maravall has put it, Catholic practice during the baroque "took delight in the marvelous."[38] The Roman Catholic experience in baroque America was shot through with miracles, consonant with the medieval period of European Christianity.[39] But since the Reformation had painted these unexplained phenomena as the causes of superstition, the baroque was forced to recognize the intelligence of those who encountered the divine, explaining miracles as the result of faith rather than as the residue of gullibility. Narratives indulged in psychological exploration of saintly individuals in order to provide legitimacy for miraculous epiphanies.

This tendency can be measured by the proliferation during the baroque of published books on the lives of the saints (*Flos sanctorum*). Frequently these tales include long soliloquies in florid prose delivered by eight- and nine-year-old future saints. More than books, however, theater was the medium of mass communication during the baroque. For those unfamiliar with the plays of Calderón de la Barca or the *autosacramentales* of Sor Juana written in Spanish, it will suffice to make a comparison with works of their English baroque contemporary, William Shakespeare. The soliloquies of Hamlet and the Plantagenet kings or the hexes and ghosts in Macbeth are replete with an exploration of the psychological dimension of human experience. Frequently without historical foundation, baroque authors felt free to accommodate the popular culture with dramatic dialogue that both educated and pleased the public.[40] And while a more skeptical age like our own would likely dismiss such baroque creations as a "constructed reality," during the baroque it was an accepted style of hagiographical writing. Baroque drama operated from a teleological premise that only a later generation could fully appreciate the importance of any spiritual event in the past. For the baroque mentality, anachronistic embellishments were intended to guarantee that the reader would not miss the theological meaning on account of an undue concern for historical accuracy.

The dramatic license of the baroque is reflected in the foundation accounts of Marian apparitions in the Americas. A comparison between the events that produced the devotions to Our Lady of Charity in Cuba[41] and Our Lady of Guadalupe in New Spain[42] demonstrates the centrality of a baroque "history" of the origins of each cult. In each case, a shrine that had witnessed marvelous cures and favors to suppliants was supplied with a narrative about an apparition of the Blessed Mother. Those who promoted the devotion supplied literary accounts of its legendary origins, adding dialogue to apparition, much in the manner of a baroque theatrical drama. Even when a sermon was delivered in Nahuatl, the style was baroque.[43] Important to this discussion about Our Lady of Guadalupe or Our of Lady of Charity is the absence of miracles or apparition narratives in texts dating from the time when the events took place. In fact, in the Mexican case, rather than allege an apparition, Franciscans such as Sahagún actually disparaged the devotion as an excess of ignorance.[44] It was not until 1630, when the baroque was flourishing, that the criollo cleric Miguel Sánchez contributed dialogue for the apparition of Our Lady of Guadalupe. With a similar license, in 1701 the second formal account of the finding of a statue of Our Lady of Charity at Nipe Bay in Cuba in 1613 reinterprets the eyewitness testimony of 1688 by adding miraculous voices and lights.[45]

Delight in the marvelous intruded into piety. Sanctity was expected to edify believers. The mystic raptures of holy nuns and descriptions of their visions were popular devotional reading. *Las siete moradas* by St. Teresa of Avila was one of a genre produced by the many *beatas* who wrote from cloistered convents, not always with the reliability of St. Teresa.[46] For nuns who did not receive these glorious visions, extreme asceticism could be used to invite God's grace. Extended fasting or physical penance in the name of religion was the obverse side of mystical glory because surviving such suffering was considered a sign of heavenly favor. In Lima, a native Dominican nun, Rosa, was to be granted the honors of the altar on account of the fame of her self-inflicted penances. The lay brother Martin of Porres was celebrated for his miracles, which rivaled those of European saints. That Martin was of the black race added to the American character of his miracles.

The attraction of the marvelous to the baroque Catholicism of the Americas did not preclude logic or erudition. In Lima, Diego de Avedaño published his six-volume *Thesaurus indicus* between 1668 and 1686. It was a learned compendium of the theological and pastoral issues of the day that demonstrates the sophistication of intellectuals in the colonies. The work of the Segovia-born Jesuit analyzed the confluence of secular and ecclesiastical powers during the period of Spanish conquest; dissected the sacramental policies in the pastoral care of the natives; attacked the moralist position of Jansenists; explained the sanctity of the recently beatified Dominican nun, Rosa of Lima; and launched a polemic against the continued enslavement of Africans.[47] This linkage of speculative issues with pragmatic and political ones by Avedaño is characteristic of the American baroque, indicating that the highly imaginative use of literary and symbolic artifice did not stand opposed to a progressive activism in areas of social justice. The native Peruvian Juan de Espinosa Medrano (c. 1628–1688), named "el Lunarejo," criticized the straying from Thomism in European Catholic theology in a book published in Rome.[48]

Of course, there was resistance to this irrational exuberance about apparitions and other expressions of faith. Juan Palafox y Mendoza (1600–1659), Bishop of Puebla in Mexico, was sober when others were expansive about the expression of faith. He sought to contain what he perceived as exploitation of the people's attraction toward miracles. His pastoral policies censured leniency toward syncretism with non-Christian beliefs and insisted the religious education of each individual was more important than collective works of piety. Yet, even if he is classified as a Jansenist island in a sea of Jesuit probabilists, his saintly faithfulness to Tridentine reform fits within the baroque period that by its nature reveled in extremes.[49]

The Council of Trent and Catholic Providentialism

The "nation-building" function of the Council of Trent in the Americas produced a special form of Catholic providentialism. For centuries, Christian writers had elaborated theological explanations of the Holy Cross as compass, an-
chor, the four winds, and similar images that resonated with the function of
the indigenous image. As described above, the Council emphasized these medieval traditions in order to assert a Catholic "difference" from Protestants who
ignored nearly a millennium of Christianity in their emphasis on the apostolic
church. However, in the Americas, the religion that had existed before the
Council was not Christianity, thus forcing theologians to invent an American
alternative. Baroque clerics in the Americas reinterpreted some religious symbols of the indigenous people as parts of God's plan to prepare the way for the
Gospel. In an age of faith such as the baroque, it was not a mere coincidence
that two religions should share the same basic symbols. Rather, such similarities proved God's providentialism in utilizing pre-Christian religions to pre-
figure Catholic doctrines.

The American variety of baroque providentialism went beyond comparison
of religious customs such as had been outlined by Las Casas during the period
of evangelization. The baroque not only accepted the similarities, but elaborated a historical setting that transformed the allegorical allusions into facts
dating back to the pre-Christian past. For instance, American theologians exploited a reference by Origen to a sailing trip of St. Thomas beyond the Med-
iterranean.[50] This passage became the basis to argue, both in Brazil and in
Mexico, that Thomas the Apostle had preached the Gospel in the Americas.
Sor Juana Inés de la Cruz elaborated the theological importance of what Carlos
Sigüenza y Góngora considered historical fact. The Mexican nun wrote in *El
divino narciso* that the Aztec custom of human sacrifice was a confused vestige
of the Eucharist wherein Catholics are urged to eat the body and blood of Christ
for salvation. At the dawn of the nineteenth century, more than a hundred
years later, Fray Servando Teresa de Mier (1763–1827) argued that, with Thomas's preaching, the claim by Spain to have brought the Christian faith to
Mexico was invalid and, therefore, the Europeans should leave the Mexicans
to their independence immediately.[51] Writing for an Enlightenment audience
after the French Revolution, Teresa de Mier's citation of baroque historical
inventiveness seems out of place. However, by recalling the suppression of the
Society of Jesus at the end of the baroque, it merits comment that the concept
of "noble savage" found in Voltaire and Rousseau was diffused in Europe by
many American Jesuits fleeing the effects of their order's suppression in Latin
America.[52] Thus, the impact of the American Trent in shaping a convergence
of theology and culture was not limited either to the Americas or to the period
of the baroque.

Nationhood for All Peoples and Theological Universality

The Tridentine Catholicism of the Americas had a transatlantic effect, since these American developments were not unconnected to the concerns of European theologians. Baroque Europe viewed acceptance of the faith as proof that Roman Catholicism was the universal religion of Christ's promise. Universality required a unity of belief, but with the embrace of cultures that did more than merely reproduce European Catholicism. The baroque statues of Mary can be examined with material theology for their inclusion of indigenous tradition within Catholicism.[53]

The artistic representations of Marian apparitions in the Americas are showered with symbols of native religion. Thus, for instance, the Mexican image of Our Lady of Guadalupe is adorned with elements derived from Aztec religious symbols, even to the location of the vision on Tepeyac hill, a site sacred to Tonantzin, an Aztec mother deity.[54] She is at once both completely Aztec and totally Christian. The native and the European faiths are fused together by juxtaposing symbols that reflect both experiences. The baroque imagination, in contrast to a Jansenistic one, invited such commingling of symbolisms. Rather than an absence of Catholic orthodoxy or a demonstration of popular resistance to Christianity, the syncretism of Marian images is an affirmation of Tridentine creativity. The influence upon cultural identity by the Mexican Our Lady of Guadalupe, or by many other American Madonnas, cannot be understood without reference to the mentality of the baroque that considered the iconic juxtapositions of native and European sacrality to be causes for celebration rather than occasions for contestation.[55]

The "con-fusion" of the Mexican Our Lady of Guadalupe with the Spanish Madonna with the same name was not merely a concession to artistic license. The Marian apparition in Mexico expressed the theological truth that the Blessed Mother had a universal love of all Catholics. Certainly, the vision of Mary in Mexico was a favorable result of the evangelization successfully carried out by the Spanish Empire, but it also demonstrated that the Queen of Heaven bestowed her blessings directly upon the native Mexicans. Thus, Marian devotion was a constituent element in America's Tridentine Catholicism because the apparitions of Mary in the Americas permitted the criollo and mestizo colonies to claim equality with European nations in terms of divine favor.[56]

Although this equality was expressed in theological terms, it was grafted onto a social and political reality. The seventeenth century subscribed to a definition of "nation" that defined a people in terms of language and customs rather than the territorial and state ascription that has been used since the nineteenth century. Based on the Roman *lex gentium*, this concept of nation allowed diverse legal codes and linguistic traditions within a single kingdom. As elaborated by the Jesuit theologian Francisco Suárez, the American and Asian nations were entitled to the same legal standing within the Spanish

Empire as the feudal kingdoms of the Iberian Peninsula.[57] To attain and safe-guard this status as a nation, the peoples of Ibero-America and Ibero-Asia were inclined to claim Mary as patroness of their nations. Her miraculous appari-tions verified claims to nationhood on behalf of the faithful who were her witnesses.

Thus, Latin American national consciousness was structured by Marian piety. In Europe, various national churches often claimed origin from the preaching of one of the apostles, thus acquiring the prestige of foundation during the apostolic age. Iberia, for instance, celebrated St. James as the founder of its Christianity, making Santiago de Campostela a pilgrimage shrine. There was a similar purpose to the effort to historicize the preaching of St. Thomas the Apostle in the Americas, as described above. But since Mary is Queen of the Apostles, Marian apparitions in the Americas or in Asia sug-gested automatic superiority for colonial Catholicism over many European churches without requiring that history contain an actual visit to the Americas from an apostle.[58]

It is no exaggeration to claim that these religious concepts provided the foundation for social, cultural, and political identities within the Iberian polity of the baroque period. Theology gave heavenly sanction to nationhood, plant-ing, in the words of Mabel Moraña, the "seeds of future nationalities."[59]

On the one hand, the baroque paradigm paid lip service to the social and political rituals of the Spanish Empire and appropriated to itself the cultural codes of the metropolis as a symbolic form of participation in the humanistic universals of the Empire. On the other hand, these intellectuals articulated a tense and pluralistic reality in the colonies through their texts over against what they already perceived and expressed as a differentiated cultural process. They utilized the imperial language to speak not only for themselves but also of themselves, their plans, hopes, and frustrations.[60]

Although the theology of Trent insisted on evidence of apparitions, throughout much of the baroque, criteria for such proof were accepted by a norm that considered oral tradition as more important than the written word. Often the mere persistence of an apparition legend among the common people confirmed its authenticity.[61] Moreover, in order to prove the Church's univer-sality and its superiority over Protestantism, the far-distant manifestations of Marian devotions were afforded prominence in Catholic Europe. As just one example of this trend, Henry Kamen reports a sodality for a Peruvian madonna, Our Lady of Copacabana, in seventeenth-century Catalonia.[62]

Trent and the Creation of Devotionalism

These considerations lead us to the final term requiring definition: devotion-alism.[63] As suggested above, the reforms of the Council of Trent required a reexamination of the accretions to Catholic piety in order to counter the arguments of Protestants. At the same time, the Church did not want to concede that all devotions to the saints were in error. By legislating that all devotions be subjected to scrutiny by clerical officials in a process of deposition, evaluation, and pronouncement, outlandish popular exaggerations could be separated from legitimate religious experiences. Moreover, only approved devotions could develop prayers that merited indulgences such as thirty days' exemption from Purgatory. The prayer was composed with theological orthodoxy, usually affirming the mediation of Jesus as Son of God and equal member of the Trinity. This ensured that every time the faithful prayed to Mary in one of her apparitions, popular piety would repeat the orthodox theological principle of the Council.

Trent added a layer of ecclesiastical and theological authenticity to devotions, making popular Catholicism after the Council qualitatively different from the medieval variety. The technology of mass printing aided devotionalism because the sacred image with its indulgenced prayer gained worldwide circulation through a network of Church-sponsored sodalities and confraternities.[64] These became parts of what Kamen calls "the machinery" of the Council.[65] While medieval devotion had been highly localized, often depending on arduous pilgrimage, baroque devotionalism extended itself across oceans by using new technologies of diffusion for holy cards, often with indulgenced prayers on the obverse side. The machinery of Trent also produced a Roman seminary, the Gregorianum, which trained seminary and chancery clerics from all parts of the world. Because of Trent, libraries in the colonies usually had the same books that had been required reading in Rome. Moreover, the technological advances of the printing press made the diffusion of such texts much easier. Thus, both devotionalism and the theological preparation of future preachers advanced in tandem during the baroque.

Another important instrument of devotionalism was the Roman breviary. By requiring Catholic clergy the world over to recite the entire Psalter every week and to read sermons of early Christian writers for feast days, Trent blended its goals of pastoral education and renewed priestly piety. Uniquely important to Spanish America was how the breviary moved Marian theology within the Latin Church beyond the shallow concepts of the medieval period.[66] The Tridentine breviary celebrated Marian feasts with readings from Eastern Christianity's richer theological domain.[67] Cyril of Alexandria and Irenaeus had developed the concept of Mary as cipher for all creation; John Damascene had brought a poetic flair to Marian attributes that resonated favorably with baroque tendencies; other authors developed still further the Neoplatonist slant of an exemplar theology in which Mary was archetype of all humanity. Even though the breviary was not the sole source of such theological ideas, these notions linked the Marian piety of baroque America to the treasures of Marian theology in the Greek writers of the Church.[68] This birthright grounded popular Marian piety upon the pillars of sound theology. In sum, the linkage of local religion to Rome and the Universal Church is the fundamental characteristic of the devotionalism created by Trent. Moreover, the exchange was not one-sided. The outreach of the Vatican to the piety within the colonies opened the door for the influence of Spanish colonial theology upon the process of Roman approval.

Conclusion

Trent in America brought about a globalized Catholicism, enriching European faith with indigenous religious symbols. The Tridentine Catholicism of the Americas contributed unique elements of imagination and creativity, even when it draped itself with the mantle of invented tradition.[69] It integrated new racial groups and non-European cultures into a globalized Catholicism. Of course, all cultural movements succumb to fatigue, and eventually the exuberance of the baroque was eclipsed by Jansenism, the Enlightenment, and Napoleonic reforms. It may be asked, however, if the decline of Trent's sixteenth-century energy into the desiccated "Tridentismo" of the nineteenth century is somehow connected to the cultural demise of the baroque as a vital mentality.

In evaluating the baroque version of Tridentine Catholicism, it is worth noting that popular Catholicism—and by extension, the baroque meaning of Trent—played a role in many of the uprisings in Latin America against European power. The riots in the streets of Cuzco in the 1750s defended the baroque popular celebration of the feast of Corpus Christi against censure by Spanish enlightened despotism.[70] At the birth of Mexican independence in 1815, the criollo cleric Miguel Hidalgo organized a procession with the banner of Our Lady of Guadalupe to protest Spanish atrocities against the rebels. One might ask if these and other historical examples make the case that Latin American nationalism includes baroque popular religion as a constitutive element. Do the 39 million Hispanics in the United States today continue the baroque traditions of Trent? One might also ask if the contemporary pursuit in the United States of Celtic spirituality and Italian popular Catholicism among many disaffected persons of Irish and Italian heritage is a new version of the baroque's "delight in the marvelous." Finally, since our world today seems to have no escape from globalism in economic, cultural, and political terms, might we learn how to anticipate our future by revisiting the past when the American Trent gave Roman Catholicism its global fullness of ethnic, racial, and cultural diversity?

NOTES

1. I will use "Spanish America" in place of the more usual "Latin America" because my focus is upon the colonial period in which the political distinctions between core and periphery were defined differently than in post-Napoleonic history, when the term "Latin America" was coined. Although among English-speaking audiences "America" and "American" usually refer exclusively to the United States, for most Spanish speakers the terms include two continents.

2. The most complete work on Spanish American theology to date is Josep Ignasi Saranyana, Carmen José Alejos-Grau, Elisaq Luque Alcaide, Luis Martínez Ferrer, Ana de Zaballa Beascoechea, and María Luisa Antonaya, *Teología en América Latina*, vol. 1, *Desde los orígenes a la Guerra de Sucesión (1493–1715)* (Madrid: Interamericana, 1999), to which I unabashedly confess a deep and abiding indebtedness. Works on the baroque in Latin America include Petra Schumm, ed., *Barrocos y modernos: Nuevos caminos en la investigación del barroco iberoamericano* (Frankfurt: Vervuert, 1998); Mabel Moraña, "Barroco y conciencia criolla en Hispanoamérica," *Revista de crítica literaria latinoamericana* 28 (1988): 229–251; Sabine MacCormack, *Religion in the Andes: Vision and Imagination in Early Colonial Peru* (Princeton, N.J.: Princeton University Press, 1991); and Colin M. MacLachlan and Jaime E. Rodriguez, *The Forging of the Cosmic Race: A Reinterpretation of Colonial Mexico* (Berkeley: University of California Press, 1980). See also Inga Clendinnen, "Ways to the Sacred: Reconstructing 'Religion' in Sixteenth Century Mexico," *History and Anthropology*, 5 (1990).

3. I refer here to the cumulative data offered in many sixteenth-century census counts of colonial cities. See John Leddy Phelan, *The Millennial Kingdom of the Franciscans in the New World*, 2nd ed. (Berkeley: University of California Press, 1970), 42. By modern standards, these population counts are deficient since they omit rural or inaccessible regions, but they do make the point about the target population of the Church's pastoral care.

4. A reliable historical perspective on the racial and generational composition of the colonial population can be found in Magnus Mörner, *Race Mixture in the History of Latin America* (Boston: Little, Brown, 1967), and in the volume edited by Mörner, *Race and Class in Latin America* (New York: Columbia University Press, 1970). More recent works have relied on computer-generated data to estimate demographic expansions and contractions, and the use of mitochondrial DNA has provided some important new perspectives on racial mixing. See Juan Carlos Martínez-Cruzado, G. Toro-Labrador, V. Ho-Fung, M. A. Estevéz-Montero, A. Lobaina-Manzanet, D. A. Padovani-Claudio, H. Sánchez-Cruz, E. Ortiz-Bermudez, and A. Sánchez-Crespo, "Mitochondrial DNA Analysis Reveals Substantial Native American Ancestry in Puerto Rico," *Human Biology* 73:4 (2001): 491–511.

5. A useful treatment of this subject published in English is Angus McKay, *Spain in the Middle Ages: From Frontier to Empire, 1000–1500* (New York: St. Martin's Press, 1977). For the legal issues, see Lewis Hanke, *The Spanish Struggle for Justice in the Conquest of America* (Boston: Little, Brown, 1965) and *Aristotle and the American Indians: A Study in Race Prejudice in the Modern World* (Bloomington: Indiana University Press, 1959).

6. James Lockhart and Stuart B. Schwartz, *Early Latin America: A History of*

Colonial Spanish America and Brazil (Cambridge: Cambridge University Press, 1983).

7. Ibid., 168.

8. Ibid.

9. Ana María Díaz-Stevens, "Analyzing Popular Religiosity for Socio-Religious Meaning," in *An Enduring Flame: Studies on Latino Popular Religiosity,* ed. Anthony M. Stevens-Arroyo and Ana María Díaz-Stevens (New York: Bildner Center for Western Hemisphere Studies, 1994), 17–36.

10. This term comes from my article "The Evolution of Marian Devotionalism Within Christianity and the Ibero-Mediterranean Polity," *Journal for the Scientific Study of Religion* 37 (1998): 50–73.

11. Hanke, *The Spanish Struggle.*

12. Iberia produced the Dominican Ramón Pennafort, who asked Aquinas to write the *Summa contra gentiles* without relying on Church pronouncements as authority, in order to better debate Muslims. The Franciscan Ramón Llull and the language school at Miramar was a signal accomplishment of missiology. See James Muldoon, *Popes, Lawyers and Infidels: The Church and the Non-Christian World, 1250–1550* (Philadelphia: University of Pennsylvania Press, 1979).

13. Diego Irarrázaval, *Inculturation: New Dawn of the Church in Latin America,* trans. Philip Berryman (Maryknoll, N.Y.: Orbis Books, 2000). See Robert Ricard, *The Spiritual Conquest of Mexico: An Essay on the Apostolate and the Evangelizing Methods of the Mendicant Orders in New Spain, 1523–1573,* trans. Leslie B. Simpson (Berkeley: University of California Press, 1966).

14. Anthony M. Stevens-Arroyo, "The Inter-Atlantic Paradigm: The Failure of Spanish Medieval Colonialism of the Canary and Caribbean Islands," *Comparative Studies in Society and History* 35:3 (1993): 515–543.

15. One will recognize here Las Casas's anticipation of the Council's distinction between *traditiones* and *consuetudines.* While the former were dogmatic in nature, explaining belief, the latter could be considered "reformable" according to time and circumstance. Thus, for instance, despite its biblical basis, the polygamy of Abraham was a "reformable custom" that had in fact been superseded by monogamy. See a summary of this position in Stevens-Arroyo, "The Evolution of Marian Devotionalism," 56, 57, 63.

16. Phelan, *The Millennial Kingdom,* 14–15; A. D. Wright, *Catholicism and Spanish Society Under the Reign of Philip II, 1555–1598, and Philip III, 1598–1621* (Lewiston, N.Y.: Edwin Mellen, 1991).

17. Phelan, *The Millennial Kingdom,* 15–16.

18. See Gustavo Gutiérrez, *Las Casas: In Search of the Poor of Jesus,* trans. Robert Barr (Maryknoll, N.Y.: Orbis Books, 1993).

19. Ricard, *The Spiritual Conquest of Mexico,* 46–49, 96–108.

20. Rather than marking a belated Catholic acceptance that Native Americans had souls, as sometimes claimed, this papal bull indicated that calling the natives "savages" could not be used as an excuse to deny their human dignity or to assign them to slavery, a position defended by Las Casas in his 1555 debate at Valladolid with the Aristotelian philosopher Juan Ginés de Sepúlveda. See Hanke, *The Spanish Struggle for Justice* and *Aristotle and the American Indians.* An incidental issue was whether

the nakedness of the natives ran counter to the biblical statement that all the descendants of Adam and Eve covered their nakedness on account of original sin.

21. Hanke, *The Spanish Struggle*, 83–108 and passim.

22. Saranyana et al., *Teología en América Latina*, 131.

23. Ibid., 135.

24. Ecclesiastical reaction to the revolt of the Chichimecas in Mexico (1541–1550) is recorded in ibid., 186–192. The hostilities continued despite truces, but the majority of the bishops and regular clergy eventually declared in 1585 that war against the rebellious natives was unjust.

25. Ibid., 270–273.

26. *De procuranda indorum salute* (1588) and *Historia natural y moral de las Indias* (1591). Saranyana et al., *Teología en América Latina*, 154–164 and passim.

27. Ibid., 238–244.

28. The manuscript was recovered in Denmark in 1908, and published in a facsimile edition in 1936. For commentary and analysis of this important reform text, see Rolena Adorno, *Guaman Poma: Writing and Resistance in Colonial Peru* (Austin: University of Texas Press, 1986).

29. Saranyana et al., *Teología en América Latina*, 304–309.

30. Ibid., 327–331.

31. Suzanne L. Stratton, *The Immaculate Conception in Spanish Art* (Cambridge: Cambridge University Press, 1994).

32. Jacques Lafaye, *Quetzalcoatl and Guadalupe: The Formation of Mexican National Consciousness, 1531–1813*, trans. Benjamin Keen (Chicago: University of Chicago Press, 1976); and Pamela Kirk Rappaport, *Sor Juana Inés de la Cruz: Religion, Art, and Feminism* (New York: Continuum, 1998).

33. Bolívar Echevarría, "La Compañía de Jesús y la primera modernidad de América Latina," in Schumm, *Barrocos y modernos*, 49–66. On p. 50, he uses the dates of the defeat of the Armada in 1588 and the Treaty of Madrid in 1764 as the temporal boundaries of the baroque. Petra Schumm in the same volume (13ff.) simply refers to "the loss of frontiers," a concept I find less problematic.

34. Walter Mignolo, *The Darker Side of the Renaissance: Literacy, Territoriality and Colonization* (Ann Arbor: University of Michigan Press, 1995).

35. Anthony M. Stevens-Arroyo, "The Radical Shift in the Spanish Approach to Intercivilizational Encounter," *Comparative Civilizations Review* 21 (1980): 80–101; see José Antonio Maravall, *Culture of the Baroque: Analysis of a Historical Structure*, trans. Terry Cochran (Minneapolis: University of Minnesota Press, 1986), and Michel Vovelle, *Ideologies and Mentalities*, trans. Eamon O'Flaherty (Chicago: University of Chicago Press, 1990).

36. Walter Moser, "Du Baroque européen et colonial au baroque américain et postcolonial," in Schumm, *Barrocos y modernos*, 67–82; and Alfredo A. Roggiano, "Acerca de dos barrocos: El de España y el de América," in *El barroco en América*, XVII Congreso del Instituto Internacional de Literatura Iberoamericana (Madrid: Ediciones Cultura Hispánica del Centro Iberoamericano e Cooperación, 1978), vol. 1, 39–48.

37. I will treat this tendency below as "devotionalism." See also Moser, "Du Baroque européen," 73ff.; and Echevarría, "La Compañía de Jesús."

38. Maravall, *Culture of the Baroque*.

39. William A. Christian, Jr., *Apparitions in Late Medieval and Renaissance Spain* (Princeton, N.J.: Princeton University Press, 1981).

40. See Maravall, *Culture of the Baroque,* for a literary exploration of this theme.

41. Olga Portundo Zúniga, *La Virgen de la Caridad del Cobre: Símbolo de cubanía* (Santiago, Cuba: Editorial Oriente, 1995).

42. The addition of miraculous elements across the centuries is analyzed extensively in David A. Brading, *Mexican Phoenix: Our Lady of Guadalupe. Image and Tradition Across Five Centuries* (Cambridge: Cambridge University Press, 2001); and Stafford Poole, *Our Lady of Guadalupe: The Origins and Sources of a Mexican National Symbol, 1531–1797* (Tucson: University of Arizona Press, 1995).

43. Louise M. Burkhart, *Before Guadalupe: The Virgin Mary in Early Colonial Nahuatl Literature,* IMS Monograph 13 (Albany: Institute for Mesoamerican Studies at the State University of New York, Albany, 2001), 2–6, 14–15 and passim.

44. Poole, *Our Lady of Guadalupe,* 77–81.

45. Portuondo Zúniga, *La Virgen de la Caridad*; Anthony M. Stevens-Arroyo, "The Contribution of Catholic Orthodoxy to Caribbean Syncretism: The Case of La Virgen de la Caridad del Cobre in Cuba," *Archives de sciences sociales des religions* 117 (2002): 37–57.

46. José L. Sánchez Lora, *Mujeres, conventos y formas de la religiosidad barroca* (Madrid: Fundación Universitaria Española, 1988); also Electa Arenal and Stacey Schlau, *Untold Sisters: Hispanic Nuns in Their Own Works,* trans. Amanda Powell (Albuquerque: University of New Mexico Press, 1989).

47. Saranyana et al., *Teología en América Latina,* 374–383.

48. Ibid., 514–521. Espinosa echoed the generalized feeling of criollos that Catholicism had been fulfilled only by its arrival in the Americas. This idea is found in his Latin epigram about Aquinas: *Nam per Te radio meliore refulget Aquinas! Candidiora coma splendet in Orbe Novo.*

49. Ibid., 362–366.

50. The St. Thomas legend was also invoked in India with the encounter there by Catholic missionaries of Christian natives who had a much more historically based claim to have been evangelized before the arrival of the Spanish.

51. Lafaye, *Quetzalcoatl and Guadalupe,* 177–187 and passim; see also Brading, *Mexican Phoenix,* 200–212 and passim.

52. Guillermo Furlong, "The Jesuit Heralds of Democracy and the New Despotism," in *The Expulsion of the Jesuits from Latin America,* ed. Magnus Mörner (New York: Alfred A. Knopf, 1965), 41–46.

53. The indispensable source on this issue is Stratton, *The Immaculate Conception in Spanish Art.*

54. To the Mexican and Cuban examples cited above can be added such others as Our Lady of Copacabana at the borders of Peru and Bolivia. See Verónica Salles-Reese, *From Viracocha to the Virgin of Copacabana* (Austin: University of Texas Press, 1997); and MacCormack, *Religion in the Andes.* For the syncretism of Santiago, Slayer of Moors, with the mock battles of Mexican religion, see Max Harris, *Aztecs, Moors and Christians: Festivals of Reconquest in Mexico and Spain* (Austin: University of Texas Press, 2000). Fear of devil possession in the seventeenth century is analyzed in Fer-

nando Cervantes, *The Devil in the New World: The Impact of Diabolism in New Spain* (New Haven, Conn.: Yale University Press, 1994).

55. Lefaye, *Quetzalcoatl and Guadalupe*, 1–4, 283–287 and passim.

56. If Edmundo O'Gorman (*La invención de América: Investigación acerca de la estructura histórica del Nuevo Mundo y del sentido de su devenir* [Mexico City: Fondo de Cultura Económica, 1984]) is partially correct to claim that Europe "invented" America as a utopian expression of itself, that statement cannot be accepted without simultaneously affirming that by use of baroque devices the Americas subverted the European effort to their own advantages. See Luis N. Rivera Pagan, *A Violent Evangelism: The Political and Religious Conquest of the Americas* (Louisville, Ky.: Westminster/John Knox Press, 1992), 5, 274, n. 9; and Iris M. Zavala, *Discursos sobre la "invención" de América* (N.p.: Rodopi Editions, 1992).

57. For Suárez's arguments, see Stevens-Arroyo, "The Evolution of Marian Devotionalism," 63. In truth, the Spanish Hapsburgs were rulers of the "Spains." Moreover, by legal tradition there were certain local requirements for legitimate rule in order for the Hapsburgs to retain their political power in each kingdom. The cultural impact of *natio* during the baroque is explored in depth in Henry Kamen, *The Phoenix and the Flame: Catalonia and the Counter Reformation* (New Haven, Conn.: Yale University Press, 1993), 371–372.

58. Stevens-Arroyo, "The Evolution of Marian Devotionalism," 63, 67–69.

59. Moraña, "Barroco y conciencia criolla en Hispanoamérica," 238.

60. Ibid., 239.

61. This logic was recently applied by Pope John Paul II to canonize the Mexican Juan Diego of the Guadalupe devotion, although there are no certain historical records to indicate that such a person existed. See Burkhart, *Before Guadalupe*, 1, n. 2; Poole, *Our Lady of Guadalupe*; and Brading, *Mexican Phoenix*, passim.

62. Kamen, *The Phoenix and the Flame*, 146.

63. Stevens-Arroyo, "The Evolution of Marian Devotionalism."

64. Felipe Fernández-Armesto, *Millennium: A History of the Last Thousand Years* (New York: Simon and Schuster, 1995), 294–295.

65. Kamen, *The Phoenix and the Flame*, 430–435.

66. Before Trent, Marian theology was focused by two theological concepts. The first, and most common, was derived from St. Bernard's notion that Mary should be served with the spiritual chivalry of a knight's devotion to his noble lady. The second came from the labored dispute between Franciscans and Dominicans over the Immaculate Conception. See Stratton, *The Immaculate Conception in Spanish Art*.

67. I am much indebted to Prof. John McGuckin of Union Theological Seminary for these details.

68. Brading, *Mexican Phoenix*, 96–98.

69. See how this idea is developed for nineteenth-century Europe in Eric Hobsbawm and Terence Ranger, eds., *The Invention of Tradition* (Cambridge: Cambridge University Press, 1983).

70. David Cahill, "Popular Religion and Appropriation: The Example of Corpus Christi in Eighteenth-Century Cuzco," *Latin American Research Review* 31:2 (1996): 67–110.

presentations, useful for preaching and teaching. Even the dogmatic canons "always offer to those who examine them with care, the possibility of further analysis and of more accurate investigation by which their contents may be more fully revealed and the breadth of their application increased."⁵ Trent had granted full freedom of expression to the fathers and theologians, and it took special care not to settle questions freely debated among theologians and not to favor one theological school over another; to avoid this, the Council had often chosen by preference the language of Scripture and the Church Fathers. The great pastoral goal of the Council had been to assure and defend the spiritual freedom of bishops, particularly from dominance by secular powers, and to sketch a portrait of an ideal bishop. In its efforts to reform the Church not only in its members but also in its head, it had distinguished the private person of the Pope, "not always a model of virtue,"⁶ from his office as successor of Peter. Urbani ended with an expression of his confidence in the sincere search for truth and in dialogue, "in the intrinsic effectiveness of the truth when presented without dissimulation or hypocrisy, without compromise or equivocation, without subterfuge or falsification. We are confident in the power of dialogue as the ecumenical premise for religious unity and universal peace."

The ceremony and the speech of Urbani reflected the ambiguity of the Council of Trent at the Second Vatican Council. Trent, which had an incomparable influence in defining the character of modern Roman Catholicism and in shaping its theology, could not be ignored, either as an event or as a set of documents. In his opening speech, John XXIII said that the chief purpose of the Second Vatican Council was a "renewed, serene and tranquil adherence to the entire teaching of the Church in its integrity and precision as it still shines forth in conciliar acts from Trent to Vatican I." But he also said that he had not called the Council simply in order to repeat what everyone knows; instead, he wanted the ancient patrimony of faith to be presented in a manner intelligible and attractive to people in the last third of the twentieth century. He did not want a series of condemnations, but a positive presentation of the faith; he wanted this conciliar exercise of the magisterium to be pastoral in character. In these respects, Trent would not be an adequate model for Vatican II.

Nevertheless, at four points in its final texts, the Second Vatican Council explicitly places itself in continuity with the Council of Trent. In its Constitution on the Sacred Liturgy (*Sacrosanctum concilium*), 55, it introduces its extension of opportunities for Communion under both kinds with the assurance that the dogmatic principles established at Trent remain firm. In its Dogmatic Constitution on the Church (*Lumen gentium*), 51, it links what it says about the living fellowship of the Church on earth with the saints in glory and the souls in Purgatory to decrees on this subject issued by the Councils of Nicaea, Florence, and Trent. In its Dogmatic Constitution on Divine Revelation (*Dei verbum*), 1, it affirms that its teaching follows in the footsteps of Trent and Vatican I. In its Decree on Priestly Formation (*Optatam totius*), 22, the concluding paragraph affirms that the decree continues "the work begun at the Council of Trent."

The phrase used in *Dei verbum*, 1, "*inhaerens vestigiis*," drew the attention of Karl Barth, who devoted a chapter to it in his little book of reflections on Vatican II. He hoped that his interpretation was valid when he wrote:

> It is not in order to remain static in its teachings (*inhaerens* can hardly be interpreted in that sense) that the Council of the twentieth century follows in the footsteps of the Councils of the sixteenth and the nineteenth centuries, but in order to fix the left foot firmly in them and then with the right foot step forward along the line they have indicated. That is, it does this in order to proceed from them and thereby make another new footprint for the Church of the future and give to the present and future another new form of her "genuine" teachings. The result is that it corresponds better with the guidelines of the first Pope of the Council to translate those words rather freely as "moving forward from the footsteps of those Councils." My interest in this question of translation will be readily understood! If this Constitution merely wished to repeat what was said at Trent and at Vatican II, if the *inhaerens* was speaking of a remaining in those footsteps, or of a "marching in place," then the very beginning of *Dei Verbum* would characterize it as a matter of little concern for us poor separated brethren.[7]

In general, Joseph Ratzinger agreed with this interpretation. He noted that the phrase Barth commented on was intended "to calm the fears of conservatives and to bring out the continuity of Vatican II with the previous councils." He hastened to add, however, that this did not mean "a rigid external identification with what had gone before, but a presentation of the old, established teachings in the midst of progress." The only way to know what this "inhaerens" means would be by careful comparison of *Dei verbum* with the earlier conciliar teachings. What Vatican II attempted was a *relecture* of Trent and Vatican I "in which what was written then is interpreted in terms of the present, thus giving a new rendering of both its essentials and its insufficiencies."[8]

To assess what Trent meant at Vatican II, an initial step will be to study not only the explicit references to Trent made in the text and footnotes of Vatican II but also certain points in debates at which what Trent had done or said entered into the deliberations and decisions of the fathers of Vatican II.[9]

Sacrosanctum Concilium

Since the Council of Trent had dealt both with dogmatic issues surrounding the Eucharist and with questions of liturgical reform, it would be expected that

Vatican II would make references to the earlier council. And indeed, both in the spoken and written interventions of the fathers of Vatican II and in the final text of the Constitution on the Sacred Liturgy (*Sacrosanctum concilium*), there are a good number of such references. Trent was invoked by both sides in the initial debate on reform of the liturgy. As early as the second speech to comment on the draft of the liturgical constitution at the first period of the Council, Cardinal Joseph Ritter appealed to Trent to argue for the need, and the legitimacy, of liturgical renewal. That council had noted that the Church had established rites and ceremonies "by which the majesty of this great sacrifice is enhanced, and the minds of the faithful are aroused by these visible signs of religious devotion to contemplation of the high mysteries hidden in it." Trent, Ritter went on, also had already taught that "the Church always had the power, given changing circumstances, times and places, in administering the sacraments of making dispositions and changes it judged expedient for the well-being of recipients, or for the reverence due to the sacraments themselves, provided their substance remained intact." The Council of Trent, then, authorized the kinds of renewal and reform being proposed in the text.[10] On the other hand, Bishop Demetrius Mansilla Reoyo, auxiliary of Burgos, in a plea to retain Latin, recalled "the infinite variety of liturgical books" that was criticized at Trent and for which Trent tried to supply a remedy.[11]

The promulgated liturgical constitution opened with a chapter titled "The Nature of the Sacred Liturgy and Its Importance in the Life of the Church," in which theological foundations for the proposed reform were offered. In composing this chapter, the preparatory commission had deliberately refused the claim made by the preparatory doctrinal commission that all matters concerning doctrine fell under its exclusive competency. Paragraph 6 of *Sacrosanctum concilium* offers a brief description of the liturgy as centering on Christ's work of salvation celebrated in sacrifice and sacraments. It speaks of the eucharistic celebration as a moment in which "his victory and triumph over death are represented." These words were taken from Trent, session 13, the Decree on the Most Holy Sacrament of the Eucharist, chapter 5 (Tanner, 696). As was noted in the conciliar debate, this was an appropriated use of words that Trent had applied not to the eucharistic celebration, but to processions on the feast of Corpus Christi.[12] No one seems to have pointed out that at Trent these processions were praised as a weapon in the war against the errors of the Reformers, an opportunity for truth to triumph over falsehood and heresy, "so that, confronted with so much splendor and such great joy of the whole Church, her enemies might be weakened and broken and fall into decline or be touched by shame and confounded and in time come to repentance."

In *Sacrosanctum concilium*, 7, Vatican II describes several ways in which Christ is present in the liturgy. The first is his presence in the sacrifice of the Mass in the person of the minister: "the same now offering himself through the ministry of priests who formerly offered himself on the cross." These words are quoted from Trent, session 22, Teaching and Canons on the Most Holy Sacrifice of the Mass, chapter 2 (Tanner, 733). To this mode of Christ's presence Vatican II adds four others, not stated or at least not prominent in Trent.

The third section of the first chapter of *Sacrosanctum concilium* begins by providing norms for the renewal of the liturgy. The part devoted to norms derived from the didactic and pastoral nature of the liturgy begins with a quote from Trent: "Although the sacred liturgy is principally the worship of the divine majesty, it likewise contains much instruction for the faithful" (*SC*, 33). What is the main clause in this sentence was at Trent the subordinate clause in a sentence that rejected a change Vatican II would bring about: "Although the Mass contains much instruction for the believing people, it has not seemed expedient to the fathers that it be celebrated regularly in the vernacular" (Trent, session 22, Teaching and Canons on the Holy Sacrifice of the Mass, chapter 8). Canon 9 anathematizes anyone who says that "Mass should only be celebrated in the vernacular" (Tanner, 735–736). Three paragraphs later, Vatican II, while asserting that use of Latin should be preserved in the Latin rites, immediately provides room for the vernacular to be introduced where this would be useful for the people (*SC*, 36).

To begin the second chapter, On the Mystery of the Most Holy Eucharist, the Council provided a brief paragraph (*SC*, 47) on Christ's establishment of the Eucharist. A number of fathers objected to phrases or offered suggestions, many of which, the reporter for the liturgical commission noted, "suppose that it was the intention of the Council to offer a full exposition of the theological doctrine about the sacrament of the Eucharist and to repeat what was set out so brilliantly by the Council of Trent (Session 22)." The paragraph, he went on, simply wished "to justify the decisions that follow about restoring the liturgy for the greater participation and benefit of the faithful."[13]

In the same initial paragraph (*SC*, 47), the Council says that in the eucharistic sacrifice, Christ entrusted "to his beloved spouse the Church a memorial of his death and resurrection: the sacrament of mercy, the sign of unity, the bond of charity, the paschal banquet 'in which Christ is received, the soul is filled with grace, and a pledge of future glory is given.'" According to Josef Jungmann,[14] one of the experts on the liturgical commission, the words "to his beloved spouse the Church" were meant to evoke a statement at Trent, session 22, Teaching and Canons on the Most Holy Sacrifice of the Mass, chapter 1, where Christ is said to have "left to his beloved spouse the church a visible sacrifice . . . by which that bloody sacrifice carried out on the cross should be represented, its memory persist until the end of time, and its saving power be applied to the forgiveness of sins" (Tanner, 733).

Along with the introduction of the vernacular, the most disputed question in the debate over the liturgy concerned allowing Communion under both kinds.[15] The question was considered so sensitive that the original version of the paragraph permitting wider use had included the phrase "sublato fidei periculo" ("provided any danger to the faith is removed").[16] In the course of the debate, some invoked this phrase as an indication that there are or can be doctrinal difficulties in the way of extending the practice, while others asked that the phrase be removed on the grounds that it was ambiguous, that whatever danger to faith had once existed no longer was a problem, and that it was offensive to Oriental Catholics. The liturgical commission accepted these criticisms, and the phrase was dropped. But in a bow to those whose criticisms on the matter were based upon an appeal to Trent, the text was altered to read: "The dogmatic principles laid down by the Council of Trent remaining in force, communion under both kinds may be granted when the bishops think fit, not only to clerics and religious but also to the laity, in cases to be determined by the Apostolic See" (SC, 55). A footnote referred to Trent, session 21, Teaching on Communion Under Both Kinds and of Children, chapters 1–3 and canons 1–3 (Tanner, 726–727). In explaining this text, the reporter for the liturgical commission took pains to indicate to the fathers of Vatican II what Trent's three dogmatic principles were: (1) that no divine law requires Communion under both kinds, nor is it necessary for salvation; (2) that the Church has the authority to determine the matter; (3) that the whole and integral Christ is received under either species.[17]

In SC, 77, the Council addressed the reform of the sacrament of marriage and quoted from Trent, session 24, Canons on the Reform of Marriage, chapter 1 (Tanner, 756): "'If any regions use other praiseworthy customs and ceremonies' when celebrating the sacrament of Marriage, 'the Sacred Synod earnestly desires that these by all means be retained.'"

Lumen Gentium

The majority of references to Trent in the Dogmatic Constitution on the Church appear in paragraphs dealing with the ministry in the Church.[18] These are anticipated in Lumen gentium, 17, where the Council asserts that it is only priests who can build up the body of Christ by the eucharistic sacrifice, which fulfills the prophecy of Malachi 1:1. A footnote refers to three patristic texts where this prophecy is related to the Eucharist and to Trent, session 22, Teaching and Canons on the Most Holy Sacrifice of the Mass, chapter 1 (Tanner, 733).

In the third chapter of Lumen gentium, titled "The Hierarchical Constitution of the Church, with Special Reference to the Episcopate," Trent is invoked with reference to all three of the ordained ministries. With regard to the episcopate, a footnote in Lumen gentium, 20, invokes Trent in defense of the statement that bishops succeed to the Apostles by divine institution; the reference is to session 23, Decree on Holy Orders, chapter 4 (Tanner, 742–743), but in fact this chapter of Trent says nothing about apostolic succession.

When Lumen gentium, 21, describes the origin of ordination in the New

Testament, a footnote states that one of the texts cited (2 Timothy 1:6–7) had been used at Trent to prove that Orders is a genuine sacrament; the reference is to session 23, Teaching on the Sacrament of Orders, chapter 3 (Tanner, 742). In the same paragraph, that ordination imprints a sacred character is bolstered by a reference to Trent, session 23, Teaching on the Sacrament of Order, chapter 4 (Tanner, 742).

In *Lumen gentium*, 25, Vatican II states that preaching the Gospel "stands out among the chief tasks of bishops" (*inter praecipua Episcoporum munera eminet praedicatio Evangelii*). In support of this statement, a footnote refers to two texts in Trent: session 5, On Reformation, paragraph 9, which calls preaching simply "praecipuum episcoporum munus" (Tanner, 669), and session 24, On Reform, canon 4, which says that the "praedicationis munus, quod episcoporum praecipuum est" (Tanner, 763). An earlier draft of *Lumen gentium* had simply echoed Trent on the point, but when it was objected that the celebration of the Eucharist was also a "praecipuum munus," it was agreed to amend the text to its final form, on the grounds that Trent was speaking positively, not exclusively,[19] that is, that Trent's statement should be translated with the indefinite article: "The task of preaching is a chief one." That this is the correct understanding of Trent may be doubted. In any case, *Christus Dominus*, the Decree on the Pastoral Office of Bishops, 12, in its only reference to Trent, repeats that the task of preaching "inter praecipua Episcoporum munera eminet" and cites the same texts at Trent as well as *Lumen gentium*, 25.

In describing the sacramental ministries of the bishop, *Lumen gentium*, 26, says that the bishop is the "original minister" of confirmation; an earlier draft had said that he was the "ordinary minister," as Trent had solemnly affirmed when it anathematized anyone who denied that "only a bishop is the ordinary minister of confirmation" (session 7, The Sacrament of Confirmation, chapter 3; Tanner, 686). The change in *Lumen gentium*, 26, was made, the July 1964 report explained, in order to take into account the practice in Oriental churches.[20]

Lumen gentium, 26, says simply that bishops are "the dispensers of sacred orders," a rather modest claim. Earlier, in response to a request that the Council teach that only bishops can ordain, the doctrinal commission said that it had decided not to say anything about whether only a bishop can ordain priests, leaving the question of right and of fact open. In defense of this decision, it referred to two documents in which Popes seem to have authorized abbots to perform presbyteral ordinations; these texts were to be collated with Trent, session 23, Teaching on the Sacrament of Orders, canon 7 (Tanner, 744), which anathematizes anyone who says "that bishops have no power to ordain or that the power they have is common to them and to presbyters."[21]

Several references to Trent occur in *Lumen gentium*, 28, a paragraph devoted to the presbyterate.[22] Trent is first invoked with reference to *Lumen gentium*'s statement that "the divinely established ecclesiastical ministry is exercised in various orders by those who already from ancient days are called bishops, presbyters and deacons." The reference is to session 23, Teaching on the Sacrament of Orders, chapter 2 and canon 6 (Tanner, 742, 744). Interestingly, canon 6 is not invoked: "If anyone denies that there exists in the Catholic Church a hierarchy, instituted by divine appointment, consisting of bishops, presbyters and ministers, let him be anathema." According to the report of the doctrinal commission given to the bishops of Vatican II in July 1964, the wording of *Lumen gentium*, 28, was deliberately chosen to avoid taking a position on "the historical origin of presbyters, deacons and other ministers, or with regard to the precise meaning of the terms used to designate them in the NT." It was enough to note that the names of the three ordained ministries can be found from very early times.[23]

When *Lumen gentium*, 28, goes on to speak of the new relationship with Christ that presbyters receive in virtue of ordination, a global reference is made to the entire teaching on the sacrament of Orders in Trent, session 23 (Tanner, 742–744), but with special attention to canon 7, which reads: "If anyone says that bishops are not of higher rank than presbyters, or have no power to confirm and ordain, or that the power they have is common to them and the presbyters; or that orders conferred by them are invalid without the consent or calling of the people or of secular authority; or that those are legitimate ministers of the word and sacraments who have neither been duly ordained nor commissioned by ecclesiastical and canonical authority, but have other origins, let him be anathema." The point was to stress that presbyters are subordinate to bishops.[24]

Two references to Trent occur when *Lumen gentium*, 28, speaks of the presbyter's eucharistic ministry. This is where, the Council says, "presbyters most especially [*maxime*] exercise their sacred role, by which, acting in the person of Christ, they unite the votive offerings of the faithful to the sacrifice of Christ their head, and in the sacrifice of the Mass they make present again and apply . . . the unique sacrifice of the NT, that namely of Christ offering himself once for all a spotless victim to the Father." The first footnote reference to Trent is appended to the phrase "acting in the person of Christ," and intends Trent, session 22, Teaching and Canons on the Most Holy Sacrifice of the Mass, chapter 2 (Tanner, 733–734). The reference seems to mean that "acting in the person of Christ" is equivalent to what Trent had to say about Christ's now offering himself through the ministry of priests who once offered himself on the cross.[25] This also seems to be the point of the second reference, which is to Trent, session 22, chapter 1 (Tanner, 732–733).

The second draft of the Constitution on the Church included a paragraph proposing to restore the diaconate as a permanent ministry; a footnote pointed out that at Trent, session of 6 July 1563, a draft text had been proposed that enumerated the duties of deacons with regard to the sacraments and the care of the Church, and proposed that they be restored.[26] In the course of the debate, Cardinal Julius Döpfner gave a lengthy defense of restoring the diaconate, referring to Trent and even arguing that the proposal before Vatican II was more cautious and restrictive than what Trent had proposed.[27] When the Council voted to restore the diaconate, the reference to Trent's discussion may have been considered no longer necessary, and it does not appear in the final text of *Lumen gentium*, 29.

The other places in *Lumen gentium* where reference is made to Trent have to do with the Church's relationship with the saints and with the Blessed Virgin Mary. *Lumen gentium,* 49, devoted to "The Communion of the Heavenly Church with the Pilgrim Church," was intended to provide dogmatic foundations for avoiding sins of excess or of defect in this material and to deal with ecumenical questions. In presenting the sentence that describes how the saints help the Church on earth by their prayers and merits, the July 1964 report of the doctrinal commission invoked Trent, session 22, chapter 3, "On Masses in Honor of the Saints," and canon 5 (Tanner, 734, 736) and session 25, The Invocation, Veneration and Relics of the Saints and Sacred Images (Tanner, 774–776). The same commission's October 1964 report quotes session 6, Decree on Justification, chapter 7 (Tanner, 673), to justify adding words about the various ways and degrees in which Christians share in the love of God. None of these references found its way into the final text of *Lumen gentium*, 49.[28]

Lumen gentium, 50, was also devoted to the pilgrim Church's relationship with the heavenly Church. For what it had to say about prayer and sacrifices for the dead and about the prayers of the saints on behalf of the living, the July report appealed to session 22, Teaching on the Most Holy Sacrifice of the Mass, chapter 2 and canon 5 (Tanner, 733–734, 736). In support of what *Lumen gentium,* 50, says about our union with the saints in charity, the same report appealed to session 6, On Justification, chapters 7 and 10 (Tanner, 673–674 675).[29] Finally, the same paragraph directly quoted from Trent about the legitimacy of Christians' "humbly invoking them, and having recourse to their prayers, their aid and help in obtaining from God through his Son, Jesus Christ, our Lord, our only Redeemer and Savior, the benefits we need." The text comes from session 25, On Invocation, Veneration and Relics of the Saints, and on Sacred Images (Tanner, 774–775).

Lumen gentium, 51, is devoted to pastoral concerns with regard to veneration of the saints. The Council declares that it receives the ancient faith about the living fellowship which exists with the saints in glory and the souls being purged, and that it again proposes the decrees of the Councils of Nicaea II, Florence, and Trent. A footnote refers to session 25, Decree on the Invocation, Veneration, and Relics of the Saints and on Sacred Images (Tanner, 774–776); to session 25, On Purgatory (Tanner 774); and to session 6, On Justification, canon 30 (Tanner, 681). Finally, *Lumen gentium,* 67, teaches that "the decrees which were given in previous times regarding the cult of images of Christ, the Blessed Virgin and the saints are to be religiously observed," and a footnote refers to session 25, On the Invocation, Veneration, and Relics of the Saints and on Sacred Images (Tanner 774–776).

Dei Verbum

Without question the most controversial issue concerning the Council of Trent debated at the Second Vatican Council was its teaching on the relationship between Scripture and Tradition. It emerged in the first debate over a doctrinal text in the first period of the Council (1962), it accompanied every subsequent draft, and it was still under discussion in the days immediately preceding the final approval and promulgation of the Dogmatic Constitution on Divine Revelation (Dei verbum) in the last period of the Council in 1965.[30]

It became almost inevitable that Trent's teaching would become controversial when the preparatory theological commission drew up for the Council a text titled De fontibus revelationis, whose first chapter was "De duplici fonte revelationis." From the beginning of its work, the preparatory commission had determined that among the most important truths in a conciliar text on revelation is that Scripture is not the only source of revelation because "besides the divine Tradition by which Sacred Scripture is explained, there is also the Divine Tradition of truths which are not contained in Sacred Scripture."[31] The intent clearly was to set the Council in opposition to a new trend among some Catholic theologians to interpret the relation between Scripture and Tradition in such a way as to maintain that the necessity of Tradition was to be explained formally or hermeneutically (that is, in order to be able to interpret the Scriptures, not materially but in the sense that only Tradition conveys certain revealed truths). This position had recently been based upon a new interpretation of Trent which argued that its decree on the canonical Scriptures had not been intended to settle the issue of the material sufficiency of Scripture. This view broke with a very common understanding of what Trent had done, and a considerable polemic broke out over the issue in the middle to late 1950s.[32]

In the draft text, De fontibus revelationis, paragraph 5, on the relation between the two sources of revelation, had stated flatly that "Tradition and it alone is the way in which some revealed truths, particularly those concerned with the inspiration, canonicity and integrity of each and every sacred book, are clarified and become known to the Church."[33] When the text De fontibus came up for discussion in the first period of Vatican II, it immediately came under fierce criticism, both for its overly cautious and suspicious attitude toward modern biblical studies and for its position on Scripture and Tradition. The very first criticisms actually quoted Trent against the draft text, pointing out that Trent, so far from having referred to Scripture and Tradition as two distinct sources (fontes), had used that word in the singular and referred it to the Gospel itself; the draft's language, then, was not traditional.[34] In addition, critics cited against the draft the principle that had guided Trent in its dogmatic decrees: that is, not to settle questions legitimately disputed among orthodox Catholic theologians.[35] On the other hand, there were those who believed that the issue had in fact been settled at Trent itself, as its language and statements clearly showed.[36] A few of the interventions even went into detail about the textual history of the decree of Trent, and in particular its removal of the words *partim, partim* (partly, partly), in referring to the transmission of the Gospel through the Scriptures and the Tradition. Monsignor Pietro Parente, assessor at the Holy Office, criticized Joseph Geiselmann by name for having "tortured" the text of Trent. Without naming him, he also criticized Yves Congar for having admitted that while the fathers of Trent were themselves in favor of the two-source theory, this was not the mind of the Holy Spirit, so that the omission of the "partly-partly" formula and its replacement by a simple "and" "left the door open for future ecumenists to favor the Protestant formula." "Ludus igitur Spiritus Sancti," Parente mocked: "The Holy Spirit's joke, therefore, which was repeated at Vatican Council I. Will it be repeated also at Vatican II?"[37]

As is well known, a proposal to remove the draft *De fontibus* from the conciliar agenda was approved by 61 percent of the fathers of Vatican II. Although this was less than the two-thirds majority required for that action, John XXIII intervened and ordered the text to be revised by a mixed commission composed of members of the doctrinal commission and of the Secretariat for Promoting Christian Unity.

As this mixed commission set to work, the question of the relation between Scripture and Tradition continued to divide its members. They soon had to report that they had reached an impasse on the question, and were told by the Coordinating Commission supervising the revision of texts between the first and second periods of the Council that if they could not reach a two-thirds majority within the commission, they should simply use the language of Trent and of Vatican I. While the members of the Secretariat were content with the latter solution, some members of the doctrinal commission continued to press for a statement that there were truths in the deposit of revelation that can be found only in the Tradition; this, they insisted, was the only way to be faithful to Trent and to Vatican I. In the end, at the urging of Paul VI, a compromise text was agreed upon and accepted by the whole Council. The final text said that Scripture and Tradition are channels flowing from the same divine wellspring—*scaturigo* is used instead of *fons*—to leave the question of one or two "sources" open. Tradition is said to exist in order to interpret and to spread the revelation contained in writing in the Scriptures, and that is why the Church does not derive her certainty about revelation from Scripture alone and also why both Scripture and Tradition are to be received and venerated *pari pietatis affectu ac reverentia* (with equal devotion and respect), a phrase borrowed literally from Trent, session 4, On the Acceptance of the Sacred Books and Apostolic Traditions (Tanner, 663). Joseph Ratzinger pointed out that at Trent the phrase was used in the same way as it had been by St. Basil, from whom it indirectly came; that is, as referring "to the realization of faith in the confession and worship of God, not to a doctrine distinct from it." Trent used it to justify the concrete ways in which the Church mediated the Gospel. But, Ratzinger says, the phrase was not the subject of new reflection at Vatican II. Instead it became "for a minority, a symbol of fidelity to Trent," and Ratzinger implies that its retention was an indication of Vatican II's failure on this point "to achieve a forward-leading *relecture* of what had been said at Trent."[38] For Barth, the inclusion of this phrase from Trent raised serious problems for Protestants.[39]

Other areas of *Dei verbum* where Trent is implicated may now be explored. In the very first paragraph of the document, the Council declares that in its teaching on divine revelation and on its transmission, it is following in the footsteps of the Council of Trent and of Vatican I. The reference here had at first been only to Vatican I, which, of course, had issued a dogmatic decree on revelation and faith. When, in the final amendment process, 175 fathers asked that Trent be included, the doctrinal commission decided to accept the proposal, "even though," they remarked, "the matter does not seem to be necessary."[40]

How Vatican II "reread" Trent is well illustrated in *Dei verbum,* 7, which refers twice to Trent, session 4, Receiving the Sacred Books and Apostolic Traditions (Tanner, 663). Parallel columns will perhaps best illustrate the continuities and the changes:

Trent

. . . that the purity of the Gospel, purged of all errors, may be preserved in the Church, [that Gospel] which was promised beforehand by the prophets in the sacred scriptures and which he then ordered to be preached to every creature through his apostles as the source of all saving truth and moral discipline. Clearly perceiving that this truth and rule are contained in written books and in unwritten traditions which were received by the apostles from the mouth of Christ himself, or else have come down to us, handed on as it were from the apostles themselves at the inspiration of the Holy Spirit

Dei verbum

. . . the Gospel which, promised beforehand by the prophets, He Himself fulfilled and promulgated by his own mouth, Christ commanded the apostles to preach to all as the source of all saving truth and moral discipline, communicating to them the divine gifts. This was faithfully done both by the apostles, who in oral preaching, examples, and institutions handed on those things which they had received either from the mouth, from the companionship, and from the works of Christ or had learned at the suggestion of the Holy Spirit, and by those apostles and apostolic men who under the inspiration of the same Holy Spirit committed the news of salvation to writing.

It will readily be seen that Vatican II does not depart from the teaching of Trent. Consistently, however, here and in other parts of *Dei verbum*, particularly in the next paragraph (number 8), it emphasizes that Tradition is not simply the transmission of words or of teachings, but of the divine realities of truth and grace themselves.

Included in this paragraph is special reference to the Fathers of the Church; their authority is put positively. At Trent there had simply been a condemnation of any who offered interpretations of the Scriptures "contrary to the unanimous consent of the Fathers" (session 4, Decree on the Vulgate Edition and on the Interpretation of Sacred Scripture; Tanner, 665). There is no reference to this Tridentine text in the documents of Vatican II.

The only other reference to Trent in *Dei verbum* occurs in a footnote to paragraph 11, where Trent, session 4, On the Canonical Scriptures (Tanner, 663), appears among a number of other authorities in support of a statement about the inerrancy of the Bible. This issue was not particularly the concern of the text from Trent, which appears to be cited because it used the phrase "salutaris veritas" (saving truth). An earlier draft of *Dei verbum* had used those words to indicate the formal object of biblical inspiration, a notion expressed in the final text by the phrase "nostrae salutis causa" (for the sake of our salvation).[41]

There is one last issue on which the relation between Trent and Vatican II can be noted. *Dei verbum*, 22, begins with the bold statement "Access to Sacred Scripture should be broadly available to the Christian faithful." This question about access to the Scriptures had been heatedly debated throughout the history of *Dei verbum*. Ratzinger interprets the paragraph as the removal of barriers to vernacular versions and to the reading of the Bible by non-theologians, and in this respect, he says, Vatican II here not only overcomes the restrictions several Popes had imposed but also represents "a *relecture* of the Tridentine decisions: the *inhaerens vestigiis* again proves to be an advance."[42] He presumably refers to Trent's statement that "the old well known Latin Vulgate edition which has been tested in the Church by long use over so many centuries should be kept as the authoritative text in public readings, debates, sermons and explanations; and no one is to dare or presume on any pretext to reject it." This statement was then reinforced at Trent by decrees with regard to the interpretation of the Vulgate and to its publication in authorized editions (Tanner, 664–665). When *Dei verbum*, 22, goes on to speak of the Vulgate, it is in more muted terms: "For this reason right from the beginning the Church received as its own that very ancient Greek translation of the Old Testament called the Septuagint; other oriental versions and Latin versions, particularly the Vulgate, she holds in honor." The Vulgate no longer appears alone, and the Church's attitude toward it is weaker than toward the Septuagint, and the next sentence encourages translations, particularly those made from the original languages. Ratzinger commented on all this:

To declare it [the Vulgate] alone as authentic would be to place tradition above Scripture; to "give it a place of honor" and at the same
time to insist on a return to the original text means, on the contrary,
a restatement of the relation between Scripture and Tradition, so
that the step that Vatican II has taken on this point is seen perhaps
more clearly in this concrete example than in the formal fundamental statements of Chapter II [On Scripture and Tradition].[43]

When Vatican II then recommends ecumenical editions of the Bible, Ratzinger
remarks that "here Trent is indeed left far behind, and the pragmatic statements of the text are, in fact, theological events of great significance."[44]

Presbyterorum Ordinis

That the Council of Trent was cited only three times in the Decree on the
Ministry and Life of Priests is itself a sign that Vatican II wished to present a
broader vision of the presbyterate than the one offered by Trent, which focused
almost exclusively on the power to celebrate the sacraments of the Eucharist
and penance. This new approach puzzled some bishops, and to meet their
desire that the text acknowledge its continuity with Trent, the latter's statement
that in virtue of ordination presbyters have "the sacred power of order, that of
offering sacrifices and forgiving sins," was included late in the history of the
text in Presbyterorum ordinis, 2; the quotation is from Trent, session 23, chapter
1 and canon 1 (Tanner, 742–743).[45] Presbyterorum ordinis, 4, says that "presbyters, as co-workers of bishops, have as a [the?] first duty that of preaching the
Gospel to all." A footnote at this point declares that the statements made in
several sources about bishops apply also to presbyters; among the sources cited
is Trent, session 5, Decree on Instruction and Preaching, chapter 9 (Tanner,
669) and session 24, Decree on Reform, chapter 4 (Tanner, 763). In Presbyterorum ordinis, 17, in support of the statement that presbyters should not "regard
an ecclesiastical office as a source of profit, and are not to spend the income
accruing from it for increasing their own private fortunes," a note invokes
Trent, session 25, Decree on Reform, chapter 1 (Tanner, 784–785). At Trent,
this effort to curb avarice was not directed at presbyters but at bishops; and
when it was extended to include anyone who had a church benefice, special
mention was made of cardinals of the holy Roman Church! Similar exhortations to the higher clergy cannot be found in the final texts of Vatican II.[46]

During the debate on this text, at least one bishop thought that Trent had
done a better job of describing the presbyteral ministry. Bishop Brian C. Foley
of Lancaster, England, was very critical of a draft that was nearly silent about
the pastoral care of souls. "Indeed, it speaks as if priestly administration consisted solely in the offering of the sacrifice of the Mass, in the giving of the

sacraments and in preaching." Trent, on the other hand, had devoted three long sessions to the care of souls and given precise rules for it.[47]

Optatam Totius

In *Optatam totius*, 22, the concluding paragraph, the Council affirms that in this Decree on Priestly Training, it has been "continuing the work begun at the Council of Trent." The debate on the treatment of seminaries in this schema turned on what fidelity to Trent means: maintaining what it had decreed or taking Trent as a model of how to meet the demands of the time by creating new institutions or adapting old ones? Bishop Jean Weber, for example, said two extremes should be avoided: "iconoclasm, the destruction of everything done by the Council of Trent, and immobilism, which, he said, would be turning a deaf ear to the crying needs of our times."[48]

One omission from the texts on the priesthood and religious life is striking. In none of them does Vatican II ever even allude to the teaching of Trent that anathematizes anyone who denies that celibacy or consecrated virginity is superior to the married state (session 24, Decree on the Sacrament of Marriage, canon 10; Tanner, 755). *Optatam totius*, 10, however, speaks of the "praecellentia" of consecrated virginity. This statement was included toward the end of the text's history, at the request of a bishop who remarked that there was little danger today that seminarians would not appreciate the value of marriage but a good chance that they would be ignorant of the *praecellentia virginitatis*. A reference was therefore added to Pius XII's encyclical on virginity that defended the superiority of that state over marriage and even spoke of Trent's teaching as a dogma.[49] It would appear that in its treatment of celibacy, or consecrated virginity, as in its treatment generally of the religious life, Vatican II was concerned to avoid referring to such a vowed life as a "state of perfection," as if other Christians are not called to perfection. If the religious life were to be recommended as something that belongs to "the Church's life and holiness," it would not be on the grounds of singling it out and elevating it to a superior status. In *Presbyterorum ordinis*, 16, what *Optatam totius*, 10, refers to as the "praecellentia" of celibacy is urged more quietly by means of comparative adjectives and adverbs (*facilius, liberius, expeditius, aptiores*).

Concluding Observations

On the level of Church practice, Vatican II reversed some decisions of Trent, most notably by permitting the vernacular to be used in the liturgy, by broadening occasions for receiving the Eucharist under both kinds, by dethroning the Vulgate as the normative biblical text, and by encouraging wide reading of the Scriptures. While a small minority of the bishops opposed one or another of these changes, fearing that they would imply that the Protestants had been right all along, the vast majority believed that whatever doctrinal issues might once have been at stake in them were no longer in play, so that reforms could be considered simply on grounds of pastoral usefulness. In this respect, Trent was in the minds of the fathers of Vatican II not only as a set of teachings and laws but also as an event, an example of how the Church could vigorously and comprehensively address serious challenges, if necessary by innovations. Trent was invoked in support of liturgical reform, of the restoration of the diaconate, and even of proposals to alter the institution it created for the training of priests, the seminary. The method employed at Trent was also recalled: free debate, refusal to settle legitimately disputed theological points or to choose among theological schools, and conciliation and compromise for as broad a consensus as possible.

Vatican II's method departed from that of Trent in one very important respect. In his opening speech, Pope John XXIII had made it clear that he did not want the Council to issue a set of condemnations. As necessary as they may have been in the past, he said, now was the time for the Church to use mercy rather than severity, and to offer instead a positive statement of the faith. Hubert Jedin saw in this one of the chief differences between Vatican II and Trent: whereas the earlier council had sought to identify and clarify in what respects the doctrines of the Reformers departed from those of the Catholic Church, Vatican II sought to identify and to express those elements of faith that Catholics and non-Catholics had in common.[50]

Because Trent had not thought it necessary to reaffirm what Protestants had not denied, the theology constructed in its wake also tended to neglect these dimensions in favor of emphasis upon the ones Reformers had denied. Vatican II sought to overcome this polemical slant and to recover the broader and deeper vision of earlier ages of Christian thought, particularly the patristic period. There is no point at which Vatican II departs from any dogmatic teaching of the Council of Trent, but at Vatican II, Trent and its problematic ceased to serve as the supreme touchstone of faith. The tradition was no longer read in the light of Trent; Trent was read in the light of the tradition. This is visible in what Vatican II has to say about the common priesthood of the faithful, the Eucharist, and the ministerial priesthood: the teaching of Trent is neither denied nor passed over in silence; it is integrated into a larger whole. As Jedin put it, Trent was not revised, it was expanded.

Finally, Vatican II tried to do for its time what Trent had done for the Reformation crisis: identify the needs of the day ("reading the signs of the times" was the Vatican II slogan), interpret them in the light of the Gospel, and determine how to meet them with two criteria at work: fidelity to the tradition and adequacy to the day. If in meeting this supreme pastoral responsibility, the Second Vatican Council found it necessary to depart from Trent's dogmatic formulas or practical decisions, even then it was still "following the footsteps" of the Council of Trent.

NOTES

1. In his speech at the end of the first period of the Council, Pope John XXIII had expressed the hope that Vatican II could complete its work by Christmas of 1963, to coincide with the fourth centenary of the close of Trent; see his speech in Floyd Anderson, ed., *Council Daybook: Vatican II*, vol. 1, *Session 1 and Session 2* (Washington, D.C.: National Catholic Welfare Conference, 1965), 119–121. In fact, Vatican II closed two years later.

2. Douglas Horton, delegate of the International Congregational Council, was quite critical of the protesters for having "suddenly ceased being observers and become demonstrators—in a negative way." One observer had remarked, "This shows who the Protestant Ottavianis are," something that Horton thought "is probably not fair to the cardinal" (*Vatican Diary 1963* [Philadelphia: United Church Press, 1964], 189–190). Robert McAfee Brown noted that "some of us were criticized for attending the session." Robert McAfee Brown, *Observer in Rome: A Protestant Report on the Vatican Council* (Garden City, N.Y.: Doubleday, 1964), 235.

3. Although delivered in Latin, it was printed in Italian in *L'Osservatore Romano*, December 4, 1963.

4. This point had been made several times by Hubert Jedin, the great historian of Trent, particularly in a widely circulated talk titled "Is Trent an Obstacle to Reunion?" (English translation in *Eastern Churches Quarterly* 15 [1962]: 209–224). Some of the themes developed by Cardinal Urbani are so close to those in Jedin's article as to suggest some sort of collaboration, but in his autobiography Jedin says only that he had thoroughly discussed the talk with Urbani some days earlier; see Hubert Jedin, *Lebensbericht* (Mainz: Matthias-Grünewald Verlag, 1984), 214–215. An article by Jedin on Trent was published in *L'Osservatore Romano* on December 3, 1963, and he gave a shortened version on Vatican Radio the same day; this was printed as an epilogue to his book *Crisis and Closure of the Council of Trent*, trans. N. D. Smith (London: Sheed & Ward, 1967), 178–187.

5. This was a point that Brown particularly appreciated. See *Observer in Rome*, 234.

6. "Un euphémisme saisissant," says René Laurentin in *L'Enjeu du Concile*, vol. 3, *Bilan de la deuxième session* (Paris: Éditions du Seuil, 1964), 183.

7. Karl Barth, "Conciliorum Tridentini et Vaticani I inhaerens vestigiis?," in his *Ad Limina Apostolorum: An Appraisal of Vatican II*, trans. Keith P. Crim (Richmond, Va.: John Knox Press, 1968), 41–55, at 44–45.

8. "Preface," in *Commentary on the Documents of Vatican II*, ed. Herbert Vorgrimler (New York: Herder & Herder, 1969), vol. 3, 168–169.

9. In what follows, references to Trent will be made to *Decrees of the Ecumenical Councils*, 2 vols., ed. Norman P. Tanner (Washington, D.C.: Georgetown University Press, 1990), abbreviated as "Tanner." References to debates and documents of Vatican II will be to the *Acta Synodalia Sacrosancti Concilii Oecumenici Vaticani II* (Vatican City: Typis Polyglottis Vaticanis, 1970–), abbreviated as *AS*.

10. *AS*, I/I, 351–353. The texts of Trent that Ritter quoted were session 22, Teaching and Canons on the Most Holy Sacrifice of the Mass, ch. 5 (Tanner, 734); and session 21, Teaching on Communion Under Both Kinds and of Children, ch. 2 (Tanner, 726).

11. *AS*, I/I, 461.

12. For criticisms of the use of the phrase, see the speeches of Cardinal Augustin Bea, *AS*, I/II, 22–26, and of Bishop Michael Arattukulam (Aleppey, India), *AS* I/II, 42–43.

13. *AS*, II/II, 296.

14. Josef A. Jungmann, "Constitution on the Sacred Liturgy," in *Commentary on the Documents of Vatican II*, ed. Herbert Vorgrimler (New York: Herder & Herder, 1969), vol. 1, 32.

15. For an example of the invocation of Trent against allowing Communion under both kinds, see the speech of Cardinal Ernesto Ruffini, in which he maintained that the "serious and just reasons" for which the Church had ceased giving the cup to the laity remained (*AS*, I/I, 600–601). Cardinal Augustin Bea offered a reply by referring to the acts of Trent themselves; see *AS*, I/II, 22–26; Archbishops Lorenz Jaeger and Jean Weber argued that the danger of which Trent spoke no longer existed. *AS* I/II, 76–78, 79–80.

16. *AS*, I/I, 280.

17. *AS*, II/II, 303–305.

18. The Tridentine profession of faith, among others, is referred to in successive footnotes in *Lumen gentium*, 8.

19. See *AS*, III/VIII, 87.

20. *AS*, III/I, 254. A similar change had to be made in the Decree on Oriental Churches, 13. See Vorgrimler, ed., *Commentary*, vol. 1, 323.

21. See *AS*, III/I, 241. The texts invoked were found in the 1963 edition of Heinrich Denziger's *Enchiridion symbolorum, definitonum et declarationum de rebus fidei et morum quod primum edidit Henricus Denzinger et quod funditus retractavit auxit notulis ornavit Adolfus Schönmetzer*, ed. Karl Rahner (Barcelona and New York: Herder, 1963). DS 1145 gave excerpts from the bull *Sacrae religionis*, February 1, 1400; DS 1290 gave excerpts from the bull *Gerentes ad vos*, to the abbot of the Cistercian monastery of Altzelle, November 16, 1427. The theological debate prompted by these cases—in particular how, or, rather, whether, they can be reconciled with the Tridentine canon—is briefly summarized in the introductory note on 312–313 of this edition of Denziger.

22. For comparisons of the teachings of Trent and of Vatican II on the presbyterate, see H. Denis, "La Théologie du presbytérat de Trente à Vatican II," in *Les Prêtres*, ed. Yves Congar and Jean Frisque (Paris: Éditions du Cerf, 1968), 193–232; Hubert Jedin, "Das Leitbild des Priesters nach dem Tridentinum und dem Vaticanum II," *Theologie und Glaube* 59 (1969): 102–124; André Legault, "La Nouveauté des perspectives offertes par Vatican II sur le ministère et la vie des prêtres," in Société Canadienne de Théologie, *Le Prêtre: Hier, aujourd'hui, demain* (Montreal: Fides, 1970), 206–219.

23. *AS*, III/I, 256.

24. See ibid.

25. See *AS*, III/I, 257.

26. *AS*, II/I, 235, 245; the reference to Trent was included in the July 1964 report of the doctrinal commission; see III/I, 261.

27. *AS*, II/II, 227–230.

28. *AS*, III/I, 343; III/V, 60.

29. *AS*, III/I, 348.

30. For the history of *Dei verbum*, see Riccardo Burigana, *La bibbia nel Concilio: La redazione della costituzione "Dei verbum" del Vaticano II* (Bologna: Il Mulino, 1998); see also Umberto Betti, *La dottrina del Concilio Vaticano II sulla trasmissione della rivelazione* (Rome: Tip. R. Ambrosini, 1985).

31. "Schema compendiosum Constitutionis De fontibus revelationis," #2. This text was prepared in the summer of 1960 as a guide for the future work of the preparatory theological commission. See Joseph A. Komonchak, "The Struggle for the Council During the Preparation of Vatican II (1960–1962), in *History of Vatican II*, vol. I, *Announcing and Preparing Vatican Council II*, ed. Giuseppe Alberigo and Joseph A. Komonchak (Maryknoll, N.Y.: Orbis, and Leuven, Belgium: Peeters, 1995), 272–273.

32. For the essential bibliography up to the eve of Vatican II, see Yves Congar, *Tradition and Traditions: An Historical and a Theological Essay* (New York: Macmillan, 1967), 156n. Congar discusses the deliberations at Trent on 156–176.

33. *AS*, I/III, 16.

34. See the speeches of Liénart, Frings, Alfrink, and Manek, *AS*, I/III, 32–36, 43–45, 55–57.

35. See the speeches of König, Maximos IV, Manek, Bengsch, Butler, and Pourchet, ibid., 42–43, 53–57, 87–89, 107–109, 159–151.

36. See the speeches of Caggiano, Florit, Parente, Landázuri Ricketts, and Ruffini, ibid., 71–74, 101–104, 133–136, 170–171, 249–251.

37. *AS*, I/III, 136. Parente was referring to *Tradition and Traditions*, 168, where Congar wonders whether the removal of the *partim-partim* formula might have "a *prophetic* meaning going beyond what the Fathers themselves could have had in mind. The completely human historicity of councils does not prevent a transcendent Moderator from realizing his intentions in them; rather does he use it as his unconscious instrument . . . it is undoubtedly true that a text of the magisterium ought to be interpreted according to the intentions of its author or authors, but it is also true that we are bound by the divine intention of the Holy Spirit, and not the human intention of men. The latter can in fact be transcended by the former, whose instrument it is and which, on the whole, it expresses."

38. Ratzinger, "Chapter II," in Vorgrimler, *Commentary*, 195–196.

39. "By what right does this chapter II direct the Catholic Church and the Catholic Christian to hold in the same manner to the Evangelist Matthew and to Thomas à Kempis or Ignatius Loyola as the interpreters of the Evangelists? Or the Protestant Church or a Protestant Christian to give the same respect to the Apostle Paul and to Luther or Calvin, or perhaps to Ainzendorf or Blumhardt? Is not such an undifferentiated equating of Scripture and tradition unjustifiable in both cases?" Barth, *Ad Limina Apostolorum*, 51. This is not a very sophisticated reading of *Dei verbum*, 9.

40. *AS* IV/V, 682.

41. See Alois Grillmeier, "Chapter III," in Vorgrimler, *Commentary*, 211.

42. Ratzinger, "Chapter VI," in ibid., 264.

43. Ibid., 264–265.

44. Ibid., 265–266.

45. See Jean Frisque, "Le Décret 'Presbyterorum Ordinis': Histoire et commentaire," in Les prêtres, 123–189, at 139.

46. At least twice, however, appeals to evangelical poverty were made, with Trent providing a model. Bishop Francis Franič argued strongly that the chief reason why bishops were no longer models of holiness for their people was their lack of poverty. The Council of Trent, he said, had effectively renewed the episcopate with regard to chastity by removing bishops who refused to dismiss their wives; with the definition of papal primacy Vatican I had fostered obedience among bishops; Vatican II should renew the Church, and especially bishops, with regard to poverty. See AS, II/III, 658–661. A year later Bishop Fulton J. Sheen made a similar point, but without the particular reference to bishops: "As chastity was the fruit of the Council of Trent, and obedience the fruit of the First Vatican Council, so may the spirit of poverty be the fruit of the Second Vatican Council." AS, III/6, 443–445; English translation in Council Daybook, vol. 2, 245.

47. AS, IV/5, 188–191; English translation in Council Daybook, vol. 3, 155–156.

48. AS, III/8, 39–42; see the summary of the debate in Council Daybook, vol. 2, 264–265. Trent provided a model for Fr. Aniceto Fernandes, who wanted better training for novice masters and hoped that what the Council of Trent did for the clergy by establishing seminaries, the Second Vatican Council should do for sisters; see AS, III/7, 448–451.

49. For careful analyses of Trent, Pius XII's Sacra virginitas, and the relevant texts of Vatican II, see Giovanni Moioli, "Per una rinnovata riflessione sui rapporti tra matrimonio e verginità: I principali documenti del magistero," Scuola cattolica 95 (1967): 201–255; see also Egidio Ferasin, Matrimonio e celibato al Concilio di Trento (Rome: Lateran University Press, 1970).

50. See Hubert Jedin, Vaticanum II und Tridentinum: Tradition und Fortschritt in der Kirchengeschichte (Cologne: Westdeutscher Verlag, 1968).

5

Robert Bellarmine and Post-Tridentine Eucharistic Theology

Robert J. Daly

A notable difference, indeed a chasm, often appears between what many liturgical scholars today agree is sound eucharistic theology and the eucharistic theology of several official documents of the Roman Catholic magisterium. Historical research suggests that Robert Bellarmine is one of the "messengers," if indeed not one of the "villains," of this unhappy story.[1]

The following summary can pass as a consensus position of contemporary liturgical theology that reflects recent developments. (1) The axiom *in persona Christi*, used to describe the role of the priest, is interpreted broadly; it is understood as including *in persona Christi capitis ecclesiae*, and also as in tandem with the axiom *in persona ecclesiae*. Accompanying this is a growing emphasis on the ecclesiological, and not just Christological, aspect of the Eucharist, as well as on its Trinitarian dynamic and on the Holy Spirit's special role. (2) There is an awareness that the mystery of the Eucharist— the sacrament and the sacrificial action in traditional terms—is spread out across the whole Eucharistic Prayer and its accompanying ritual action, and that it cannot be atomized or located merely in one part, such as the Words of Institution. (3) There is an awareness that the dynamic of the eucharistic action flows from Christ to the Church to the Eucharist, and that the role of the priest is embedded in the Christ–Church relationship, and not as something standing between Christ and the Church.

The following can pass as a description of the position of the contemporary Roman magisterium. (1) The axiom *in persona Christi* is construed somewhat narrowly, eliminating, for the most part, the ecclesiological perspective and strongly emphasizing the Christological perspective, to the concomitant overshadowing of the Trinitarian aspect of the Eucharist and the special role of the Holy Spirit. (2) There is still a strong focus on the Words of Institution (formerly identified as the *forma essentialis* of the sacrament). (3) The dynamic of the eucharistic action is conceived as flowing from Christ to the priest to the Eucharist to the Church—thus leading to an overemphasis on priestly power, position, and privilege against which many have protested.[2]

The discrepancy between these two views is striking. The late Edward Kilmartin, for instance, characterized this "modern average Catholic theology of the eucharistic sacrifice" as "bankrupt" and "without a future."[3] The question, therefore, for the historian of doctrine is How did this discrepancy come about?

"Modern Average Catholic Theology of the Eucharist"

This phrase refers to a specific line of the teaching of the Roman magisterium from Pius XII's 1947 *Mediator Dei*[4] to John Paul II's 1980 *Dominicae cenae*[5] and the 1983 "Letter of the Congregation for the Doctrine of the Faith on the Subject of the Role of the Ordained Ministry of the Episcopate and Presbyterate in the Celebration of the Eucharist."[6] The phrase "specific line of the teaching" refers to an aspect, often the dominant aspect, of contemporary magisterial teaching that seems to circumvent or pass over in silence (and thus, at least implicitly, to reverse) some of the important developments of Vatican II's Constitution on the Liturgy, *Sacrosanctum concilium,* and the subsequent liturgical reform in the Roman Catholic Church.[7]

In *Mediator Dei*, it is stated that "[t]he priest acts for the people only because he represents Christ, who is head of all his members and offers himself for them. Thus he goes to the altar as the minister of Christ, inferior to Christ, but superior to the people."[8] This is an obvious paraphrase from Robert Bellarmine (to whom the encyclical's footnotes refer): "The sacrifice of the Mass is offered by three: by Christ, by the Church, by the minister; but not in the same way. For Christ offers as primary priest, and offers through the priest as man, as through his proper minister. The Church does not offer as priest through the minister, but as people through the priest. Thus, Christ offers through the inferior, the Church through the superior."[9]

On this Kilmartin has pointed out: "This theological approach . . . subsumes the ecclesiological aspect of the eucharistic sacrifice under its christological aspect. In other words, the priest represents the Church because he represents Christ the head of the Church who offers the sacrifice in the name of all the members of his body the Church."[10] In other words, the dynamic line is not Christ–Church–Eucharist, in which the role of the priest is embedded in the relationship Christ–Church, but, rather, submerging the ecclesiological aspect under the Christological, and elevating the role of the priest: Christ–Priest–Eucharist–Church. That latter viewpoint is basically what is developed in *Mediator Dei*, as is clear from the following passage:

> For that unbloody immolation, by which at the words of consecration Christ is made present upon the altar in the state of victim, is performed by the priest and by him alone, as representative of Christ and not as representative of the faithful. But it is because the priest places the divine victim upon the altar that he offers it to God the Father as an oblation for the glory of the Blessed Trinity and for the good of the whole Church. Now the faithful participate in the oblation, understood in this limited sense, after their own fashion and in a twofold manner, namely, because they not only offer the sacrifice by the hands of the priest, but also, to a certain extent, in union with him. . . . Now it is clear that the faithful offer by the hands of the priest from the fact that the minister at the altar, in offering a sacrifice in the name of all his members, represents Christ, the head of the mystical body. Hence the whole Church can rightly be said to offer up the victim through Christ. But the conclusion that the people offer the sacrifice with the priest himself is not based on the fact that, being members of the Church no less than the priest himself, they perform a visible liturgical rite; for this is the privilege only of the minister who has been divinely appointed for this office; rather it is based on the fact that the people unite their hearts in praise, impetration, expiation, and thanksgiving with the prayers or intentions of the priest, even of the High Priest himself, so that in the one and same offering of the victim and according to a visible sacerdotal rite, they may be presented to God the Father.[11]

This is the line of teaching repeated and, in some respects, promoted even further by present-day magisterial teaching. As is well known, Vatican II and its subsequent liturgical reforms took steps toward a much broader understanding of the Eucharist. But the Council did not in fact make a clean break from the traditional narrower approach. In the Constitution on the Church, *Lumen gentium*, 10, we read: "In the person of Christ he [the ministerial priest] brings about the Eucharistic sacrifice [*sacrificium eucharisticum in persona Christi conficit*] and offers it to God in the name of all the people."[12] The Constitution on the Liturgy, *Sacrosanctum Concilium*, also includes this line of thinking when it states:

> The Church, therefore, spares no effort in trying to ensure that, when present at this mystery of faith, Christian believers should not

be there as strangers or silent spectators. On the contrary, having a good grasp of it through the rites and prayers, they should take part in the sacred action, actively, fully aware, and devoutly. They should be formed by God's word, and be nourished at the table of the Lord's Body. They should give thanks to God. Offering the immaculate victim, not only through the hands of the priest but also together with him, they should learn to offer themselves. Through Christ, the Mediator, they should be drawn day by day into ever more perfect union with God and each other, so that finally God may be all in all (48).

While there is indeed more emphasis on the participation of the faithful, the traditional dynamic line of Christ–Priest–Eucharist–Church (rather than Christ–Eucharist–Church), remains intact, and there is no mention of the role of the Holy Spirit. A few years later, the *Missale romanum* (1969) of Pope Paul VI made a significant advance by introducing an explicit epiclesis of the Holy Spirit, but in such a way (especially by placing it before rather than after the consecration) as to leave intact the traditional Western overemphasis on the Words of Institution. This is clear from the "General Instruction on the Roman Missal," which, after speaking of the Eucharistic Prayer as "the climax and the very heart of the entire celebration,"[13] proceeds, under the heading "The Institution Narrative and Consecration," to say, "Through the words and actions of Christ there is accomplished the very sacrifice which he himself instituted at the Last Supper when, under the species of bread and wine, he offered his Body and Blood and gave them to his apostles to eat and drink, commanding them in turn to perform this same sacred mystery."[14] The result is that the Eucharistic Prayer and the Communion of the faithful may still be considered as pertaining to the integrity of the liturgical rite, but not to the integrity ("essential form" in traditional scholastic terms) of the sacrament or the sacrifice.

Before moving on to the subsequent development of magisterial teaching in John Paul II and the Congregation for the Doctrine of the Faith, it may be helpful to summarize how Kilmartin, under the headings "Words of Consecration" and "Representation of the Sacrifice of Christ," described this "modern average Catholic theology of the Eucharist." The core of this position is the theology of the "moment of consecration." Kilmartin writes:

> In the Western tradition, the words of Christ spoken over the bread and wine are [also] understood to be the essential form of the sacrament. These words thus constitute the moment when the sacrament is realized, namely, when the bread and wine are converted into the body and blood of Christ. Thus, while the words are spoken by the presiding minister, they are understood as being spoken by Christ through his minister. This act is one accomplished only by the minister acting *in persona Christi* in the midst of the prayer of faith of

the Church. . . . The representation of the death of Christ occurs with the act of conversion of the elements. The somatic presence of Christ and the representation of the sacrifice of Christ are simultaneously achieved in the act of the consecration of the elements.

But what is meant by the idea that the death of Christ is "represented at the moment of the consecration of the elements"? The post-Tridentine theories, which sought to find the visible sacrifice of the Mass in the separate consecration of the elements, proposed a "mystical mactation" of Christ at the level of the sacramental signs. *Thus they espoused the idea of a sacrificial rite, the structure of which was the sacrifice of the self-offering of Christ in the signs of the food. This is a pre-Christian concept which is now generally discarded in current Catholic theology* [emphasis mine].

Nowadays the average Catholic theology of the Mass . . . affirms that the representation of the sacrifice of the cross is a sacramental reactualization of the once-for-all historical engagement of Jesus on the cross. The idea that in the act of consecration a sacramental representation of the sacrifice of the cross is realized in the sense that the historical sacrifice is re-presented or reactualized also seems to be favored by official Catholic theology today. However, Pius XII in *Mediator Dei* did not attempt to settle this basic question.[15]

It should be noted that this idea of sacramental representation, although now quite characteristic of contemporary Catholic theology, is actually one of the weak points of that theology. For this theory—that the historical saving acts of Christ are "metahistorically" made present to us—is not significantly supported by the biblical witness, nor by the Jewish background, nor by broad patristic evidence. Still more, it is also the kind of theory that creates further problems, since there is little agreement among scholars on how to explain what is being asserted.[16]

John Paul II, in his 1980 Holy Thursday letter, "On the Mystery and Worship of the Holy Eucharist" (*Dominicae cenae*), points out that the sacredness of the Eucharist is due to the fact that Christ is the author and principal priest of the Eucharist, and that this ritual memorial of the death of the Lord is performed by priests who repeat the words and actions of Christ, and thus offer the holy sacrifice "*in persona Christi* . . . in specific sacramental identification with the High and Eternal Priest, who is the author and principal actor of this sacrifice of his."[17] Commenting on this, Kilmartin pointed out that here and throughout this letter, "John Paul II limits himself to the typical scholastic approach to the theology of the Eucharist, passing over the trinitarian grounding of the holiness of the Eucharist. In modern Catholic theology, the sacred character of the Eucharist is grounded on more than just this christological basis. Its sacredness is not merely based on the fact of originating in a historical act of institution by Christ. Rather, what grounds the holiness of the Eucharist is the initiative of the Father: the self-offering by the Father of his only Son for the salvation of the world."[18]

John Paul II's description does not highlight the role of the Holy Spirit in the Eucharist suggested by Vatican II's *Sacrosanctum Concilium* and subsequently implemented by the insertion of epicleses of the Holy Spirit in the new Eucharistic Prayers of the missal of Paul VI. John Paul II's description of the role of the ministerial priesthood omits the pneumatological dimension. Rather, basing himself on Trent's decree on priesthood, canon 2, concerning the *potestas consecrandi* (DS 1771), the ministerial activity of priests is mentioned under the presupposition of its Christological grounding. Priests are said to be the acting subjects of the consecration: "they consecrate [the elements of bread and wine],"[19] "by means of consecration by the priest they become sacred species."[20]

This neglect of recent magisterial and theological developments is characteristic of *Dominicae cenae*. Three more examples stand out. As first example, one can note that appeal is made to chapters 1 and 2 of the Council of Trent's Decree on the Sacrifice of the Mass: "Since the Eucharist is a true sacrifice, it brings about the restoration to God. Consequently, the celebrant . . . is an authentic priest performing . . . a true sacrificial act that brings men back to God."[21] Also in the same chapter it is stated: "To this sacrifice, which is renewed in a sacramental form . . ."[22] Kilmartin pointed out that this reflects the same kind of confusion as that caused by Trent using *offerre* to refer both to the historical sacrifice of the cross and to the (phenomenological, history-of-religions) liturgical-ritual sacrificial act of the eucharistic celebration, not attending to the fact that sacrifice, in the history-of-religions sense of the word, had been done away with by the Christ-event. The theological and terminological problem caused by Trent's failure to distinguish the historical self-offering of Christ and its ritual expression can be resolved, Kilmartin insisted, only by rethinking both the inner relation of the personal sacrifice of Jesus and his body the Church, and the outward form of the meal as its efficacious sign.[23]

A second example may be noted. *Dominicae cenae* follows Trent in viewing the Last Supper as the moment when Christ instituted the Eucharist and, at the same time, the sacrament of the priesthood.[24] But the Pope also goes beyond Trent in teaching that the Last Supper was the first Mass.[25] This view was once favored by Catholic theologians; but most now argue that the Church was constituted in the Easter-event, and that the sacraments are also Easter realities grounded on the sending of the Holy Spirit.[26]

A third and final example is available. *Dominicae cenae* also slips back into older and outmoded terminology when it speaks of the sacrifice of Christ "that in a sacramental way is renewed on the altar (*in altari renovatur*)."[27] It is hard to imagine that the Pope wanted to take up again the infelicitous implications of the saying of Pope Gregory the Great that "[Christ] in the mystery of the holy sacrifice is offered for us 'again.' "[28] One must presume that "John Paul II did not intend to state anything more than that the newness of the eucharistic sacrifice can only be ascribed to the repetition of the ecclesial dimension."[29]

Two documents of the Congregation for the Doctrine of the Faith continue this narrow line of interpretation. The "Letter of the Congregation for the Doctrine of the Faith on the Subject of the Role of the Ordained Ministry of the Episcopate and Presbyterate in the Celebration of the Eucharist" (1983) states the traditional teaching: "For although the whole faithful participate in one and the same priesthood of Christ and concur in the oblation of the Eucharist, nevertheless only the ministerial priesthood, in virtue of the sacrament of orders, enjoys the power of confecting the eucharistic sacrifice in the person of Christ and of offering it in the name of the whole Christian people.[30] Later on, there is more detail regarding the representative function of the presiding minister:

> However those whom Christ calls to the episcopate and presbyterate, in order that they can fulfill the office . . . of confecting the eucharistic mystery, he signs them spiritually with the special seal through the sacrament of orders . . . and so configures them to himself that they proclaim the words of consecration not by mandate of the community, but they act "in persona Christi," which certainly means more than "in the name of Christ" or even "in place of Christ" . . . since the one celebrating by a peculiar and sacramental way is completely the same as the "high and eternal Priest," who is author and principal actor of this his own sacrifice, in which no one indeed can take his place.[31]

The "Declaration of the Congregation for the Doctrine of the Faith on the Question of Admission of Women to the Ministerial Priesthood" (1976) continued this narrow line of teaching when it put special weight on the Christological argument to show that only men can represent Christ in the act of eucharistic consecration: "It is true that the priest represents the Church which is the body of Christ; but if he does so it is primarily because, first, he represents Christ himself who is head and pastor of the Church."[32] In response to this, Kilmartin had noted that this meant that since the priest represents Christ in strict sacramental identity at the moment of consecration, the role must be taken by a man.

Recent papal teaching, however, as in *Mane nobiscum Domine*, the "Apostolic Letter of the Holy Father John Paul II to the Bishops, Clergy and Faithful for the Year of the Eucharist" (October 7, 2004),[33] happily puts more emphasis on the transforming effects of the Eucharist in the lives of the faithful. This letter speaks of "the impulse which the Eucharist gives to the community for *a practical commitment to building a more just and fraternal society*" (28). But ultimately, this largely exhortatory document reverts to the same line of teaching whose weaknesses Kilmartin has exposed. It does so by explicitly referring its readers (see section number 3) to the teaching of *Ecclesia de Eucharistia,* the "Encyclical Letter of His Holiness Pope John Paul II to the Bishops, Priests and Deacons, Men and Women in the Consecrated Life, and All the Lay Faithful on the Eucharist in Its Relationship to the Church" (April 17, 2003).[34] This document suffers from several additional theological deficiencies. The first is a biblical literalism, almost a fundamentalism, that is quite at odds with the Church's own official approval of the methods of modern historical criticism. The second is an embarrassing insertion of unscholarly personal piety into a formal teaching document when, for example, early on, the letter speaks of the Cenacle of Jerusalem as the place where Jesus instituted the Eucharist. The third is the constant conflation of the existential and the historical when speaking of the relationship between the Eucharist and the Church. *Existentially,* the Eucharist is indeed the source and summit, the center and foundation of all that the Church is and is supposed to be. But *historically,* the Eucharist—if we mean by that what the Church now celebrates—came from the Church, not vice versa. It took the Church, under the guidance of the Holy Spirit, more than three centuries to learn how to celebrate and begin to understand the eucharistic mystery as we now celebrate and understand it.[35]

Accordingly, if the consensus position of contemporary critical liturgical theology described at the beginning of this chapter is basically correct, there is indeed an alarming divide between that position and contemporary magisterial teaching now exposed as being in need of renewal. I shall now try to contribute toward such a renewal by examining some of the sixteenth-century antecedents—eroded theological foundations, so to speak—of this contemporary magisterial teaching.

The Sixteenth-Century Antecedents

Pius XII's *Mediator Dei* and subsequent magisterial teaching on the Eucharist appeals to Robert Bellarmine to support its typically Western emphases on the words of consecration and on the Christological aspects of the Eucharist, to the neglect of its Trinitarian, pneumatological, and ecclesiological aspects. In this sad story of division between the Church's teaching and that of its best liturgical theologians, is Bellarmine the "villain" or just the "messenger"? The answer, it seems, is "a bit of both."

Marius Lepin[36] summarized the teaching of the theologians who formulated Trent's teaching on the Eucharist:[37]

> From all the preparatory discussions, several important facts stand
> out which it is important to underline.
>
> First, at no point in the Council's deliberations can one find a

suggestion of the idea that the Mass contains any reality of immolation. No theologian and no [council] father pretended to find anything but a figure or a memorial of the immolation once realized on
the cross. There is no trace of the theories one will see arising in the
following years, theories that tend to require of the eucharistic sacrifice a change in the victim equivalent to some kind of destruction,
as if, for a sacrifice to be real, there would have to be a real immolation.

Second, the idea of the sacrifice of the Mass appears to be connected practically to three fundamental elements: the consecration,
the oblation, and the representative commemoration of the past immolation.

If diverse theologians seem to place the formal reason of the eucharistic sacrifice in one or other of these elements apart from the
others, they are the exceptions. The largest number of them, and the
most important, tend to locate the formal reason of the sacrifice in
the three elements together, i.e., in (1) the oblation of Christ, (2) rendered present under the species by the consecration, (3) with a mystical figuring of his bloody immolation. In doing so they seem to be
recapitulating the best ancient tradition.[38]

To understand what developed later, one must remember that Trent never
explained what it meant by "sacrifice." That was left to the theologians to argue
about. The Catholic theologians inherited Trent's confusing conflation of
the self-offering of Christ and the ritual liturgical offering. And they joined the
Protestants in looking first to the practice of sacrifice in the religions of the
world, and in finding there that some destruction of the (a) victim was essential
to true sacrifice. In doing so, both sides fatefully overlooked the fact that
Christ's sacrifice had done away with sacrifice in the history-of-religions sense
of the word; both sides tragically failed to look first at the Christ-event in order
to understand the Eucharist. Destruction-of-the-victim thinking thus became
the false touchstone in the debates over whether and how the Eucharist could
be, as Trent put it, a true and proper sacrifice. Inevitably, the Catholic theology
of the Eucharist after Trent became extremely complicated. Lepin distinguishes
four major theories, most with subgroups, for explaining this destruction-of-
the-victim idea of eucharistic sacrifice.[39]

Theory I

The sacrifice does not require a real change in the victim; the Mass contains
only a figure of the immolation of Christ.[40]

This theory was explained in two different ways. First, for Melchior Cano,
Domingo de Soto, and others, the figure of the immolation of Christ is found

outside of the consecration. Melchior Cano (1509–1560) saw neither the consecration nor the subsequent oblation as sufficient to constitute the sacrifice for which, following Saint Thomas, "there must be a certain action exercised with the breaking and the eating of the bread understood as symbolic of the past immolation." However, hardly anyone else placed this kind of significance on the breaking of the host.

Domingo de Soto (1494–1560) saw the essence of the eucharistic sacrifice in three parts: the consecration, the oblation, and the communion. But, like Cano, he needed to find an action exercised *concerning/around,* but *not on,* the sensible appearances of the eucharistic Christ. This he found only in the communion (he did not mention the fraction). The Jesuits Louis de la Puente (1554–1624) and Pierre Coton (1564–1626) followed the reasoning of de Soto.

Second, for two Jesuits, Alfonso Salmeron and Juan de Maldonado, the figure of the immolation of Christ was seen to be found in the consecration. They followed in principle the lines developed by the Dominicans Cano and de Soto, but they concentrated the representation of the immolation of Christ wholly on the consecration itself.

Alfonso Salmeron (1518–1585) saw the immolation figured in the double consecration, in the separate species of body and blood. All that follows the consecration contributes to the perfection of the mystical signification, and thus to the perfection of the sacrifice, but not to its substantial truth. He found a "death of a victim" to be "represented" in the Eucharist; for he pointed out that the actual death of a victim is required only when the victim is present *in propria specie,* but not when present, as Christ is in the Eucharist, *sub aliena specie.* This became a very popular theological explanation.

Juan de Maldonado (1515–1583) found that what is called sacrifice in Scripture is not the death of the victim, but its oblation. The actual oblation of Christ on Calvary does not need to be repeated, for the Eucharist looks back to it, just as the Last Supper looked ahead to it.

Theory II

The sacrifice requires a real change of the material offered; in the Mass the change takes place in the substance of the bread and wine.

This theory was held, for instance, by Michel de Bay (Baius), Francisco Torrès, Matthew van der Galen, Francis Suarez, and Francisco de Toledo.[41] In general, all the other theologians of the end of the sixteenth century agree in putting the idea of change into the definition of sacrifice. Many see this change only in the bread transubstantiated by the consecration. But since the bread and the wine are not the true victim offered to God, they are led practically to justify the eucharistic sacrifice in some other way.

Michel de Bay, or Baius (1513–1589), in a small work of 1563,[42] claimed, with some equivocation,[43] that the Eucharist is called sacrifice simply because it is the principal sacrament. He allowed that the bread and wine, as dedicated for change, are rightly called sacrifice, and the body and blood of Christ, as the term of the change, are rightly called sacrifice. However, sacrifice is, properly, an act (of oblation); de Bay reduced it to a mere quality, the quality of victim.

That sacrifice is a change affecting the bread and wine is presented in a form that is more orthodox—but theoretically hardly more satisfying—by the following theologians.

Francisco Torrès (1509–1584) locates it in the change of the bread and wine into the body and blood of Christ in the consecration as transubstantiation, which is seen as the sin-forgiving (and thus sacrificial) *opus operatum* work of Christ.

Matthew van der Galen (1528–1573), after building an elaborate definition of sacrifice from an analysis of a broad spectrum of ancient sources, and finding that the only change he could locate is in the bread and wine converted into the body and blood of Christ, then, in effect, abandoned his elaborate theory and went back to the more constant tradition of the Church by finding the sacrifice in the oblation of Christ rendered present under the transubstantiated species.

The position of Francis Suarez (1548–1617), while more beautiful and more sophisticated, follows the same pattern as that of van der Galen. He built an elaborate definition of sacrifice that focused on change; but since, in the positive term of the change *(immutatio)*, namely Christ, who is alone truly the host of our sacrifice, there can be no change, he ends up with a beautiful and profound interpretation of eucharistic sacrifice that, however, had little to do with his own elaborate definition of sacrifice. Francisco de Toledo followed a very similar course.

Theory III

The sacrifice requires a real change of the material offered; in the Mass, the change affects Christ himself.[44]

A certain number of theologians actually took the "logical" step in applying this change *(immutatio)* to Christ himself. These can be organized into three principal groups.

The first group (Jan Hessels, Jean de Via, Gaspar de Casal) argued that there was a change of Christ in the consecration. Jan Hessels (1522–1596), following Ruard Tapper (1487–1559), stated, for example, that "The New Law . . . contains an image of what takes place in heaven where Christ, in exercising his priesthood, stands before God and intercedes for us in representing his passion to his Father and in consummating the sacrifice of the cross. . . . On the altar Christ does what he is doing in heaven."

Jean de Via (d. ca. 1582) held a similar position, expressed with remarkable richness: "But if his priesthood is eternal, so too should his sacrifice be eternal, not only in the effect that is produced but also in the function that is exercised, although in a different manner: in heaven in its proper form, here below by the mysterious action of a different minister [*in caelo in propria forma, in altari hic infra in aliena operatione arcana*] . . . in the Church militant, a new sacrifice is not made by the ministry of the priest, but it is the same sacrifice once offered which he continues to offer."

Hessels followed Thomas Aquinas and Tapper in holding for a distinction between oblation and sacrifice, but he modified the Thomistic axiom that sacrifice is when a certain action is exercised with regard to (about) the matter offered. His new formula read: "Sacrifice occurs when the things offered are destroyed [*consumantur*] in honor of God." Thus, with destruction essential to the definition of sacrifice, he was unable to apply it satisfactorily to the Eucharist. All he can do is affirm that, above all, the Mass is an oblation, an oblation that is one with (and only formally distinguished from) the concrete reality of the consecration. "The consecration . . . puts at our disposition the Body of the Lord so that we can offer it."

Gaspar de Casal (1510–1585) combined two statements of Aquinas: (1) action with regard to (about) the victim and (2) an act done in honor of God in order to propitiate him (*ad eum placandum* [*ST* 3, q. 48, a. 3]) in order to come up with a definition of sacrifice that requires, essentially, a destruction. The "immolation" he needed, he found verified in the double consecration. Casal tried to go further, but each step he took only revealed further the difficulty or impossibility of trying to find a real "destruction" or "immolation" in the Eucharist.

The second group was led by Robert Bellarmine (1542–1621), who argued that the change of Christ occurs in the communion. Bellarmine saw the Mass as having two essential parts, the consecration and the communion. He failed to find the needed destruction in the consecration, for there the immolation is entirely mystical. The *real* destruction that constitutes the consummation of the sacrifice is the communion by the priest. For Christ suffers no diminishment in *acquiring* sacramental being (consecration), but in *losing* it (communion). As Bellarmine pointed out from his analysis of the Old Testament, sacrifice requires a *real* destruction.[45] For their influence on later Catholic theology, Bellarmine's words are ominous: "The consumption of the sacrament, as done by the people, is not a part of the sacrifice. As done by the sacrificing priest, however, it is an essential part, but not the whole essence . . . For the consumption carried out by the sacrificing priest is not so much the eating of the victim [what the people do] as it is the consummation of the sacrifice. It is seen as properly corresponding to the combustion of the holocaust."[46]

Bellarmine's influential and much repeated definition of sacrifice reads: "Sacrifice is an external offering made to God alone by which, in order to acknowledge human weakness and confess the divine majesty, some sensible and enduring thing is consecrated and transformed (*consecratur et transmutatur*) in a mystical rite by a legitimate minister."[47] He followed the Thomistic line in seeing the sacrifice as a mystical rite, as an action *circa rem oblatam*, apparently convinced that his whole theory was in accord with that of Aquinas. His great authority helped solidify the idea that true sacrifice requires a real destruction of the victim, but hardly anyone followed him in seeing that destruction in the sacramental consumption of the species.

Finally, a third group held composite theories that were more or less dependent on Bellarmine. Among these theologians were Henrique Henriquez [Enríquez], Pedro de Ledesma, Juan Azor, Gregorio de Valencia, and Nicolas Coeffeteau.

Henri Henriquez (1536–1608) modified Bellarmine's definition: "Sacrifice is an external ceremony by which a legitimate minister consecrates a thing and, consuming it in a certain way, offers it cultically to God alone in order to appease him."[48] Thus, to Bellarmine's two essential parts of the Mass is added a third, oblation. But it is the consumption or destruction that transforms the victim pleasing to God, separates it from all other use, and consumes its substance in order to attest the sovereign dominion of God over being and life. This is accomplished by the communion *of the priest!*[49] But elsewhere Henriquez seems to speak of the priest's communion only as a "more clear signification" of the death that has already been represented by the consecration under the two species.[50]

Peter de Ledesma (d. 1616) spoke of a figurative immolation consisting in the separation of the species.[51]

Gregory of Valencia (1549–1603) defined sacrifice as "a function of an external order by virtue of which a man, particularly chosen for this purpose, offers something to God by way of confection or transformation—as when an animal is slaughtered or burned, or when bread is broken and eaten—in a certain ritual ceremony in recognition of the divine majesty and also in proclamation of the interior devotion of the man, i.e., his homage and servitude, towards the Sovereign Master of all things."[52] One recognizes the language of Suarez and the ideas of Bellarmine. But in addition to Bellarmine's essential elements of consecration and communion as he would have it, Gregory added a third, the fraction. But, like so many others, it is in the consecration that he saw the constitutive essence of the sacrifice.

Theory IV

The sacrifice requires a real change; nevertheless, there is in the Mass a change only in the species of the sacrament.[53]

A final group of theologians admitted that sacrifice requires a change in the material offered, but nevertheless placed the essence of the eucharistic sacrifice elsewhere than in a real change in Christ. The resulting contradiction was ignored by some, while others tried to save the theory by restricting the rigor of its application to the Eucharist.

Some of these theologians—such as William Allen, Jacques de Bay, and Willem van Est [Estius]—were satisfied with a simple affirmation of the principle and of the fact. William Cardinal Allen (1532–1594) saw in the consecration a proper act of sacrifice simply because Christ is put to death there in (only) a figurative or sacramental manner (*mactatur sacramentaliter*). But he did not attempt to resolve the contradiction with contemporary theories of sacrifice (including his own) that required a real change/destruction of the victim.[54]

Jacques de Bay (Baius) (d. 1614) also saw the sacrifice of the Mass concentrated in the consecration (as did Salmeron) and, like Allen, left the contradiction unresolved.[55]

Willem van Est (1542–1613), when commenting on *The Book of the Sentences*, had similar contradictions. But when commenting on the Epistle to the Hebrews, he followed a more promising line that consisted in identifying (or at least associating) the sacrificial action of the eucharistic Christ with that which he accomplishes before his Eternal Father in heaven. Thus, the eucharistic oblation and the heavenly oblation are one and the same: Christ, the High Priest, offering himself to his Father for his Church.

Other theologians, such as Gabriel Vasquez and Leonardus Lessius, attempted to reconcile the principle and the fact. Both of these Jesuits exercised considerable influence in the ages to follow.

Gabriel Vasquez (1549–1604) pointed out the "absurdity" of Bellarmine's communion/destruction theory that the sacrifice takes place in the stomach of the priest. He also rejected the theory of Suarez that the eucharistic sacrifice consists not in a change/destruction, but in a confection/production. He saw, with most of his contemporaries, the essence of sacrifice in the act itself of the change that takes place in the victim. He distinguished between an *absolute* sacrifice and a *relative* sacrifice (uniquely the Eucharist). He defined sacrifice as "a mark or note existing in a thing, by which we profess God as author of death and life."[56] This change, realized in the consecration of the two species, is a *figurative* or *mystical*, but not a real immolation of the body and blood that represents/signifies the death of Christ. Vasquez's theory exercised great influence, but he, too, was unable to reconcile his theology of the Eucharist with his general theory of sacrifice. His idea of a *relative* sacrifice, unique to the Eucharist, did not catch on.

Leonard Lessius (1554–1623) defined sacrifice as "an external oblation, offered to God alone, by a legitimate minister, in which a sensible substance undergoes a change, or even a destruction, in witness to the divine sovereignty and our servitude thereto."[57] He was influenced primarily by Suarez's seeing the "destruction" as a kind of *production* taking place in the consecration, and actually came to locate the whole essence of sacrifice in the consecration, seeing there a *virtual* or *mystical immolation* of Christ on the altar by reason of the *separate* consecration. In other words, "under the species of bread is placed only the Body, not the Blood; under the species of wine only the Blood, not the Body."[58] He also wrote that "[t]he words of consecration are a kind of sword. The Body of Christ which is now living in heaven, is to be slaughtered here instead of a living victim. The Body, placed under the species of bread, and the Blood under the species of wine, are like the body and blood of a lamb now immolated."[59] Like Aquinas, he did not insist on a change of the victim (*mutatio hostiae*), but on a *mutatio circa hostiam*—a change that takes place with regard to the host/victim—and insisted that this change suffices to assure (Trent's) "true and proper sacrifice."[60]

From this detailed outline of post-Tridentine theologies of eucharistic sacrifice, Marius Lepin concluded, finally:

> As we cast a retrospective eye over the half-century since the Council of Trent, we can see that the theologians follow one or the other of two clear tendencies.
>
> 1. The theologians of the first group propose in principle that sacrifice consist essentially in a destruction or real change of the victim. They are thus forced to find this real change (or destruction) in the Sacrifice of the Mass. No one found sufficient the pure and simple change of the bread and wine by transubstantiation. The idea of a simple acquisition by Christ of his sacramental essence (Hessels) also did not satisfy. Two theories received most of the attention: that of Casal, which sees the destructive change of Christ realized in the consecration itself; and that of Bellarmine, where it is accomplished in the communion [of the priest].
> 2. An equally large number insist, on the contrary, that the eucharistic Christ does *not undergo any real change,* neither at the consecration, nor at the communion; there is only a figure of his past immolation and an appearance of death.
>
> Consequently, those who maintain that sacrifice in general requires the change (destruction) of the victim suppose that the Sacrifice of the Mass is an exception to the common rule. Salmeron and Jacques de Bay justify the exception from the fact that Christ is not rendered present under his own species. Vasquez justifies it by reasoning that the Mass is a relative sacrifice. The others are of the opinion that sacrifice can be conceived apart from a real change/destruction of the thing offered. Suarez replaces the idea of destruction with the quite opposite idea of *production.* Melchior Cano, Domingo de Soto, and Maldonado require, following Thomas Aquinas,

a simple *action* carried out with regard to the sacrificial matter. Lessius, finally, with whom one can place van Est, holds on to the term "change—*immutatio*" and, applying it to the same reality as the just-mentioned theologians, talks about change "with regard to" the host/victim.[61]

Bellarmine and the "Modern Average Catholic Theology of the Eucharist"

Returning to the question with which we opened this chapter, we can now see that Bellarmine was much more the messenger than he was the villain in mediating a decadent theology to some contemporary Catholic thinking. Catholic eucharistic theology on the eve of Trent was much broader and much more in continuity with earlier traditions than it was at the end of the sixteenth century. None of the pre-Tridentine or Tridentine theologians suggested any *reality* of immolation in the Mass. But neither did any of them have a sense of the content and structure of the whole Eucharistic Prayer in its ritual context. But somewhat saving the day was their general understanding that, along with the consecration that always held pride of place, there were always two other essential elements in the Mass: the oblation and the representative commemoration of the past immolation. Most important, they generally refrained from reducing the Eucharist to just one of these essential elements.

Reacting against the Reformers, Trent defined the Mass as a "true and proper sacrifice—*verum et proprium sacrificium*,"[62] but left it to the theologians, as we have seen, to argue over what sacrifice is. Trent's earlier definition about the reality of the change of the bread and wine into the Body and Blood of Christ[63] inevitably freighted the whole discussion with heavily physical connotations that disrupted the fragile balance between the symbolic and the realistic that, up to this time, had never totally been lost. Further clouding the issue was the dawning of modern science. Protestant and Catholic theologians, in an infelicitous instance of ecumenical "agreement," both made the same fateful mistake of inductively analyzing the practice of sacrifice in the world's religions in order to establish a definition of sacrifice from which to examine the so-called sacrifice of the Mass. They approached the matter backward. Instead of looking first to the Christ-event and letting that define their thinking, both Protestants and Catholics first defined sacrifice phenomenologically and then applied that definition to the Mass. An awareness of the content and structure of the classical Eucharistic Prayer, which could have been a corrective, was no longer present in the Western Church. No one was conscious of what, after Gregory Dix, we now call the "shape of meaning" of the Eucharist.

This massive methodological mistake was then matched by a mistake in content that apparently no one thought to question: namely, the idea, increasingly accepted by almost all involved, that a *real* sacrifice requires a *real change* or *destruction* of the victim, and then the application of this idea to the Mass. There was no clear awareness that the Christ-event had done away with sacrifice in the history-of-religions sense of the term. Theologians still dealt with the Old and New Testaments in a relatively undifferentiated way, that is, without any historicizing or differentiating hermeneutic, applying to the Mass ideas of sacrifice taken from the Old Testament almost as if Christ never existed. Some Catholic polemicists came up with more or less workable understandings of the Eucharist, but none of them were able to do so in a way consistent with their own (unquestioned) definition of sacrifice as involving the destruction of a victim. The most successful theories were those which emphasized not a real, but a mystical or sacramental, immolation. But often this "mystical immolation" was described in terms so graphically realistic as to undercut the symbolic or mystical meaning. Jan Van Eyck's famous painting *The Adoration of the Mystical Lamb* is a graphic illustration of this.

By the beginning of the seventeenth century, with no one any longer following Bellarmine's idea that the eucharistic sacrifice was consummated in the priest's communion, the only essential element that survived was the consecration carried out, as the infelicitous modern rendering of one of the classical eucharistic hymns put it, "by the action of the priest."

In sum, the eucharistic theology of Bellarmine and of the outgoing sixteenth century, to which Pope Pius XII's *Mediator Dei* and the subsequent magisterial teaching of the Catholic Church appeal, suffers from the following theological shortcomings:

1. Lack of Trinitarian perspective and massive overemphasis on the Christological perspective; no mention of the role of the Holy Spirit; no acknowledgment that the Eucharistic Prayer is addressed to the Father.
2. Neglect of the ecclesiological perspective. There is an allusion to the ecclesiological in the insistence that the rite is to be celebrated by a legitimate or properly ordained minister. This minister, however, is the sole essential performer of the action. He is not conceived as standing there as part of the Church, embedded in the Christ–Church relationship, but as standing between Christ and the Church.
3. Neglect of the role of the participating faithful. They are not even necessary for the essential integrity of the Eucharist. They take part in it only by a kind of association, by consenting to the action of the priest that is, in any case, essentially complete without them.
4. Minimal awareness of the ultimate (or eschatological) goal of the Eucharist, namely, the reorienting transformation of the participants in the direction of the dispositions of Christ. So much emphasis

was put on the real presence of the body and blood of Christ, on verifying a real—or at least symbolic (but with graphically real descriptors)—destruction of the victim that the real goal and ultimate reality of the Eucharist—transformation into Christ—was obscured.

This helps explain the embarrassing dichotomy between the teaching of the contemporary official Roman magisterium and that of most contemporary liturgical theologians. It is due to the magisterium's continued acceptance of some of the shortcomings of post-Tridentine Catholic eucharistic theology. Thus, if there is to be movement toward a more broadly shared Catholic understanding of the Eucharist, the Roman magisterium will need to become less attached to explanations of the Mystery of Faith that are less than satisfactory. Theologians must do their part also. They must do a better job of pointing out that their attempts to provide the Church with a more adequate understanding of the Eucharist are not a challenge to, but are in continuity with, the fullness of the Catholic tradition.

NOTES

This chapter, here somewhat revised, updated, and more compactly presented, appeared originally in *Theological Studies* 61 (2000): 239–260.

1. The principal source for this historical research is Edward J. Kilmartin, *The Eucharist in the West: History and Theology,* ed. Robert J. Daly (Collegeville, Minn.: Liturgical Press, 1998).

2. Ibid., 346–347, 350–351.

3. Ibid., 384. My task is not to substantiate Kilmartin's thesis. I assume that the force of his argument is strong enough to require serious attention by scholars.

4. *Acta apostolicae sedis* (*AAS*) 39 (1947): 521–600.

5. Ibid., 72 (1980): 113–148.

6. Ibid., 75 (1983): 1001–1009.

7. See Kilmartin, *Eucharist in the West,* 187–201.

8. *AAS* 39 (1947): 553. The text is also found in Heinrich Denzinger, auxit Alois Schönmetzer, eds., *Enchiridion Symbolorum,* 36th ed. (Freiburg: Herder, 1967), no. 3850. Hereafter cited as DS.

9. Robert Bellarmine, *Controversiarum de sacramento eucharistiae,* lib. 6.6, *Opera Omnia,* vol. 4 (Paris: Vivès, 1873), 373.

10. Kilmartin, *Eucharist in the West,* 190.

11. Pius XII, *Mediator Dei, AAS* 39 (1947): 555–556.

12. Vatican II translations are taken from *The Basic Sixteen Documents, Vatican Council II,* ed. Austin Flannery (Northport, N.Y.: Costello, 1996).

13. Paul VI, *Institutio generalis missalis romani,* no. 54, in *Missale romanum* (Rome: Vatican Press, 1970), 39; also in *Enchiridion documentorum instaurationis liturgicae: Ordo Missae,* ed. Reiner Kaczynski (Turin: Marietti, 1976), no. 1449, 1. 488; also in *The Conciliar and Postconciliar Documents: Vatican Council II,* ed. Austin Flannery (Collegeville, Minn.: Liturgical Press, 1975), 175.

14. Paul VI, *Institutio generalis missalis romani* no. 55(d); Kaczynski, *Enchiridion*, no. 1540d, 1. 488; Flannery, *Vatican Council II*, 176.

15. Kilmartin, *Eucharist in the West*, 294–295.

16. Ibid., 268–300.

17. *Dominicae cenae*, II, 8 (*AAS* 72 [1980]: 128).

18. Kilmartin, *Eucharist in the West*, 196–197.

19. *Dominicae cenae*, II, 11 (*AAS* 72 [1980]: 141).

20. Ibid., II, 9 (*AAS* 72 [1980]: 133).

21. Ibid. (*AAS* 72 [1980]: 131).

22. "Ad hoc igitur sacrificium, quod modo sacramentali in altari renovatur. . . ."

23. Kilmartin, *Eucharist in the West*, 198–199.

24. Trent, session 22, canon 2; DS 1752.

25. *Dominicae cenae* (*AAS* 72 [1980]: 119–121).

26. Kilmartin, *Eucharist in the West*, 200–201.

27. *Dominicae cenae*, II, 9 (*AAS* 72 [1980]: 133); see also 131.

28. The sentence in which this phrase occurs reads: "Haec namque singulariter victima ab aeterno interitu animam salvat, quae illam nobis mortem Unigeniti per mysterium reparat, qui licet resurgens a mortuis jam non moritur, et mors ei ultra non dominabitur (Rom. 6:9), tamen in semetipso immortaliter atque incorruptibiliter vivens, pro nobis iterum in hoc mysterio sacrae oblationis immolatur." Gregory the Great, *Dialogorum libri IV*, 4.48 (PL 77, 425C–D).

29. Kilmartin, *Eucharist in the West*, 201.

30. Congregation for the Doctrine of the Faith, Letter of August 6, 1983, I, 1 (*AAS* 75 [1983]: 1001–1009, at 1001). This letter conveniently contains footnote references to all the major statements of recent official teaching of the Roman magisterium on this point.

31. Ibid., III, 4 (*AAS* 75 [1983]: 1006). The quotation that occupies the second half of this citation is from Pope John Paul II's *Dominicae cenae*, 8 (*AAS* 72 [1980]: 128–129).

32. *Inter insigniores*, October 15, 1976 (*AAS* 69 [1977]: 98–116, at 112–113), as quoted in Kilmartin, *The Eucharist in the West*, 196.

33. English translation is available on the Vatican Web site, www.vatican.va/phome_en.htm.

34. Official text is in *AAS* 95 (2003). English translation is available on the Vatican Web site, www.vatican.va/phome_en.htm.

35. For further details see Robert J. Daly, "Eucharistic Origins: From the New Testament to the Liturgies of the Golden Age," *Theological Studies* 66 (2005): 3–22.

36. Marius Lepin, *L'Idée du sacrifice de la Messe d'après les théologiens depuis l'origine jusqu'à nos jours* (Paris: Beauchesne, 1926). Marius Lepin (1870–1952), a Sulpician, who was the founder of the congregation Servantes de Jésus, Souverain Prêtre (1938), published prolifically on modernism and the eucharistic teaching of the Catholic Church. *L'Idée du sacrifice de la Messe*, honored by the Académie Française, was his major work of enduring scholarly value. See *Dictionnaire de théologie catholique, Tables générales*, 2 (1967): 2972–2973.

37. Contained specifically in the first two chapters of the *Doctrina de ss. Missae*

sacrificio (DS 1739–1743) and the first three canons of the *Canones de ss. Missae sacrificio* (DS 1751–1753) of session 22, September 17, 1562, of the Council of Trent.

38. Lepin, *L'Idée du sacrifice*, 326 (my translation from the French). This 815-page study extensively quotes theologians' writings on this theme, beginning with the ninth century and covering the next eleven centuries. It constitutes the indispensable and single most important scholarly work for this research.

39. Ibid., 346–415.

40. Ibid., 346–357.

41. Ibid., 357–374.

42. *De sacrificio*, in *Michaelis Baii, celeberrimi in Lovaniensi Academis theologi Opera, cum bullis pontificium, et aliis ipsius causam spectantibus . . . studio A. P. theologi* (Cologne, 1596), 1.160; see Lepin, *L'Idée du sacrifice*, 359.

43. Lepin, *L'Idée du sacrifice*, 361.

44. Ibid., 375–393.

45. "Id vero probatur, primum ex nomine sacrificii. . . . Secundo probatur ex usu Scripturarum. . . . Et omnia omnino in Scriptura dicuntur sacrificia, necessario *destruenda* erant: si viventia, per occisionem; si inanima solida, ut similia, et sal, et thus, per combustionem; si liquida, ut sanguis, vinum et aqua, per effusionem: Lev., i et ii. Neque his repugnat exemplum Melchisedech. . . ." Robertus Bellarminus, *Disputationes de controversiis fidei* (Ingolstadt, 1586–1593; Paris, 1608), *De missa*, i, V., c. xxvii, t. III, col. 792).

46. Ibid., cols. 792–793.

47. Ibid., col. 792; Lepin, *L'Idée du sacrifice*, 383–384. See note 36.

48. Henricus Henriquez, *Summae theologiae moralis libri quindecim* (Salamanca, 1591; Mainz, 1613), i, IX, c. iii, 498b; Lepin, *L'Idée du sacrifice*, 345, 387.

49. Lepin, *L'Idée du sacrifice*, 388.

50. Ibid.

51. Ibid., 389.

52. Gregory of Valencia, *Metimnensis, De rebus fidei hoc tempore controversis* (Lyons, 1591); *De sacrasancto missae sacrificio, contra impiam disputationem Tubingae nuper a Jacobo Herbrando propositam, atque adeo contra perversissimam Lutheri, Kemnitii aliorumque novatorum doctrinam*, i, I, c. ii, 504a; Lepin, *L'Idée du sacrifice*, 344, 390–391.

53. Lepin, *L'Idée du sacrifice*, 393–415.

54. Ibid., 394–397.

55. Ibid., 397–399.

56. Gabriel Vasquez, *Commentarii ac disputationes in III^m partem S. Thomae* (Lyons, 1631), disp. 220, c. iii, no. 26, p. 394a; Lepin, *L'Idée du sacrifice*, 406.

57. Leonardus Lessius, *De sacramentis et censuris, praelectiones theologicae posthumae, olim in Academia Lovaniensi ann. 1588 et 1589 primum, iterum 1596 et 1597 propositae*, q. 83, art. i, no. 7, in *In divum Thomam, de beatitudine, de actibus humanis, de Incarnatione Verbi, de sacramentis et censuris, praelectiones theologicae posthumae* (Louvain, 1645), 152; Lepin, *L'Idée du sacrifice*, 344–345.

58. Lessius continues, acknowledging his debt to Vasquez: "Et hoc sufficit ad rationem hujus sacrificii, tum ut sit verum sacrificium (fit enim circa hostiam, dum sic ponitur, sufficiens mutatio, qua protestamur Deum habere supremam in omnia potestatem), tum ut sit sacrificium commemorativum, repraesentans nobis sacrificium

crucis et mortem Domini. Qui plura hac de re desiderat, legat Gabr. Vasquez." Leonardus Lessius, *Opuscula in quibus pleraque theologiae mysteria explicantur, et vitae recte instituendae praecepta traduntur: Ab ipso auctore, paulo ante mortem, varie aucta et recensita* (Antwerp, 1626) *De perfectionibus moribusque divinis* (1620), 1, XII, c. XIII, no. 97, 128; Lepin, *L'Idée du sacrifice*, 413.

    59. Lessius, *Opuscula in quibus . . .* , no. 95, 128; Lepin, *L'Idée du sacrifice*, 413.

    60. Lepin, *L'Idée du sacrifice*, 414.

    61. Ibid., 414–415.

    62. Trent, Session 22, September 17, 1562, canon 1 of *Canones de ss. Missae sacrificio* (DS 1751).

    63. Trent, Session 13, October 11, 1551, in *Decretum de ss. Eucharistia*, cap. 4, *De transsubstantiatione* (DS 1642); and canon 2 of *Canones de ss. Eucharistiae sacramento* (DS 1652).

6

The Latin of the Roman Rite: Before Trent and After Vatican II

Gerard S. Sloyan

So much of the Catholic tradition of the West is enshrined in the Latin language. For almost two millennia, Latin was the official language of the Church's teaching, ritual, and theology. With the Second Vatican Council, the vernacular has emerged along with a less Eurocentric and a much greater multicultural Church. No discussion of the Council of Trent and the Second Council of the Vatican could take place without a careful historical understanding of the Catholic mother tongue—its history, its role in the official life of the Church, and, finally and apparently, its demise.

From the Beginning to Trent

In the first century of the Christian era, during the reigns of Tiberius, Claudius, Nero, Domitian, and, at the close, Trajan, Latin would have been spoken among the upper classes, in the imperial court, by the legates sent abroad, and in the higher echelons of the army. Greek was the language heard on the streets of Rome—indeed, everywhere in the empire, as the lingua franca that Jews, Syrians, Copts, and Persians had to master for commercial purposes. As early as the second century B.C., the gentleman farmer and public official Marcus Porcius Cato (234–149) was the declared enemy of Greek culture as enervating of the Roman character. We do not have his history of Rome, *Origenes*, but his *De agricultura* is the oldest surviving work of prose in Latin. He concluded his every public address with the demand, delivered against the luxury and wealth of the Punic capital: *Cartago delenda est.*

Alexander the Great's conquest was far more cultural and linguistic than political in its lasting effects. We can assume the same of the speeches of the bishops of Rome, beginning with Linus, in the list of Irenaeus (d. ca. 200), who was himself a native of Asia Minor and a Greek missionary to Gaul, and who later wrote from Rome.[1] All twelve names after "the blessed apostles" are Greek except for Clement, the third in line, and Pius, the ninth, counting Peter and Paul as first. But if this Clement wrote the letter to the Corinthians attributed to him, and if Pius was the brother of Hermas, author of *The Shepherd*, as the Muratorian canon says, then both operated in Greek. Irenaeus's list ends with Eleutherus, to whom the dates 174–189 have been assigned ("now in the twelfth place"), allowing us to date his *Adversus Haereses* in 190 or later. The Bishop of Rome after Eleutherus was Victor I, an African by birth and the first Latin speaker in that office.[2] This forceful figure would have had to be bilingual, both to govern the Church at Rome and to enforce the Roman practice of celebrating Easter on the Sunday following the fourteenth of Nisan (the first day of Pesach). Previously, the Christian East had celebrated Christ's resurrection on the fourteenth of Nisan, whichever day of the week it occurred. The Quartodecimans or "Fourteenthers" included Irenaeus and the martyred Polycarp of Smyrna, but all capitulated, if ungraciously, to the synods Victor mandated on the question from Gaul to Mesopotamia. In what language were these synods? Surely, Latin was used in Rome and North Africa, and almost certainly Greek elsewhere.

Meanwhile, some apologetic and even theological writings began to emerge in the Latin tongue. The first piece of Christian writing that can be dated with certainty is the *Passio Martyrum Scilitanorum* of A.D. 180 (Scili of Numidia in modern Algeria), which also exists in Greek translation.[3] Six men were put to death by the sword under the proconsul Saturninus at Carthage in 180.

Marcus Minucius Felix wrote a Latin apology, *Dialogus Octavius*, in the form of a probably fictitious philosophical dialogue sometime after 197.[4] He was a lawyer as was his friend Octavius, in whose memory the dialogue was written. It was an attempt to convince the pagan Caecilius of the truth of Christianity, who in the event departed the company, at the end of their excursion, a believer. Quintus Septimius Florens Tertullianus (ca. 160–after 220) was a well-educated pagan, possibly in law, born at Carthage (founded by the Phoenicians out of Tyre), who returned there as a Christian from Rome. He did some writing in Greek, but mostly in his native Latin. Tertullian's *Apologeticum* was probably the basis for that of Minucius Felix, although the influence may have gone in the other direction. He wrote another three dozen treatises and letters in a vigorous Latin—most of which are extant—coining along the way some 980 new words. *Trinitas* is the best known of them; the Greek continued to use the ordinary numeral *triás* for the mystery. Berthold Altaner says of Minucius Felix, "Apart from the *Vetus Latina* [the Bible translation that preceded Jerome's *Versio Vulgata*] his writings have exercised the greatest influence on old Christian Latin."[5] The popes from Callistus to Felix (217–274), three of them probably of Greek descent, wrote letters in Latin that are attested to in other writings. Cornelius (251–253) did the same, but also wrote three letters in Greek.[6] Meanwhile, the liturgy in Latin was emerging, more in North Africa than in Rome. "No complete text of the African Mass has come down to us, but scattered references give us sufficient grounds for believing that in many points it coincided with the [later] Roman."[7] Josef Andreas Jungmann speaks of what must have been the steps in translating the liturgy from Greek into Latin in third- and fourth-century Rome because of the changed community there, but says that not much light can be shed on the problem. If before Constantine's time, as Optatus of Milevi reports in 365, there were more than forty churches in the capital, there could well have existed Latin-speaking congregations there even before the days of Pope Cornelius, on whose tomb an inscription in that language first appears.[8]

Since there were Latin-speaking congregations in Rome and possibly Milan in the mid-200s, what Bible translation was read from and incorporated into the sacramental texts? *The Acts of the Scillitan Martyrs* of 180, cited above, speaks of a manuscript of "the letters of Paul, a just man," presumably but not necessarily in Latin translation. A Latin translation of the epistle attributed to Clement of 96 or 97 was circulating in second-century Europe. Late in the century, Tertullian was citing texts from both Testaments, while Cyprian (d. 258) did the same from a Latin Bible. It has been computed that the martyr bishop of Carthage quoted one-ninth of the New Testament in his treatises, letters, and homilies. The places of origin of the various books of the Old Latin version cannot be determined other than North Africa and Europe by comparison of forms of the text, with Rome and Gaul proposed for Europe.[9]

St. Jerome (d. 420) remarked in his "Preface to Joshua" that there were "as many forms of the text for Latin readers as there are manuscripts." Interestingly, he did not retouch or revise five of the books later disputed as to canonicity: 1 and 2 Maccabees, Wisdom, Sirach, and Baruch. They are pure Old Latin, are extant in full text, and are apparently the work of a single translator.[10] Most of the translations of Old Testament books from the Hebrew are Jerome's work except for the Psalter, "an Old-Latin text which was corrected by Jerome to agree with the Greek text of Origen's *Hexapla* . . . In the New Testament, all books have an Old Latin base; but this base has been revised in the light of the Greek with varying degrees of thoroughness—in the Gospels rather hurriedly, in most other books more carefully. The reviewer of the Gospels was certainly Jerome: the reviser(s) of the other books, or groups of books, are altogether unknown."[11] This scholarly summary is followed by the judgment that the Vulgate is far from being a unity and that the translation is called Jerome's Vulgate only because there is more of his work in it than anyone else's. It began to win out in popular (hence *vulgata*) usage by the year 600, although various versions of the Old Latin continued in use. The Vulgate text is attested by many manuscripts from Italy, Spain, Gaul, and Ireland. Charlemagne set Bishop Theodulf of Orléans (d. 821) to revising it. Some manuscripts that resulted from his labors remain, but the far better-known recension is that of the Benedictine Alcuin of York (d. 804). His preference for the Vulgate text contributed to its final acceptance in the West. It became the "Paris Bible" of the thirteenth century, which was the first book set in movable type by Johannes Gansefleisch (Gutenberg) in 1461.

If one asks why vernacular liturgies in the West did not emerge, as occurred in the Byzantine rite translated into Old Slavonic, the answer probably is that while missionaries from the Italian and Irish monasteries did go out to previously pagan populations as did Cyril and Methodius, something of great historical importance took place in that age. The peoples of northern Europe came south to the Alps and beyond. The Celts of the continent, the Franks and the other Teutonic tribes, the Slavs, and the Magyars were brought into the Church not by evangelization in many cases but by command of their kings and chieftains. The clergy knew enough Latin to read the Bible, they had a liturgy of the sacramental rites, and they could communicate in Latin with each other and with the patriarchal see at Rome. The latter was convinced of the fittingness of evangelizing in Latin but knew it could not bring it about by fiat. The apostles of the nations, such as Benedict's black monks and the independently founded Irish monks, already had Latin. So did Patrick, Willibrord, Ansgar, the men at the courts of Wenceslaus and Stephen, and the clergy in the company of Clovis. They therefore continued to celebrate the liturgical rites, including the readings from the gospels and epistles, in Latin, but they expounded them in the people's tongues as they managed to come abreast of them. Catechizing outside the liturgy was necessarily in the vernacular, often in the exact terms of the Latin catechetical lists of Isidore of Seville (d. 636) through to the question-and-answer catechisms of the Carolingian period (eighth–ninth centuries).[12] The preaching of the mendicant friars was in the vernacular, needless to say, as were the catechisms of Luther, Bellarmine, Canisius, and Ripalda 300 years later.

Why, then, were the texts of the Mass, of baptism, confirmation (the same rite become separated), and extreme unction not also put in the vernacular? Penance was in the people's language except for the formula of absolution; so, too, was the marriage rite, especially the preliminary exhortation and the promises of a lifetime of fidelity that the bishop or priest accepted, responding with the nuptial blessing in Latin. The probable reason was cultural inertia. It was, after all, the *Roman* Rite, and it had been in place for well over a millennium. Latin had acquired a sacral character in the popular clerical, and even the lay, mind. For centuries, as a result, the baptized never understood, and in fact could not even hear (*submissa voce*), the wording of the Eucharistic Prayer or Canon at the heart of the Mass. They believed, incorrectly, that only the consecrating words of the priest effected the change of elements, when in fact it was the prayer of the Church, their prayer, to which a choir sang or servers spoke an affirmative "Amen" in their name. The Mass or Lord's Supper, whether celebrated silently in a wayside chapel or with full panoply in a cathedral church, was viewed by the people as the means to bring the eucharistic Christ whom they could look on adoringly, and for the most part did not either eat or drink.

From Trent to Vatican II

Session XXII of the Council of Trent (September 17, 1562) produced a decree on the Mass, the first chapter of which reiterated the ancient faith in the sacrificial character of the rite.[13] The second chapter reaffirmed its rich fruits as propitiatory for the sins of the living and "the dead in Christ not yet fully purged." Subsequent chapters stated that not only God was honored by it but also the saints, that no erroneous teaching might be admitted into the canon, and that human frailty should not allow any but meticulous "observance of the rites of holy mother Church"—for example, that "certain parts of the Mass spoken be in a low tone, others in a higher." It went on to say that while the ideal was that all present should communicate, those Masses at which the priest alone consumed the eucharistic elements while the worshipers communicated spiritually were neither invalid nor illicit. The eighth chapter of the decree speaks most directly to our present concerns: "Even though the Mass contains much for the instruction of a faithful people, the [Council] Fathers do not judge it expedient that the Mass be celebrated *passim* (indiscriminately) in the vernacular tongue." The ambiguous adverb may testify to the strong advocacy of a vernacular liturgy by several bishops on the floor of the small gem that is the Trent cathedral, but canon 9 states that anyone who holds that the Mass must be celebrated only *in lingua vulgari* is to be considered anathema.[14] We possess condensed versions of the interventions and a tally of the votes, but nothing of the debates on the various topics. The negative votes on the vernacular proposal were undoubtedly cast by a combination of *nihil innovetur* traditionalists and others who, though convinced of the proposal's merits, nonetheless thought it tarnished by the protagonists of reform who held heretical views of the Eucharist. That was certainly the case of the rejected proposition that the laity and children under the age of reason had to receive the Sacrament under both species.[15]

The *Roman Missal* was published in 1570 under Pius V and went basically unchanged for 400 years. Many Frankish elements had been added to the austere Roman rite around the time of the second millennium, making it very wordy. Some clerics could commit all the prayers of the Mass to memory in those days of scanty theological education, but altar charts were produced con-

taining the canon and the prayers before and after it, the prayers of the preparation of the gifts and the hand-washing, and the prologue of John's Gospel.
The *Roman Ritual* mandated by the Council for the sacraments other than the
Mass appeared only in 1614 under Paul V, probably because there were so
many local rituals in use that were never entirely replaced. Numerous local
dioceses and regions of bishops had portions translated into the vernacular.
The *Ritual* was enlarged in 1752 and revised in 1925.[16]

Vatican II and Beyond

After Vatican II, the liturgies of baptism, marriage, penance (or reconciliation)
in three forms, including one for general absolution, ordination, the anointing
of the sick, and the funeral rites, each promulgated separately, were rendered
into vernacular languages throughout the Catholic world. All were produced
in *editiones typicae* and immediately translated into the people's languages. That
had been made possible by the Constitution on the Sacred Liturgy, *Sacrosanctum Concilium*, promulgated at the close of the second session of Vatican Council II by Paul VI on December 4, 1963. It read in part that while

> (1) the use of Latin language . . . is to be preserved in the Latin rites
> . . . (2) a wider use of the vernacular may be made whether in the
> Mass, the administration of the sacraments or in the other parts of
> the liturgy . . . especially in readings, directives, and some prayers
> and chants . . . (3) [I]t is for the competent territorial ecclesiastical
> authority . . . to decide whether, and to what extent, the vernacular
> language is to be used; [their] decrees are to be approved, that is,
> confirmed by the Apostolic See. And, whenever it seems to be called
> for, this authority is to consult with bishops of neighboring regions,
> which have the same language. (4) Translations from the Latin text
> into the mother tongue intended for use in the liturgy must be ap-
> proved by the competent territorial ecclesiastical authority men-
> tioned above.[17]

The Divine Office or Liturgy of the Hours went largely unchanged from
the time of its approval after the Council of Trent to its complete revision on
the specific terms laid out in *Sacrosanctum Concilium*, 83–101. The English-
language version, overseen by the International Committee on English in the
Liturgy, was published in 1975. A major change, however, had previously taken
place when Pope Pius XII appointed a committee of six scholars at the Pontifical Biblical Institute in 1941 to do a new Latin translation. It was completed
in 1944 and promulgated for private and choral prayer in 1945. Christine Mohrmann deplored its resort to classical Latin in many places, deserting the looser,
freer Christian Latin of the third and fourth centuries. Thus, *levare* became

attollere, tabernaculum became *tentorium, accipere* (Vulgar Latin for *sumere*), *auferre,* and *contristatus,* the milder *maestus.* But the word changes were not the major matter; rather, it was the syntax and phrasing. The present writer became acquainted with the Gallican Psalter in the breviary as a deacon, often having been stumped by phrases that were meaningless because of corrupt Hebrew or Greek texts that underlay the Latin. With priestly ordination and a new set of breviaries, he was sent to a classical dictionary more than once. The study of theology in textbooks and Thomas's *Summa* had familiarized him with the vocabulary and style of the Bible portions and patristic and later era second nocturnes of matins, but the elegant wording and phrasing of the new translation sent him back to the Livy, Horace, and Plautus of college study.

Two things of interest had happened in the papacy of John XXIII (1958–1963) that prepared for the heated floor discussions that ended in the above settlement. His baptismal name was Joseph and, out of devotion to this saint, he inserted by fiat that name after Mary in the canon prayer *Communicantes.* The popular eruption that followed is not easy to reconstruct in imagination at a distance of forty years, so sacrosanct was the Mass text thought to be. In the apostolic constitution *Veterum Sapientiae* of February 22, 1962, at the urging of the curia's chief Latinist, speaking for others, Pope John XXIII promulgated the necessity of the continued use of that tongue in seminary classroom instruction and in the various sacramental rites where it was losing ground. The document had a very brief effect, for two reasons: there were not enough seminary professors capable of lecturing in Latin, not to speak of students understanding it, and the growth of the Church in the so-called Third World in the twentieth century had made it an increasingly less Eurocentric communion and more multicultural in every respect, including the multilingual. The latter reality characterized the Second Council of the Vatican and made it a turning point in the life of the global Church. It had been Catholic in name since St. Ignatius of Antioch so denominated it in writing to the Church at Smyrna from shipboard in 109 or 110.[18] He meant by the term the inclusion of the entire apostolic teaching in contrast to emerging heretical groups, such as the Gnostics. By the late second century, "catholic" had taken on the geographic connotation testified to in Irenaeus's mention of the churches established in Germany and among the Iberians and Celts in addition to those already found in Egypt and Libya.[19] That catholicity of the West included the Latin language as the medium of public prayer, theological scholarship, and communication within the Church. Greek served the churches evangelized out of Constantinople in the same manner. This bipolar fact and the cultures that accompanied the languages had more to do with the tragic division between East and West in the eleventh century than any differences in theology or papal jurisdiction.

Two minor occurrences before Vatican II may illustrate the sensitive character the question of Latin in public worship had acquired in this country. John

Pope John XXIII (1958–1963) convoked the Second Council of the Vatican in 1959.
Art Resource, NY ART19813

Ross Duggan, a retired Australian army colonel, had come to the United States after World War II and founded the Vernacular Society, its membership confined to subscribers to the modest, leaflet-sized periodical *Amen*. The masthead on the first page under the title read, "How can anyone say 'Amen' to your prayer of Thanksgiving if he does not know what you are saying? (1 Cor. 14: 16)." The colonel came regularly to the annual Liturgical Weeks, but he was never given the place at a general session that he craved. Meantime, he lobbied curial cardinals regularly to make his case. On a smaller stage, the present writer was told by the rector of The Catholic University of America in the late spring of 1962 to cancel the course to be given by Dom Godfrey Diekmann from the upcoming summer session. He had offered it triennially over the previous twenty-one years. The reason, the rector finally acknowledged, was that Diekmann, as editor of the journal *Worship,* had published a symposium containing a paper that advocated the vernacular liturgy, about which some archbishop on the board of trustees had complained. This was a position Diekmann had never taken publicly, nor had the Liturgical Conference (because of well-known episcopal opposition to the idea). Francis Spellman, Cardinal Archbishop of New York, made an intervention at Vatican II, framed by his *peritus* in Latin, favoring the Divine Office in vernacular translation but opposing any similar move with regard to the Mass. This might well have been the position of those Council fathers whose grasp of Latin was deficient and who had in consequence suffered over many years from the obligation of the breviary.

Because the Council's Decree on the Sacred Liturgy had spoken guardedly of vernacular use ("whether and to what extent it was to be employed . . . wider use may be made of it . . . especially in readings, directives, some prayers, and chants"), the United States bishops shortly after Vatican II approved and received Vatican confirmation *ad experimentum* of a macaronic missal. The gospel and epistle readings of the Roman missal had been translated into English at high speed by members of the Catholic Biblical Association before the completed New American Bible was to appear on September 30, 1970. Many congregations were surprised and delighted to hear much besides the canon, secret, and post-communion prayers in their own tongue. Some others were displeased by the break with tradition, and a number expressed unhappiness with the quality of translation. Much was made of the rendering "this fellow" (John 9:29) as an unconsciously disrespectful way to speak of Jesus, when in fact the evangelist's Pharisees meant to dismiss him in precisely this fashion. That outcry was the opening salvo in the language wars that have continued. One of the first tasks of the International Committee on English in the Liturgy (ICEL) was to provide a translation of the Sacramentary, including the *Novus Ordo* of the Mass, in language acceptable to the bishops of the several English-speaking countries and regions. That, too, was done in haste. There was less to complain about the translation than the infelicitous wording of certain of the great mysteries of faith, such as the Incarnation and the triune life of God, coupled with frequent silences about the work of grace in human actions. The long deferred *Roman Missal* in English dress, overseen by a reconstituted, cu- rial puppet ICEL, will, according to report, be more concerned with hieratic speech—faux seventeenth-century—than the forceful speech already in use that conveys faith in the body and blood of the Lord offered, eaten, and drunk for the forgiveness of sins. Not many phrases in the "dynamic equivalence" that is the essence of all good translation need be altered, although it seems many have been, in the interests of a literal rendition.

When the Consilium for the Implementation of the Constitution on the Sacred Liturgy had completed the *Lectionary for Mass* as part of *Missale Ro- manum* (promulgated in an apostolic constitution of April 3, 1969), it was ordered to be used beginning on the First Sunday of Advent, November 30 in that year. The *editio typica* was based on the Clementine Vulgate. This meant that the verse enumeration of the Psalms and other biblical passages differed notably from that found in modern Bible translations from the Greek and Hebrew. The *Lectionary* promulgated in Latin did indicate the times when Old Testament verse numbers differed in the Vulgate from the Greek of the Sep- tuagint but not when New Testament textual scholarship had proposed a dif- ferent enumeration. As to the places where the Latin wording of an Old Tes- tament passage made it a clearer type of a New Testament antitype than a translation from the Hebrew would do, nothing could be done.

Whether Pope Paul VI was moved by liturgical considerations or the need to have a better Latin Bible for purposes of allocutions and *motibus propriis* (self-motivated communications), he called on Archbishop Pietro Rossano, re- cently involuntarily retired from the number-two position in the Congregation for Relations with Non-Christian Religions, to oversee a new translation of the Bible from the Hebrew, Aramaic, and Greek. The Pope died in 1978 and in 1979 there appeared a purported new edition of the Vulgate, doubtfully the fruit of the Rossano team of translators. Rossano spoke to the present writer, when in Philadelphia for a lecture, of his discouragement over the project. "The scholars expert in the ancient tongues whom he could draft were not good Latinists, and those in Rome and elsewhere who knew Latin best were unfamiliar with the finer points of Hebrew, if not also the *koinē* Greek with a Semitic accent of the New Testament."[20] He had not been expected to draft three distinct teams of linguists for the project.

The Neo-Vulgate is meant to replace the version ordered by Clement VIII that appeared in 1590, twenty-seven years after the adjournment of Trent.[21] It was a revision with some 3,000 corrections of the work initiated by Sixtus V just two years before. The New Vulgate is not especially new except for some readings from critical texts that the earlier translators could not have known and a new translation of Ecclesiasticus (Sirach or Ben Sira). It continues to be "she" (*ipsa*) who will strike the head of the serpent's seed or progeny at Genesis

3:15, whereas the Hebrew text has the pronoun "he" (namely, her seed or off-spring) who will do the striking. Other choices can be based on a single letter in a Hebrew word, as in "loves" rather than "breasts" in the Stuttgart 1983 Vulgate at Song of Songs 1:1. "Let us cut down the tree in its strength and get rid of him" (Jeremiah 11:19) is a great improvement on the older Vulgate, "Let us put wood on his bread and eliminate him," as are "He shall sustain me with raisin cakes" rather than "flowers" (Song 2:5) and "such is your *decus* (distinction? honor?)" over "your *decet* (your due)." All these improved readings, like that of Job 19:21–27 that retains *redemptor* for go'el but continues "shall stand upon the earth," are the result of recourse to the Hebrew text. The sole regret is that such recourse is not thoroughgoing in the many cases where the Septuagint lies behind the Clementine Vulgate and provides a less dependable reading.[22]

Something has been lost in the Catholic West with the diminished knowledge and use of the Latin tongue. As a medium of communication between the world's bishops and the Roman See, its passing was inevitable. Just as French served as the international tongue for commerce, world politics, and culture up to World War II, so English has come to replace it. Understandably, much of Europe, including the hardworking people at the Vatican (where in fact Italian is the everyday medium), resent this. But history has a way of tarrying for no one. One important loss for the theological world, Protestant as well as Catholic, is the inability to deal with perfect ease with the literary monuments of the patristic, early and late medieval, and modern periods. In publications and in the spoken media, even in university lectures, one encounters serious gaffes in syntax and pronunciation (e.g., *ex post factum, stigmáta*, a long e and a short in second and third conjugation infinitives consistently confused, the fugitive recessive accent). Legal terms are one offender, but the unforgivable is mangled Latinity on the lips of an otherwise educated person or the voice on a classical music station.

Is familiarity with the Latin tongue fated for total discard in the Catholic West? Church usage quite apart, it is already not required, and in many instances not offered, in *lycée, Gymnasium*, or the English-speaking Catholic secondary school. It is possible to earn a Ph.D. in theology in the United States without having gotten past "Amó, amás, I loved a lass," the basic pronunciation solecism. A small but not endangered species is the canon lawyer, who is happily required to come abreast of Latin, whether for dissertation research purposes or simply communication with the Sacred Roman Rota. The same requirement still holds for any other branch of theology in the more respectable university programs. Few need to read Galileo's *Sidereus Nuncius* or Newton's *Philosophiae Naturalis Principia Mathematica* nowadays except for their scholarly purposes, but the theologian's struggle with the Latinity of John Duns Scotus or Huldreich Zwingli, and the political scientist's with the Magna Carta, is another matter. Even the easier to comprehend Aquinas and Calvin send many to translations, at times not thoroughly dependable, for a fine point in theology.

Is there any relief in sight, or are the worlds of learning and culture fated to a continued and even profounder ignorance? The world of choral song seems to be retaining and even growing in the use of motets and longer pieces in Latin. Public high schools in economically well-favored school districts are increasingly offering Latin as a language option, a move that even fee-paying Catholic secondary schools appear not to be making. Most encouraging of all, perhaps, is the adoption by parish congregations, under good musical leadership, of simpler chant pieces such as the *Gloria, Sanctus,* and *Agnus Dei,* even if not sung with the arsis and thesis that characterize that flowing mode of song. The day when congregations worldwide sang the final two verses of longer hymns, *O Salutaris Hostia, Tantum Ergo,* and *Pange Lingua,* without knowing their meaning may never return, and that is just as well. Christ hidden under the veil of bread is bad eucharistic theology and gazing upon him instead of consuming him is worse, but at least a centuries-old tradition of language was being kept alive.

Is it folly to prophesy that a resurgence of that tradition may yet be in prospect? The prophecy has nothing to do with nostalgia nor bemoaning the look to the present and future of the Second Vatican Council, but with the fact that so much of the Catholic tradition of the West is enshrined in Latin. When the language is lost, the treasure in which it speaks may be lost. While enrichment of the Catholic tradition proceeds apace with the great variety of languages and cultures, many of them oral, being either added or restored to it, impoverishment of its heritage of Latinity, so long predominant in the West, would be a bad bargain indeed, *quod Deus avertat!* Interestingly, since none of the bishops at the October 2005 Synod on the Eucharist asked for a return to Latin in the Church's prayer, the retention of the tongue must be the work of the scholarly community in the near future.

NOTES

1. *The Refutation and Overthrow of the Knowledge Falsely So Called,* III. iii, 3, in *The Apostolic Fathers with Justin Martyr and Irenaeus,* ed. Alexander Robinson and James Donaldson (Edinburgh: T. & T. Clark, 1867; repr. Grand Rapids, Mich.: Eerdmans, 1996), 416; Cyril C. Richardson, ed., *Early Christian Fathers* (New York: Touchstone, 1996), 372–373.

2. For a summary account of what is known or speculated about each of these Roman incumbents from Peter forward, identified as the first bishop of that church ca. 200, to Victor, see John N. D. Kelly, *The Oxford Dictionary of the Popes* (Oxford: Oxford University Press, 1986), 5–12.

3. See Berthold Altaner, *Patrology,* trans. Hilda C. Graef (New York: Herder & Herder, 1960), 7, 162, 249. He writes: "To the Africans falls the honor of having exer-

cised the greatest influence on the formation and development of the so-called Christian Latin. . . . Probably as early as the middle of the second century, at least substantial parts of the Bible were translated into Latin in N. Africa" (162).

4. M. Minucii Felicis, *Octavius: Prolegomena, Text and Critical Notes*, ed. A. D. Simpson (New York, 1938); *The Octavius of Marcus Minucius Felix*, trans. G. W. Clarke (English and annotation only) (New York: Newman Press, 1974).

5. Altaner, *Patrology*, 166. The Dutch scholar of early Christian Latinity, Christine Mohrmann, attributes its "exotic" character to the Hebraic influence on the Septuagint and distinguishes between the classical style retained by Minucius Felix and Lactantius and the innovative style of Tertullian and Cyprian. The early Latin liturgical texts took on a hieratic or sacral tone, she maintains, influenced by imperial language— *gloria* for *doxa*, for example—thus becoming a language of ritual expression rather than of communication (her terms). See Mohrmann's *Liturgical Latin, Its Origins and Character* (Washington, D.C.: Catholic University of America Press, 1957) and *Études sur le latin des chrétiens*, 2 vols. (Rome: Edizioni di Storia e Letteratura, 1958).

6. Altaner, *Patrology*, 190.

7. Josef A. Jungmann, *The Mass of the Roman Rite: Its Origins and Development*, translation of *Missarum sollemnia* by Francis A. Brunner (New York: Benziger Brothers, 1950), 45, citing Fernand Cabrol, "Afrique (Liturgie)," in *Dictionnaire d'archéologie chrétienne et de liturgie*, ed. Fernand Cabrol, vol. 1 (Paris: Latouzey and Ané, 1907), 591–657.

8. See Jungmann, *Mass of the Roman Rite*, 50.

9. See Kevin G. O'Connell, "Texts and Versions," in *The New Jerome Biblical Commentary*, ed. Raymond Brown et al., (Englewood Cliffs, N.J.: Prentice-Hall, 1990), § 68, 131. See the *Vetus Latina* volumes of the Archabbey at Beuron, edited by Bonifacio Fischer, Beuron: Vetus Latina Institute, volumes on Genesis (1951–1954); the Wisdom of Solomon (1977–1985); Isaiah, Ephesians, Philippians, and Colossians were published in between.

10. O'Connell, "Text and Versions," 132.

11. B. Fischer, J. Gribomont, and R. Weber, "Preface," in *Biblia sacra iuxta vulgatam versionem*, 3rd rev. ed., vol. 20 (Stuttgart: Deutsche Bibelgesellschaft, 1983). This critical text is new, meant to replace the official Roman edition authorized by Clement VIII in 1593. It acknowledges the work on the Old Testament manuscripts of the monks of Saint Jerome Abbey in Rome, and on the New Testament of J. Wordsworth and J. H. White (Oxford: Oxford University Press, 1898). St. Jerome's translation of the Psalms from the Hebrew according to the Septuagint of Origen's *Hexapla*, the Gallican Psalter (so called because of its adoption in Gaul), *The Apostolic Fathers with Justin Martyr and Irenaeus*, and his later translation of the Psalter directly from the Hebrew are printed on facing pages. The former made its way into editions of the Vulgate and the breviary.

12. For some examples see Gerard S. Sloyan, *Shaping the Christian Message* (New York: Macmillan, 1958), 22–37; also (Glen Rock, N.J.: Paulist Deus Books, 1963), 30–45.

13. H. Denzinger and A. Schönmetzer, eds., *Enchiridion Symbolorum*, 32nd ed. (Freiburg: Herder Verlag, 1963), 1738 [937a]–1778 [968]. Hereafter DS.

14. Ibid., 1749, 1759.

15. Ibid., 1725–1734, on the matter from session XXI (July 16, 1562), reiterated as DS 1760 after the decrees and canons on the Sacrifice of the Mass. For the identity of the speakers (by diocese only) and the vote tallies on successive questions, see *Acta authentica S. Oecumenici Concilii Tridentini*, vol. 2 (Zagreb, n.d.), 58–129. In the previous century, some among the Bohemian Brethren of Jan Hus had held that without the chalice containing the Precious Blood, the Eucharist was not validly received. See "Utraquists," in *New Catholic Encyclopedia*, vol. 14 (New York: McGraw-Hill, 1967), 505.

16. "Rituale Romanum," in *The Oxford Dictionary of the Christian Church*, 3rd ed., ed. E. A. Livingstone (New York: Oxford University Press, 1997), 1401.

17. "The Constitution on the Sacred Liturgy," III, C, 36, in *The Documents and Postconciliar Documents of Vatican II*, ed. Austin Flannery, vol. 1 (Northport, N.Y.: Costello, 1992).

18. See "Critical Observations on the New Latin Psalter: Its Diction and Style," in Christine Mohrmann, *Études sur le Latin des Chrétiens*, vol. 1 109–131, repr. from *American Benedictine Review* 4 (1953): 7–33. For the complete text see "Liber Psalmorum . . . cura Professorum Pontificii Instituti Biblici," in *Biblia Sacra Iuxta Vulgatam Clementinam* (Tournai: Desclée, 1956), 1–120.

19. See Ignatius, "To the Smyrnaeans" 8, 2, in Richardson, *Early Christian Fathers*, 115.

20. See "Irenaeus Against Heresies," I, 10, 2, ibid., 360.

21. Gerard S. Sloyan, "Some Thoughts on Bible Translations," *Worship* 75, 3 (May 2001): 245.

22. See *Nova Vulgata Bibliorum Sacrorum Editio* (Rome: Libreria Editrice Vaticana, 1979).

7

Priestly Formation

Kenan B. Osborne

Both the historians and theologians of the Roman Catholic Church have found the relationship between the Council of Trent and the Second Vatican Council of great interest, since the two councils profoundly influenced the Catholic Church during the second millennium. In many ways, however, the Council of Trent and the Second Vatican Council were worlds apart. Trent and Vatican II, separated by four centuries, took place in vastly different situations. They differed in their respective epistemes, their central problems and issues, and their goals. In both councils, the highest leadership of the Roman Catholic Church developed a doctrinal and pastoral message that was based on the Word of God and the traditions of the Church. Nonetheless, the messages reflect different ages and dissimilar worldviews, as well as changing foci and diverse goals. If one does not understand both the common and the distinctive elements of the two councils, one will never appreciate the depth and breadth of these two historic events in the Roman Catholic Church.

In this chapter, the focus is on a single theme central to both councils, the formation of priestly leadership. The goal is twofold: on the one hand, to indicate the clear differences, and, on the other hand, to emphasize the undeniable similarities regarding the respective positions of the two councils on the issue of formation of priestly leadership. To do this, I have arranged the material under the following topics: first, an overview of the basic official statements regarding the Tridentine reform of priestly formation; second, a historical background, listing the major factors that occasioned such a reform in priestly formation in the sixteenth century; third, a review of the major developments of the seminary system in the seventeenth century, immediately following Trent; fourth, an overview of the basic official material on priestly formation as developed by Vatican II and its postconciliar reception; finally, some concluding remarks.

An Overview of the Basic Official Statements Regarding the Tridentine Reform of Priestly Formation

In his bull of 1542 convoking the Council of Trent, Pope Paul III made it very clear that not only doctrinal questions, but also issues of reform, were to be discussed. The agenda was to include "the restoration of what is good and the correction of bad morals."[1] In 1545, the *Decretum de inchoando concilio* of Paul III, which officially and formally opened the Council, was read to the small gathering of bishops at Trent. In this decree, the reform issue was made explicit. The bishops were officially asked: "Does it please you . . . for the reform of the clergy . . . to decree and declare that the holy and general Council of Trent begins and has begun?" The bishops then answered: "It pleases us."[2] With this agreement, a *doctrinal* and a *reform* council of the Church began. One of the major goals was, therefore, the reform of the clergy.

As the sessions of the Council of Trent took place, the reform of the formation of priests appeared repeatedly, and the issue was considered essential to the broader goal of reform of the clergy. Starting with the fifth session of the Council, in 1546, each session issued a doctrinal decree and a reform decree (*decretum de reformatione*). In the Decree Concerning Reform issued in 1546, the bishops mandated two particular issues bearing on our theme. First, only competent Scripture scholars should train seminarians (chapter 1); and second, preaching the Word of God was a major task of bishops and priests, and such preaching should be done regularly on all Sundays and solemn festivals (chapter 2). This second mandate implied that seminarians should receive competent training for preaching.[3] In 1547, the seventh session of the council issued its Decree Concerning Reform that stressed the competency of the clergy for the *cura animarum*. Special attention was given in chapters 11, 12, and 13 to the suitable training of seminarians, focusing specifically on precautions and regulations for the promotion of any seminarian to major orders.[4] In the fourteenth session, held in 1551, one finds a similar focus on formation of clergy in its Decree Concerning Reform in chapters 1, 2, 3, and 7, in which the promotion or advancement to orders of unworthy seminarians was once again the concern.[5] At the twenty-first session in July 1562, the Decree Concerning Reformation, chapters 2 and 6, concentrated on priestly formation. Seminarians who had no means of livelihood were not to be ordained, and since illiterate rectors and vicars should not be given beneficiary positions, the decree implied that illiterate seminarians should not receive holy orders.[6] In September 1562, at the twenty-second session, the Reform Decree, in chapters 1 and 2, focused specifically on the spiritual life and the moral conduct of those in formation.[7]

It was in the twenty-third session in July 1563, however, that the Decree Concerning Reform developed in extensive and intensive detail the seminary system for the formation of the clergy. The entire reform decree of this session of Trent, in eighteen chapters, was devoted to the details of seminary training.[8] The main themes of this lengthy decree were the following: the *cura animarum* in a diocese is a matter of highest priority, implying that formation for the *cura animarum* is also a matter of high priority; the bishop is responsible for all ordinations in his respective diocese, and this includes the admission to the clerical state or tonsure; a seminarian must be at least fourteen years old; competent examiners must vouch for a seminarian's ordination; ordinations must be public events, and the interstices between orders must be observed; a seminarian must be at least twenty-two years old to receive the subdiaconate, at least twenty-three years old to receive the diaconate, and at least twenty-five years old to receive the presbyterate; vagrants and incompetent seminarians are excluded from ordination; and, finally, seminaries are to be established in every diocese or at least in a provincial diocese. In the span of roughly seventeen pages, a general program for seminarians and seminaries was promulgated by the conciliar bishops.

All of this material indicates that reform of priestly formation was a central task for the Tridentine bishops. The specific details indicate a widespread deficiency in the training and formation of priests. Too many seminarians were illiterate, unable to provide for their basic needs, morally unfit, ordained too quickly and without discernment of their solid spiritual and ethical life, unfit for the *cura animarum*, woefully ignorant of the Holy Scriptures, and incompetent in regard to preaching the Word. The very mention of these major shortcomings of seminarians indicates that the status of priestly vocations was in a major crisis. Let us consider the historical basis for this needed reform of priestly formation.

A Historical Background: The Major Factors in Priestly Formation in the Sixteenth Century

Each of the decrees mentioned above was officially titled *Decretum de reformatione* (Decree Concerning Reform). Today, at the beginning of the third millennium, the very word "reform" sounds ominous. Today, Roman Catholics are far more comfortable with the word "renewal." The Second Vatican Council has been described as a council of renewal, and few authors have spoken of Vatican II in terms of "reform." However, at the time of Trent, even with the Protestant Reformation still active, "reform" was a treasured term. Indeed, "reform" had enjoyed a long and even privileged history in the late medieval world. In a most remarkable way, the period from approximately 1000 to 1500 witnessed the appearance of a number of disparate reform movements, initiated by a wide variety of Catholic Christians from all levels of medieval society. During this lengthy period, one cannot speak of a single reform movement; rather, there were many reform movements with varying degrees of interconnection and interdependency. Within monasticism, there was the Cluniac reform (927–1157), led by five outstanding abbots. There was the Cistercian reform, begun by Robert of Molesme (ca. 1028–1112). Other monastic reformers followed: Robert of Arbrissel (d. 1117), Vitalis of Sauvigny (d. 1122), Bernard of Tiron (d. 1120), and Gerald of Salles (d. 1120). The list could go on. In 1046, the Holy Roman Emperor, Henry III, began a reform of the papacy with the installation of a German Pope, Clement II. There followed a series of German Popes down to Urban II in 1088. This Germanic reform movement has been given the name Gregorian Reform, since Gregory VII (1073–1085) was its most notable leader. During the period 1000–1300, hundreds of lay reform movements can be added to the "reform" tendency. New religious communities— for example, the Franciscans, Dominicans, Servites, Carmelites, Hermits of St. Augustine, Williamites, and Mercedarians—developed as well, and all them were reform-minded. In the sixteenth century, the establishment of the Jesuits was a continuation of this reform spirit. The Protestant reformations were part of this same movement, and after the reform Council of Trent, an officially designated "Catholic Reformation" was furthered by Paul III (1534–1549), and even more forcibly by his successor, Paul IV (1555–1559).

The Counter-Reformation or, as it is also called, the Catholic Reformation, continued using the notion of reform up to the American Revolution and the French Revolution. These two revolutions with their own agendas for reform created an atmosphere in which the term "reform" became anathema to Roman Catholic leadership. "Renewal," rather than "reform," became the acceptable term, and this preference continues to the present day in the Roman Catholic Church.

However, for the bishops at the Council of Trent, "reform" was the proper term, and reform of priestly formation was a major part of their agenda. Although the "seminary system" was mandated by the Tridentine bishops, it predated the Council of Trent. Historians note that the reform movements in the Church of Spain at the end of the fifteenth and the beginning of the sixteenth centuries played a major role in the development of the "seminary system" throughout the Roman Catholic Church.[9] Three episcopal leaders were key to the Spanish reform movement: Hernando de Talavera, Archbishop of Granada; Cardinal Mendoza (d. 1495); and Ximénes de Cisneros (d. 1517). Besides the efforts of these three men, two regional councils were held in Toledo (in 1473 and 1512), at which reform decrees were promulgated and effectively applied. Mendoza wrote a catechism of Christian life, and he established a number of colleges and universities. The seminary program at Granada provided a model that the bishops at Trent appealed to when they were developing their material on the seminary system.[10]

One should not conclude, however, that the "seminary system" thrived throughout Europe before Trent. It did not. Most candidates for the priesthood did not have any seminary training at all. Before Trent and even during its sessions, a large number of priests and not a few bishops lived openly in concubinage, that is, they lived on a permanent basis with a woman.[11] Other issues also indicate that priestly formation in the late Middle Ages was below standard. First, at Trent the residency of bishops in their dioceses, which had become a major problem, was enjoined on several occasions.[12] Bishops, at this time, were notorious for not staying at home. In their absence, scandalous leadership often took over the direction of dioceses, and such a leadership did not have "priestly formation" at the top of its agenda. Second, historians have consistently noted that just prior to the Council of Trent there were too many priests.[13] Such an overgrowth of priests had been mentioned at the regional Council of Sens in 1528; a similar mention can be found in the sessions of Trent in 1547 and 1562. Not only were there too many priests, but a large number of them were morally deficient, intellectually unqualified, or professionally incompetent.[14] Some men became priests for economic reasons; poorer people sought ordination in order to have a modicum of economic security, and those better off in life entered the clergy in order to have a more affluent life or more power within society. Based on historical data, the cause for this overgrowth seems to lie primarily with the benefice system. Given this set of circumstances at the time of Trent, the Tridentine bishops had every reason to be concerned about the formation of priests.

If the diocesan clergy was in shambles, one might expect that the religious clergy were better off. They were, but hardly in a significant way. First, in contrast to diocesan priests, religious postulants for ordination were required to undergo a lengthy period of spiritual formation. This formation was, of course, the formation of the candidate for religious life that took place before the novitiate, during the novitiate, and the few years after the novitiate. Second, in the more established religious communities, care was generally taken to provide intellectual and theological formation. Unfortunately, in some monastic communities prior to Trent, a two-track system existed regarding ordination. Postulants or religious seminarians were ordained with a minimum of theological training, but as priests, they were not given any ministerial office. Because of their lack of intellectual and theological training, they could not exercise the *cura animarum*. They had enough education to read Latin and to celebrate Mass, but they had no training for preaching and other ministerial or pastoral duties. The historical data indicate that the custom of daily Masses in monastic communities, with the concomitant financial stipends that they engendered, played a major role in ordaining many to the priesthood but prevented many of them from active participation in the pastoral ministry. They were simply "Mass priests." Once again, the conclusion is obvious: at this time, there were too many priests, both religious and diocesan, and a large majority of these ordained men were not adequately trained for the *cura animarum*.

Abbots and major priors were, in too many instances, similar to bishops in their absence from the monastery for long periods of time. If they were in residence, they had other issues to take care of than the religious life of the monks. Since they were in charge of wealth, they could live in more elegant ways than ordinary religious could, and in many instances this allowed them to live in some form of concubinage. Many of these abbots, considered princes of the Church, often held the title "prince of the land" as well. Accordingly, they lived as many princes lived: with great moral or, perhaps better, immoral latitude.

Given all of this, one cannot view the Council of Trent simply as a council that was called to reestablish true Catholic doctrine. Clearly, the leaders of the Protestant Reformation, such as Luther, Calvin, and Zwingli, had presented a theology that challenged the operative theology of the Roman Catholic Church in the sixteenth century. Clearly, the operative theology itself, as found in the Roman Catholic Church of the sixteenth century, needed a major realignment; theological issues were significant and deserved a major reply. However, the many reformations mentioned above, which began more or less around 1000, were not generally concerned with theology itself, but with the spiritual life of the Church. Two quotations are of major importance in making this point. The first is from S. Harrison Thompson:

> It is commonplace to assert that the Protestant Reformation did not come unheralded onto the European historical scene. It had a long preparation. Every failure to remove the abuses that had crept into the Church only made it more certain that the effort would have to be repeated in a more forceful manner. If any of the reform endeavors—for example, those of the councils, the mystics, certain progressive popes or cardinals, the reformers within the older orders, the reform-minded laymen, or the humanist reformers—had succeeded, the Protestant Reformation would probably not have occurred, or at least it would have been postponed for a long time.[15]

Thompson's words are painfully accurate. Abuses had indeed infested the Roman Catholic Church, and these abuses were not primarily theological but spiritual. Almost every reform movement that Thompson notes was spiritual, not theological. Since 1000, there had been a call to lead an apostolic life, that is, a call to go back to the Gospels and make them the center of one's Christian living. The Word of God nourished the reform spirit of many lay movements, of the new communities of religious such as the Franciscans, and of the mystics, many of whom were women. In the "standard" forms of the Roman Catholic Church from 1000 to the mid-1500s, the Gospel, the Word of God, was woefully missing.

The second quotation, from the outstanding historian of doctrine Jaroslav Pelikan, speaks of a major lack in the late medieval church. He writes:

> The institutions of medieval Christendom were in trouble, and everyone knew it. Intended as windows through which men might catch a glimpse of the Eternal, they [the institutions] had become opaque, so that the faithful looked at them rather than through them. The structures of the Church were supposed to act as vehicles for the spirit—both for the Spirit of God and for the spirit of man. . . . Instead what he [the individual] found was a distortion of the faith. . . . Captive in ecclesiastical structures that no longer served as channels of divine life and means of divine grace, the spiritual power of the Christian gospel pressed to be released. The pressure exploded in the Reformation.[16]

Once again, as Pelikan points out, the spiritual aspects of Christian life were pressing for release from the institutional structures. Clearly, both theological and spiritual issues were involved. The spiritual indigence that Thompson and Pelikan discuss might have been remedied had there been better Church leadership. In late medieval times, leadership of the Catholic Church was in the hands of the clergy. However, if the formation of priests was spiritually deficient, then the leadership itself could not help but reflect these same defects. From 1000 on, reform-minded people and reform-minded groups had expressed their frustration with these spiritual shortcomings. Some of these groups succeeded in bringing about a more spiritual Church, and these people provided enormous nourishment to many laymen and laywomen who were hungering and thirsting for spiritual depth. A number of priests were active in this search for spirituality, and a smaller number of bishops were leading the way as best they could. While the late Middle Ages was not a complete wasteland, the spiritual situation of the Church was in crisis.

Complicating the entire period from 1000 to 1550 was the rancorous battle between the *imperium* and the *sacerdotium*. Even Paul III's bull of convocation of the Council of Trent examines in great detail the social and political world of his time. Paul was strong enough to convoke a council, but he made sure that the bishops at Trent in no way tried to diminish the power and prestige of the papacy. Hubert Jedin notes: "The fact that the pope [Paul III] was filled with anxiety, lest his authority would be tampered with at Trent, is abundantly proved by the frequent directives to the legates not to tolerate any narrowing of the papal authority, even in small matters, such as the granting of indulgences."[17] Paul III's defensive stance toward the powers of the papacy, even in small matters, included a similar protective cover for the papal curia. For most of the Tridentine fathers, however, the call for Church reform at the Council of Trent was directed toward both head and members. By the term "head," the bishops and the vox populi certainly meant the Pope, but with him they also included the bureaucratic curia. The call for a reform of head and members began in the eleventh century with the reformation efforts of the Holy Roman Emperor and the German bishops. At Trent, no substantial reform of the papacy or the papal curia took place. Thus, the call for curial reform has continued to the present day, but in spite of some minor personnel and titular changes, no Pope has made vital changes in the curia. In other words, structural reform of the Church has been, and remains, significantly blocked by the deliberate refusal to allow internal changes in the structure of the curia. This failure to reform the curia at Trent, at Vatican II, and since Vatican II remains an important obstacle to the renewal of priestly formation.

Gregory VII had ended with a failed reform because he viewed his every gain and his every loss at such a reform through the criterion of a gain or a loss for the papacy. Working with this premise, he doomed his reform to failure from its inception. His reform efforts did not focus on the major causes of abuse in the Church. For most Christians in the medieval West, the issue was not who was greater, Pope or Emperor—Gregory's main issue—but the desire to live out the Gospels, the good news and the message of Jesus himself. Theological issues, spiritual issues, and political issues came together and struggled together. Nonetheless, historical data indicate that there were very few "bad guys" and very few "good guys" among the leadership of the period from 1000 to 1500. In those centuries, great Catholic men and women lived their lives and enriched thousands of Catholic Christians. In those same centuries, people and movements were responsible for major ecclesial abuses. The formation of clergy during those centuries was touched by both these positive and negative factors. Unfortunately, at the time just preceding Trent, the Roman Catholic Church's formation of priests was mainly in a state of disrepair. Thus, the bishops at Trent were very courageous to mandate the reforms for the seminary system and the formation of priests.

A Review of the Major Developments of the Seminary System in the Seventeenth Century

Let us now consider the immediate aftermath of the Council of Trent, with a particular focus on the reforms in the formation of priests. In the seventeenth century, we begin to see the reception of Trent on the issue of these reforms. During the first century after the Council of Trent, bishops throughout the Roman Catholic Church began to develop diocesan seminaries, perhaps not universally but at least in a major regional way. The efforts of Jean-Jacques Olier (1608–1657) are a good case in point. Olier was ordained a diocesan priest in 1633 and engaged in parish ministry with St. Vincent de Paul (1580–1660). Olier eventually founded the Society of St. Sulpice (the Sulpicians), and Vincent de Paul founded the Congregation of the Missions, commonly called the Vincentians. Both of these communities of priests were strongly dedicated to the training of seminarians. Both leaders were strongly influenced by the spiritual movement of Barbe Acarie (1566–1618), who established the Carmelite reform in France. Olier's book *Traité des saints ordres*, published posthumously in 1676, captures his long experience in the formation of seminarians.

This volume eventually became a *vade mecum* for seminarians throughout Europe and the Americas. It presented norms for a "good seminarian" and a "good priest." Its influence can hardly be stressed enough, since the development of the post-Tridentine seminary system owes much to its vision. In 1984, three Sulpician scholars, Gilles Chaillot, Paul Cochois, and Irénée Noye, published a critical edition of this work, titled *Traité des saints ordres (1676) comparé aux écrits authentiques de Jean-Jacques Olier (d. 1657)*.[18] They found that the third Superior General of the Sulpician community, Louis Tronson, who had personally arranged for the publication of Olier's work in 1676, had actually rewritten parts of Olier's work but had failed to mention that he had done so. Of major importance was a change in the image of the priest that Tronson introduced into the text. In the preface to the critical edition, C. Bouchard mentions that the image of the priest in Olier's writings was essentially paschal, baptismal, and mystical, while that of Tronson was clerical and ascetic. Olier had emphasized the pastoral dimension; Tronson, the ascetic dimension.[19] From 1676 to 1966, it was Tronson's view that dominated the seminary system. The priest was a man apart and a cleric separated from the laypeople. Seminarians should be trained to keep themselves distinct from laypersons and separate from the nonspiritual life of ordinary Christians.

In the twentieth century before Vatican II, the ideal diocesan priest was a "rectory priest" or a "sacristan priest." His contact with the laity was official rather than casual. The apostolate was Church-centered, not society-centered. The *horarium* of a priest's day was governed by the Eucharist and prayer, in particular the breviary. The times for the Eucharist and the praying of the breviary were two spiritual parts of the priest's day that were considered sacrosanct and ordinarily merited a priority above all else in the daily *cura animarum*. During the years of seminary formation, the diocesan seminarians were trained for this kind of eucharistic-breviary *horarium*. Both the ideal seminarian and the ideal priest were judged, in no small way, on their daily preparation for and celebration of the Eucharist and on their conscientious praying of the breviary at specified times during each day. This was the ideal presented repeatedly to the diocesan seminarian.

When one considers the general status of a diocesan priest prior to the Council of Trent, as we saw above, with the general status of a diocesan priest who had been trained in a Sulpician or Vincentian way from 1700 onward, the quality of difference is quite apparent. From the latter date, the Roman Catholic diocesan priest was both an educated individual and a spiritual person. This image of an educated and spiritual priest continued throughout the twentieth century to the time just prior to Vatican II. There is no doubt at all, historically considered, that the reception of the seminary system, as mandated by the Council of Trent, ultimately improved the quality of priests throughout Europe and in the non-European countries as well. The reception of the Tridentine mandate on priestly formation had been profoundly enhanced by Olier and Vincent de Paul, who, in major ways, injected a strong spiritual tenor into seminary life. While both men were committed to the intellectual life of the seminary formation, their influence on the spiritual formation of the seminarian was especially distinctive.

Protestant churches, from the 1600s on, have emulated the Roman Catholic seminary system, so that in the same period, Protestant pastors largely came to be regarded as well-educated and deeply Christian individuals. Even the name "seminary" was slowly attached to the schools in which the formation of Protestant clergy took place. In novels, movies, dramas, and short stories, both American and European, the authors generally depicted the priest or the clergyman as well educated and spiritually integrated. Exceptions to this image did occur, but the social standing of a priest or clergyman was generally respected and honored. For many a seminarian, the goal of the priesthood was fostered by relatives and friends. To have a priest in the family brought honor to a family. For all its faults and failures, the seminary system developed and received after the Council of Trent accomplished a major reformation in regard to the formation of a priest. The Second Vatican Council, unlike the Council of Trent, was not convened in order to reform the clergy and the formation of seminarians.

An Overview of the Basic Official Material on Priestly Formation at Vatican II and Its Postconciliar Reception

Let us move from Trent and its reception to the Second Vatican Council. In this council, the bishops eventually addressed the issue of priests and priestly formation. However, these two topics were not on the original agenda. Only in the course of the Council did the bishops realize that they could not return home without a statement on priests, and this involved, consequently, a second statement on the formation of priests. We have, then, two major conciliar documents: the Decree on the Training of Priests, *Optatam totius*, promulgated on October 28, 1965, and the Decree on the Ministry and Life of Priests, *Presbyterorum ordinis*, promulgated in the final session of the council on December 7, 1965. It is essential that both documents be studied through the lens of the primary doctrinal document of Vatican II, *Lumen gentium*. *Lumen gentium* was, and remains, the major statement of the Council on the theology of the Church. In many ways, the document has defined the meaning of the Roman Catholic Church from 1965 to the present.[20] Since a theology of the priest can be understood only in the light of a theology of the Church, and since the formation of priests can be accomplished only in the light of a theology of the Church, the ecclesiology of *Lumen gentium* is foundational. One cannot lose sight of the fact that ecclesiology determines the meaning and role of the ordained person in the Church. The theology of the ordained person does *not* determine ecclesiology.

An entire volume is needed to elucidate the ways in which *Lumen gentium*, the basic ecclesiology of Vatican II, has affected the theology of the priesthood. Since this chapter does not allow such a lengthy and detailed examination, I can offer only a few major themes regarding the integration of Vatican II's ecclesiology, on the one hand, and a theology of ordained ministry, on the other. These major themes, as a consequence, become crucial for the formation of candidates for the priesthood.

The documents of Vatican II on priestly formation focused primarily on the diocesan priest. Throughout all the conciliar documents, with the exception of chapter 6, on religious life, in *Lumen gentium;* the decree on the renewal of religious life, *Perfectae caritatis* (October 28, 1965); and some other obiter dicta remarks in *Ad gentes* and *Apostolicam actuositatem*, the issue of religious communities of men and women was not center stage at Vatican II. On the specific issue of the priesthood, there was no extended focus on the meaning of the priesthood in the religious life. Consequently, the presentation on the formation of priests and the presentation on the priesthood itself in the documents of Vatican II are centered exclusively on the diocesan form and life of priestly ministry. Since I presuppose this focus in the following pages, the seminaries to which I refer are primarily diocesan seminaries.

The important themes from Vatican II that have had significant impact on the formation of priests, as well as on the identity of priests, are the following. First, the foundational ecclesiology of Vatican II was deliberately linked to Christology by the conciliar bishops.[21] While Christology itself never became a detailed question in any of the conciliar documents, the selection of the title *Lumen gentium* was made by the bishops to indicate that Jesus alone is the Light of the World.[22] The Church itself is not the light of the world. The conciliar bishops were in total agreement on this issue. Jesus, not the Church, was, and is, and will remain the Light of the World. Bonaventure Kloppenburg, one of the *periti* at the council, elucidates this relationship by a comparison of the sun and the moon. In our world, the sun is the major source of light; the moon has no light of itself, but it does reflect the light of the sun. So, too, Jesus is the major light of the world; the Church has no light of its own and, therefore, fulfills its identity only when it reflects Jesus.[23] Kloppenburg writes:

Only Christ is the light of the world. He is the Sun, sole source of light. At the side of this Sun, which is Christ, stands the Church like the moon, which receives all its light, brilliance and warmth from the Sun. We can understand the Church only if we relate it to Christ, the glorified Lord. *The Church lives by Christ.* If the Church is absolutized, separated from Christ, considered only in its structures, viewed only in its history and studied only under its visible, human and phenomenological aspects, it ceases to be a mystery and becomes simply one of countless other religious societies or organizations. It does not then deserve our special attention and dedication.[24]

This lunar relationship of the Church to Jesus has an immediate effect on the identity of the priest and thereby plays a major role in the formation of the priest. A priest is truly a priest if and only if, when and only when, he reflects Jesus. The formation of seminarians is a formation into a lunar reflection of the one Light of the World, Jesus. When this ceases to be the major guiding principle in seminary training, the training itself has ceased to be of value. Ecclesiology is constitutively dependent on Christology. This is the mystery and identity of the Church as traced out in chapter 1 of *Lumen gentium.* Such a Christology and ecclesiology are the authentic basis for seminary formation.

Likewise, the decision by the bishops at Vatican II to place the material on the "people of God" in the second chapter of *Lumen gentium* was an important moment.[25] Strong voices among some of the bishops, who insisted that chapter 2 be a chapter on the hierarchy, turned the debate into a lengthy and at times abrasive one. The final decision to devote chapter 2 to the people of God influences the way one considers the ordained person or the hierarchy. "The people of God" is only one of the terms used for the common matrix of all Christians. Two other phrases were also used: "believers of Christ" (*Christifideles*), and "the priesthood of all believers" (*sacerdotes generales*). This means that the ordained priesthood cannot be understood apart from, unrelated to, or prior to the priesthood of all believers. Although the documents of Vatican II present both "priesthoods" and give preference in chapter 2 to the priesthood of all believers, the bishops also approved the passage which states that an essential difference exists between the two priesthoods (*Lumen gentium,* 10).

Two points on this matter need to be kept in mind. The first is the use of the term "essential." In the common and operative theology of the priesthood just before Vatican II, the term used by theologians was not "essential" but "ontological." This is found in many of the manuals of theology, the official theological textbooks for seminary curricula. While they provided no reason for their decision, the bishops at Vatican II deliberately avoided the term "ontological." Second, the bishops used the term "essential," but never defined in a clear way what the essential difference might be. In several sessions prior to the eventual promulgation of Vatican II, groups of bishops met with various theologians who attempted to indicate the difference between the priesthood of all believers and the ordained priesthood. Some of the distinctions that the theologians presented to the bishops included the following:

PRIESTHOOD OF ALL BELIEVERS	ORDAINED PRIESTHOOD
1. A figurative priesthood	a real priesthood
2. A spiritual priesthood	a real priesthood
3. An interior priesthood	an exterior priesthood
4. A nonsacramental priesthood	a sacramental priesthood
5. A private priesthood	a public priesthood

While this list includes more, in the end the bishops decided not to settle the question of the difference between the two, leaving the issue open for further theological precision. After the Council, when the committee was established to revise the Code of Canon Law, its members invited theologians to present the difference between the priesthood of all believers and the ordained priesthood. Once again, the listing of differences by reputable theologians and biblical scholars was diverse, and the committee, much like the conciliar bishops, decided not to indicate any basis for the distinction in the revised Code of Canon Law. The new code simply states that there are a priesthood of all believers and an ordained priesthood. Further precision was left up to theologians and biblical scholars.[26] Nonetheless, one cannot speak about ordained priesthood today in a vacuum. The two issues regarding priesthood are interrelated. The formation of seminarians must include an identity of ordained priesthood in relationship to their own identity as part of the priesthood of all believers.

Thus, the bishops at Vatican II deliberately changed the meaning of an ordained priest, and this newly presented understanding of priest belongs to the current teaching of the Church. The full assembly of bishops was presented with this change when the Archbishop of Rheims, François Marty, told them that "the scholastic definition of priesthood, which is based on the power to consecrate the Eucharist," was no longer the operative theology of the priest at the Vatican Council. "The priesthood of presbyters must be looked at . . . as embracing not one function but three," namely the *tria munera*: prophet, priest, and king.[27] The *tria munera* understanding of the priest became an essential part of the revised Code of Canon Law, and it was also used in the later writings of Paul VI and in the writings of John Paul II. In the *Catechism of the Catholic Church*, the ministerial priesthood "is entirely related to Christ and to men." The office "is in the strict sense of the term a service" (1551). It is "measured against the model of Christ, who by love made himself the least and the servant of all" (1551)[28] In the *Catechism*, the teaching office is called the "first task," namely, to preach the Gospel of God (888). Second is the sanctifying office, especially visible in the Eucharist but also in the prayer and work of the priests, in the ministry of the Word and in sacramental celebrations (893). Third is the governing office, and the Good Shepherd is presented as the model and form of this pastoral dimension of the *tria munera* (894).

In his essay "Clerical Reform," Christian Dequoc presents a well-argued position that the documents of Vatican II moved in disparate ways when the bishops began to reconsider priestly ministry in today's socioecclesial world. The rethinking of priestly ministry in a triadic fashion, especially in a Gospel-centered priesthood, while at the same time retaining the traditional hierarchical elements that had dominated Trent, creates a major problem. He writes: "The determination, already expressed in practice, to change the situation of the clergy in the Church is manifesting itself everywhere. If this [changing of the situation] is not done, we shall end with restoration, not reform—the very thing that Vatican II wanted to avoid."[29]

Repeatedly, in the documents from Rome on priestly ministry, the primacy is given to the preaching of the Word. This has major ramifications for the formation of priests: seminarians must have a very solid training in the biblical word of God. This comes through competent professors of biblical studies in the individual seminaries, and it comes through competent professors of homiletics as well. Moreover, preaching the Word of God will become the major task of priestly ministry only if the Word of God becomes one of the primary sources of personal spirituality. If there is one book with which a seminarian should be thoroughly conversant, it is the New Testament. The same book should be the spiritual nourishment of bishops, priests, and deacons. An academic and intellectual appreciation of the New Testament is not enough for the formation of priests today. The Word of God should be a major source of their spiritual life. In this sense, Catholic clergy are called on to be more "Protestant." For Protestant clergy, the Word of God has been, since the Reformation, the major source of their spiritual life, often more so than sacraments. For the Roman Catholic clergy, the stress in the past was on sacramental nourishment, especially the sacraments of the Eucharist and reconciliation. Today, since Vatican II, the Word of God has begun—but in practice only just begun—to be a major source of priestly spirituality. If the preaching of the Word of God is the primary task of a priest, then the Word of God must enter into the life of a priest—and by implication of a seminarian—not only intellectually but spiritually as well.

In the development of the conciliar document on the ministry and life of priests, *Presbyterorum ordinis*, a tug-of-war developed over which section should come first: the function of the priest or the life of the priest. In many ways, this argument mirrored the Olier–Tronson division. Is the priest primarily a person of service to the community? The emphasis in the *Catechism* on the priesthood as essentially service (*diakonia*) indicates this. Alternatively, is the priest before all a man called to perfection, a spiritual person? After heated discussion, the majority of bishops voted that the priest as a person of service should come first. Thus, chapter 2 of this document contains a threefold division: the function of the priest; the relation of the priest to others; and the distribution of priests and priestly vocations. Only in chapter 3 does the focus move to the life of the priest, with its threefold division: the priest's call to perfection; the special spiritual requirements in the life of the priest; and the helps for the priest's life.

Postconciliar material on priesthood and priestly formation, which includes papal, curial, and episcopal documents, has vacillated between an emphasis on the mission and function of the priest and/or on the life and spiritual growth of the priest. This ambivalence plays a major role in the seminary training today, with some seminaries emphasizing the mission and function of the priest first, and other seminaries emphasizing life and spiritual growth as primary. This is not a question of either/or; rather, it is a question about which is primary. The selection of one over the other has as its major influence the way in which a young man develops himself for the priesthood. The primacy issue affects the self-identity of the priest. If the emphasis is on function and ministry, the spiritual life can be seen as secondary and only secondary. If, on the other hand, the young man sees himself as a spiritual person, the role of ministry can be seen as secondary and only secondary. As of today, there is still a tension between these two "primacies." Some seminaries are considered "conservative" because they give the primacy to the "spiritual life," that is, to a life apart from people and functions. Other seminaries are termed "liberal" because of their primacy on "function," the *cura animarum*. Such appellations are damaging. In the history of the priesthood, some priests have been too aloof from people and the *cura animarum*; other priests have been too involved in the *cura animarum* and have not given time to their own spiritual and mental health. Clearly, what is called for is a holistic formation.

In the decree on the training of priests, *Optatam totius*, many issues of practical import, all of major help to seminary directors, are taken up by the conciliar bishops. One area presents serious questions. In sections 9 and 10, the spirituality of a diocesan priest is described in terms of poverty, chastity, and obedience. This same focus found at greater length in *Presbyterorum ordinis*, 15–17. This approach to priestly spirituality antedates Vatican II by hundreds of years. However, it should be pointed out that such a spirituality, which has its origin in monastic life and religious life with the three evangelical vows, has tried over the centuries to make diocesan priests into "mini-monks." What is needed for the third-millennium Church is a spirituality for the formation of diocesan priests that is priestly and not monastic. The 1977 document from the National Conference of Catholic Bishops, *As One Who Serves*, provides only a few paragraphs on priestly spirituality, with the emphasis on prayer, reception of the sacrament of penance, and the celebration of the Eucharist. The 1990 synodal working document *Formation of Priests in Circumstances of the Present Day* presents a priestly spirituality that is basically personal, ethical, and private, and not ministerial, social, and public. In number 14, however, this document states clearly that all priests are called to mission, namely, "to announce the gospel of God to all." The implication should be clear: every candidate for the priesthood who is not profoundly and spiritually anxious to bring the Gospel to others should be considered far from the mark of readiness for ordination. Priestly spirituality *is* pastoral spirituality, and seminarians should be formed in this way. Priests who are too timid to leave either the monastery or the rectory are by no means the priests that today's world needs. Robert Schwartz's book *Servant Leaders of the People of God*, with its focus on the spirituality of the North American priest, forthrightly faces the issue of a contemporary priestly spirituality, at least for priests in a basically Euro-American world.[30]

Finally, collegiality is part of the theology of priesthood presented by Vatican II. The priest is an essential part of a *presbyterium*, and the bishop also is an essential part. Whenever the *presbyterium* of a diocese meets together or has a convocation, the bishop should be there during the entire time. The bishops as well form a *collegium*, and they cannot be seen as isolated from each other. Interrelationship and interdependence form part of the very essence of priestly ministry. Moreover, the relationship of the priest/bishop—the ministerial priesthood—is unthinkable and unlivable apart from, and must be in collegial union with, the priesthood of all believers. The same emphasis of interrelationship is found in the documents of Vatican II that consider the papal ministry in which the Pope's rights are fully recognized but are presented in the broader framework of ecclesial collegiality.

Concluding Remarks

The reception of Vatican II continues. It took several centuries for the reception of Trent to reach its end. So, too, Vatican II will continue the process of reception throughout the twenty-first century. The contemporary situation of sexual abuse by clergy and the concomitant question of episcopal credibility tend to focus the discussion of priesthood and episcopacy in a very circumscribed area. As a result, the leadership of today's bishops tends to center on the "resolution" of the credibility crisis, and the identity of the priest tends to focus on sexual behavior. Meanwhile, the structural changes in the Church that Vatican II visualized are being placed to one side. The credibility of the Roman Catholic Church wanes. Leaders of vision are urgently needed, and these Church leaders are not confined to priestly or hierarchical persons. In the long history of the Church, there have been leaders—men and women—who have refocused even the hierarchical leadership on the meaning of Church: reflecting the *Lumen gentium*, Jesus, the Light of the World. The Church stands in dire need of leaders who can bring it back to its lunar identity, its sacramental identity, for the Church is the sacrament of Jesus. Jesus in his humanity is the sacrament of God. Jesus is the Light *of* and *for* the world. Jesus is also Light from the God who is Light from Light.

NOTES

1. See *Canons and Decrees of the Council of Trent: Original Text with English Translation*, translated by H. J. Schroeder (St. Louis, Mo.: Herder, 1941), 1–9 (Eng.), 281–289 (Lat.). Future citations will read Schroeder, *Canons*. The quotation is from the *Bulla indictionis*, Schroeder, 9 (Eng.), 288 (Lat.).

2. *Decretum de inchoando concilio*, ibid., 11 (Eng.), 290 (Lat.).

3. Schroeder, *Canons*, 24–28 (Eng.), 303–307 (Lat.).

4. Ibid., 59–60 (Eng.), 337 (Lat.).

5. Ibid., 107–108, 111 (Eng.), 381–382, 385 (Lat.).

6. Ibid., 136–137, 139–140 (Eng.), 410–411, 413 (Lat.).

7. Ibid., 152–154 (Eng.), 425–426 (Lat.).

8. Ibid., 164–179 (Eng.), 436–450 (Lat.).

9. See Hermann Tüchle, C. A. Bouman, and Jacques le Brun, *Réfome et Contre-Réforme: Nouvelle Histoire de l'Église* (Paris: Éditions du Seuil, 1968), 9–11.

10. Ibid., 10.

11. Ibid., 34: "Parmi les nombreux écarts individuels dans la vie du clergé de cette époque, le concubinage était fréquent. Les comptes rendus de visites épiscopales parlent d'un quart (Pays Bas), voire d'un tiers (Rhénanie 1569) des prêtres vivants dans cette situation. Le registre des punitions de l'officialité de Châlons vise un quart du clergé."

12. See Robert Birley, "Early Modern Germany," in *Catholicism in Early Modern History: A Guide to Research*, 11–30, who states that residency for prince-bishops in the German area did not become normative until they were removed during the secularization of 1803.

13. A. Duval, "The Council of Trent and Holy Order," in *The Sacrament of Holy Orders* (Collegeville, Minn.: Liturgical Press, 1962), 221.

14. Kenan Osborne, *Priesthood: A History of the Ordained Ministry in the Roman Catholic Church* (New York: Paulist Press, 1988), 276.

15. S. Harrison Thompson, *Europe in the Renaissance and Reformation* (New York: Harcourt, Brace and World, 1963), 459.

16. Jaroslav Pelikan, *Spirit Versus Structure: Luther and the Institutions of the Church* (New York: Harper & Row, 1968), 5.

17. Hubert Jedin, *A History of the Council of Trent*, translated by Ernest Graf, 2 vols. (St. Louis, Mo.: Herder, 1957–1961), vol. 2, 42.

18. G. Chaillot, P. Cochois, and I. Noye, eds., *Traité des saints ordres (1676) comparé aux écrits authentiques de Jean-Jacques Olier (1657)* (Paris: Procure de la Compagnie de Saint-Sulpice, 1984).

19. Ibid., "Les Enjeux de la présente édition critique," xxiii–xxvii.

20. It is clear that *Lumen gentium* is not the only document on ecclesiology that Vatican II promulgated. Nonetheless, it is the primary one. It would be difficult to arrange the other Vatican II documents on this matter in any order of importance, but the Pastoral Constitution on the Church in the Modern World, *Gaudium et spes*,

deserves a major emphasis. So, too, does the Decree on the Church's Missionary Activity, *Ad gentes*, since from Paul VI to John Paul II, evangelization is seen as central to the very identity of the Church, and *Ad gentes* articulates the meaning of evangelization in a major way. Since a priest is a sacramental and liturgical leader, the Constitution on the Sacred Liturgy, *Sacrosanctum concilium*, is of prime importance, especially the section that presents the criteria for all liturgy. These criteria are conciliar criteria, and therefore next to an infallible papal or conciliar statement in terms of being of the highest importance. Since Vatican II reinstated the office of bishop into the sacrament of orders, and since it refers to episcopacy as the "fullness of priesthood," the Decree on the Pastoral Office of Bishops in the Church, *Christus Dominus*, also must play a major role in the understanding and formation of priests. The remainder of the documents relate to priestly formation in one way or another, but they focus on specific aspects of a relationship to priestly formation. That they are important cannot be denied; that they are as important as the ones just mentioned cannot be asserted in a generalized way.

21. The Christological relationship between the Church and Jesus, found in the documents of Vatican II, continues the emphasis of Pius XII, as found in the encyclical *Mystici corporis*. In fact, the bishops at Vatican II went further than Pius XII in their theological understanding of the Church's relation to Jesus. The phrase "Mystical Body of Christ" or simply "Body of Christ," as designating the Church is indeed found in the documents of Vatican II, but it is not the centralizing theme.

22. The selection of the title *Lumen gentium* was made by the bishops at Vatican II for many reasons. One of them was that John XXIII had used this term in preparatory documents for the Council, and the choice of this phrase was an honor that the bishops wanted to give to him. However, the Christological import of the phrase was clearly the most important reason for the selection of the title.

23. Bonaventure Kloppenburg, *The Ecclesiology of Vatican II*, translated by M. J. O'Connell (Chicago: Franciscan Herald Press, 1974). See especially chapter 1, "The Nature of the Church."

24. Ibid., 19–22.

25. See Gérard Philips, *La chiesa e il suo mistero* (Milan: Jaca, 1975).

26. See Kenan Osborne, *Ministry: Lay Ministry in the Roman Catholic Church. Its History and Theology* (New York: Paulist Press, 1993; Eugene, Ore.: Wipf and Stock, 2003), 535–536. Details of these theological presentations at the Council are provided in this volume. See also Philips, *La chiesa e il suo mistero*, 131–137. Excellent coverage of the common priesthood can be found Hans-Martin Barth, *Einander Priestersein: Allgemeines Priestertum in ökumenischer Perspektive* (Göttingen: Vandenhoeck & Ruprecht, 1990).

27. See Osborne, *Priesthood*, 316, for the quotation from Archbishop François Marty. Also see François Marty, "Décret sur le ministère et la vie des prêtres," in *Documents conciliaires* (Paris: Centurion), vol. 4, 159–182.

28. See Friedrich Wulf, "Decree on Priestly Ministry: Commentary on the Decree," in *Commentary on the Documents of Vatican II*, ed. Herbert Vorgrimler (New York: Herder & Herder, 1969), vol. 4, 215–217. Also see Joseph Lécuyer, "Decree on the Ministry and Life of Priests," ibid., 183–209.

29. Christian Duquoc, "Clerical Reform," in *The Reception of Vatican II*, ed.

Giuseppe Alberigo, Jean-Pierre Jossua, and Joseph Komonchak, trans. Matthew J. O'Connell (Washington, D.C.: Catholic University of America Press, 1987), 308.

30. Robert Schwartz, *Servant Leaders of the People of God* (New York: Paulist Press, 1989). At the very end of this book, Schwartz writes of priestly identity and its roots (213ff.). He does not devote many pages to this very insightful view. I have tried to elaborate on Schwartz's position in "Mixed Signals: Priestly Identity and Priestly Spirituality Since Vatican II," in *The Candles Are Still Burning: Directions in Sacrament and Spirituality*, ed. Mary Grey et al. (London: Geoffrey Chapman, 1995), 70–81.

8

Singing a New Song unto the Lord: Catholic Church Music

James J. Boyce

The Council of Trent and the Second Vatican Council made pronouncements about music in response to calls for change in the years preceding them, and their decisions have had a significant impact on liturgy until the present time. The purpose of this essay is to discuss the legislation of these two councils regarding liturgical music, the conditions affecting their decisions, and the effects of such legislation upon the spiritual life of the faithful.

Liturgical Music before the Council of Trent

Liturgical music in the years immediately before the Council of Trent reflected trends that had been forming for several centuries.[1] The Mass had progressively acquired textual and/or musical accretions to established chants such as the *Kyrie cunctipotens genitor*,[2] for example, as well as entirely new pieces such as the prosa and sequence sung between the Alleluia and the Gospel.[3] During the Middle Ages, the number of feast days expanded exponentially, so that in some dioceses proper feasts preempted even the Sunday liturgy.[4] The number of liturgical texts for the Divine Office and Mass also steadily grew, yielding an enormous corpus of liturgical poetry and rhymed offices,[5] but obscuring the general cursus of the liturgical year itself. The local nature of many of these special and versified offices also meant that the liturgy of the Church had expanded at the expense of uniformity. These new offices with poetic and prose texts continued to be sung in Gregorian chant, either newly composed or adapted from existing offices.[6]

In addition to the proliferation of texts, new forms of music evolved, especially in southern France at the abbey of St. Martial de Limoges;[7] the progressive development of polyphony, beginning with the addition of a single voice over the traditional chant, eventually led to three-voice or four-voice compositions, all under the title organum.[8] The most famous compendium of organum is the *Magnus liber organi*, written at the cathedral of Notre Dame in Paris by Master Leoninus (fl. 1150s–c. 1201) and revised and expanded by his successor, Perotinus (fl. c. 1200).[9] The sacredness of the chant itself was respected, but the need for musical innovation generally relegated the chant line to the bass, where it became known simply as the *cantus firmus*.[10] The new style of fourteenth-century composition known as the a*rs nova* organized both pitches and rhythms of the Gregorian chant into specific recurring patterns known as isorhythm, the most famous example of which is the *Messe de Notre Dame*, written by Guillaume de Machaut for the cathedral of Rheims.[11]

Renaissance composers gradually moved the chant melody to the top voice and harmonized it, as in the case of the harmonized hymns of Guillaume Dufay (1397–1474),[12] or assigned it in imitative polyphony among all the voice parts in the Mass. Some of these restated an established melody under new Mass texts and became known as paraphrase Masses. A prime example of this is the *Missa Pange Lingua* of Josquin Desprez (c. 1450/1455–1521),[13] which paraphrased the melody of the famous Gregorian *Pange Lingua* chant in the standard Ordinary chants of the Mass: the Kyrie, Gloria, Credo, Sanctus, and Agnus Dei.[14] Gradually even secular tunes such as *"L'Homme armé"* (the armed man) became the object of paraphrase, as in the *Missa L'Homme armé* by Guillaume Dufay.[15] The overlapping repetition of the same text in several voice parts could, especially in the longer and more elaborate texts such as the Gloria or Credo, compromise the intelligibility of the texts, even though the listeners probably knew them by heart. Thus, while these newer styles of composition offered wonderful cultural and spiritual opportunities for both composer and listener, they were nonetheless open to criticism on liturgical grounds. The popularity of polyphonic Masses, especially in cathedrals and other large churches, necessarily meant the waning of Gregorian chant. This was essentially the situation on the eve of the Council of Trent.

If fifteenth- and sixteenth-century imitative polyphony seemed to make music more complex, the sixteenth century also saw a general desire to simplify the musical sound, especially in its worship context. Luther's criticism of Catholic practices in his treatise *De captivitate babylonica*[16] and other works eventually led him to put his reformed services in the vernacular in order to make them intelligible to the faithful and to develop the new, simpler style of singing, normally with one note per syllable, which became the Lutheran chorale.[17] In the Anglican reform, a similar situation obtained, for the new style of English hymn known as the anthem also featured clearly intelligible text using one note per syllable, according to Archbishop Cranmer's directive.[18] In the French secular tradition, the new style of music known as *musique mesurée à l'antique*[19] emphasized the richness of the language itself by having the voice parts sing in chords, using one note per syllable, with long and short notes to render the French metrical accent correctly.

The necessity for a musical reform within the Catholic tradition paralleled trends in secular music, as the Church sought to move away from an elaborate and potentially distracting music that entertained the faithful to a simpler, more austere music that edified them. The problems were outlined in a report sent to Pope Paul II by Fridericus Nausea Blancicampianus, Bishop of Vienne, in 1543, two years before the convening of the Council of Trent. In it, he cited as reasons for reform the use of nonscriptural texts in lessons and chants of Catholic worship, the careless manner and poor musical training of canons in many cathedrals, and the use of uncorrected books and poor-quality music by singers.[20]

The Legislation of the Council of Trent

The Council of Trent (1545–1563) actually spent more time discussing liturgy[21] than is evident from its minimal pronouncements on music, which almost have to be gleaned from the documents themselves. Session 22, chapter 5, maintains that "some parts of the mass should be said in quieter tones and others in louder,"[22] and that through its rituals, "the minds of the faithful are aroused by those visible signs of religious devotion to contemplation of the high mysteries hidden in it."[23] Thus music, at least by implication, should edify the minds of the listeners. The only specific reference to music comes in the Decree on Things to Be Observed and Avoided in Celebrating Mass: "And they should keep out of their churches the kind of music in which a base and suggestive element is introduced into the organ playing or singing, and similarly all worldly activities, empty and secular conversation, walking about, noises and cries, so that the house of God may truly be called and be seen to be a house of prayer."[24]

The "base and suggestive element" engendered a great deal of debate by the Council fathers, and was the focus of much correction in the years after the Council. Thus, canon 12 of session 24 prescribed for cathedral canons that all "are obliged to attend the divine office personally and not through substitutes, and to assist and serve the bishop when he is celebrating mass or other pontifical rites, and when in choir for sung worship to praise the name of God reverently, distinctly and devoutly in hymns and canticles."[25] The same canon enjoined the provincial synod to establish "a precise rule in the light of the good and the customs of each province about the appropriate style of singing and chanting, about the determined manner of gathering and remaining in choir, and all that is necessary about church ministers and anything else of the kind."[26] Session 18 of February 26, 1562, called for a commission to study "suspect and dangerous books";[27] session 24, canon 7, concerned itself with an adequate explanation of the sacraments;[28] and session 25 linked the revision of the missal and breviary to that of the catechism.[29]

What is specifically mentioned only in vague and oblique terms, nonetheless, had been the subject of considerable discussion. The reference to the "base and suggestive element"[30] may reflect the oral tradition whereby liberties were taken with the written chant that was not always sung in its purest form.[31] The discussion focused explicitly on the intelligibility of the text:

> In the case of those Masses that are celebrated with singing and with organ, let nothing profane be intermingled [presumably referring to secular tunes such as "L'Homme armé"] but only hymns and divine praises. If anything is to be sung with the organ from the sacred services while they are in progress, let it be recited in a simple clear voice beforehand so that no one will miss any part of the eternal reading of the sacred writings [presumably a criticism of the imitative entries of polyphonic music]. The whole plan of singing in musical modes should be constituted not to give empty pleasure to the ears, but in such a way that the words may be clearly understood by all, and thus the hearts of the listeners be drawn to the desire of heavenly harmonies, in the contemplation of the joys of the blessed.[32]

Canon 8 of the Council decrees from September 10, 1562, thus emphasized the importance of the intelligibility of the text and the decorum with which it was announced, whether by the priest saying the Mass or the singers chanting it.[33] Session 23 of May 10, 1563, legislated that the training of seminarians include the fine arts as well as Gregorian chant.[34] Canon 7 of the reform decree required clerics to take part in the Divine Office personally, to serve the bishop at the altar, and to sing the required hymns and chants.[35] This ensured that their experience of liturgical music was not confined to reading textbooks, but was in fact part of their actual practice. In a letter of August 23, 1563, Emperor Ferdinand I of Spain strongly endorsed the retention of polyphonic music, presumably because of the music of Spanish composers such as Cristóbal de Morales (c. 1500–1553) and Tomás Luís de Victoria (1548–1611);[36] as a result, the decree of session 24 of November 11, 1563, allowed provincial councils to establish normative usage for each country.[37]

The Results of the Council Legislation

The Council of Trent imposed the Roman rite on the Universal Church but allowed any religious order or diocese with a distinctive liturgical tradition to revise it and submit it to the Holy See for approval.[38] While the process itself was cumbersome, it did ensure the continuation of an established rite for the following several centuries. The invention of printing by movable type in the fifteenth century and the steady advances made in this process during the sixteenth century enabled the revised versions of chant texts and music to be disseminated efficiently. In response to the Council of Trent, every diocese and religious order either had to accept the Roman rite or to conduct a thorough revision of its own rite in order to retain it. The mendicant orders, such as the Dominicans, Franciscans, and Carmelites, and most of the older and larger dioceses went through the process of revising their liturgies, eliminating local saints or those of dubious origin and making sure that the resulting music conformed to the aesthetic of the Council of Trent and the national synods charged with implementing its directives. Specifically, in plainchant, the tonal formularies for the responsories had to adhere to the established patterns for each of the eight Gregorian modes; virtually all rhymed offices were eliminated from the repertoire; only proper offices based on Scripture or the approved vita of the saints were permitted; and only four sequences were retained from the large medieval repertoire of these chants.[39]

New Books and Melodies

After the Council of Trent, new standard books were printed for those dioceses and orders which were required to adopt the revised Roman rite; thus the Apostolic Letter "Quod a nobis" of July 9, 1567, promulgated the reformed breviary, and the letter "Quo primum tempore" of July 14, 1570, promulgated the reformed missal in accordance with session 25 (mentioned above).[40] A *motu proprio* of Pope Pius V of December 17, 1571, granted an exemption for countries under Spanish rule and basically allowed them to follow the rite of the Church in Toledo, the primal see.[41]

By a brief of October 25, 1577, Pope Gregory XIII[42] commissioned Giovanni Pierluigi da Palestrina (1525/1526–1594)[43] and Annibale Zoilo (c. 1537–1592) to revise and publish the chant melodies and texts to conform to the revisions of the breviary and missal, respectively; they gave up on the project. It was subsequently entrusted to Felice Anerio (c. 1560–1614) and Francesco Soriano (1548/1549–1621), who published what is called the *Editio medicea* in 1614.[44] Anerio and Soriano made extensive changes in the melodies, excised the long passages over a single syllable known as melismas, and reorganized the music according to the principles of a humanist pronunciation of the Latin text.[45] This edition offered a version of chant that emphasized correct textual declamation at the expense of good musical style.[46] David Hiley has suggested that the composers who produced the *Editio medicea* were influenced primarily by the polyphonic music of Palestrina and his contemporaries.[47] This explains the rhythmic note values, the curtailing of melismas,[48] and the actual truncating of many of the pieces, especially the prolix or great responsories for Matins.[49] Since the Medicean version was never made mandatory, however, it is difficult to assess what impact, if any, it had on Church music in general.

The production of a new edition of chant books gave rise to a new type of book, known as the *directorium chori*; this was a manual designed for use by the choir director to train the singers to perform the revised version of chant, including its rhythms. The Roman printer Giovanni Guidetti published the *directorium chori* of the Vatican Basilica in 1582,[50] and religious orders and dioceses with distinctive rites followed suit; for example, Father Archangelus Paulus, a Carmelite, published one in Naples for the order in 1614 and issued a supplement for particular Carmelite feasts in 1627.[51]

Polyphony

The imitative entries of musical lines so characteristic of Renaissance polyphony threatened to obscure the meaning of the text; thus the Masses of Josquin Desprez, for instance, were generally too ornate for Tridentine taste, even though an average congregation was entirely familiar with the Mass texts. An eight-member commission of cardinals was appointed in 1564–1565 to oversee the implementation of the decrees of Trent; one of their number, Cardinal Vitellozzi, summoned the papal choir to his home on April 28, 1565, for the purpose of singing Masses to determine the intelligibility of the text.[52] The story recounted by Palestrina's biographer, Giuseppe Baini, that Palestrina's *Missa Papae Marcelli*, ostensibly part of the sung repertoire that evening, persuaded the Pope to allow the retention of polyphonic singing in Catholic worship is generally considered apocryphal;[53] nonetheless, Palestrina remained the favorite polyphonic composer in most Catholic churches until Vatican II. The *Preces speciales pro salubri generalis concilii successu* of Jacobus de Kerle (1531–1591),[54] stylistically similar to the writing of Palestrina, were sung at the Council itself, as were Masses by Palestrina, Giovanni Animuccia (c. 1520–1571),[55] Orlando di Lasso (1532–1594),[56] Vincenzo Ruffo (c. 1508–1587),[57] Marc Antonio Ingegneri (1535/1536–1592),[58] and others who favorably disposed the Council fathers to polyphony.[59] In his Pope Marcellus Mass, Palestrina tended to group the six voice parts into contrasting choirs of either three and three or two and four, thus having each group follow the other in an echo effect rather than having overlapping imitative polyphony.[60] Throughout the Tridentine era, this unaccompanied polyphony continued to flourish in the Vatican and in any other church that could support a choir. A generation of composers writing in the more conservative style of Palestrina enjoyed great prominence in the post-Tridentine period.[61] This tradition was carefully safeguarded especially in Spain, where works by composers such as Tomás Luís de Victoria (1548–1611) and Cristóbal de Morales (c. 1500–1553) enjoyed great popularity in the "golden age" of Spanish liturgical music.

New Trends

The Council of Trent, in seeking to rid liturgical music of what it considered impure and lascivious elements, could define such elements only in terms of earlier or contemporary music, not music that had yet to be written. Further-more, its directives on what constituted good music, apart from Gregorian chant, were almost nonexistent. In fact, the changing styles of music rendered the problems before Trent, and hence the solutions proposed after the Council, obsolete. Since it is far beyond the scope of this paper to discuss all the musical styles and their composers between the two councils, a few highlights must necessarily suffice.

The Tridentine era encouraged the declamation of the text in polyphonic works known as motets. These were settings of scriptural texts rather than the ordinary of the Mass. The other voices aligned themselves with the main voice proclaiming the text, whose influence was preeminent in the work. The varied texts offered great opportunity for musical expressiveness, promoting devotion in the listeners. Composers such as Orlando di Lasso, Luca Marenzio (1550–1599), and Jakob Handl (or Jacobus Gallus, 1550–1591) developed this form.[62] Adrien Willaert (c. 1490–1562) and Giovanni Gabrieli (1557–1612), among oth-ers, expanded upon the musical sections of a choir echoing each other to works for more than one choir, a style developed further by Italian composers such as Paolo Agostini (1593–1627), Antonio Maria Abbatini (1595–1677), Virgilio Mazzocchi (d. 1648), and Orazio Benevoli (1605–1672).[63]

Claudio Monteverdi (1567–1643) contrasted what he terms the "prima prat-tica," the traditional polyphony of earlier composers that emphasized the text, with his own "secunda prattica,"[64] which used instrumental accompaniment to emphasize the music. The baroque period in which he lived saw the devel-opment of a modern harmonic sound. Monteverdi rewrote the instrumental toccata beginning his opera *Orfeo* (1607) to accompany the text "Domine ad adiuvandum" beginning his Vespers of 1610.[65] This explicit use of operatic music in a sacred context indicates that the development of new secular mu-sical styles had a direct influence on Church music in the wake of Trent. The general nature of the Council of Trent's legislation concerning music permitted good music to be sung in a liturgical context. Since the music was of a highly professional caliber, it also implicitly encouraged professional musicians, in-

cluding opera singers, to perform in Catholic liturgy. The development of the
missa concertata, the Mass that featured the use of instruments, is a significant
outgrowth of this "secunda prattica."[66]

The Vespers composed in 1710 by Handel for the Carmelites in Rome,
for their patronal feast of Our Lady of Mount Carmel (July 16), represents
a pastiche of antiphons and psalms for soloists and choir that has occasioned
considerable reconstruction efforts[67] because the entire Vespers service has
not survived intact. Surviving antiphonaries from the Roman Carmelite convents of Santa Maria in Traspontina and San Martino ai Monti from around
1700 reveal the structure of the chanted Vespers liturgy, but not of the choral
and orchestral elements that might be added to it. Handel's Vespers not only
shows an operatic musical style but also requires a trained chorus and professional soloists to perform it, all of which abounded in eighteenth-century
Italy.

The Italian practice of doubling polyphonic voice parts instrumentally in
a manner known as colla parte led composers to double the voice parts of the
a cappella vocal works of Palestrina with instrumental accompaniment. These
Italian practices traveled north to the court of Dresden, where they in turn
influenced J. S. Bach in the writing of his monumental Mass in B Minor.[68] In
Naples, composers wrote the parts of the Mass as separate movements, just as
they would write separate pieces for the parts of an opera. Thus arias and duets,
commonly featured in opera, made their way into Mass settings. Technical and
emotional aspects of arias also found their way into Mass texts, giving the
pieces an emotional as well as a spiritual appeal.[69]

While the Council of Trent clearly defined parish boundaries in which
Catholics were expected to worship, particular churches, cathedrals, or noble
families frequently competed with the parish liturgy by sponsoring individual
composers and their works. The cardinal protector of the Italian Carmelites,
for example, who presumably subsidized the Handel Vespers, was a member
of the prestigious Colonna family. Franz Joseph Haydn's (1732–1809) employment with the Esterházy family included writing music for Masses and other
worship services in the court chapel. During the years he served as kapell-
meister to the younger Prince Nikolaus Esterházy, Haydn produced a Mass
each year to be performed in celebration of the name day of Princess Maria
Hermenegild on September 8, for performance the following Sunday. He
wrote the Nelson Mass in 1798, the Theresienmesse in 1799, the Creation Mass
(Schöpfungsmesse) in 1801, and the Harmoniemesse in 1802. Other compositions
include the Cecilia Mass of 1766, consisting of a number of self-contained
arias and choruses, and the "Stabat Mater" of 1767.[70] These religious works
combined Haydn's mastery of orchestral and choral writing with a deep personal devotion. All of them were intended for liturgical performance and were
generally reflections of both the taste and the demands of his employers.

Eighteenth-century Viennese tradition distinguished between the *missa solemnis*, a full-length work for important occasions, and the *missa brevis*, a shorter work for less solemn occasions in which, especially in the longer pieces such as the Credo, the text was telescoped to overlap among the voice parts in the interest of brevity.[71]

Mozart's (1756–1791) sacred music includes his *Exsultate, Jubilate* (K. 165/ 158a), a three-movement vocal work whose last movement is the famous "Alleluia." Mozart wrote Church sonatas, works for strings and organ to be performed between the Epistle and Gospel of the Mass. In addition to the shorter Masses in the *missa brevis* style, he wrote larger works such as the Coronation Mass (K. 317) of 1779, thought to have been written for the ceremonial crowning of an image of the Virgin for a church near Salzburg. His most famous sacred pieces are probably his *Ave Verum Corpus* of June 1791 and the Requiem, left unfinished at the time of his death in 1791.[72] In the absence of specific directives from Church authorities, Haydn, Mozart, Schubert, and other Viennese composers necessarily had to formulate their own style of Church music, employing the musical resources of the orchestras and soloists available to them, as well as the compositional devices such as sonata form, in the works they composed.[73] The policies of Emperor Joseph II restricted the use of the orchestra for such Masses in the smaller parish churches in the interest of his Enlightenment utilitarian policies, views that Mozart's employer, Archbishop Collaredo, shared.[74] Austrian cathedrals and other churches maintained a choir and an orchestra for regular performance of these works. This practice continues today: in Vienna's St. Augustine's Church; for instance, the Masses of Haydn, Mozart, and other Viennese masters are regularly featured at the principal Sunday service.

Beethoven's (1770–1827) sacred works include his Mass in C (op. 86) of 1807 and his Missa Solemnis in D (op. 123) (1819–1823).[75] Originally written for the installation of his student and friend, Archduke Rudolf, as Cardinal of Ölmutz on March 9, 1820, the Missa Solemnis was not completed in time for the actual ceremony;[76] its length and complexity normally preclude its being performed during the celebration of a Mass, at least in its entirety. Beethoven's *Missa Solemnis* inaugurated the Romantic idea of expressing personal feelings in a conventional setting; this surely must be the case with the prolonged "Dona nobis pacem" section of the Agnus Dei, since it clearly reflects a personal struggle for peace.[77]

Franz Schubert's (1797–1828) sacred music[78] includes six Masses, a *Deutsche Messe*, and settings of the hymn "Tantum Ergo," the Marian antiphon "Salve Regina," and other sacred pieces. The lyrical qualities of Schubert's Mass in G Major (1815) and *Deutsche Messe* are particularly appealing, and the Mass in A-flat Major (1822) and Mass in E-flat Major (1828) are renowned for their expressiveness.[79] The Masses in particular not only were suitable for sacred performance at the time but also are now part of the general repertoire of classical music.

In Italy, opera composers such as Gaetano Donizetti (1797–1848) and Gioacchino Antonio Rossini (1792–1868) produced religious music for choir and orchestra, and in France, Luigi Cherubini (1760–1842) and Hector Berlioz (1803–1869) composed large concert works as well as shorter compositions suitable for church performance. Of these pieces, the Requiem of Berlioz is the most famous.[80] A later generation of French composers includes Charles Gounod (1818–1893), whose famous "Ave Maria," based on the C Major prelude of Bach, is still part of the repertoire; Charles Ambroise Thomas (1811–1896); and César Franck (1822–1890).[81] Franz Liszt's sacred compositions include his Gran [Cathedral] Mass of 1855 and his Coronation Mass of 1867, and Anton Bruckner (1824–1896) wrote Masses in D Minor (1864), F Minor (1866), and E Minor (1868), in addition to two settings of the "Te Deum" (1881 and 1884).[82]

An important development in nineteenth-century French sacred music took place in the establishment of the École de Musique Classique et Religieuse in Paris by Louis Niedermeyer, who taught plainsong and composition there. The school specifically sought to improve the caliber of church music in France and to emphasize its spiritual dimension. Upon the death of Niedermeyer in 1861, Camille Saint-Saëns took over the piano class there. The school's most illustrious student was Gabriel Fauré (1845–1924),[83] whose famous Requiem expresses his personal musical style both harmonically and spiritually. Fauré deliberately omitted the "Dies Irae" from his work because of its harsh tone; in fact, his Requiem was thought to make the passage from death to resurrection seem too easy.[84]

Music for the Mass in ordinary parish churches during the eighteenth and nineteenth centuries was probably on a much less sophisticated level; in fact, by the nineteenth century, numerous complaints had arisen about the quality of Church music. In general, participation in the liturgy was passive rather than active; the congregation listened to the music sung by professionals instead of participating in the singing. Active participation meant either joining the choir or singing the Latin or vernacular hymns at devotional services such as Benediction or celebrations in honor of the Virgin Mary. Eucharistic devotional chants such as "Tantum Ergo" or "O Salutaris Hostia" featured music ranging from plainchant to the style of the day. By the early twentieth century, the Saint Gregory Hymnal included settings of numerous hymns, normally sung homophonically with organ accompaniment or in four-part harmony, with or without accompaniment;[85] these ranged from sixteenth-century works by Palestrina to pieces that reflected the nineteenth-century style. Numerous settings of the "Ave Maria" by Schubert, Bach-Gounod, and others, as well as "Panis Angelicus" by César Franck, were (and still remain) staples for soloists throughout the twentieth century.

Solesmes and Its Reform

The most significant force in Church music between the two councils was the movement to revive Gregorian chant that took place at the Benedictine monastery of Solesmes in France from the middle of the nineteenth century until Vatican II. Under the direction of Dom Prosper Guéranger (1805–1875)[86] and his successors, the revival approached the question of chant from three perspectives: first, to collect and study a large number of manuscripts, comparing versions in the hope of identifying a single authentic one; second, to publish chant books that disseminated the most accurate melodies to the Catholic faithful; and third, to produce recordings of chant in keeping with the available technology: first records, then cassettes, and eventually CDs that would permit listeners to hear how the chant should be sung. One of their great achievements was the publication in facsimile edition of a number of chant manuscripts in the series Paléographie Musicale. While manuscripts, of themselves, cannot indicate the original sound of the music, and while the Solesmes Benedictines' methodology has come under scrutiny, their version of the chant did produce a pleasing result. Winning the official approval of Church authorities, beginning with Pius X in his *motu proprio, Tra le sollecitudini,* of November 22, 1903,[87] allowed the Solesmes Benedictines to promote their views on chant virtually unchallenged. Primary among their views was the idea that every note should have the same duration. The generally poor quality of singing chant in the early nineteenth century further encouraged the Solesmes views on chant performance. In unilaterally rejecting any notion of rhythm in chant, they of course contravened the ideas promoted by Palestrina and Zoilo discussed above. Only in recent years has there been a proliferation of chant recordings by Schola Hungarica and other groups, some of which have challenged the often inflexible viewpoints of the Solesmes Benedictines.

The Church on the Eve of the Vatican II

While twentieth-century composers continued to write religious music, such as Francis Poulenc's Mass in G Major (1937) and Igor Stravinsky's Mass (1948),[88] music in the average church in the years before Vatican II essentially consisted of a choir singing Gregorian chant, motets by Palestrina, and various hymns for choir or soloist at the Offertory or Communion at Masses that featured singing. Where resources permitted, more elaborate sacred music of the classical masters was presented. The choir was usually accompanied by the organ, and arrangements of Gregorian chant with organ accompaniment were produced by the Solesmes monks. The study and popularization of Gregorian chant was promoted at schools and universities, particularly in the United States at the Pius X School of Sacred Music at Manhattanville College of the Sacred Heart in Purchase, New York, and at Notre Dame University in Indiana.

Many Masses had no singing at all, and congregational singing was generally limited to hymns for Benediction or Marian devotions.

Vatican II and Its Legislation

Vatican II (1962–1965), unlike Trent, at least had something specific to say about liturgy and liturgical music. Its Constitution on the Sacred Liturgy, approved at session 3 on December 4, 1963, included an entire chapter on liturgical music. Chapter 6, *De musica sacra*, paragraph 112, specifically called the Church's musical tradition a "priceless treasure, more so than other artistic expressions, especially insofar as the sacral chant which is superimposed onto words makes a necessary and integral contribution to solemn liturgy."[89] Paragraph 114 urged that "very great efforts should be made to preserve and develop the rich heritage of music in churches. The growth of choirs should be energetically fostered, especially in cathedral churches. At the same time, bishops and others in positions of pastoral responsibility should make strenuous efforts to see that the whole gathering of believers are able to take the active part which is proper to them in any event of worship meant to be conducted through song, in keeping with articles 28 and 30."[90] Article 116 recognized the value of Gregorian chant and polyphony for worship,[91] and article 117 mandated the completion of the "standard edition of the books of Gregorian chant,"[92] also advocating that "an edition comprising simpler melodies could be prepared, for use in smaller churches."[93] The Council respected the musical tradition of native peoples in mission areas (article 119), advocating the musical training of missionaries,[94] and in article 120 advocating the honor in which the pipe organ was held, while conceding that "other instruments may be brought into the worship of God."[95]

The most striking liturgical legislation of the Second Vatican Council was to promulgate the new rite of the Mass according to Paul VI and to make the vernacular language normative for the Mass. This meant that the universal use of the Latin language was now generally to be abandoned so that the text might be fully intelligible to the congregation. The Council also allowed for the Divine Office to be sung or said in the vernacular languages and opened its recitation to any interested participants, including the laity.

While the Council did not ban the use of Latin Church music in the liturgy, by making the vernacular language normative for the liturgical texts, it in effect made it normative for the music as well. In calling for the greater liturgical participation of the laity, the Council also gave the whole congregation a role that had previously been restricted to the choir. Expecting the entire congregation to sing required them to participate in the liturgy in a more active and entirely unfamiliar way. Turning the altar around to emphasize the Eucharist as meal rather than sacrifice required the priest-celebrant to face the people rather than have his back to them, thus entailing much more interaction with the congregation. Vatican II allowed more instruments than just the organ, which, at least in theory if not in practice, had been the only musical instrument generally used after the Council of Trent. This opened the way for other instruments, especially the guitar, to be introduced into the liturgy. The role of the priest was changed from being concerned with the correct rendition of the unchanging liturgy to presiding over it and motivating the congregation to prayer, while the congregation's role was changed from passive recipients to active participants; all of this produced enormous differences of opinion and much tension, particularly in the years of rapid change following the Council.

This atmosphere of tension was reflected in a secular work from this time: in 1971 the *Mass* of Leonard Bernstein,[96] commissioned by the Kennedy family in memory of the late President John F. Kennedy, opened the newly built Kennedy Center in Washington, D.C. *Mass* was called a "theater piece" rather than a Mass in the traditional sense; it was not designed for performance in church but served as a very personal commentary by Leonard Bernstein and Stephen Schwartz (in the additional texts they added to the Mass of Paul VI) on the tensions in the Church and particularly in the larger society, since the Vietnam War was still a deeply troubling issue for many Americans. At the outset of *Mass*, one hears a polyphonic Kyrie, which gradually grows in complexity and dissonance until it is abruptly curtailed by a guitar chord played by the celebrant, who then begins to sing his "Simple Song." In juxtaposing these two styles, Bernstein sums up the tension in the Church between traditionalists and innovators, especially where music is concerned. *Mass* also depicts theatrically the tension between celebrant and congregation as they adjust to new roles, as well as the tension between singers of traditional polyphony and the new folk music.

Vatican II essentially replaced an established style of music, either plainchant or classical music pieces, with an entirely new one, either hymns borrowed from established Protestant traditions, which previously had been prohibited from Catholic worship, or newly composed music. The problem was that the new music did not yet exist, nor were there established composers to write it, as Palestrina had done after the Council of Trent. By the twentieth century, a chasm had grown between popular and serious music that was unknown at the time of Trent. In the absence of people who could supply this new music and of any particular direction for doing so, the churches at every level had to do the best they could to supply what was now necessary and not readily available. Whereas the direct borrowing of music from the Protestant traditions had previously been unthinkable, after Vatican II it became normative, simply because little else was available. Hymns were now to be sung at various times during the Mass, particularly at the entrance and exit of the celebrant, at the Offertory and Communion—in other words, at any point in the Mass where silence might be awkward. Far less emphasis was placed initially on singing the chants of the ordinary of the Mass and of singing some new acclamations, despite their avowed liturgical importance. Within the course of a few years, however, this situation did correct itself, so that numerous settings of the ordinary of the Mass are readily available and singing of these and other parts of the Mass (e.g., the Preface by the celebrant) is encouraged.[97] The new hymns were taken from Anglican (Episcopalian), Lutheran, Methodist, Baptist, and other traditions, and reflected the collective experience of widely disparate worshiping communities. Traditional and older Catholics typically felt more comfortable with these standard hymns, many of which were written in a musical style of the baroque period, especially the German hymns of the Lutheran tradition. At the same time, new and more informal styles of celebrating liturgy began to develop along with a new folk music to sing at Mass. The first wave of composers of this new music tended to be younger clerics and religious who felt inspired by the Muse to compose and generally were undaunted by a lack of formal training in music, although most of them could chart their way through a few guitar chords if required to do so. Thus, new hymns such as "Take Our Bread" by Joseph Wise became the favorites of the younger generation and the bane of the older one. At the same time, dissatisfaction with the Vietnam War and other political issues made its way into a sacred space; for example, protest songs such as "We Shall Overcome" found their way into the liturgy, either intact or with new text, even though most of the worshipers did not have anything in particular to overcome.

Various styles of writing hymns and antiphons reflect different preferences in prayer styles, different national traditions, and generational issues as well. The music of the French priest Lucien Deiss, for instance, generally consists of refrains sung by the congregation with a soloist singing the verses, and directly relates to his own vision of singing as an integral function of the worshiping community.[98] A French Jesuit, Joseph Gelineau, composed his psalm settings using more extended psalm texts with a simple accompaniment, usually on the organ; these also reflected his viewpoint that singing at Mass should essentially be done by the congregation.[99] Hymns continue to be written in a traditional or academic style, such as the Masses of C. Alexander Peloquin (1918–1997) or "Gift of Finest Wheat" by Robert Kreutz, commissioned as the official hymn of the Eucharistic Congress at Philadelphia in 1976. The writing of hymns in various traditions has led to a great deal of borrowing from one to the other and translating from one language to another, so that the old standard Protestant hymn "Nearer My God to Thee" is now sung to Spanish and Polish texts as well as its original English one.

The search for new prayer forms since Vatican II has also entailed new musical forms. One of the more successful of these is the music of Jacques Berthier from Taizé, the ecumenical monastic community in France (and now elsewhere in the world). Based on short Latin or vernacular texts and usually performed as ostinato responses and chorales, litanies, acclamations, or canons, the pieces convey a generally pleasing sound and promote a prayerful experience.[100]

Numerous groups have arisen since the Second Vatican Council to write and perform music, some of which has entered the repertoire on a more or less permanent basis, while most of it has fallen into disuse. The monks of the Weston Priory in Vermont, the Dameans, and the St. Louis Jesuits are a few such groups, but they now seem to have been gradually replaced by Christopher Walker, David Haas, and many others. The quality of this new music has improved, and the number of instruments has greatly expanded beyond a few guitars. There is also more of a rapprochement between organists and players of other instruments, the traditionalists and the innovators, in the search for suitable music for worship.

In the United States, the huge influx of people from other nations, particularly from Spanish-speaking countries, has required enormous efforts on the part of the local Church to accommodate their needs even as the new immigrants make a significant contribution to its spiritual life. Thus, new music and new styles of singing have merged with traditional practices, and singing hymns in various languages or providing translations of texts from one language to another has become a standard feature of many liturgical celebrations. These Hispanic hymns, like their English counterparts, have had various levels of success as they add a new dimension to the traditional English liturgy; one hymn in particular, "Pescador de hombres" by Cesáreo Gabaraín, has enjoyed great popularity.

Reflections on the Councils of Trent and Vatican II and the Music They Generated

People who find themselves disillusioned with the contemporary state of music in the Church may take heart from the example of the Council of Trent. The pronouncements of Trent came from the side of liturgy and theology rather than music. Thus, the intelligibility of the text for worship purposes became paramount; polyphony in the later Renaissance style was tolerated, providing that it allowed for the preeminence of the text. The musical and liturgical sound created by Palestrina and the composers of his generation remained popular for centuries after the Council. The Council fathers' preoccupation with textual declamation and infatuation with the humanism of their time led them to endorse the primacy of Gregorian chant and then to produce a version of it that completely distorted its musical shape. Since its application was never legislated as mandatory or enforced by subsequent papal commissions, its effect remained limited.

The development of the modern sound in music, including the establishment of modern tonality and harmony, along with the progressive systemati-zation of polyphony, culminated in the fugues of J. S. Bach by the middle of the eighteenth century. The Council of Trent, in basing its directives concern-ing liturgical music on the prevalent trends of the sixteenth century, in effect did virtually nothing to set the course for liturgical music in the years that followed it, nor did it offer specific guidelines for what constituted good litur-gical music.

Since the Church was not especially interested or able to enforce its own ideology concerning liturgical music, and since it did not engage in ongoing dialogue with later musicians, these composers were left on their own to write suitable liturgical music. Thus, despite the prohibition of using orchestral in-struments in liturgical music, by the eighteenth century the practice in fact had become widespread. In the absence of any explicit directives from the Vatican, the classical Viennese composers forged their own style of liturgical music based on symphonic techniques combined with choral writing to create what they considered the ideal liturgical music. As a result, the sacred works of Haydn, Mozart, Beethoven, Schubert, and many lesser composers comprise an important corpus of good music, much of which can still be used in the context of worship. Nineteenth-century liturgical music, too, reflected prevail-ing tastes of the time more than a Vatican ideal; while some may consider much of the music too operatic, on the one hand, or overly personal or senti-mental, on the other, music after Trent nonetheless ensured a high caliber of liturgical performance, at least in many churches.

The nineteenth-century revival of Gregorian chant at Solesmes, including the study, publication, singing, and recording of chant based on early sources, resulted from the Benedictines' initiative rather than any Vatican mandate. The endorsement of their work by Pope Pius X in 1903 made a fundamental shift in our approach to Gregorian chant away from the Medicean edition to a more authentic version of it.

The state of music on the eve of the Second Vatican Council probably reflected the state of music through much of the last several centuries, in that the quality of music varied widely from church to church. While the great works of music from late Renaissance polyphony through the choral works of the nineteenth century were sung in cathedrals and churches able to support a good organist and choir director, publications such as the *St. Gregory Hymnal* put at least some of the material at the disposal of the average parish.

While Vatican II encouraged the development of the "rich heritage of mu-sic," at the same time it made it almost impossible to do so. It created this dilemma by making the vernacular language normative and emphasizing the preeminent role of the congregation in the communal singing of the parts of the Mass and some of the accompanying hymns. In the process, the Council rendered obsolete the existing heritage of music, normally written for a trained choir and predominantly sung in Latin. Like Trent before it, Vatican II did not legislate on how this development was to be accomplished, nor did it provide any specific guidelines that would facilitate its happening. Unlike Trent, Vatican II did not issue any definitive model for singing analogous to the Medicean edition of chant books. Again, like Trent, Vatican II has let Church music more or less evolve on its own, so that the style of singing varies considerably from one country to another and even from one parish to another.

Since the liturgy is now celebrated in the vernacular rather than the universal Latin language, the effects of globalization have been felt in liturgical music after Vatican II in a manner that would have been unthinkable after Trent. Thus, hymns from one national tradition are regularly translated and sung elsewhere in different languages. While not all styles of music can possibly please the entire worshiping community, the variety of options available for the liturgy in many parishes at least allows people to find a worship format that suits their personal taste. Since the close of the Council, the most perceptible changes in Church music have been the rapprochement between traditionalists and innovators, and the willingness to retrieve the essential elements of our Catholic music tradition as well as to investigate new ways of creating liturgical music for worship. If, in the aftermath of the Council of Trent, it took a long time for the process of liturgical revision to be completed in most religious orders and dioceses, we can expect to be in a state of flux with liturgical music well into the near future. If the four centuries between the two Councils saw the composition of numerous works in as many different musical styles— from imitative polyphony to Masses with orchestral accompaniment; to Masses in the various operatic styles of Church music developed by Italian and French composers; to the more consciously religious style of Gabriel Fauré—we can only hope that the quest for a religious and distinctively liturgical music will continue to be pursued in the post–Vatican II epoch.

NOTES

1. For a brief history of these musical trends, see Jan Michael Joncas, "Liturgy and Music," in *Handbook for Liturgical Studies*, vol. 2, *Fundamental Liturgy*, edited by Anscar J. Chupungco (Collegeville, Minn.: Liturgical Press, 1997), 281–321.

2. Richard L. Crocker, "Kyrie Eleison," in *The New Grove Dictionary of Music and Musicians*, 2nd ed., edited by Stanley Sadie (London: Macmillan Reference; New York: Grove, 2001), vol. 14, 71–73, distinguishes between texts set to preexisting melodies, as in most Kyries, and tropes that are textual or musical additions to an existing piece; thus the text added to the Kyrie in *Kyrie cunctipotens genitor* simply accompanied the music that was already there.

3. The terms "prosa" and "sequence" were sometimes distinguished, with "prosa" referring to the text sung to the sequence melody, but eventually came to be used interchangeably, each referring to both melody and text. See Richard L. Crocker, "Prosa," in *New Grove Dictionary*, 2nd ed., vol. 20, 430–431; and Richard L. Crocker, John Caldwell, and Alejandro E. Planchart, "Sequence (i)," ibid., 23, 91–107. This pro-

cess of adding sequences, prosas, and tropes is discussed in Joncas, "Liturgy and Music," esp. 299.

4. Keith F. Pecklers, "History of the Roman Liturgy from the Sixteenth until the Twentieth Centuries," in Chupungco, *Introduction to the Liturgy*, vol. 1, 157.

5. A rhymed office or, less frequently, rhymed Mass, featured metrical chants written in poetic rhyme; many of these texts are published in the monumental work of Guido Maria Dreves and Clemens Blume, *Analecta hymnica medii aevi*, 55 vols. (Leipzig: O. R. Reisland, 1886–1922).

6. Among the most famous of these later rhymed offices is that of St. Thomas of Canterbury, discussed in Andrew Hughes, "Chants in the Rhymed Office of St. Thomas of Canterbury," *Early Music* 16 (1988): 185–201; and Kay Brainard Slocum, *Liturgies in Honour of Thomas Becket* (Toronto: University of Toronto Press, 2004). Owain Tudor Edwards, in *Matins, Lauds and Vespers for St. David's Day* (Cambridge: D. S. Brewer, 1990), shows how the office of St. David of Wales was directly based on the office of St. Thomas of Canterbury. The Carmelites of Mainz also fashioned their office of the Presentation of the Virgin Mary on preexisting chants, primarily from the office of Thomas of Canterbury; see James Boyce, "The Carmelite Feast of the Presentation of the Virgin: A Study in Musical Adaptation," in *The Divine Office in the Latin Middle Ages*, ed. Margot E. Fassler and Rebecca A. Baltzer (New York: Oxford University Press, 2000), 485–518. Edwards discussed this application of established music to new texts in "Chant Transference in Rhymed Offices," in *Cantus Planus, Papers Read at the Fourth Meeting, Pécs, Hungary, 3–8 September 1990* (Budapest: Hungarian Academy of Sciences, Institute for Musicology, 1992), 503–519.

7. David Fenwick Wilson, *Music of the Middle Ages: Style and Structure* (New York: Schirmer Books, 1990), discusses these new forms, such as the *versus*, developed at St. Martial; see esp. chapter 6, "The Sacred Music of Southern France," 135–163.

8. Fritz Reckow, Edward H. Roesner, Rudolf Flotzinger, and Norman E. Smith, "Organum," in *New Grove Dictionary*, 2nd ed., vol. 18, 671–695.

9. The achievements of Leoninus and Perotinus in compiling and then revising the *Magnus liber organi* are outlined in Edward H. Roesner, "Leoninus," in *New Grove Dictionary*, 2nd ed., vol. 14, 565–567; and "Perotinus," ibid., vol. 19, 446–451; he deals specifically with Perotinus's revision of the *Magnus liber organi* on 446.

10. Wilson, *Music of the Middle Ages*, 155ff.

11. Wulf Arlt, "Machaut . . . , Guillaume de . . . ," in *New Grove Dictionary*, 2nd ed., vol. 15, 478–490.

12. Alejandro Enrique Planchart, "Du Fay . . . , Guillaume," ibid., vol. 7, 647–664.

13. Patrick Macey, Jeremy Noble, Jeffrey Dean, Gustave Reese/Patrick Macey, "Josquin . . . des Prez . . . ," ibid., vol. 13, 220–266.

14. For a discussion of the paraphrase Mass with particular reference to Josquin's *Missa Pange Lingua*, see Allan W. Atlas, *Renaissance Music: Music in Western Europe, 1400–1600* (New York: Norton, 1998), esp, 302–304.

15. For a discussion of Dufay's *Missa L'Homme armé*, see ibid., 124–126.

16. For a detailed overview of Protestant, particularly Lutheran, criticisms of Mass practices and the Catholic response to them, including the statements of theologians at the Council, see Reinold Theisen, *Mass Liturgy and the Council of Trent* (Col-

legeville, Minn.: St. John's University Press, 1965). Theisen, however, does not specifically address the musical issues. Also see Pecklers, "History of the Roman Liturgy,"
153–178. For a good dicussion of Catholic Church music after the Council of Trent,
see Joseph Dyer, "Roman Catholic Church Music," in *New Grove Dictionary*, 2nd ed.,
vol. 21, 544–570.

17. Robert L. Marshall and Robin A. Leaver, "Chorale," in *New Grove Dictionary
of Music,* 2nd ed., vol. 5, 736–746.

18. Edith Weber, *Le Concile de Trente et la musique: De la Réforme à la Contre-
Réforme* (Paris: Honoré Champion, 1982), 50.

19. Weber discusses the importance of this type of music within the French tradition and in connection with the Council of Trent in ibid., 19.

20. The definitive work on the reform of chant by the Council of Trent is P.
Raphael Molitor, *Die Nach-Tridentinishe Choral-Reform zu Rom: Ein Beitrag zur Musik-
geschichte des XVI. und XVII. Jahrhunderts,* 2 vols. (Leipzig: Leuckart, 1901–1902; repr.
Hildesheim: G. Olms, 1976). Robert F. Hayburn summarizes much of this material
in *Papal Legislation on Sacred Music, 95 A.D. to 1977 A.D.* (Collegeville, Minn.: Liturgical Press, 1979), esp. 25–27.

21. Kenneth Levy, John A. Emerson, Jane Bellingham, David Hiley, and Bennett
Zon, "Plainchant," in *New Grove Dictionary,* 2nd ed., vol. 19, 825–887, discuss the
Tridentine legislation, 849–853.

22. Norman P. Tanner, ed., *Decrees of the Ecumenical Councils,* vol. 2, *Trent to
Vatican II* (Washington, D.C.: Georgetown University Press, 1990), 734.

23. Ibid.

24. Ibid., 737.

25. Ibid., 767.

26. Ibid.

27. Ibid., 723.

28. Ibid., 764.

29. Ibid., 797.

30. Ibid., 737.

31. For instance, as late as the eighteenth century in some cathedrals in France,
the style of singing known as "sur le livre" called for tenors, countertenors, and so-
pranos to improvise over the chant line, sung by the basses. See Abbé Jean Prim,
"*Chant sur le Livre* in French Churches in the 18th Century," *Journal of the American
Musicological Society* 14 (1961): 37–49.

32. Hayburn, *Papal Legislation,* 27; Florentius Romita, *Jus musicae liturgicae: Dis-
sertatio historico-iuridica* (Rome: Edizione Liturgiche, 1947), 59.

33. Hayburn, *Papal Legislation,* 27; Romita, *Jus musicae liturgicae,* 59.

34. Hayburn, *Papal Legislation,* 28; Romita, *Jus musicae liturgicae,* 61.

35. Hayburn, *Papal Legislation,* 28; Romita, *Jus musicae liturgicae,* 62.

36. Allan Atlas discusses the achievements of Morales and Victoria in *Renaissance Music,* 408–412, and 613–615, respectively.

37. Hayburn, *Papal Legislation,* 28–29; Edith Weber discusses some of these local councils in detail in *Le Concile de Trente et la musique,* 137ff.

38. See Molitor, *Die Nach-Tridentische Choral-Reform*; Hayburn, *Papal Legislation,*
34.

39. The four sequences that were retained are *Victimae paschali laudes* for Easter, *Veni sancte spiritus* for Pentecost, *Lauda Sion* for the feast of Corpus Christi, and the *Dies irae* for the requiem Mass; the sequence *Stabat mater* for the feast of the Seven Sorrows of the Virgin Mary was restored in 1727; see Atlas, *Renaissance Music*, 605.

40. Hayburn, *Papal Legislation*, 34.

41. Ibid., 34–35.

42. The papal brief of October 25, 1577, is cited in Atlas, *Renaissance Music*, 604–605.

43. Lewis Lockwood, Noel O'Regan, and Jessie Ann Owens, "Palestrina . . . , Giovanni Pierluigi da," in *The New Grove Dictionary*, 2nd ed., vol. 18, 937–957. Also see Atlas, *Renaissance Music*, 583–597.

44. Atlas, *Renaissance Music*, 605.

45. David Hiley discusses their work in *Western Plainchant: A Handbook* (Oxford: Clarendon Press, 1993), 615–618.

46. Hayburn discusses the legislation and numerous problems and intrigues associated with the production of this edition in *Papal Legislation*, 33–67.

47. Hiley, *Western Plainchant*, 616.

48. The term "melisma" refers to a large number of notes over a single syllable of text, particularly common in the great responsories of Matins for the Divine Office and in Graduals and Alleluias for the Mass. The most elaborate melismas generally occur in the Alleluia chant; the concluding part of the Alleluia, emphasizing the beauty of the music itself, is known as the *jubilus* because it conveys the idea of rejoicing. For a discussion of melismas and the *jubilus* in the Alleluia chant, see Hiley, *Western Plainchant*, 130–139.

49. These prolix responsories follow each of the readings for the night service known as Matins as a musical reflection on the text that has been read. The term "prolix" refers to their textual and musical length, often involving ornate music. See ibid., 25–30, 273–279.

50. Hayburn, *Papal Legislation*, 43–44.

51. See James Boyce, "Carmel in Transition: A Seventeenth-Century Florentine Carmelite Supplement," *Manuscripta* 39 (1995): 56–69.

52. Weber, *Le Concile de Trente*, 111.

53. Leeman L. Perkins, *Music in the Age of the Renaissance* (New York: Norton, 1999), 873–874.

54. The dedication to these *Preces speciales* has been published in *Source Readings in Music History*, selected and annotated by Oliver Strunk (New York: Norton, 1950), 355–356.

55. Lewis Lockwood and Noel O'Regan, "Animuccia, Giovanni," in *New Grove Dictionary*, 2nd ed., vol. 1, 686–688.

56. James Haar, "Orlande . . . de Lassus," in ibid., vol. 14, 295–322.

57. Lewis Lockwood and Alexandra Amati-Camperi, "Ruffo, Vincenzo," in ibid., vol. 21, 874–875.

58. Steven Ledbetter and Laurie Stras, "Ingegneri . . . , Marc Antonio," in ibid., vol. 12, 380–382.

59. Council decisions on sacred music and the circumstances that brought them

about are discussed in Gustave Reese, *Music in the Renaissance*, rev. ed. (New York: Norton, 1959), 448–451.

60. Karl Gustav Fellerer discusses the musical style initiated by Palestrina and further developed by Tomás Luís de Victoria and others in *The History of Catholic Church Music*, trans. Francis A. Brunner (Baltimore: Helicon Press, 1961), esp. 94–100; this is the authorized translation of the 2nd ed. of *Geschichte der katholischen Kirchenmusik* (Düsseldorf: Schwann, 1949).

61. See Weber, *Le Concile de Trente*, 175–189, for a discussion of composers who produced works according to the Tridentine aesthetic.

62. This style of music is discussed in greater detail in Fellerer, *The History of Catholic Church Music*, 105–108.

63. See ibid., 108–110, for this discussion.

64. Monteverdi discussed these differences in the foreword to his *Fifth Book of Madrigals* of 1605; see Oliver Strunk, ed., *Source Readings in Music History*, rev. ed., ed. Leo Treitler (New York: Norton, 1998), 536–544.

65. Tim Carter and Geoffrey Chew, "Monteverdi . . . , Claudio . . . Antonio," in *New Grove Dictionary*, 2nd ed., vol. 17, 29–60, esp. 40–41.

66. George B. Stauffer, *Bach: The Mass in B Minor* (New York: Schirmer, 1997), 6.

67. Graham Dixon, "Handel's Music for the Carmelites. A Study in Liturgy and Some Observations on Performance," *Early Music* 15 (1987): 16–29, and "Handel's Vesper Music: Towards a Liturgical Reconstruction," *The Musical Times* 126 (1985): 393, 395–397; J. S. Hall, "Handel Among the Carmelites," *Dublin Review* 233 (1959): 121–131.

68. George B. Stauffer discusses the influence of musical practice from Venice, Rome, Naples, Bologna, and Vienna on the Dresden court, and by extension on J. S. Bach, in his *Bach: The Mass in B Minor*, particularly 1–23.

69. Ibid., 8.

70. James Webster and Georg Feder, "Haydn, (Franz) Joseph," in *New Grove Dictionary*, 2nd ed., vol. 11, 171–271.

71. James W. McKinnon, Theodor Göllner, Maricarmen Gómez, Lewis Lockwood, Andrew Kirkman, Denis Arnold, and John Harper, "Mass" in *New Grove Dictionary*, 2nd ed., vol. 16, 58–85, esp. "III. 1600–2000," 77–84.

72. Cliff Eisen and Stanley Sadie, "(Johann Chrysostom) Wolfgang Amadeus Mozart," in *New Grove Dictionary*, 2nd ed., vol. 17, 276–347. For a discussion of Mozart's sacred music, see Daniel Heartz, *Haydn, Mozart, and the Viennese School, 1740–1780* (New York: Norton, 1995), esp. 643–674.

73. See Konrad Küster, *W. A. Mozart und seine Zeit* (Laaber: Laaber-Verlag, 2001), esp. "Liturgische Musik in Mozarts Zeit," 213–261.

74. Reinhard G. Pauly, "The Reforms of Church Music Under Joseph II," *The Musical Quarterly* 43 (1957): 372–382.

75. Joseph Kerman, Alan Tyson, Scott G. Burnham, Douglas Johnson, and William Drabkin, "Beethoven, Ludwig van," in *New Grove Dictionary*, 2nd ed., vol. 3, 73–140.

76. William Drabkin gives background information concerning the composition of the *Missa Solemnis* in *Beethoven: Missa Solemnis* (Cambridge: Cambridge University Press, 1991), esp. 11–15.

77. For Drabkin's discussion of the "Agnus Dei" of the *Missa Solemnis*, see ibid., 83–95.

78. Robert Winter, Maurice J. E. Brown, and Eric Sams, "Schubert, Franz (Peter)," in *New Grove Dictionary*, 2nd ed., vol. 22, 655–729.

79. Joncas, "Liturgy and Music," 308.

80. These and other composers are discussed in more detail in Fellerer, *The History of Catholic Church Music*, 169–171.

81. Ibid., 174–175.

82. Ibid., 175–178.

83. Jean-Michel Nectoux, "Fauré, Gabriel (Urbain)," in *New Grove Dictionary*, 2nd ed., vol. 8, 594–607; Jessica Duchen, *Gabriel Fauré* (London: Phaidon Press, 2000); Carlo Caballero, *Fauré and French Musical Aesthetics* (Cambridge: Cambridge University Press, 2001).

84. Caballero discusses the reactions to Fauré's Requiem and the composer's defense of his approach in *Fauré and French Musical Aesthetics*, 188–192.

85. An example of this hymnal is *The Saint Gregory Hymnal and Catholic Choir Book*, abridged ed., compiled, edited, and arranged by Nicola A. Montani (Philadelphia, Pa.: The Saint Gregory Guild, 1979). The original hymnal dates to 1920. See also *Unison, Two and Four Voice Choirs with Organ*, compiled by Carroll Thomas Andrews (Chicago: G.I.A. Publications, 1979).

86. Dom Louis Soltner, *Solesmes and Dom Guéranger, 1805–1875*, trans. Joseph O'Connor (Orleans, Mass.: Paraclete Press, 1995).

87. See Joncas, "Liturgy and Music," 310.

88. For a discussion of the spiritual aspect of Stravinsky's music, including his Mass, see Robert M. Copeland, "The Christian Message of Igor Stravinsky," *The Musical Quarterly* 68 (1982): 563–579.

89. Tanner, *Decrees of the Ecumenical Council*, vol. 2, 839.

90. Ibid., 840.

91. Ibid.

92. Ibid.

93. Ibid.

94. Ibid., 840–841.

95. Ibid., 841.

96. For a discussion of Bernstein's *Mass* in the context of the new liturgy and of social unrest, see W. Anthony Sheppard, "Bitter Rituals for a Lost Nation: Partch's *Revelation in the Courthouse Park* and Bernstein's *Mass*," *The Musical Quarterly* 80 (1996): 461–499.

97. Jan Michael Joncas discusses in detail the relationship of music to the specific parts of the Mass in "Musical Elements in the *Ordo Missae* of Paul VI," in Chupungco, *Handbook for Liturgical Studies*, vol. 3, *The Eucharist* (Collegeville, Minn.: Liturgical Press, 1999), 209–244.

98. Lucien Deiss, *Visions of Liturgy and Music for a New Century*, trans. Jane M.-A. Burton, ed. Donald Molloy (Collegeville, Minn.: Liturgical Press, 1996).

99. For a critique of Joseph Gelineau's *Chant et musique dans le culte chrétien* (Paris: Éditions Fleurus, 1962), translated by Clifford Howell as *Voices and Instruments in Christian Worship: Principles, Laws, Applications* (Collegeville, Minn.: Liturgical

Press, 1964), see Peter Jeffery, *Re-Envisioning Past Musical Cultures: Ethnomusicology in the Study of Gregorian Chant* (Chicago: University of Chicago Press, 1992), 78–86.

100. For a detailed study of this music, see Judith Marie Kubicki, *Liturgical Music as Ritual Symbol: A Case Study of Jacques Berthier's Taizé Music* (Leuven: Peeters, 1999), esp. "Musicological Analysis of Jacques Berthier's Music for Taizé," 41–91.

9

Moral Theology

James F. Keenan

Few explicit references regarding moral theology can be found in the documents of either the Council of Trent or the Second Vatican Council. At the Council of Trent, the twenty-fourth session reformed the sacrament of marriage canonically. Other than upholding conscience in *Gaudium et spes*, 16, there is little else at Vatican II than a passage from *Optatam totius*, the Declaration on Priestly Formation, that reads: "Moral theology's scientific presentation should draw more fully on the teaching of Holy Scripture and should throw light upon the exalted vocation of the faithful in Christ and their obligation to bring forth fruit in charity for the life of the world."

Still, the doing of moral theology before and after the two councils witnesses to extraordinary changes regarding the method of theology, its standard of authority, and its understanding of moral truth. I will divide this essay into two sections. First, I will look at two major works, one thirty years before, and the other thirty years after, the Council of Trent. Second, I will examine developments before and after Vatican II.

Before and after Trent

John Mair's *Commentary on the Fourth Book of the Sentences* (1509) and Francisco de Toledo's *Summa casuum conscientiae sive De instructione sacerdotum, libri septem* (1598) appeared thirty years away from either end of the Council of Trent. Mair (1467–1550) died five years after the Council began, and until 1530 was the most influential figure in ethics at the University of Paris. Toledo began teaching his popular courses on the priesthood a year before the Council's close. The two men serve as bookends of the Council of Trent, and few were more relevant to the field of moral theology in their period and in the subsequent centuries. James Farge remarks that the courses of the nominalist John Mair were among the most popular ones at Paris (1506–1518, 1521–1522, 1526–1531) on the eve of the Reformation.[1] Mair's nominalism afforded him some footing in a world no longer comfortable with older systems.[2] When his scholastic nominalism engaged new practical concerns, the result resembled what we today call casuistry.[3]

Three insights support that claim. First, Mair wanted to experiment with method. He asked, "Has not Amerigo Vespucci discovered lands unknown to Ptolemy, Pliny and other geographers up to the present? Why cannot the same happen in other spheres?"[4] The new questions that Mair entertained prompted him to reexamine old ways of thinking. Second, as a result, the concept of authority, so significant in the scholastic method, was radically changed. Mair's new insights required, to some degree, a rejection, albeit nuanced, of the sanctioned views of Gregory the Great, Huguccio, Thomas Aquinas, and even Augustine. As the world expanded, local cultures and practices demanded newer directives, and tradition, failing to provide sufficient insight, had less influence. In a world of competing authorities, Mair and his disciples offered no longer certain, but only probable, arguments. Third, in this probable world, Mair employed the scholastic dialectic, but instead of using it to examine moral and immoral "objects" as the earlier scholastics had done, he drew analogies through a comparison of situations, experiences, and cases.

Mair's desire to explore previous teachings, his ability to contest earlier expressions of authority, and his study of cases typify moral theology in the early sixteenth century. To appreciate his work, we can study how he treated the case of maritime insurance.[5] In 1237, Pope Gregory IX issued the decretal *Naviganti vel eunti ad nundinas*, ruling that this insurance was a form of usury, and therefore morally illicit. John Noonan called the decretal "the most important single papal decree on the usury question with the exception of those containing the basic prohibition itself."[6]

In 1530, a group of Spanish merchants living in Flanders asked the University of Paris to address certain commercial practices. One question concerned whether one who assumes the risk that another runs may receive payment for assuming that risk. Mair responded, using the solution from his already published *Commentary on the Fourth Book of the Sentences*.[7] He employed the scholastic method to consider two common objections: that insurance is useless and that it is prohibited. The first objection contended that unlike the soldier or the captain, the insurer does not prevent possible loss of cargo; a sinking ship sinks whether it is insured or not. Mair responded by addressing not the state of the cargo, but the psychological state of the shipping merchant: his worries were allayed, because were the cargo lost, its worth would be saved. Moreover, by providing the insurance, the agent enters into a partnership with the owner in which the worth of the cargo and their attendant concerns are borne equally by agent and owner.

Mair then answered the second objection by examining three sets of laws. From Scripture, he noted that all adults are required to work, and referred to the law that we are to eat our bread earned from the sweat of our brow (Genesis 3:19) and the injunction that we humans were born to work (Job 5:7). Since the agent only underwrites the cargo, he seems to fail to heed the Scriptures. Mair again wrote that the agent assumes the merchant's worry and fear of loss, and thus enters into a partnership. Then Mair added a theme that he repeated elsewhere. The children of wealthy families do not work, but play and recreate with the amassed riches of their parents. Why, then, are the Scriptures used against the working agents and not against the shiftless wealthy?

Next Mair examined positive law and noted that the law has no injunctions against maritime insurance, but outlines, instead, conditions for when it would be fraudulent. Finally, he examined the papal decretal *Naviganti*. Mair argued that the Roman Pontiff did not prohibit maritime insurance per se, but rather usury, receiving a fee for a loan. The insurance agent does not receive a fee for a loan, but for his share in the partnership and for the service he provides by underwriting the cargo and sharing in the anxiety. A usurious contract is different, then, from a morally legitimate contract of maritime insurance.

This case is an example of high casuistry. It addresses a dilemma, uses analogies, examines circumstances, resolves doubt, examines the intentionality of personal agents, and gives its solution. In short, it makes its case. It does not presume that the reader agrees, but provides argumentation to prompt the reader's assent. The authority of the solution rests on two points: what Albert Jonsen and Stephen Toulmin call internal and external certitude. Internal certitude is the cogency of the argument itself. External certitude is that which derives from the recognizable authority of the author. For casuistry, then, a case needs to be made, argued, and demonstrated by an author with evident authority.[8]

Moreover, while Mair enjoyed obvious authority in the argument's "external authority," he undermined the Pope's external authority by putting the Pope's decretal in a new interpretative context. In other words, he subdued the internal certitude of the Pope's teaching and thus overrode a 300-year-old prohibition.

Francisco de Toledo's *Summa casuum conscientiae sive De instructione sacerdotum, libri septem,* is very different.[9] In 1569, Toledo was made preacher of the papal court and later, theologian of the Sacred Penitentiary (the Roman Inquisition) and consultant to several Roman Congregations. Ultimately, he served seven Popes. He was made Cardinal in 1593, the first Jesuit to receive that honor.[10]

Toledo developed his summary from the courses of theology that he taught at the Roman College from 1562 to 1569, lecturing on the priesthood, the administration of the sacraments, the Ten Commandments as they were used for the hearing of confession, and, finally, the sacrament of marriage. These lectures were the material for the *Summa casuum*. Copies of them as well as students' notes were probably in circulation before their publication in 1598.[11]

When the lectures were published, they were among the first of a series of Jesuit summaries of cases of conscience that began to appear in the 1590s. Prior to Toledo's work, Pietro Alagona published a compendium of the manual of Martin of Azplicueta (1495–1586) (also known as "Navarro") in 1590. The following year, Enrico Henriquez wrote a summa of moral theology in three tomes, a systematic treatment of the ends of human action including some reserved cases. Finally, Emmanuel Sà published a summa of cases listed alphabetically.[12] Though Sà's work went through several editions, Toledo's work was the first major breakthrough: seventy-two editions and multitudinous translations, remaining in print until 1716.[13]

Ninety years after Mair's *Commentary*, Francisco de Toledo's *Summa casuum conscientiae* does not look like casuistry. Rather than making a case, it gives summaries of cases. Commentators, both historians and ethicists, often fail to differentiate works of casuistry that are demonstrable or argumentative from case summaries that are pedagogical judgments.[14] Summaries of cases do not consist of demonstrable arguments; neither do they depend on internal certitude (there are no arguments made), but rather on their external certitude, on the authority of the writer. Moreover, the purpose of the text is not to receive validation from the reader. Mair's case needed to receive validation from the reader; Mair made his case to prompt the reader's assent. Toledo, however, was simply interested in guiding his readers. Unlike Mair, he had nothing to prove. Toledo's *Summa casuum conscientiae* is divided into seven books: priesthood; the administration of the sacraments; the practice of confession; the first three commandments; the remaining seven; the six precepts of the Church; and matrimony.

The first book answered the question "What is a priest?" Toledo underlined the unique dignity of priests and the heavy responsibilities expected from those acting on God's commission. He began, therefore, with a definition that he subsequently parsed throughout the first chapter: a priest is a man commissioned by divine authority communicated through specific persons for the true worship of God.[15]

Toledo was concerned with power: by power, the priest is ordained; through power, priests exercise their ministry. In chapter 3, he discussed the twofold power of the priesthood: orders and jurisdiction. The former was the power to confect the body of Christ and to administer the other sacraments. The latter was the power of rendering judgment on the excommunicated, granting dispensations, conferring indulgences, and applying the laws of the Church.[16] The second book was on the sacramental ministry of the priest, with similar concerns for power and its right exercise. By this point, Toledo had established the seriousness of the priestly vocation, and priests reading this work would probably have been overwhelmed by the onerous responsibility of their vocation. Still, they would want to read further to find the directions about how to exercise wisely and prudently the power that they have. Rather quickly, Toledo established that he was a man of great authority who was willing to share his wisdom in mentoring fellow priests.

Toledo developed a significant agenda: priesthood was effectively an institutional position to determine the law and to administer the sacraments. Paramount among the latter was the power to absolve in the sacrament of penance.[17] No other sacrament or task scrutinized the complex personal matter of human conduct; no other sacrament or task so definitively relied on the particular skills and judgment of priests; and no other sacrament or task so directly related to the salvation of an individual soul. In sum, no other divine action was so vulnerable to the fallibility of human judgment as absolution, and yet no other divine activity was as significant as that which absolved a person from eternal damnation.

Like his contemporaries, Toledo added a new feature to the confessional: by focusing the matter of sin on decidedly institutional concerns, he outlined which social structures were morally permitted and which were sinful. He brought the world of commerce under the jurisdiction of the confessional.

In simply counting the number of folios dedicated to each commandment, it was the seventh that was the most considered. While nineteen folios were devoted to the Fifth Commandment and its exceptions, eighteen to the Fourth Commandment, and a mere twelve to the Sixth Commandment, eighty-eight folios focused on the Seventh Commandment, where he discussed usury and related matters. Similarly, the Eighth Commandment was the subject of thirty-one folios, and the Ninth Commandment of a surprising thirty-five folios. Furthermore, Toledo's evident lack of interest in sexual matters is reiterated in his dismissal of the Tenth Commandment by simply stating that it was treated under the sixth.[18]

Under the Seventh Commandment, Toledo examined the fundamental structures of financial institutions. Rather than being about simple personal or even private acts of theft, lying, or concupiscence, the subject matter was the structures of relationships in civil and ecclesiastical societies. After an introduction, he spent eleven chapters (17–27) on restitution, that is, the social repair of an act of theft. Then he turned to usury and stipulated five conditions without which an action was not usury.[19] After four chapters (28–31) on usury, he discussed mutual compensation for loans (*lucrum in mutuo*) in three chapters (32–34), restitution of gains accrued from usury in three chapters (35–37), and the innovative public pawnshops-turned-commercial banks (*De monte pietatis*) in four chapters (38–41). His longest section (chapters 42–49) was dedicated to annuities (*census*), and he concluded his comments on the Seventh

Commandment with a discussion on credit agencies (*cambium*) (chapters 50–55).

After these chapters, the Eighth Commandment addressed the duties in a court of law. A chapter was dedicated to each of the different functionaries in the court: the accused, the state, witnesses, advocates, notaries, and procurators. The final chapters were about what would constitute detraction. Though Toledo described the Ninth Commandment as the social impact of avarice,[20] it was actually about the financial responsibilities of ecclesiastics. After extensive comments (chapters 72–75) on stipends, he turned to six chapters (76–81) on benefices. Here, as elsewhere, he explained what specifically was prohibited. He concluded the fifth book with two chapters (82–83) on pensions and ten (84–93) on simony.

Toledo's work is a summary of already resolved cases of conscience. Stringing those summaries together allowed Toledo's readers to appreciate important distinctions between the permitted and the prohibited. Then, Toledo presented ground rules, new categories, and clearly drawn lines. These became laws, and their deductive applications were made in a decidedly self-conscious institutional context. These were not demonstrative acts of moral argumentation reasoning. The powerful Toledo had nothing to prove. Unlike Mair, he was not making "new" headway.

Jonsen, Toulmin, and others differentiate the inductive or "high" casuistry of the early sixteenth century from the later deductive or "low" casuistry of the case summaries or moral manuals, of which Toledo's is among the first. The former was innovative and depended upon creating analogies between one case and another. The latter are applications of principles to cases; they are more explications than they are arguments.[21] Albert Jonsen explains that there are three phases to high casuistry: first, a morphological dissection of the circumstances and maxims in conflict in a case; then a taxonomy to line up the cases to search for congruence among them; finally, there is the kinetic that develops emerging insights and articulates them into rules.[22] All three were in place in Mair's presentation, but in Toledo, we see only the conclusion of the entire casuistic process, the so-called kinetic phase (that is, its summaries). Within those summaries, we find occasional explications that we can call an application of a principle to a case, or what today we call low casuistry.

Mair's age was marked by innovation. The fifteenth and early sixteenth centuries allowed moralists to explore major economic questions from maritime insurance and triple contracts to stipends and benefices. Toledo's voluminous summa is a testimony, however, to how many of these discussions became settled, institutionalized, and standardized.

This move from innovative casuistry to institutionalized norms appears in all the areas of moral theology in the sixteenth century. On the topic of abortion, for instance, Antoninus of Florence (1389–1459) endorsed a position held by John of Naples (dates unknown) regarding a therapeutic abortion of an early

or unformed fetus. Antoninus's stance unleashed an important casuistic debate about the legitimate grounds and means for what constituted a therapeutic
abortion of a not yet formed fetus. In 1588, Sixtus V introduced *Effraenatam*,
which excommunicated anyone involved in an abortion, and by 1591, Gregory
XIV had modified it to apply the penalty to the abortion of a formed fetus. This
remained the standard position for another 300 years, and theological debate
focused solely on the legitimacy of Antoninus's exception.

Regarding sexuality, we find before Trent the question of "parvity" or light-
ness of matter, which asked whether every sexual action that was not an intended procreative act with one's spouse was always mortally sinful. Besides
John Mair and Martin of Azplicueta, Martin the Master (1432–1482) was among
those casuists who entertained such cases of parvity and promoted the legitimacy of such exceptions (see Vereecke). By 1612, however, the Superior General
of the Society of Jesus (the Jesuits) condemned the position that excused from
mortal sin some slight pleasure in deliberately sought venereal desires. Not
only did he bind Jesuits to obey the teaching under pain of excommunication,
he also imposed on them the obligation to reveal the names of those Jesuits
who violated even the spirit of the decree (Boyle, 14–16). These and other
sanctions dissuaded moralists from entertaining any of the circumstantial exceptions as earlier casuists had.[23]

The theological mentality that followed Trent, therefore, convinced many
that ending debate, establishing standards, and writing summas, rather than
doing high casuistry, was the right way to proceed. Above all, the spirit of Trent
prompted the Church to its course of standardization. As time passed, the
Church would claim its newly established norms on each of the commandments as universal and, in time, as ones that "the Church had always taught."

Moral theology needed, however, new instruments to navigate between the
certainly prohibited and the probably safe. At this time, then, moral theology
possessed not only specific moral norms such as those from Toledo, but also
a variety of methodological principles, such as toleration, cooperation, and double effect, that were first articulated in the second half of the sixteenth century.
For instance, though Joseph Mangan argued that Thomas Aquinas first articulated the principle of double effect,[24] Josef Ghoos proved otherwise.[25] Ghoos
showed that the moral solutions from the thirteenth century through the sixteenth century were of isolated concrete cases. In the sixteenth century, Bar-
tolomeo Medina (1528–1580) and Gabriel Vasquez (1551–1604) began to name
the common factors among relevant cases. Finally, John of St. Thomas (1589–
1644) articulated the factors into the conditions of the principle as such.

At the end of the sixteenth century, moral theologians had developed summaries of cases by first studying the original cases "morphologically," then
setting them into related categories "taxonomically," and finally articulating
them "kinetically." They arrived at the newly minted principles in the same
way: by considering cases of actions with two effects, or those requiring simple

toleration or more complex actions of legitimate cooperation. These principles gave moralists a flexibility with the small number of instances that were not yet settled. Though much had been determined in the summaries, the theologians anticipated yet unnamed circumstances that could place the summaries into doubt. Thus, by offering the methodological principles, they left us tools to resolve any doubt raised by the circumstances.

These manualists who applied moral principles were not like John Mairs, looking, as Amerigo Vespucci had, for new lands to explore. Rather, they were careful escorts across the terrain of already discovered landmasses riddled with sinful actions. The authoritative moral theologian was able to guide others by sanctioning an indirect intention or indirect action, so as to avoid an already known morally evil action.

Trent ended the speculation that moralists such as Mair and Azplicueta produced, and endorsed a mentality that accepted the summaries of cases as everlasting norms. Moreover, for anything still undefined, methodological principles were in place to guarantee that no new norms needed to be articulated. Trent left as its moral legacy these textbooks that secured as everlasting the indisputably settled norms regarding moral conduct and the more flexible principles that described other actions by what they were not: for example, an indirect abortion, passive euthanasia, an unprovoked ejaculation, or an indirect attack on civilian populations. In this way they left moralists with norms to apply and, when in doubt, methodological principles to resolve the question. In either case, the application was always done deductively. There was no need for the inductive logic from the fifteenth and early sixteenth centuries. No wonder, then, that for almost four centuries Catholics were fascinated with the principle of double effect. They had nothing else with which to work.

Before and after Vatican II

The first English summary of cases, or moral manual, was *A Manual of Moral Theology* (1906) by Thomas Slater (1855–1928). In the preface, Slater acknowledged that other manuals had already appeared in German, Italian, Spanish, and French, and asserted that moral theology's singular and exclusive preoccupation was with sin. By focusing on sin, he affirmed that there was no need for moral theology to engage spiritual or ascetical theology, that is, a theology that supported and encouraged the spiritual betterment of oneself. He wrote:

> [Moral theology] is the product of centuries of labor bestowed by
> able and holy men on the practical problems of Christian ethics.
> Here, however, we must ask the reader to bear in mind that the
> manuals of moral theology are technical works intended to help the
> confessor and the parish priest in the discharge of their duties. They

are as technical as the textbooks of the lawyer and the doctor. They are not intended for edification, nor do they hold up a high ideal of Christian perfection for the imitation of the faithful. They deal with what is of obligation under pain of sin; they are books of moral pathology.

Slater noted the "very abundant" literature of ascetical theology, but added that "moral theology proposes to itself the much humbler but still necessary task of defining what is right and what wrong in all the practical relations of the Christian life. . . . The first step on the right road of conduct is to avoid evil."[26] The notion of moral truth as simply an evil to be avoided—rather than also a good to be pursued—predominated throughout the moral manuals from Toledo's to Slater's.

Two features of the manuals were particularly noteworthy. First, tolerance was an institutional virtue for the manualists. Although they asserted long-held norms as universal and eternal, still, by considering newly admitted cases and their circumstances, and by applying the methodological principles to an evaluation of these cases, they considered their specific judgments as simply prudential. They would claim that in many instances other manualists arrived at different judgments. These differences were not simply accidental; they were constitutive of the manualist method. Moreover, there were schools within the manualist tradition, often drawn across the lines of religious orders, notably the Dominicans, Jesuits, and Redemptorists, although other orders and the secular clergy had their preferred manualists as well. A certain "gentlemen's agreement" existed in which manualists, while not endorsing another's writings, certainly rarely attacked or, worse, denied another's claims to teach. Second, there was some development in this tradition. The application of principles to newly emerging cases eventually led to the development of new understanding of the principles themselves.[27]

By the mid-twentieth century, however, many moral theologians began to abandon manualism and embraced a new integrated relationship with ascetical or spiritual theology. From the 1920s through the 1950s, three major figures insisted on looking for moral truth not in determinations about acts of sin but as an essential part of the context of faith: a Benedictine, Dom Odon Lottin; a diocesan priest, Fritz Tillman; and a Jesuit, Gérard Gilleman. These and others claimed that moral truth was not realized as much in solitary external actions as in overarching internal personal dispositions. Moreover, integral to this claim was the belief that moral truth was not found primarily in negative principles—about what was to be avoided—but rather in the person who pursued the good. The locus of moral truth began to change, therefore. At the beginning of the century, moral truth was found in the long-held norms and, analogously, in their application by moral theologians. By century's end, moral truth was found in the lives of active Christians.

What happened, then, to the norms and to the moral theologian's particular judgments? They became "premoral," that is, the norms and their applications were no longer considered the final word on specific moral topics but,
rather, one of the objects worthy of consideration *before* moral agents expressed
moral truth in their particular lives. This shift from moral truth in norms to
its expression in the lives of conscientious Christians took 100 years to attain.
Yet, throughout the entire change, moral theology remained true to its vocation,
that is, to the search for moral truth in an ecclesial context.

This more positive, interior, and integrated direction for finding moral
truth was of extraordinary moment. A look at Gilleman's contribution helps
to highlight the nature of this innovation. In his work on charity,[28] Gilleman
provided a counterpoint to the manualists' occupation with external sin-actions
by studying the importance of the most internal and gracious of all virtues,
charity. He did this by studying the *Summa theologiae* of Aquinas in light of
the work of Émile Mersch. In three successive works, Mersch examined the
mystical body of Christ: first through historical investigations, then its relevance for morality, and finally, its own theological significance.[29] Gilleman
found compelling grounds in Mersch for identifying the Christian with the
filial self-understanding of Jesus, the Son of God. In that self-understanding,
Gilleman found charity that establishes our union with God.

Moral theology's congruence with ascetical theology became apparent. The
reunion of the former, identified by the manualists as the avoidance of evil,
with the latter's interest in the personal pursuit of the good reintegrated the
first principle of the natural law—to do good and avoid evil—under one discipline. This was a remarkable departure from Thomas Slater's manual or
Toledo's summary. Now moral theology studied moral truth primarily in the
deeper reality of being human and living humanly, rather than in norms prohibiting solitary, specific, external actions. This shift restored to moral theology
the very dynamism that makes the task of searching for moral truth so fruitful.
Gilleman writes, "The task of Christian morality and of asceticism which is
intimately linked to it, is to render the intention and exercise of charity in us
always more and more explicit."[30]

The turn to human interiority led to an understanding of moral truth as
needing to be realized in the human being. By 1960, moral truth was no longer
propositional, but rather ontological. An illustration of this change is found in
Sacramentum mundi's entry "Truthfulness."

> Truth is defined primarily as ontological, the basic intelligibility of
> things, with God as the First Truth. Further, God is held to be know-
> able but incomprehensible, while man is understood as a being cre-
> ated in order to know and love God, who finds therefore his true
> self in being blessed by God and giving himself to God. The main
> task of an ethics of truth is then to remain as absolutely open as

possible for the truth in whatever guise man encounters it, and to unconditionally follow out the known truth in action. The ethics of truth will mainly take the form of an ethics of the disposition, insisting on the formal attitude. Hence an ethics of truth cannot do without reflection on one's personal consciousness and its implications.[31]

As moral theologians turned to the person to find moral truth, the hierarchy, particularly in Rome, began to appropriate the methodology of the manualists that contemporary theologians were repudiating. Like the manualists, Popes and bishops believed that moral truth was found in norms and principles. While moral theologians were searching for truth-to-be-realized in the lives of Christians, hierarchical leaders were still thinking of truth as propositional, since this is what they had learned from their manualist teachers in seminary days. Furthermore, Popes and bishops began to consider themselves as competent in moral matters. At first, they commented on social issues, speaking as social ethicists would, but by the papacy of Pius XII, Popes and bishops were writing about birth control, abortion, pain relief, life support, ectopic pregnancies, and a host of other issues.

Likewise, they began to assert the claim that consistency was a constitutive guarantor of the truthfulness of their claims and began to preserve their own teachings as normative by updating and commenting on them. Progressively, throughout the century, Popes, bishops, and curial officials promulgated moral teachings in a variety of fields: fundamental, medical, sexual, and social ethics. Like the moral manuals that were commentaries on earlier important manualists' summaries, Church documents became updated commentaries on predecessors' utterances. Thus, a central feature of any contemporary papal or episcopal document is the frequent citation of previous teaching moments by such authorities. The same self-generating and self-validating practices that the manualists used for three centuries became the tools of twentieth-century Popes and bishops. The positivism that emerged from the manualists likewise emanated from these documents—David Kelly calls it an "ecclesiastical positivism."[32]

When the manuals were the authority for moral truth from Trent through the mid-twentieth century, papal, episcopal, and curial offices generally responded to any petitions regarding newly admitted circumstantial questions by directing petitioners to the judgments of "approved" manualists. But with the repudiation of the manuals by moralists themselves, papal, episcopal, and curial offices began giving their own answers, and along the way, with the exception of certain social statements, most of these judgments were, not surprisingly, about actions to be avoided.

Other episcopal leaders also looked less to their own moral theologians and with greater frequency turned to the very office that appointed them to their positions. By the end of the twentieth century, bishops saw the Pope and his curial officials as competent to decide moral matters. Not surprisingly, just as for three centuries moral truth had been identified in this context with the utterances of the manualists, so in the twentieth century, with this emerging papal magisterium, moral truth became identified with papal and episcopal utterances.[33]

These papal teachings enjoy evident similarities with the manualists' work, but they depart from the manualist tradition in four significant ways: there are no diverse viewpoints nor a constitutive structural tolerance; the Popes and curial bishops are usually not trained in moral theology; local pastors earlier had the freedom to choose from among the manualists, but pastors today have no such choice about these new papal, curial, and episcopal magisteria; and, finally, moral manualists were never guardians of the Church's identity, and therefore did not confuse the need for a community's historical identity with the need to determine their own moral claims as truthful.[34]

In light of these differences, Popes and bishops assumed a competence from their self-understanding of themselves as guarantors of the moral truth of the communities that they shepherded. Inevitably, the statements of Popes, bishops, and curial officials reflected the judgment of someone who knows moral theology only to the extent that he has allowed himself to be influenced by the consultants whose service he necessarily solicits. Much here depends on whether the bishop chooses those with adequate competence, who can understand and express professionally and fairly the viewpoints of his colleagues. The fact that many continue to follow a method based on the belief that moral truth is found in utterances about external actions, and often derive "expert" advice from those considerably at odds with recent developments in moral theology, suggests that for all the goodwill in the world, a fair understanding of the claims of most contemporary moral theologians is nearly impossible. The promulgation and reception of *Veritatis splendor* highlights, for instance, this painful inability to achieve mutual understanding.[35]

The moral theologians' critical abandonment of the method of the manualists and the papal, episcopal, and curial decisions to replace the manualists has had an extraordinary effect. The scientific research of moral theologians— that is, their continuous search for critical moral truth—goes on in the precincts of their own investigations: in their classrooms, their publications, and their conferences. But in an entirely different way, Church teaching emerges more interested in order and uniformity than in critique and diversity, more interested in consistency and universality than in the contextual questions, more willing to suppress legitimate moral beliefs, differences, and exceptions for the sake of identity.

Moral teaching is presently taking place and developing on two different tracks. One pursues moral truth in the person of Christ as to be realized in the very human lives of Christians; the other, in specific and (possibly) long-held propositional utterances. The gulf between these two tracks widens. For instance, those who advise magisterial authority participate less frequently in professional conferences of moral theologians, at which most moral theologians present their research for scientific critique. They are instead more at the disposition of those officials who rely on their judgments not only to write statements of instruction, but also to review, to estimate, and, if they deem it necessary, to censure the work of contemporary moral theologians.

To highlight these two tracks, we can look at the intellectual conversion of one of the major figures of twentieth-century moral theology, Josef Fuchs. Fuchs was appointed by Pope Paul VI to the commission studying the Church's teaching on birth control (of which Bernard Häring was also a member). Purportedly because the commission's first meetings tended toward reform of the teaching on birth control, the Pope desired more traditional moral theologians on the commission, among them, Fuchs. On the commission, Fuchs began listening to the testimony of others and abandoned his conviction that moral truth was founded necessarily and primarily on long-held norms.

In Fuchs's own life, we find that the shift of locating truth not in propositions but in persons was not a simple intellectual one. Moral theologians do not come to these convictions in simple meditations. Rather, these convictions arose from seminal experiences. By listening to the testimony of married couples, Fuchs slowly recognized that his original supposition was inadequate, and began to explore critically whether the method of directly applying a norm to a case is also adequate for determining moral truth. If the question were posed to Josef Fuchs in 1952, his answer would have been a resounding yes; by 1968, it was an equally decisive no.[36]

Fuchs's conversion became an important impetus for others. Fuchs became the draftsman of the report that represented the views of fifteen of the nineteen theologians on the commission.[37] This report recognized that moral truth regarding birth control could be articulated only by those married persons who in conscience need to determine whether the serious issue of birth control ought to be a means toward realizing themselves as responsible parents. In presenting the report, Fuchs explained that the locus for finding moral truth had shifted from utterances to persons: "Many confuse objective morality with the prescriptions of the Church. . . . We have to realize that reality is what is. And we grow to understand it with our reason, aided by law. We have to educate people to assume responsibility and not just to follow the law."[38]

Later the commission's governing group of cardinals and bishops asked Fuchs why he had changed his entire understanding of moral decision-making. He responded by narrating his own doubts arising in 1963; how he stopped teaching for a year (1965–1966) at the Gregorian University because he could not take responsibility for teaching a doctrine he did not accept; and how in 1965 he ordered the university press not to reprint his work *De castitate*.[39] In light of his answers, the episcopal committee voted first on whether contraception is an intrinsic evil (nine, no; three, yes; three, abstentions), then appropriated and formally approved the majority report that he wrote for the theologians.[40]

The majority report was later rejected by Pope Paul VI, who contended, in *Humanae vitae* (para. 6), that "certain approaches and criteria for a solution to this question had emerged which were at variance with the moral doctrines on marriage constantly taught by the Magisterium of the Church." With *Humanae vitae*, we see, then, the first significant papal endorsement of moral manualism after Vatican II and, concurrently, an implicit rejection of the moral theologians' approach.

With its publication, an inevitable collision between the two approaches to moral theology arose. Previously, proponents from one track did not deny the others' right to teach, but with the encyclical, the Pope claimed that the consciences of all the faithful must adhere to the continuous teaching of an utterance defined as universally, and absolutely, morally true. In 1983 Fuchs provided some commentary on this phenomenon.

> Since the Council of Trent, but especially in the last century, a strong juridical understanding of the magisterium as "demanding assent," has become central; this was not so earlier. According to this understanding, the moral theologians' task should be understood primarily and extensively as the scholarly reflection and confirmation of already existing magisterial directives in moral questions. This is how it is expressed above all in Pius XII's encyclical *Humani Generis* (1950). Even today, this understanding is widespread although the Second Vatican Council began to shift the emphasis by its reference to the whole People of God as bearer of the Holy Spirit.[41]

Fuchs's concern was that the neomanualism of the magisterium lacked the tolerance and diversity of even the manualists themselves, and inhibited the Christian conscience and, thereby, moral truth. He stipulated four particular dangers. First, the tendency to positivism that "can hinder the research of moral theology as well as the living process of the establishment of moral truth. This process is never definitively finished." The second danger was the encouragement of the belief that we encounter God's instructions, made known through positive revelation, in concrete moral directives. Third was a "cramping or narrowing of moral-theological reflection." Finally, "the situation sketched here is apt to promote a permanent 'moral immaturity' in the establishment of moral truth (in L. Kohlberg's sense), or the formation of 'superegos' in Freud's sense—as one may observe in lay people, priests, moral theologians, and bishops."[42]

Fuchs's assessment in 1983 captures our experience of moral theology today, more than twenty years later and more than forty years since the Second

Vatican Council. The revisionism by moral theologians of their own tradition in light of the reforms that were expressed before Vatican II were repudiated by the restorationists, especially in the last quarter of the twentieth century. This situation remains the same in the first decade of the new millennium.

In conclusion, we are able to see in the sixteenth century how moral theology evolved from the innovative high casuistry at the beginning of the century to the fixed and settled judgments at the end of the century that were embodied in a sophisticated textbook mentality. In time, this mentality endowed these judgments with peculiar transhistorical claims. In the beginning of the twentieth century, we find moral theologians progressively abandoning this method in favor of a more person-centered approach. By the end of Vatican II, the hierarchy had begun to reject the revisionism of the moral theologians and develop a method that bears some resemblance to the case summaries after Trent. Still, in fairness to Toledo and his constituents, this newer method in moral theology lacks the robust epistemological features that gave the case summaries a 400-year-long legacy.

NOTES

1. James Farge, *Biographical Register of Paris Doctors of Theology 1500–1536* (Toronto: Pontifical Institute of Mediaeval Studies, 1980).

2. J. H. Burns, "New Light on John Major," *The Innes Review* 5 (1954): 83–101; John Durkan, "John Major: After 400 Years," *The Innes Review* 1 (1950): 131–157; Aeneas Mackay, *Memoir of John Major of Haddington* (Edinburgh: Edinburgh University Press, 1892); Thomas Torrance, "La Philosophie et la théologie de Jean Mair ou Major (1469–1550)," *Archives de philosophie* 32 (1969): 531–547. On experience, Mair argues against Augustine and Huguccio; see John Thomas Noonan, *Contraception: A History of Its Treatment by the Catholic Theologians and Canonists* (Cambridge, Mass.: Harvard University Press, 1965), 310–322; Louis Vereecke, "Mariage et plaisir sexuel chez les théologiens de l'époque moderne (1300–1789)," *Studia moralia* 18 (1980): 245–266, and "Mariage et sexualité au déclin du Moyen-Âge," *La Vie spirituelle* 57 (supp.) (1961): 199–225.

3. In a variety of places, Martin Stone has considered the scholastic contribution to casuistry: "The Origins of Probabilism in Late Scholastic Thought," *Recherches de théologie et philosophie médiévales* 67 (2000): 114–157; "Theology, Philosophy and 'Science' in the Thirteenth Century," in *The Proper Ambition of Science*, edited by M. Stone and J. Wolff (London: Routledge, 2000), 28–55; *The Subtle Arts of Casuistry: An Essay in the History of Moral Philosophy* (Oxford: Oxford University Press, 2000). See also James F. Keenan, "The Return of Casuistry," *Theological Studies* 57 (1996): 123–129; and "Casuistry," in *Oxford Encyclopedia of the Reformation*, 4 vols., edited by H. Hillerbrand (New York: Oxford University Press, 1996), vol. 1, 272–274.

4. From Mair's *Commentary of the Fourth Book of the Sentences*, quoted in Durkan, "John Major," 135.

5. On his case regarding *cambium bursae*, see James F. Keenan, "The Casuistry of John Major, Nominalist Professor of Paris (1506–1531)," in *The Context of Casuistry,*

ed. James F. Keenan and Thomas Shannon (Washington, D.C.: Georgetown University Press, 1995), 85–102 (hereafter *Context*). See also Mair, *Commentary*, dist. 15, q. 36, fol. CVII. The case and its analysis appear in Louis Vereecke, "La Licéité du cambium bursae chez Jean Mair (1469–1550)," *Revue historique de droit français et étranger* 30 (1952): 124–138.

6. The translation is from John Thomas Noonan, *The Scholastic Analysis of Usury* (Cambridge, Mass.: Harvard University Press, 1957), 137.

7. Mair, *Commentary*, dist. 15, q. 31, case 15, fol. CIII. An analysis appears in Louis Vereecke, "L'Assurance maritime chez les théologiens des XVe et XVIe siècles," *Studia moralia* 8 (1970): 347–385.

8. Albert Jonsen and Stephen Toulmin, *The Abuse of Casuistry: A History of Moral Reasoning* (Berkeley: University of California Press, 1988), 252; Yves Congar discusses the authority derived from the *quod* (the argument itself) and the *quo* (the authority figure who articulates the argument) in his important article "A Brief History of the Forms of the Magisterium and Its Relations with Scholars," in *Readings in Moral Theology*, no. 3, *The Magisterium and Morality*, ed. Charles Curran and Richard McCormick (New York: Paulist Press, 1982), 314–331.

9. Francisco de Toledo, *Summa casuum conscientiae sive De instructione sacerdotum, libri septem* (Konstanz: Nicolaus Kalt, 1600).

10. See James F. Keenan, "The Birth of Jesuit Casuistry: *Summa casuum conscientiae, sive De instructione sacerdotum, libri septem* by Francesco de Toledo (1532–1596)," in *The Mercurian Project: Forming Jesuit Culture, 1573–1580*, ed. Thomas McCoog (Rome: Institutum Historicum Societatis Iesu, 2004), 461–482.

11. John O'Malley, *The First Jesuits* (Cambridge: Harvard University Press, 1993), 147.

12. Giancarlo Angelozzi, "L'insegnamento dei Casi di Coscienza nella pratica educativa della Compagnia di Gesù," in *La "ratio studiorum": Modelli culturali e pratiche educative dei Gesuiti in Italia tra Cinque e Seicento*, ed. Gian Carlo Brizzi (Rome: Bulzoni, 1981), 121–162.

13. Feliciano Cereceda, "Tolet, François," in *Dictionnaire de théologie catholique*, edited by Bernard Loth and Albert Michel (Paris: Letouzey et Ané, 1953–1972), vol. 15, 1223–1225; "En el cuarto centenario del nacimiento del P. Francisco Toledo," *Estudios eclesiásticos* 13 (1934): 90–108.

14. See James F. Keenan, "Was William Perkins' *Whole Treatise of Cases of Consciences* Casuistry?: Hermeneutics and British Practical Divinity," in *Contexts of Conscience in Early Modern Europe: 1500–1700*, ed. Harald E. Braun and Edward Vallance (New York: Palgrave, 2004), 17–31.

15. Toledo, *Summa*, fol. 1.

16. Ibid., fol. 5.

17. Thomas Tentler, *Sin and Confession on the Eve of the Reformation* (Princeton, N.J.: Princeton University Press, 1977). On the evolution of casuistry and the institution of confession, see Miriam Turrini, *La coscienza e le leggi: Morale e diritto nei testi per la confessione della prima età moderna* (Bologna: Il Mulino, 1991).

18. Toledo, *Summa*, fol. 463

19. Ibid., fol. 344.

20. Ibid., fol. 428.

21. On the two forms of casuistry see James F. Keenan, "Applying the Seventeenth Century Casuistry of Accommodation to HIV Prevention," *Theological Studies* 60 (1999): 492–512. On the development of the tradition of these summaries, see John Thomas Noonan, "Development in Moral Doctrine," in *Context,* 188–204; Thomas Kopfensteiner, "Science, Metaphor and Moral Casuistry," in *Context,* 207–220.

22. Albert Jonsen, "The Confessor as Experienced Physician: Casuistry and Clinical Ethics," in *Religious Methods and Resources in Bioethics,* ed. P. F. Camenisch (Dordrecht: Kluwer Academics, 1994).

23. On the history of the Church's teaching on sexuality, see James F. Keenan, "Catholicism, History," in *Sex from Plato to Paglia: A Philosophical Encyclopedia,* ed. Alan Soble, 2 vols. (Westport, Conn.: Greenwood Press, 2005).

24. Joseph Mangan, "An Historical Analysis of the Principle of Double Effect," *Theological Studies* 10 (1949): 41–61.

25. Josef Ghoos, "L'Acte à double effet: Étude de théologie positive," *Ephemerides theologicae lovanienses* 27 (1951): 30–52. See James F. Keenan, "The Function of the Principle of Double Effect?" *Theological Studies* 54 (1993): 294–315.

26. Thomas Slater, *A Manual of Moral Theology,* 2nd ed., 2 vols. (New York: Benziger Brothers, 1908), vol. 1, 5–6.

27. Noonan, "Development in Moral Doctrine"; Kopfensteiner, "Science, Metaphor and Moral Casuistry"; Raphael Gallagher, "Catholic Medical Ethics: A Tradition Which Progresses," in *Catholic Ethicists on HIV/AIDS Prevention,* ed. James F. Keenan (New York: Continuum, 2000), 271–281.

28. Gérard Gilleman, *Le Primat de la charité en théologie morale* (Louvain: Nauwelaerts, 1952).

29. Émile Mersch, *Le Corps mystique du Christ: Études de théologie historique* (Brussels: Desclée de Brouwer, 1936); *Morale et corps mystique* (1937); *La Théologie du corps mystique,* 2 vols. (Paris: Desclées de Brouwer, 1944).

30. Gérard Gilleman, *The Primacy of Charity in Moral Theology,* trans. William F. Ryan and André Vachon (Westminster, Md.: Newman Press, 1959), 82.

31. Waldemar Molinski, "Truthfulness," in *Sacramentum Mundi: An Encyclopedia of Theology,* ed. Karl Rahner et al. (New York: Herder & Herder, 1970), 313–318, at 313.

32. David Kelly, *The Emergence of Roman Catholic Medical Ethics in North America* (New York: Edwin Mellen Press, 1979), 230.

33. See Peter Black and James F. Keenan, "The Evolving Self-understanding of the Moral Theologian: 1900–2000," *Studia moralia* 39 (2001): 291–327.

34. Brian Johnstone raises this distinction in "Can Tradition Be a Source of Moral Truth? A Reply to Karl-Wilhelm Merks," *Studia moralia* 37 (1999): 431–451.

35. See, for instance, some of the reactions to *Veritatis splendor:* George Cottier, "Una lettura della Veritatis Splendor," *Rassegna di teologia* 34 (1993): 603–614; Cataldo Zuccaro, "La 'Veritatis Splendor.' Una triplice chiave di lettura," *Rivista di teologia morale* 25 (1993): 567–581; Konrad Hilpert, "Glanz der Wahrheit: Licht und Schatten. Eine Analyse der neuen Moralenzyklika," *Herder Korrespondenz* 47 (1993): 623–630; Dietmar Mieth, ed., *Moraltheologie im Abseits? Antwort auf die Enzyklika "Veritatis Splendor"* (Freiburg: Herder, 1994); Peter Knauer, "Zu Grundbegriffen der Enzyklika 'Veritatis Splendor,'" *Stimmen der Zeit* 212 (1994): 14–26; Joseph Selling and Jan Jans, eds., *The Splendor Accuracy* (Grand Rapidds, Mich.: Eerdmans, 1995); Marciano Vidal,

La propuesta moral de Juan Pablo II. Comentario teológico-moral de la encíclica "Veritatis Splendor" (Madrid: PPC, 1994); Sabatino Majorano, "Il teologo moralista oggi," *Studia moralia* 33 (1995): 21–44; Raphael Gallagher, "The Reception of *Veritatis Splendor* within the Theological Community," *Studia moralia* 33 (1995): 415–435.

36. Mark Graham, *Josef Fuchs on Natural Law* (Washington, D.C.: Georgetown University Press, 2002); James F. Keenan, "Josef Fuchs and the Question of Moral Objectivity in Roman Catholic Ethical Reasoning," *Religious Studies Review* 24, 3 (1998): 253–258.

37. Robert McClory, *Turning Point* (New York: Crossroad, 1995), 98–99.

38. Robert Kaiser, *The Politics of Sex and Religion: A Case History in the Development of Doctrine 1962–1984* (Kansas City, Mo.: Leaven Press, 1985), 154.

39. Ibid., 161.

40. McClory, *Turning Point*, 127.

41. Joseph Fuchs, *Christian Ethics in a Secular Arena* (Washington, D.C.: Georgetown University Press, 1984), 137.

42. Ibid., 138.

10

The Virgin Mary

Lawrence S. Cunningham

The Council of Trent

Anyone minimally acquainted with late medieval and Renaissance art knows that the Catholic world reflected a robust devotion to the Blessed Virgin Mary. She is honored in sculpture, painting, and architecture. The Renaissance Madonna with child is almost a cliché. The devotion to the Blessed Mother, so visually present in the art of the period, has deep roots that go back well before the Middle Ages, into the patristic period. The theological foundations of that devotion, at a minimum, must be grounded in the definition of Mary as God Bearer (Latin: *Deipara*; Greek: *Theotokos*) enunciated at the fifth-century ecumenical council of Ephesus, which met in 431 as a response to the heretical notion, associated with Nestorius, that Mary was only the mother of the human Jesus.

It is equally well known that the Protestant Reformers, first hesitantly with Luther and then more vigorously with the subsequent Reformers, repudiated devotion to the Blessed Virgin as part of their general reaction against what was seen as the heterodox path taken by the old Church. The repudiation comprised not only a doctrinal shift but also a spasm of iconoclasm in which churches were renamed, shrines dismantled, and art erased from the public displays that hitherto had been part of the late medieval cityscape and landscape.

It was inevitable that the reforming Council of Trent would have to take up the issue of the Protestant reaction against the Marian tradition of Catholicism. It is clear from the conciliar documents that this was not a primary concern of the Tridentine reformers, but the Council did reassert the legitimacy of Catholic belief and practice as part of its overall strategy of confronting both the challenge of the Protestant reality and the needs for reform within the body Catholic. The Council of Trent met sporadically from 1545 to 1563. With respect to the Blessed Virgin Mary, it satisfied itself at session 25 in 1563 with asserting that the veneration of Mary and the other saints was a legitimate part of Catholic faith. It insisted, furthermore, that it was proper to display images of Mary and the saints for veneration in churches. It did warn, however, against abuses that may "have crept into these holy and saving practices."[1]

The main concern of the Council of Trent, in this regard, was to combat the iconoclasm of the Reformation as well as its reaction against Marian devotional practices. In the Tridentine Profession of Faith (1564) appended to the Nicene Creed, it made the points enunciated at the Council itself briefly but clearly: "I firmly declare that the images of Christ and of the Mother of God Ever Virgin and of the other saints are to be kept and preserved, and that due honor and veneration should be given to them."[2]

The only other mention of the Blessed Virgin, apart from assertions in the historic creeds that Christ was born of the Virgin Mary, was the statement in its decree on the doctrine of original sin that the Council did not intend "to include in this decree, when it is dealing with original sin, the blessed and immaculate Virgin Mary, the Mother of God. . . ." The Council left open the doctrine of the immaculate conception of Mary (that is, that she was born free of the stain of original sin) because it was still an idea that had not matured enough for final articulation. There would be no declaration on the Immaculate Conception until the nineteenth century.

Mary and the Catholic Reformation

If the Council of Trent satisfied itself with affirming the legitimacy of venerating the Blessed Mother and further stipulated the right use of religious imagery in the context of that veneration, the Catholic reaction to the Reformation tended to highlight devotion to Mary in order to contrast the practices and beliefs of the ancient Church with those of the Reformers. That reaction took several forms.

First, theologians focused on the doctrinal justification for the role of Mary in the plan of salvation. Such discussions typically took place within the context of apologetical and/or polemical works directed against Reformation adversaries. One new element did appear in this period: the development of separate dogmatic treatises devoted solely to the Virgin Mary. The first time that the neologism "Mariology" appeared in the Catholic world was in the title of a treatise written by a Sicilian Jesuit, Nigido Placido (1570–1650), who published a volume titled *Summa Mariologiae* (Palermo, 1602; expanded version, 1613). From the early seventeenth century on, there appeared, with some regularity, volumes dedicated to a doctrinal discussion of Mary. Most of these discussions were indebted to the first serious dogmatic treatise on the Blessed Mother, found in the expansive commentary written by the Jesuit Francis Suarez (1548–1617) on the *Summa* of Saint Thomas Aquinas. Suarez treated the Blessed Virgin in the context of the mystery of Christ in his commentary on questions 27–37 of the third part of Thomas's *Summa*.[3] Similar treatises on Mary, written explicitly as polemical works against the Reformers, were penned by Peter Canisius (died 1597) and the greatest of the Catholic apologists, Robert Bellarmine (died 1621), who studded his apologetic works with defenses of Marian devotion. Other writers, such as the Capuchin Lawrence of Brindisi (died 1619), as Hilda Graef has noted, developed their ideas about Mary less in direct confrontation with Reformation critics and more in the tradition of pre-Reformation piety and practice.[4]

Perhaps the most influential book on the Blessed Mother in the post-Tridentine period was Alphonsus Liguori's *The Glories of Mary*, compiled by the saint over a period of sixteen years. Since its first publication in 1750, it has been republished in innumerable editions, and still may be found in print. It is a sprawling work, studded with quotations from earlier sources and written in a somewhat florid style not uncharacteristic of the baroque period. It is less a doctrinal work and more a compendium of doctrine, devotion, and homiletics. The first part consists of reflections on every line from the medieval hymn "Salve Regina." The second part consists of a series of sermons keyed to the major feasts of the Virgin Mary in the Roman calendar. *The Glories of Mary* carries forward from the medieval period the concept that Jesus rules the Kingdom of God with justice, and Mary tempers that justice with mercy. He emphasizes Mary as mediatrix and advocate, and accepts the notion of Bernard of Clairvaux that all graces come to us through Mary, just as she was the vehicle for the Incarnation itself. Many of the more daring speculations about Mary, characteristic of Marian devotionalism in the modern Church before Vatican II, have their roots in the work of Saint Alphonsus.[5]

Theological and devotional works on Mary were a staple of the Catholic response to the Reformation, but they were not the only weapons in the armory of militant Catholicism. The reforming orders of Catholicism, such as the Jesuits, Franciscans, Capuchins, and Theatines, also fostered devotional practices as a badge of Catholic fidelity. Recitation of the rosary, a devotion that took its modern form in the fifteenth century, became a staple of Catholic practice.[6] Indeed, Pope Pius V attributed the victory of Don Juan of Austria over the Turks at Lepanto in 1571 to the intense recitation of the rosary by Roman confraternities. As a tribute, he extended the feast of the Holy Rosary to the Universal Church and set October 7, the date of the victory, as the commemorative day in the liturgical calendar.

In his history of the Reformation, Diarmaid MacCulloch has argued that the energetic preaching of the cult of Mary was a particular concern of the Catholic Reformation. It served as a marker of Catholic fidelity in the self-identification of those who had not gone over to the Reformed churches. There was a particular emphasis on the revival of Marian shrines as a destination for pilgrims, and lay confraternities dedicated to the Virgin were a prominent feature of Catholic evangelization. By the end of the sixteenth century, once the revival of shrines gained momentum, the cult of Mary was made the chief symbol and agency of Counter-Reformation renewal.[7]

It is also striking that in the Counter-Reformation period new religious communities of men and women under the patronage of Mary were founded. These communities were often instruments of Catholic revivalism, especially in France, where they found inspiration in the highly affective spirituality of the so-called French School of spirituality. Louis-Marie Grignion de Montfort (1673–1716) not only founded a community of priests and brothers for apostolic work but also became famous for his *Treatise on True Devotion to the Blessed Virgin* (sometimes called *The Secret of Mary*), with its emphasis on becoming slaves or servants of Mary. This rococo pious work has had a lasting influence, serving as one of the key texts for the spirituality of the contemporary lay group known as the Legion of Mary, and it also had a particular influence on Pope John Paul II. In the same period, the former Oratorian John Eudes (1601–1680) developed from the popular devotion to the Sacred Heart a further intensification directed toward the heart of Mary. He not only wrote a full liturgical Mass and Divine Office, celebrated for the first time in 1672, honoring the sacred hearts of Jesus and Mary, but also spread that devotion widely. His own religious congregation, the Eudists, founded in 1643, was more formally known as the Company or Society of Jesus and Mary. Both Eudes and de Montfort crystallized Marian ideas already present in the spiritual teachings of the French School—a fertile matrix for the founding of innumerable religious congregations of both men and women in the eighteenth and nineteenth centuries (consider, for example, the Marists, Marianists, and Oblates of Mary Immaculate, among others), as well as the inspiration for many forms of devotionalism characteristic of Catholicism in the pre–Vatican II Church.[8]

The Nineteenth Century

Two conspicuous events characterized the Marian character of Catholicism in the nineteenth century: the definition of the doctrine of the Immaculate Conception by Pope Pius IX in 1854 and the rise of Marian apparitions and subsequent pilgrimage locations, most conspicuously at Lourdes in France. Each of these events will be discussed in order.

Was Mary, the Mother of God, herself sinless, as would befit the bearer of the Son of God? That question had been debated as far back as the patristic period. A strong tradition in the West stated that Mary could not have been exempt from original sin for the simple reason that Jesus Christ died for all people. If Mary had been sinless at her conception, then the salvific work of Christ would not have been total. Resistance to the idea of Mary's immaculate conception had a powerful theological pedigree behind it: the writings of Saints Augustine, Ambrose, Anselm, Bernard of Clairvaux, Bonaventure, and Thomas Aquinas. It was only in the fourteenth century that the suggestion by some, notably the Franciscan John Duns Scotus (died 1308), that Mary could have been saved by the anticipated work of Christ, that the tide in favor of the doctrine began to shift, albeit slowly. Dominican theologians generally were not disposed to the doctrine, and Franciscans, and later the Jesuits, were staunch proponents. Popular piety also favored the idea of Mary as pure and immaculately preserved from the stain of sin. As early as the late seventeenth century, delegations were sent to Rome asking for the definition to be proclaimed as part of Catholic doctrine.

Pope Pius IX decided to inquire of the world's hierarchy about the advisability of defining the doctrine of the Immaculate Conception. Of the more than 600 bishops consulted, the vast majority—543 out of 606—urged the definition. After multiple drafts, the Pope finally made the solemn declaration in the constitution *Ineffabilis Deus* on December 8, 1854: "We declare, pronounce and define that the doctrine which holds that the Blessed Virgin Mary, in the first instant of her conception, by a singular grace and privilege granted by Almighty God, in view of the merits of Jesus Christ, the savior of the human race, was preserved free from all stain of original sin, is a doctrine revealed by God and therefore to be believed firmly and constantly, by all the faithful."[9]

That infallible pronouncement, the first use of papal infallibility in modern times, most likely was partially inspired by the Catholic public's enthusiastic reception of the private revelations of a French nun, Catherine Labouré (1806–1876), in 1830. In 1832, the Archbishop of Paris permitted a medal to be struck (later known as the "Miraculous Medal") that rapidly was distributed in the millions. On the medal were stamped the words "O Mary, *conceived without sin*, pray for us who have recourse to thee" [my emphasis].

After the papal definition of 1854, the doctrine of the Immaculate Conception received a further impetus in Catholic circles when a French peasant teenager, Bernadette Soubirous (1844–1879), reported a series of apparitions of the Virgin Mary, who, among other things, said to the girl (as reported in Bernadette's patois), "I am the Immaculate Conception." After various vicissitudes, the visions were accepted as authentic, and in the latter half of the nineteenth century Lourdes became a national, and then an international, pilgrimage destination. The Lourdes pilgrimage became a strong instrument of the Catholic Church in its struggles with the increasingly secular and anticlerical governments of France. Our Lady of Lourdes became almost iconic as a representation of modern Marian piety with innumerable churches, shrines, and other church agencies placed under her patronage. A feast in honor of Our Lady of Lourdes was common in many dioceses in the late nineteenth century and was inserted into the universal calendar in 1907.[10] In a sense, the definition of the doctrine of the Immaculate Conception followed an old path: certain popular practices, permitted by the Church, led to a desire for clarification in the realm of doctrine. Doctrine, in other words, tended to follow practice, not the other way around.

If Lourdes was the most famous apparition site in the modern period, it was not the only one. Indeed, it is interesting to speculate why there has been such a rash of reported visions of the Blessed Mother, of which Lourdes was only the most conspicuous. In the nineteenth century, there were apparitions reported at LaSalette in 1851 and at Fontmain in 1871. In the twentieth century, the Church recognized three apparition sites out of the many that were reported: Fatima in Portugal in 1917; Beauraing in Belgium in 1932; and Banneux in the same country in the same year. While other reported occurrences have gained a certain local currency—Knock in Ireland and the "weeping Madonna" in the Sicilian city of Siracusa—it has been Lourdes in France and Fatima in Portugal that have gained the greatest number of devotees and the largest encouragement of the Universal Church.[11] Of course, the thirst for such apparitions has not abated in our own day, as the evidence of pilgrimages to, among other sites, Medjugorje in the former Yugoslavia, attests.

The Twentieth Century

The increased interest in Mary in the Roman Catholic Church, reflected both in popular piety and in theological development, reached its high point in the twentieth century with the definition of the Assumption of the Blessed Virgin Mary into heaven, proclaimed by Pope Pius XII on November 1, 1950, in the bull *Munificentissimus Deus,* which promulgated, as part of the Catholic faith, that the Blessed Virgin Mary, having completed her earthly life, was assumed body and soul into heavenly glory. The definition left ambiguous the question of whether Mary died or, as the ancient formulary of the Christian East phrased it, "fell asleep" (in Greek: the *Koimesis* or "falling asleep" or "dormition" of the Virgin). Along with the proclamation of the dogmatic truth of Mary's assumption, the Pope also issued a new Divine Office and a new Mass for the feast, which was to be observed on August 15. The order of the Mass was modified in 1969.

The proclamation of the dogma of the Assumption took place within the context of the celebration of the 1950 Holy Year. Four years later, Pius XII declared 1954, the hundredth anniversary of the dogma of the Immaculate Conception, the Marian Year. In 1957–1958, special observances were held in

Rome to honor the centennial of the apparitions at Lourdes. The same Pope had consecrated the whole world to the Immaculate Heart of Mary during World War II, thus giving an early modern Marian devotion a more solemn cast. Likewise, he dedicated Russia to the Immaculate Heart in 1951, in the midst of the Cold War.

On the eve of the convocation of the Second Vatican Council, then, the Catholic world of Pius XII had a strong Marian character to it, both in official celebrations in Rome and in the vitality of separate branches of theology devoted specifically to the study of Marian themes. In addition, vigorous forms of popular piety, often connected to devotional practices deriving from such popular pilgrimage sites as Lourdes and Fatima, were flourishing. Indeed, in this era it was clear that there were theological and popular pressures to further advance Marian privileges from the status of deeply held devotional formulations to the status of dogma, especially the concept of Mary as the mediatrix of all graces and, beyond that, the idea of Mary as co-redemptrix. Thus, there was intense interest in Marian matters not only at the popular level but also among Mariologists, who both mounted congresses of study and published in scholarly journals available to them.

Despite the vigor of such Marian piety, there were good reasons to worry lest that very zeal might also carry with it some worrying distortions. Such worries, although different theologically, had a variety of aspects that may be reduced to the following fundamental issues:

1. Had the developments in Mariology, an area of theological research of modern provenance as we have already seen, advanced too independently from the larger context of traditional theology?

2. More to the point of the first question, had Mariology become so independent that it had detached itself from the very fundamental roots it should have in the absolute centrality of Christ? Were its methodology and its presuppositions too independent of the larger theological task? Was it positive that Mariology had developed into a separate track in the traditional curriculum of scholastic theology?

3. At a time when ecumenical consciousness was on the rise, did the particular strands of Marian doctrines found only in the Western Church exacerbate rather than conciliate the Roman Catholic tradition with the ancient traditions of Orthodoxy, which had its own well articulated understanding of Mary rooted in the shared truth of Mary as *Theotokos*? The question was all the more urgent when one analyzed trends in Catholic Mariology in the light of Reformation critiques. Such preoccupations, carefully expressed by any number of theologians, form an essential backdrop for the deliberations preparatory to and part of the Second Vatican Council.[12]

Vatican II

In the closest vote recorded during the Second Vatican Council, the assembly in 1963 voted 1,114 to 1,074 *not* to have a separate document on the Blessed Virgin but to incorporate the Council's teaching on Mary into the document on the Church. The records of the Council, and the vote itself, indicate that this discussion was extremely lively, but the majority vote indicated both the fear that a separate schema might give the impression that the Council was teaching new doctrine, which it manifestly did not want to do, and, further, that a separate document might exacerbate tensions between Catholics and the other Christians. Finally, there was the widespread feeling among theologians that theological reflection on Mary needed to be placed within the wider frame-work of the whole of Catholic theology in general, and within the mystery of Christ in particular. The result of that decision was, as is clear in retrospect, that the independent strain of Mariological speculation was brought more closely in line with larger theological themes, with the result that Mary was considered more contextually in the light of the great mysteries of salvation, especially in terms of Christology and ecclesiology, which was the intention of the Council fathers (although not all of them) from the beginning.

It was one thing to place the Council's declaration on Mary within the context of the Dogmatic Constitution on the Church; it was another thing to decide what the chapter would and would not say. The debates, both in the formal sessions and in the various attempts to draft a satisfactory statement, make for fascinating reading, but it was clear that the debates could not be reduced, as is often reported, to a struggle between "maximalist" and "mini-malist" tendencies within the Church. The final statement, incorporated as chapter 8 of the Dogmatic Constitution on the Church, *Lumen gentium*, had as its title "The Blessed Virgin Mary, Mother of God [*Deipara*], in the Mystery of Christ and the Church."[13]

A close reading of that chapter indicates that the Council wanted to sum up the Church's teaching about the Virgin Mary but, as it explicitly noted, it did not intend "to put forward a complete doctrine concerning Mary or of settling questions which have not yet been brought fully to light through the work of theologians" (*Lumen gentium*, VIII.1.54). Later in the same chapter, sensitive to the ecumenical situation, the document insists that devotion to Mary "in no way hinders the direct union of believers with Christ; rather, it fosters that union" (*Lumen gentium*, VIII.3.60). At the same time, the Council warned the faithful to sedulously avoid "both in what they say and in what they do, anything that might lead our separated brothers and sisters or any other people into error concerning the true teaching of the church" (*Lumen gentium*, VIII.4.67).

Notwithstanding all of those cautions, the Council did not diminish its authentic understanding of the role of the Virgin Mary in the unfolding of the plan of salvation. Drawing on sacred Scripture, the liturgy, and the teaching of the Church, the Council insisted that Mary, by her free consent and active participation, held a fundamental role in the plan of salvation. As a contemporary theologian has put it, Mary was not a passive or accidental person in the plan of salvation, but personally cooperated with grace as an active agent in God's plan. Thus, the Council's understanding of Mary was consistent with "the entire understanding of grace underlying the document. This understanding of grace, which appreciates the necessity of human cooperation and agency, enables the council to explain the evangelical and sacramental character of the church as a whole."[14]

In the discussions over the draft of this chapter, much dissension revolved around the use of the term "mediatrix" with reference to Mary. There was real fear by some that its use in such a solemn assembly would amount to a definition by the Council, while those who were supporters of the term, and the doctrinal possibilities implied in the term, urged its use. There were pressures from regional episcopal bodies, as well as from other interested groups, to use the term. The compromise solution, which is reflected in the chapter, was to use the term as a devotional title along with other epithets traditionally ascribed to Mary, with a clarifying note: "Therefore in the church the Blessed Virgin is invoked by the titles of advocate, benefactress, helper, mediatrix. This, however, must be understood in such a way that it takes nothing away from the dignity and power of Christ the one mediator, and adds nothing on to this [Latin: *nihil superaddat*]" (*Lumen gentium*, VIII.3.62).

As the chapter ended, reinforcing a fundamental theme of the entire Constitution on the Church, the Council cast Mary in eschatological terms. It spoke of Mary who stood by the primitive Church with her prayers and who now, with all the angels and saints, is exalted in heaven and intercedes for the entire human race until that point when all are "gathered together in peace and harmony into one people of God to the glory of the most holy and undivided trinity" (*Lumen gentium*, VIII.5.69). This further contextualization of Mary within the communion of saints is reminiscent of the liturgical usage both of the Christian West and of the Christian East.

After Vatican II

It is now more than four decades after the close of the Second Vatican Council. What trajectories can be traced out from the decisions and deliberations of the Council, especially in the light of the judgment of the Council that the Church's reflections on Mary should be located in the larger context of the Church's theological tradition? It is clear, as some feared, that there would be a shift in the Church with respect to devotion to Mary, with a certain waning of some forms of devotionalism, and, as might have been predicted, a certain reaction that would attempt to revive the older devotional models once popular among Catholics. While the pressures to proclaim new Marian doctrines are heard from a very small but vocal minority, such voices do not predominate because, among other things, there is a counterpressure coming from the Church's serious engagement with ecumenical dialogue.

Contemporary thinking about Mary in the Catholic Church makes use of four criteria set out by Pope Paul VI in his apostolic constitution *Marialis cultus*. A recent study sets out those criteria economically:

1. Marian reflection must be set out in the light of contemporary biblical understanding.
2. Such reflection must heed current liturgical renewal and be in conformity with the historic development of the liturgy.
3. Theological reflection must be sensitive to, and supportive of, the conciliar sense of ecumenical thought and practice.
4. Finally, there must be an anthropological sensitivity to the thought and life experiences of people in their cultural situation today.[15]

It is certainly the case that the theological framing of the Blessed Virgin Mary at Vatican II fortuitously resulted in encouraging a spate of studies, conferences, and ecumenical dialogues on the role of Mary in the context of the Christian Gospel. Theologians often note the ecumenical amity within which these exchanges take place and the ecumenical seriousness within which the place of Mary in the larger picture of theology is treated.[16]

It is also the case that the rise of feminist theology in the period after Vatican II has reconceptualized the way we portray Mary in the Christian tradition. Serious efforts have been made to deconstruct the somewhat antiseptic vision of Mary, coming from the imaginations and speculations of celibate males, and to think of Mary in ways more congruous with the aspirations of women today. As the British theologian Sarah Boss has written, the common images of Mary as a woman who bears a baby, nurses him, and protects him from harm have been "recently supplanted in Catholic devotion by images of a prayerful young woman whose body had no ostensible association with maternal functions."[17]

The turn to the more historical reality of Mary as a peasant woman who lived in a colonial culture, bore Jesus in the poorest of circumstances, fled with him to escape oppression, hymned in her own words the poor (in the *Magnificat* of Luke 2), and watched her son die on a cross (Mother of an executed son) has found a particular resonance among feminist theologians who write out of the Latin American context. Indeed, liberation theologians in general have pointed people back to the rich images of *religión popular* in order to recover the strong identification that oppressed people have for the Virgin as protector and liberator. Excellent studies have been done on Our Lady of Guadalupe to show how that Virgin—depicted as an indigenous person—has unified people to the degree that one can speak of *Guadalupismo* as a popular but fundamental strand of Mexican Catholicism.[18]

In a similar vein, inspired by feminist and liberation themes, the North American theologian Elizabeth Johnson has attempted to refocus our attention on Mary not in the vertical language of patroness or intercessor but as sister, thus drawing on resources from a renewed theology of the communion of saints and the solidarity theme found in both feminism and liberation theology. Johnson argues that the memory of Mary is "dangerous" in that she recalls, as we learn of her in the New Testament, a prophetic voice, a strong woman, and one who is in solidarity with the poor.[19] This notion of the dangerous memory of Mary parallels, of course, the famous formulation of Johannes Baptist Metz about the subversive power of the dangerous memory of Jesus.

The development of liberationist, feminist, and other contemporary theological themes has been a trend in post–Vatican II theology, but there has also been a revival of traditional Marian piety largely fostered by the personal example and constant teaching of Pope John Paul II from the beginnings of his pontificate in 1978. In 2003, the twenty-fifth anniversary of his election to the papacy, the Pope designated the year as the year of the rosary. The Pope, it may be recalled, added another set of "mysteries" to the traditional ones that have been called the "luminous" mysteries. They are the baptism of Jesus in the Jordan; Jesus at the wedding feast in Cana; the proclamation of the reign of God; the Transfiguration; and the institution of the Eucharist. That addition may be seen as part of the effort of Pope John Paul II to align the veneration of Mary to the larger picture of the Gospel.

In many of his utterances in 2003 and at other times, the Pope spoke of his desire to contemplate the face of Christ "in the school of Mary." Indeed, he proposed, as a fundamental theme for the new millennium, the contemplation of the face of Christ with Mary. Using a profound line from Luke's Gospel, he asked all the faithful to emulate Mary, who, as Luke puts it, "treasured all these words [i.e., of the shepherds at the Nativity] and pondered them in her heart" (Luke 2:19; see Luke 2:51 for a parallel passage).[20] The Pope applied the Marian trope of "pondering" in the heart to a wide range of topics, from philosophizing in the school of Mary, in *Fides et ratio*, to his somewhat mystical meditation on the relationship of Mary to the Eucharist.[21]

Indeed, it could be said that Pope John Paul's thinking had been profoundly shaped by his intense Marian piety. His motto, *Totus tuus* (Everything Is Yours), is Marian in inspiration. His piety was both very traditional, drawing on baroque devotionalism, and deeply thought out in a manner not unlike that of one of his favorite theologians, the late Hans Urs von Balthasar.[22] Von Balthasar's thesis is that the Church has different profiles: the contemplative profile of the Apostle John; the missionary profile of Saint Paul; a Petrine profile of jurisdiction; and a Marian profile of discipleship. This approach to ecclesiology struck a resonant note in the Pope's thinking that one finds throughout the corpus of his writing and preaching.

Some Trajectories

It is not easy to obtain a full picture of Mary's place in the Roman Catholic Church today. If one were to attempt such a picture, it would be more in the likeness of a mosaic made up of very different tesserae. There is still a strong devotional streak of popular veneration of the Virgin Mary. Traditional pilgrimage sites such as Lourdes and Fatima, to say nothing of Guadalupe in Mexico, still draw large numbers of people.[23] Nor has there been any decline in reported apparitions, which have garnered their own pilgrims and devotees. One piece of the mosaic picture, then, would have to include the fact of popular Marian devotion that takes many and various forms.

Popular devotion itself, however, has gotten a second look from liberationist theologians in particular, who have probed deeply into the motivations behind such popular fervor as well as the solidarity that arises from a people who express both their pain and their hope through devotion to the Virgin. This interest in popular religion has not always received the attention of theologians. While traditional Mariology has tended to work at the level of doctrine and magisterial documents, these newer approaches to the significance and theological riches of popular religion include serious theological reflection illumined by history, sociology, and anthropology.[24]

Roman Catholic theologians have also been in dialogue with other Christian churches to speak about the ecumenical implications of the Roman Catholic emphasis on Marian themes. Those exchanges, as we have seen, have borne fruit as this kind of exchange has progressed. One particular value of this dialogue is a better incorporation of the doctrinal statements about Mary into the larger picture of Christology.[25] Then, there is, of course, the strong Mariological character of the papal teachings that the Church has received over the past generation. While that focus has been a clear and consistent one, it is not clear how much of it has filtered down to the people in the pews or how seriously it has been received in the theological community.

As part of the liturgical reforms following on the Second Vatican Council, January 1 has been designated the Solemnity of the Blessed Virgin Mary, Mother of God. This feast supplanted the older practice of honoring the circumcision of Christ on that day. The liturgical prayers for that day are particularly rich with the authentic piety and doctrine of the Catholic Church. Perhaps it would be appropriate to end this essay with one of the gathering prayers used on this feast, for, as is often the case, the liturgy is capable of expressing the true faith of the Church regarding Mary in a succinct and compelling fashion:

Father,
Source of light in every age,
The Virgin conceived and bore your Son
Who is called Wonderful God, Prince of peace.
May her prayer, the gift of a mother's love,
Be your people's joy through all ages,
May her response, born of a humble heart,
draw your Spirit to rest on your people.
Grant this through Christ Our Lord. Amen.

NOTES

1. All quotations from the ecumenical councils are from Norman Tanner, ed., *Decrees of the Ecumenical Councils*, 2 vols. (Washington, D.C.: Georgetown University Press, 1990). Specific notation will appear in the body of the text.

2. The full text is in Jaroslav Pelikan and Valerie Hotchkiss, eds., *Creeds and Confessions of Faith in the Christian Tradition* (New Haven, Conn.: Yale University Press, 2003), vol. 3, 873–874.

3. See the entry "Mariology," in *Theotokos: A Theological Encyclopedia of the Blessed Virgin Mary*, ed. Michael O'Carroll (Wilmington, Del.: Galzier, 1986), 231–232.

4. Hilda Graef, *Mary: A History of Doctrine and Devotion* (Westminster, Md.: Christian Classics, 1987), vol. 2, 18 and passim for these developments.

5. The context of Alphonsus's writings is brilliantly explored in Frederick M. Jones, *Alphonsus de Liguori: The Saint of Bourbon Naples* (Westminster, Md.: Christian Classics, 1992); for a selection, see *Selected Writings: Alphonsus de Liguori*, ed. Frederick M. Jones (New York: Paulist Press, 1999), 246ff.

6. The most reliable account of the development of the rosary is Anne Winston-Allen's *Stories of the Rose: The Making of the Rosary in the Middle Ages* (University Park: Pennsylvania State University Press, 1997).

7. Diarmaid MacCulloch, *The Reformation: A History* (New York: Viking, 2004), 441.

8. For a survey and some selected texts, see Raymond Deville, *The French School of Spirituality: An Introduction and Reader* (Pittsburgh, Pa.: Duquesne University Press, 1994).

9. A succinct treatment is found in Elizabeth Johnson, "Immaculate Conception," in *HarperCollins Encyclopedia of Catholicism*, ed. Richard McBrien (San Francisco: Harper, 1995), 665–666; for a fuller dogmatic treatment, see Karl Rahner, "The Immaculate Conception," in *Theological Investigations*, trans. Cornelius Ernst, vol. 1 (Baltimore: Helicon, 1966), 201–213.

10. Ruth Harris's *Lourdes: Body and Spirit in the Secular Age* (New York: Viking, 1999) brilliantly shows how the cultivation of devotion to the shrine of Lourdes was a strong apologetic tool for combating the anticlericalism of post-Revolutionary France.

11. On the apparitions, see Sandra Zimdars-Swartz, *Encountering Mary: From LaSalette to Medjugorje* (Princeton, N.J.: Princeton University Press, 1991).

12. Two excellent books attempting to think about Mary in a more restrained

fashion are Karl Rahner, *Mary, Mother of the Lord*, trans. W. J. O'Hara (New York: Herder and Herder, 1963); and Edward Schillebeeckx, *Mary, Mother of the Redemption*, trans. N. D. Smith (London and New York: Sheed & Ward, 1964).

13. A complete discussion of these deliberations may be found in the fourth volume of *History of Vatican II*, ed. Giuseppe Alberigo and Joseph Komonchak (Maryknoll, N.Y.: Orbis, 2003), 52 and passim (see Komonchak's comment, chap. 4, n. 31.). For a briefer consideration, see John J. Markey, *Creating Communion: The Theology of the Constitutions of the Church* (Hyde Park, N.Y.: New City Press, 2003), 78–80.

14. Markey, *Creating Communion*, 79.

15. See the survey, with good bibliography, in Walter Brennan, "Recent Developments in Marian Theology," *New Theology Review* 8, no. 2 (May 1995): 49–58.

16. A few more recent publications include Alain Blancy, Maurice Jourion, and the Dombes Group, *Mary in the Plan of God and in the Communion of Saints*, trans. Matthew J. O'Connell (New York: Paulist Press, 2002), a report of the ecumenical Dombes Group; Beverly Gaventa and Cynthia Rigby, eds., *Blessed One: Protestant Perspectives on Mary* (Louisville Ky.: Westminster/John Knox, 2002); Dwight Longnecker and David Gustafson, *Mary: A Catholic-Evangelical Debate* (Grand Rapids, Mich.: Brazos Press, 2003); Carl Braaten and Robert Jenson, eds., *Mary: Mother of God* (Grand Rapids, Mich.: William Eerdmans, 2004).

17. Sarah Boss, *Empress and Maiden: On Nature and Gender in the Cult of the Virgin Mary* (London and New York: Cassell, 2000), 40.

18. The standard liberationist volume is Ivone Bebara and Maria Clara Bingemer, *Mary: Mother of God, Mother of the Poor* (Maryknoll, N.Y.: Orbis, 1989). On Guadalupe, see Virgil Elizondo, *Guadalupe: Mother of the New Creation* (Maryknoll, N.Y.: Orbis, 1997). From a Protestant perspective, see Max Johnson, *The Virgin of Guadalupe* (Lanham, Md.: Rowman & Littlefield, 2002).

19. Elizabeth A. Johnson, *Truly Our Sister: A Theology of Mary in the Communion of Saints* (New York: Continuum, 2003); Johnson builds on her earlier essay "Mary and the Female Face of God," *Theological Studies* 50, no. 3 (1989): 500–526. For another feminist perspective on Mary, see the intriguing Boss, *Empress and Handmaid*.

20. The Pope's most systematic treatment of the Blessed Mother is in his 1987 encyclical *Redemptoris mater*.

21. See the extended reflections in *Ecclesia de eucharistia* in *Origins* 32, no. 46 (May 1, 2003): nos. 53ff.

22. On the connection, see George Weigel, *Witness to Hope: The Biography of Pope John Paul II* (New York: HarperCollins, 1999), 576–577.

23. For an exhaustive list of Marian shrines in global perspective, with examples not restricted to the First World, see Anthony Chiffolo, *100 Names of Mary: Stories and Prayers* (Cincinnati: St. Anthony Messenger Press, 2002).

24. Maxwell Johnson's *The Virgin of Guadalupe: Theological Reflections of an Anglo-Lutheran Liturgist* (Lanham, Md.: Rowman & Littlefield, 2002) provides an excellent survey of both Roman Catholic and Protestant research, with a valuable bibliography.

25. The conclusions of the Dombes Group (see note 16 above) have been particularly balanced in this assessment.

early Church, in a sense everyone was lay, everyone was one of the People of God (*laikoi*). And when, as inevitably happened, some individuals were distinguished from the rest in virtue of particular charisms or responsibilities (*kleroi*), there was at first no suggestion that this meant levels of power or authority. There were different gifts, but all were understood to flow from the sacrament of baptism. In baptism, the Christian not only entered the Church; through baptism, the individual acquired the responsibilities of mission and witness that went with it. Thus, for example, in the early Church the extent of lay participation in decision-making, or at least in declaring their consent to decisions of the Church, was important and highly developed, whereas today it is nonexistent and would be vigorously opposed by the institutional Church. This role of the laity was replaced by a notion of hierarchy that owed a great deal to the imperial Roman system, and perhaps still more to the hierarchies of Pseudo-Dionysius, in which ranks were signals of gradations in being and in power.

The nature and relationship of the common priesthood of the faithful and the ordained priesthood has been one of the most neglected of teachings in the life of the Church. In virtue of baptism, the whole people are a priestly and prophetic people, called to discipleship to Christ, the servant-leader. In virtue of the Church's ratification of the individual's sense of a divine calling, some are ordained to serve in sacramental ministry as deacons, priests, and bishops. But when the Church adopted the Constantinian/Dionysian understanding of hierarchy, the common priesthood was all but buried under excessive attention to the sacramental priesthood. In consequence, the kinds of corruptions to which the medieval Church became subject, and which became the object of the Reformers' attentions, tended to have their foundation in deficient understandings of ecclesiology in general and the theology of orders in particular.

Despite the critique of priesthood and hierarchy offered by the Reformers, the Council of Trent had little or nothing to say about the role of the laity in the Church, or the nature of the lay state. However, a considerable amount was implied by the Council's words on the sacrament of baptism and on the closely connected question of the nature of priestly orders. In the decrees on baptism, the bishops were responding to Luther's views on the common priesthood of all the faithful. For Luther, there was only one priesthood, shared in by all in virtue of baptism. Thus, baptism and priesthood could not be more closely connected. Ministry is one Christian vocation among others, within the common priesthood. Opposite this view, the Catholic tradition had held that the "sacramental" or "hierarchical" priesthood was a special establishment by Christ himself, a priesthood different in kind, and not only in degree, from the common priesthood, and not reducible to it. Both the power of orders and the power of jurisdiction were thus connected to Christ himself and, in a way, understood as chronologically preceding the formation of the community. Indeed, Yves Congar has argued this very thing precisely in order to protect the teaching that the priesthood was established by Christ himself, though in the end he no longer found it necessary to claim chronological priority for hierarchy over community. But the Church held consistently that, at the very least, hierarchy and priestly orders were understood to be given with the Church, from the moment of its inception, by a special constituting act of Christ himself.

Trent's view of baptism was that it imparts a character or ontological mark to the soul, which makes it unrepeatable. As in confirmation and holy orders, the newly baptized person becomes a new creation: "If anyone says that in the three sacraments, namely, baptism, confirmation and orders, a character, namely a spiritual and indelible mark, is not imprinted on the soul . . . let him be anathema."[4] The decrees on baptism take issue with some Reformers' beliefs that baptism could be repeated after a lapse of faith; the Council insisted on the practice of baptizing children, that baptism is necessary for salvation, and that it can be validly performed even by a heretic or a woman. If we ask, as we should, what the decrees are meant to protect, it seems clear that the ontological change which baptism effects is at stake here; it is most emphatically not just a rite of entry into the community. It changes the soul. But the attention to the ontological change that baptism imparts is in order to distinguish the baptized from the unbaptized, and is not used by Trent to make a case for the fundamental equality of all those gifted and the common priesthood. Indeed, ordination is a further ontological change added on to that of baptism—and, in fact, that of confirmation, too. Nevertheless, the focus on baptism was in itself something healthy, and would be taken up again by Vatican II in very different fashion: precisely to assert the fundamental equality of all the baptized.

The extent of Trent's concern to restrict Communion for laypeople to one species only is also illuminating. For Luther, the restoration to the laity of Communion under both kinds, bread and wine, was an important symbol of the unity and equality of all Christians. For Trent, the rejection of this move had less to do with whether the laity ought or ought not to be receiving the cup than it had to do with making the point that the Church could legitimately develop traditions which did not depend upon literal justification in the words of Scripture. Indeed, in the catechism of the Council of Trent, itself often a clearer indication of the intent of the Council than the decrees themselves, the arguments first adduced against Communion under both species are entirely practical: the wine may be spilled, reserved wine will quickly turn acid, "there are many who cannot at all bear the taste or even the smell of wine," and wine is scarce in many countries. Only then is reference made to the polemical purpose: to oppose the heresy which would deny that the whole Christ is present under either species.[5] In other words, the debate had more to do with the relationship of Scripture and tradition than with its ostensible subject, withholding the cup from the laity.

While Trent had nothing to say directly about the meaning of the lay state, and while its silence echoes down the centuries, through the almost equally silent Vatican I to the threshold of Vatican II itself, many individual laypeople held prominent responsibilities within the Church.[6] Trent was the age of such enormously important laypeople as Thomas More, deeply influenced by the humanism of Erasmus; a better example might be the Venetian Casparo Contarini, who devoted great energies to the Church but was ordained only late in life. At the Council itself, Pope Paul III appointed a group of laymen to the office of Cardinal in order to strengthen his reforming hand. Thus, the early sessions of the Council in 1546 were presided over by Reginald Pole, though he was not ordained priest until some ten years later. Count Ludovico Nogarola, another layman, served as secretary at the theological discussions and preached on St. Stephen's Day before the assembled legates and bishops. Indeed, Jan Grootaers has argued that Trent was quite paradoxical. While "one of the effects of this Council was an increasing clericalization of the Church," it was occasioned by the need to assert ecclesial independence from temporal power. At the same time, says Grootaers, the Council was trying "to a certain extent to associate laymen [members of the *laos*, the People of God] intimately with a great enterprise of renewal and reorganization."[7]

While it would be possible to provide a long list of thoughtful, prominent, and saintly laypeople whose work belies any suggestion that laypeople were merely passive over the centuries following Trent, this would not in itself amount to theological progress in understanding the lay role in the church. Prominent among those listed by Grootaers, for example, are Gaston de Renty (1611–1649), Joseph Goerres (1776–1848), Joseph de Maistre (1751–1821), Charles de Montalembert (1810–1870), Frederic Ozanam (1813–1853), Madame de Swetchine (1782–1857), William George Ward (1812–1882), and Lord Acton (1834–1902). But after a fascinating sketch of the extent of lay influence and involvement in the Church, Grootaers rightly concludes that it does not present "the picture of a well-articulated and well-balanced community, in which, in accordance with the words of St. Paul, each member has his own appointed task."[8] This remark continues to resonate in the Church, where today the steady expansion of lay ministry is not matched by a concomitant level of theological reflection on the lay state, and in fact is more likely to be accompanied by dire warnings about the clericalization of the laity.

Although Trent had stressed the difference between clergy and laity, the next two centuries showed some development of thought.[9] Striking ideas can be found, as in Charles de Condren's remark that "the Eucharist is the sacrifice of the whole church."[10] Henri Brémond reported that seventeenth-century resistance to the translation of the eucharistic prayer into the vernacular or active lay participation in the liturgy was motivated by a fear that the faithful would start thinking of themselves as "priests just like the priest."[11] At this time, too, the writings of Francis de Sales began the process of developing a lay spirituality in which the particular "secular" character of lay life was seen as a way toward God.[12] And the challenges of Enlightenment rationalism heralded a new urgency to apologetics in which laypeople were also involved. Consequently, Congar suggests, the term "apostolic" came to be liberated from its exclusive ties to the work of the original Twelve and attained its modern meaning, in which the laity could be said to participate in the apostolate.[13] Nevertheless, the Church was still a long way from Vatican II's Decree on the Apostolic Activity of the Laity (*Apostolicam actuositatem*).

The nineteenth-century Church was engaged in a struggle with modernity in which the laity were deeply implicated. The process of secularization led both clergy and laity to a withdrawal from the world, no doubt reflecting the Enlightenment's privatization of religion, and to a simultaneous aggressive reaction to the loss of ecclesial influence in the secular realm. The world became both the enemy to be feared and avoided, and at the same time the "unchurched" to be conquered for Christ. The laity, too, emerged as a bifurcated community. On the one hand, there were those who needed protection from the depravities of the secular world. On the other, it was clearly to the laity that the responsibility to reclaim the world for Christ largely fell. This in its turn created a problem for Church leadership. How could the appropriately hierarchical conception of the Church—an idea that came to full flower in the nineteenth century—be protected while the laity were given apostolic responsibilities? The eventual answer, offered by Pius XI, was that of Catholic Action, which the Pope defined as lay "participation in the hierarchical ministry of the church," though his successor's subtle adjustment to "collaboration in the hierarchical ministry of the church" says a great deal about how cautious the twentieth-century Church remained about the role of the laity.[14]

The nineteenth-century Church's answer to the problem of defending, controlling, and harnessing the laity to the task of evangelization proceeded on several fronts. During this century, a multitude of pious confraternities and societies of every conceivable description were launched. Congar describes this as "a kind of Catholic doubling of secular activities," as sports clubs, hospitals, and schools proliferated and pious popular literature abounded, so that the ordinary faithful would have no need to expose themselves to the blandishments of the ungodly world. Accompanying this creation of a Catholic parallel world was an enormous flowering of popular devotions, the best-known of which, though there were many others, was devotion to the Sacred Heart of Jesus. While these steps constituted something of a rearguard action on the part of the Church because it was responding too late to the loss of the urban working classes, they nevertheless did create a high-profile, distinctive Catholic culture that lasted well into the twentieth century.

At the same time, as the ordinary faithful were being protected from the world, prominent Catholics often took leadership roles in promoting what one might call "the Catholic view of things" in the world of public opinion, at a time when society had become so anticlerical that laypeople often had to be the vanguard. The work of such groups and individuals as the Munich circle of Joseph Gorres and the Münster circle of Amelia Gallitzin; the writings of Chateaubriand and Veuillot; of Newman, Ward, and Acton; of Ozanam and Vincent Pallotti, were highly significant. However, they frequently did not destroy that suspicion held by the extraecclesial world of the institutional Church, which in the same period of time gave us the *Syllabus of Errors* and the definition of papal infallibility. Ecclesiastical control was maintained by a rhetoric of submission to hierarchical authority. The draft schema for Vatican I, *Supremi pastoris*, affirmed that "the church is an unequal society in which God has ordained that some will command, and others obey. The latter are the laity, the former the clergy."[15] Much the same wording, as we have seen, was repeated in Pius X's 1906 encyclical letter *Vehementer nos*, and this understanding certainly did not simply disappear from ecclesiastical consciousness. While Vatican II would reject this attitude toward the laity, subsequent ecclesiastical grumblings about the dangers of the "clericalization of the laity" testify to the vitality of what Congar once called "hierarchology," in which the study of the Church is reduced to the study of the power of the hierarchy.[16]

The immediate preparation for the sea change that Vatican II brought about in an understanding of the lay state can be found above all in France in the first half of the twentieth century, in that loose association of mostly Dominicans and Jesuits that proudly wore the label derisively assigned to it by its enemies, "la nouvelle théologie."[17] The Modernist crisis of the early twentieth century had led to a well-attested atrophy of Catholic theological scholarship, a flight into historical and liturgical studies that were relatively safe from the anti-Modernist forces marshaled by the Vatican. Thanks to a happy blend of the cunning of reason and ironies of history, these very same studies were a subtle factor in Vatican II's theological revolution. Liturgical scholarship not only revivified sacramental theology but also restored a full role in worship to the laity. But even more important, the shift into historical scholarship was the immediate cause of the overthrow of the reigning neoscholastic ideology that Leo XIII had made the official philosophical and theological method in the Church. Fighting back, historians such as Pierre Rousselot and Etienne Gilson had demonstrated how neoscholasticism was an unhistorical reading of St. Thomas that did violence to his intent. Thus, they freed Thomism from the unhistorical straitjacket in which it had been placed by neoscholastic thinkers; suddenly a new excitement gripped European theology. Nowhere was it more in evidence than in France at midcentury, and nowhere more so than in the writings of Yves Congar who, while not alone, was undoubtedly the overwhelming influence upon Vatican II's nascent theology of the laity. It is also surely not coincidental that Congar, who wrote the first great book on the laity in the Catholic Church, was by self-definition primarily an ecumenical theologian. Vatican II's steps toward developing a theology of the laity represent, at least implicitly, a rapprochement with Luther.

Congar's commitment to ecumenism brought him under suspicion in Rome, beginning with the publication in 1935 of his first book, *Chrétiens désunis*.[18] The very month it was published, he was ordered by Cardinal Pacelli, then Pius XI's secretary of state, and soon to succeed him as Pius XII, to refuse an invitation to attend the Oxford Ecumenical Conference as a Catholic observer. Some years later, he was prevented from publishing a new edition of the book, and in 1950, he was one of the unnamed objects of concern in the papal encyclical *Humani generis*, which attacked "relativism" and "historicism" in theology. The encyclical in effect attempted to resurrect the specter of Modernism, and it eventually resulted in Congar's being silenced and sent into exile with the English Dominicans in Cambridge, who seem to have quite cheerfully shouldered the burden of placing him under virtual house arrest. This occurred in 1954, but the previous year he had had no difficulty publishing his book on the laity, a text with which the censors seem to have had no problem. Perhaps the field was too new; perhaps they did not pay much attention to a theology of the laity; perhaps they saw only the relatively conservative tenor of the book, something that took its author another ten years to correct. In any event, John XXIII rapidly rehabilitated Congar in 1958, and he was brought into a central role at the first session of Vatican II in 1962. Reading the Vatican Council's treatment of the laity is like reading Congar himself, though we should not underestimate the influence of either Msgr. Gérard Philips, who wrote a valuable theology of the laity,[19] or that of Karl Rahner, for that matter.[20]

The Laity in the Documents of Vatican II

In order to understand correctly the Second Vatican Council on the laity, it is necessary to look at three documents: the Dogmatic Constitution on the Church, *Lumen gentium*; the Decree on the Apostolate of the Laity, *Apostolicam actuositatem*; and the Pastoral Constitution on the Church in the Modern World, *Gaudium et spes*. Each makes a particular contribution. *Lumen gentium* provides a theological breakthrough with its image of the Church as the People of God and its emphasis on baptism, though it does not follow through as far as some had hoped. *Apostolicam actuositatem* spells out in detail the kinds of work that are legitimately done by laypeople in virtue of their inclusion through baptism in the common priesthood. And *Gaudium et spes* is important in defining the relationship between the Church and the world, which make *Lumen gentium*'s identification of the laity as "secular" more hopeful than it otherwise might have been. Taken together, it is fair to say that they are revolutionary documents in their implications for the understanding of the lay vocation. But like all revolutions, they leave much hard work to be done if the old, nonhistorical ways are not to return.

Lumen Gentium

While some debate exists about the central image of the Church at Vatican II, it is difficult to deny that the idea of the People of God is the most striking indication the bishops offer of their line of thinking.[21] Chapter 1 of the document lists a series of biblical images, all of them interesting and fruitful. But it is in chapter 2 that the "People of God" motif makes its appearance, obviously offered as a more comprehensive model than those in the previous chapter, or perhaps as one particularly suited to the present age. As the Council fathers write, quoting the First Letter of Peter, Christ brought about the new covenant, a race of "Jews and Gentiles which would be one, not according to the flesh, but in the Spirit, and this race would be the new People of God."[22] These believers in Christ, through the power of the Spirit, are finally established as "a chosen race, a royal priesthood, a holy nation . . . once no people but now God's people."[23] In this new people, "the baptized, by regeneration and the anointing of the Holy Spirit, are consecrated as a spiritual dwelling and a holy priesthood."[24] All are called to share in the priestly character of the people. All are called to share actively in worship. All are called to witness to the light of Christ. And all are called to prophecy. While the chapter makes clear that the "common priesthood of the faithful and the ministerial or hierarchical priesthood" in fact "differ in essence and not simply in degree,"[25] its location before the chapter on hierarchy and its references to the universality of the call to holiness radically change previous institutional understandings of the common priesthood. Now the priestly people, in virtue of baptism, actually have something *to do.* Moreover, the language of the chapter importantly makes clear that "the faithful" is not a synonym for the laity, but includes all the baptized. Membership of the common priesthood is not abrogated by ordination. The ordained priesthood is an addition to the possession of the common priesthood held in virtue of baptism.

While chapter 2 of *Lumen gentium* establishes the conditions for a theological renaissance in the understanding of the Church and the roles of all the baptized, the remainder of the document fails to live up to the promise. Some of this is due to the inevitable compromising character of Vatican documents, crafted as they were in order to pass by overwhelming votes. Often, what is given with one hand is taken away again with the other. Nowhere is this clearer than in the tension between an understanding of the Church rooted in baptism and one that is essentially hierarchical. The second chapter of *Lumen gentium* thus gives way immediately to a chapter on hierarchy that reasserts a stratified understanding of the Church, in which different levels are distinguished by the possession of powers. Then, when the laity return to center stage in chapter

4, they are described in terms of their secularity. True, there are renewed references to baptismal equality, but the bishops are clear that "their secular character is proper and peculiar to the laity" (para. 30), and that "it belongs to the laity to seek the kingdom of God by engaging in temporal affairs and directing them according to God's will" (para. 31). While there is obviously a measure of truth to this claim, it unfortunately tends to lend credence to older approaches to laity and clergy, which stressed their essential difference from one another, rather than pursue the logic of chapter 2, in which all distinctions of ministry are seen in the light of the one common priesthood that all assumed through their baptism. In fact, at just the time that Congar's stress on the secularity of the laity was being incorporated into the Council documents, he himself was beginning to have second thoughts; he subsequently proceeded to recast his whole understanding in terms of "different ministries." Such an approach in which, as Congar wrote, "the clergy must now be defined relative to the laity," is entirely consistent with the baptismal approach of chapter 2, but is less accommodating to chapter 4.[26]

Some theologians, Cardinal Léon-Joseph Suenens and Edward Schillebeeckx among them, have suggested that the Council not only missed an opportunity but also may have suffered a loss of nerve at this point, taking refuge in the relatively uncontroversial concerns about the lay apostolate rather than dealing with the infinitely trickier matters of a theological reflection on the lay state. Specifically, Suenens thought that immediately after the Council, the Church rather conveniently forgot what he understood to be the co-responsibility of the whole People of God for the Church.[27] Schillebeeckx was more critical. He thought that the Council's "laborious search for the layman's place in the church" was wrong on two counts. First, it exactly reversed the real problem: "What is the place of the Church's office in the people of God?" Second, its emphasis on baptism, which he applauded, was only a description "simply of the state of being a Christian itself" and said nothing specific about the lay state.[28]

Whether Suenens and Schillebeeckx were right or not, there was a clear shift at this point in *Lumen gentium* to a discovery of what laypeople *do* in the Church rather than simply who they *are*. This is not in itself a bad thing. Indeed, the apostolic tasks of the laity are treated in a refreshingly positive light, and there are stirring passages about an appropriately healthy relationship between clergy and laity. Christ, we are told, "desires that his kingdom be spread by the lay faithful." They are evangelizers who "enjoy a principal role in the universal fulfillment of this task."[29] And even if the pastoral role of the clergy continues to be stressed in a way that is at best paternalistic, at worst oppressive, it is striking to see that, on the other hand, the laity are expected to speak out when they deem it necessary. "By reason of the knowledge, competence or pre-eminence that they have," say the bishops, "the laity are empowered—indeed sometimes obliged—to manifest their opinion on those things which pertain to the good of the church." Moreover, the bishops describe a climate of mutuality between pastors and faithful, and affirm that "many benefits for the church are expected to flow from this familiar relationship between the laity and the pastors."[30]

Apostolicam Actuositatem

The strengths and weaknesses of *Lumen gentium* are matched in the decree on the lay apostolate, *Apostolicam actuositatem*, though it has to be said that this document has been the springboard for an extraordinary flowering of lay ministry since Vatican II, especially in the American Church. That there has been no concomitant development of theological reflection on the character of the lay vocation explains why in very recent years lay apostolic activity has been defenseless in the face of Vatican efforts to reassert the "essential" difference between the two priesthoods. It also helps to bring into focus one of the most difficult questions with which the Council left the Church: What is the theological status of what has come to be called, since the Council, "lay ecclesial ministry"? Given the identification of the laity primarily with their secularity, and hence their essential mission with the work of evangelization in the secular world, what are we to make of the many thousands of laypeople, full- and part-time, paid and volunteers, who seem at least to be exercising a ministerial vocation within the Church community itself? Are we, when all is said and done, to envisage their work as simply a kind of supplement to the work of the clergy, who "properly" exercise these ministries, so that laypeople then become stand-ins for the shortage of clergy? Or are we to imagine, as Congar certainly came to believe, that the shortage of clergy is a moment of opportunity exploited by the Holy Spirit to signal that this time is opportune for a thorough re-visioning of ministry in the church? *Apostolicam actuositatem* certainly did not attempt to answer these questions, and perhaps even sidestepped them. But the document at least provides some directions in which to look for an answer.

The Decree on the Apostolate of the Laity is one of those documents hurriedly completed at the end of the fourth and final session of the Council, and it shows all the signs of this haste in its somewhat breathless style and fragmented structure. However, it is instructive in a number of ways. First, it locates lay ministry in the context of charisms; this is a significant advance on *Lumen gentium* and is engaging in its freshness. It then immediately proceeds to discuss the question of a lay spirituality, obviously an important topic. However, the characteristics it suggests as components of lay spiritual life are clear illustrations of the truth of Schillebeeckx's claim that the Council fathers never get to the specifics of lay life, but only manage a description of the Christian life as such. So, they say, it must be aided by the liturgy; be grounded in faith, hope, and charity; be marked by discipleship of Christ; and take Mary as its model. None of this is any truer of lay than of clerical spirituality. It is Christian discipleship, *tout court*. True, the Council fathers do go on to refer to a spirituality that acquires its specificity "from the circumstances of one's state in life . . . and from one's professional and social activity,"[31] but no specific theological reflections follow. Indeed, the frequent references to the "hiddenness" of the lay apostolate or the humility with which the laity must live out their spiritual lives seem reminiscent of an age when it could be more or less assumed that the laity were less professionally accomplished than the clergy or employed in less public positions. This is obviously no longer the case.

Perhaps the single most important reason why the Council never achieved serious theological reflection on laity and clergy or on the nature of orders is that issues of lifestyle obscure the discussion. This is one of the problems that surfaces in this decree. The question of what is proper to clerical and lay ministry may be a worthwhile question to ask, but it has nothing essential to do with distinctions because of marriage, celibacy, gender, or, above all, the clerical lifestyle. Accidentally, of course, lay people in the Catholic Church can be identified as those who may marry if they wish, and clergy as those who (mostly) must be celibate. It is also possible to argue that this state of affairs should not be changed, that the law of celibacy for the clergy is appropriate, and that women should not be included in the ranks of the ordained. But even so, these characteristics remain accidental. What is ministry and what is vocation for clergy and laity alike have to be determined in the light of their common baptismal calling into the priestly people, not because of biological accident, lifestyle choice, or happenstance. That ordained ministers are called to lead the community of faith is beyond dispute. However, in what manner they live their lives may not be at all relevant, although the Church's fixation on such questions has hopelessly obfuscated the central issue of what it is to minister.

When *Apostolicam actuositatem* examines different forms of lay ministry, more problems arise. The appropriate distinctions are made between individual lay apostolates and those conducted in groups and, given the times, energy is expended to explain once again what it means to refer to Catholic Action as "collaboration in the hierarchical ministry of the church." But in the examination of which ministries pertain to lay individuals, the bishops suggest that in extraordinary situations—in mission lands, for example, where priests may be very few in number (or, for instance, in jail)—laypeople may "take over as far as possible the work of priests."[32] They envisage activities such as teaching Christian doctrine or catechetics. In the Decree on Missions, *Ad gentes*, they even include preaching.[33] We could extend the list, including everything from the role of eucharistic minister—which has lately become a battleground of the new clericalism—to that of pastoral associate, who in essence does everything except preside at Mass and hear confessions in increasingly common priestless parishes.

What does it tell us about ministry when in exceptional circumstances, however these are defined, laypeople may take over ministries "more closely connected with the duties of pastors"?[34] One thing that seems indisputable is that the dividing lines between clergy and laity, or between clerical and lay ministry, become much less clear-cut than we might have imagined. The long-maintained traditional theological posture that ordination results in a kind of ontological change in the individual, in virtue of which "he" acquires special powers attached to "his" position in the hierarchy, is placed under the severest stress. Without the clerical leader present, or present in sufficient numbers, someone else must take up the responsibilities previously exercised by the priest alone. Eucharistic ministry, parish administration, and preaching can all be appropriately the ministry of laypersons in special circumstances. Obviously, the Council did not imagine that the list could be extended further, so that it could be said that lay ministers might celebrate the Eucharist in the absence of a priest. But if the bishops could be weaned off an ontological understanding of priesthood and toward one in which presiding at the Eucharist follows from ordination to be the servant-leader of the community, such a step might not be so difficult to imagine, and a much more fluid understanding of ministries in the church might follow.[35]

Gaudium et spes

In the end, the Pastoral Constitution on the Church in the Modern World, *Gaudium et spes*, is more important for understanding the roles of the laity than either *Lumen gentium* or *Apostolicam actuositatem*. This reason is *Gaudium et spes*'s challenge to the dualistic approach between the secular and the sacred, between the world and the Church. This dualism has plagued Catholicism since Trent, identifying the laity with the secular realm and the clergy with the sacred. Once the distinction collapses—recognizing that the Church is also a worldly reality, that it exists within the world, and that, relative to the world, it is both a teaching and a learning body—then lay ministry comes to be seen in a different light. In the traditional model, lay apostolic activity is foraging behind enemy lines in the name of the Gospel. In the model of *Gaudium et spes*, the laity are in the vanguard of the Church's mission. Ordination to the priesthood becomes, then, leadership of an essentially missionary community, one that is within the world, not over against it, albeit with a message that in the end transcends it.

A theology of the laity that prefers chapter 4 of *Lumen gentium* and *Apostolicam actuositatem* could be relatively conservative, while one that favors chapter 2 of *Lumen gentium* and *Gaudium et spes* would seem much more progressive. This flexibility of Vatican II is something of a two-edged sword. It enables and even encourages, on the one hand, the kind of polemical confrontations that sometimes occur between those who want to stress the Council's continuity with the past and those who prefer to highlight its fresh approaches. All they have to do is engage in a partial reading of the Council texts. On the other hand, attempting the challenging task of holding all the texts as uniform can lead toward new understandings that are indeed in continuity with the past, if not always the bits of the past that this or that prelate might prefer.

Conclusions

When we understand Vatican II in the light of all that its documents say and imply, the understanding of the lay role in the Church is implicitly revolutionized. From passive recipients of the benefits accorded by a clergy called to the exercise of sacred powers and divinely bestowed jurisdiction, the laity become active ministers of the Gospel. They are led by the ordained, but this is mere tautology. Ordination is confirmation of calling to leadership. The laity and the clergy together, the whole Church, come to be understood as a missionary body in history, called into dialogue with the world that is not the Church; at the same time, this world, in virtue of its being loved by God, exists in relation to the Church, the People of God. It is often said, rightly enough, that Christ is the sacrament of God and the Church is the sacrament of Christ. It is rare to hear, though equally true, that *the laity are the sacrament of the Church*. They represent Christ's Church in the world, and they are this Church. And, if indeed the laity are "secular," then so, in a sense, is the Church itself.

Examining the time span from Trent to Vatican II through the lens of the laity, it is quite apparent that as the Catholic tradition attempts to fashion a new theological understanding of the lay vocation, it will have to reengage Luther on the matter of the common priesthood. When Congar abandons the sacred/secular distinction in favor of the language of different ministries; when the Council blurs some of the lines between the ministries of the ordained and the laity; when postconciliar thought takes up the Council's unexplored suggestion that it is in baptism that we may find the solution to our questions, it would be churlish not to reexamine Luther's legacy. Hence, any future Council would need to approach the question of lay vocation and that of orders in the Church from the sacrament of baptism; it should take its lead from the strong hints that Vatican II offered, but that it failed to develop or explain fully.

In the end, a theological understanding of the laity is an entire ecclesiology, and one that cannot be healthily constructed without honestly facing the problems that a cultic understanding of priesthood has bequeathed to the Church. If baptism involves an ontological change, by which we become a new creation, born again of water and the Holy Spirit, and through which we are anointed into ministry, then perhaps the traditional understanding of ordination is just one ontological change too many. However, a theology of vocation that flows from baptism most certainly does not reduce ordained servant-leadership to the category of a function delegated by the community. However, it does mean that ordination is *for* the community, and so, borrowing an image from today's computer jargon, we can proudly proclaim: the priest must be understood relative to the laity, for the layperson is the default Christian.

NOTES

1. Yves Congar, *Jalons pour une théologie du laïcat* (Paris: Cerf, 1954; rev. ed., 1964), translated as *Lay People in the Church: A Study for a Theology of the Laity* (Westminster, Md.: Newman Press, 1955; 2nd rev. ed., 1965). All references here are to the revised English edition.

2. Para. 8; the text is most easily available in Claudia Carlen, comp., *The Papal Encyclicals* (Wilmington, N.C.: McGrath, 1981), vol. 3.

3. There are shades of opinion upon how and when the clergy emerged as a distinct group. The middle position is maintained by Yves Congar in "Laïc et laïcat," in *Dictionnaire de spiritualité ascétique et mystique*, ed. Marcel Viller et al. (Paris: Beauchesne, 1976), vol. 9, cols. 79–108. Alexandre Faivre maintains vehemently that there was no lay/clergy distinction in the early Church in his *The Emergence of the Laity in the Early Church* (New York: Paulist Press, 1990). A more conservative position that finds the laity appearing somewhat sooner, though still without the hierarchical emphases of a later time, is presented in a seminal essay by Ignace de la Potterie, "L'Origine et le sense primitive du mot 'laïc,'" *Nouvelle Revue Théologique* 80 (1958): 840–853.

4. Norman P. Tanner, *Decrees of the Ecumenical Councils*, vol. 2, *Trent to Vatican II* (Washington, D.C.: Georgetown University Press, 1990), 685. All subsequent references to conciliar documents are to this text.

5. John A. McHugh and Charles J. Callan, eds. and trans., *Catechism of the Council of Trent for Parish Priests* (New York: Wagner, 1934), 252–253.

6. I am greatly indebted in this paragraph to the work of Jan Grootaers. See his "The Roman Catholic Church," in *The Layman in Christian History: A Project of the Department on the Laity of the World Council of Churches*, ed. Stephen Charles Neill and Hans-Ruedi Weber (Philadelphia: Westminster Press, 1963), 298–336.

7. Ibid., 304–305.

8. Ibid., 335.

9. The indispensable source for this discussion, which I have used extensively here, is Congar, "Laïc et laïcat."

10. Charles de Condren, *L'Idée du sacerdoce et du sacrifice de Jésus-Christ*, part IV (Paris, 1677), 323, quoted in Congar, "Laïc et laïcat," col. 94.

11. Henri Brémond, *Histoire littéraire du sentiment religieux en France*, 11 vols. (Paris: Bloud et Gay, 1924–1933), vol. 9, 159.

12. Above all, of course, Francis de Sales's *Introduction to the Devout Life* (Garden City, N.Y.: Image Books, 1972).

13. Congar, "Laïc et laïcat," col. 98.

14. Congar, *Lay People in the Church*, 362, 365.

15. The schema is available only in a Latin text in Johannes Mansi, *Sacrorum conciliorum nova . . . collectio*, 55 vols. (Paris: H. Welter, 1901–1927), vol. 51, 539–553.

16. Congar, *Lay People in the Church*, 58–59.

17. The best treatment of this topic is to be found in Étienne Fouilloux, *Une église en quête de liberté: La pensée catholique française entre modernisme et Vatican II, 1914–1962* (Paris: Desclée de Brouwer, 1998).

18. Yves Congar, *Chrétiens désunis* (Paris: Éditions du Cerf, 1935), trans. John R. Gilbert and James W. Moudry as *Divided Christendom* (London: Geoffrey Bles, 1939).

19. Gérard Philips, *The Role of the Laity in the Church* (Chicago: Fides, 1957).

20. See Karl Rahner, "Notes on the Lay Apostolate," in his *Theological Investigations*, trans. C. Ernst, vol. 2, *Man in the Church* (Baltimore: Helicon, 1963), 319–352.

21. See, for example, José Comblin, *People of God*, trans. Philip Berryman (Maryknoll, N.Y.: Orbis, 2004), which is written to show that the institutional Church's current preference for the model of "communion" is a plot to undermine Vatican II and in particular to undercut theologies of liberation, with their enthusiasm for the People of God image. While Comblin may go a little far, since the model of "communion" is certainly to be found in the Vatican documents, he may well be right that it has distinct ideological connotations that would lead those who wish to downplay Vatican II to prefer it over "People of God."

22. Tanner, *Decrees*, vol. 2, 855.

23. 1 Peter 2:9–10.

24. Tanner, *Decrees*, vol. 2, 856.

25. Ibid., 857.

26. See especially Yves Congar, "My Pathfindings in the Theology of Laity and Ministries," *The Jurist* 2 (1972): 169–188, and the fuller bibliography available in Paul Lakeland, *The Liberation of the Laity: In Search of an Accountable Church* (New York: Continuum, 2003), 291, n. 2.

27. See Léon-Joseph Suenens, *Co-responsibility in the Church*, trans. N. D. Smith (New York: Herder and Herder, 1968).

28. Edward Schillebeeckx, *The Mission of the Church* (New York: Seabury Press, 1973), 122.

29. Tanner, *Decrees*, 878.

30. Ibid., 879.

31. Ibid., 983.

32. Ibid., 992–993.

33. Ibid., 1030.

34. Ibid., 1996.

35. This is the burden of Richard Gaillardetz's outstanding essay, "The Ecclesial Foundations of Ministry Within an Ordered Communion," in *Ordering the Baptismal Priesthood: Theologies of Lay and Ordained Ministry*, ed. Susan K. Wood et al. (Collegeville, Minn.: Liturgical Press, 2003), 26–51.

12

Christian Marriage

William P. Roberts

Aside from the dramatic changes in the celebration of the Eucharist and the sacraments, perhaps no other development from the Tridentine and post-Tridentine era to the Vatican II and post–Vatican II period has affected, on a practical level, the lives of more Catholics than the pronounced shifts in the theological understanding of Christian marriage. This topic is the focus of this essay.

Our treatment of this paradigm shift will be divided into five main parts. The first will summarize the main points of the Council of Trent's position on marriage. In the second, we will consider the post-Tridentine understanding of the meaning of marriage as reflected in the 1917 Code of Canon Law. The third part will consider the principal developments of the Church's perception of marriage as presented by the bishops at the Second Vatican Council. The fourth will explore some of the practical implications emanating from this change of understanding. The final section will explore further questions that emerge from this new perception of marriage, questions that the hierarchical magisterium has not yet sufficiently addressed.

The Council of Trent

The Council of Trent's treatment of the sacrament of matrimony took place at its twenty-fourth session on November 11, 1563.[1] The Council began its treatment of marriage by summarizing the doctrine on the sacrament of matrimony. It recalls the Yahwist account of creation in Genesis, chapter 2: "The first parent of the human race, under the inspiration of the Divine Spirit, proclaimed the perpetual and indissoluble bond of matrimony when he said, 'This now is bone of my bones, and flesh of my flesh. . . . Wherefore a man shall leave father and mother, and cleave to his wife: and they shall be two in one flesh'" (Genesis 2:23f.; see Ephesians 5:31).[2]

The Council goes on to speak of Christ, who "taught more clearly that only two persons are joined and united by this marriage bond."[3] Christ, it points out, referred to those closing words of the Genesis text on marriage as "words spoken by God," and then proceeds to say that what God "has joined together, let no man put asunder."[4] In this way, Christ "confirmed the stability of that same bond which had been declared by Adam so long before."[5] The bishops at Trent then reiterate that Christ instituted the sacraments and brought them to perfection. He "merited for us by his passion the grace that brings natural love to perfection, and strengthens the indissoluble unity, and sanctifies the spouses."[6]

After completing the doctrinal section, the Council turned its attention to "the evil, foolish men of our day" who entertain wrong notions about the sacrament of matrimony and spread "many ideas that are foreign to the understanding of the Catholic Church."[7] To refute these errors, the Council issued twelve canons that anathematize those who propose them. Among the errors condemned: that marriage is not a sacrament instituted by Christ, that Christians can practice polygamy, that the Church does not have the power to determine diriment impediments to marriage (circumstances that render the marriage invalid, such as age, an existing marriage, or a close blood relationship), and positions that oppose the Church's teaching on indissolubility or on clerical celibacy.[8] Also anathematized is anyone who says "that the marriage state is to be preferred to the state of virginity or of celibacy and that it is not better and holier to remain in virginity or celibacy than to be joined in marriage."[9]

After issuing these anathemas, the Council turned its attention to reforming certain marriage practices. It put an end to clandestine marriages by requiring for validity the presence of an authorized priest and two witnesses.[10] It prohibited marriage between persons with a spiritual relationship and within certain degrees of affinity. The bishops prescribed punishments for abductors, for concubinage, and for temporal lords and magistrates who violated a person's freedom to marry whom he or she chooses. The Council set down a caution regarding the marriage of vagrants, and reaffirmed the "ancient prohibitions" of solemn nuptials from Advent to Epiphany and from Ash Wednesday through the octave of Easter.[11]

It is clear from this overview that the Council of Trent assumed the theological understanding of the meaning of marriage that had been handed down for a number of centuries. The bishops' purpose for treating the sacrament of matrimony was not to advance this theology further, but rather to refute what they perceived as heresies in its regard, and to correct certain abuses. As far as the official teaching of the Church was concerned, the medieval perception of the meaning of marriage perdured until the Second Vatican Council, and was reaffirmed in the 1917 Code of Canon Law, to which we now turn.

The 1917 Code of Canon Law

Since the focus of this chapter is to trace the development of the theology of marriage from the Tridentine era to the post–Vatican II period, my concentration here will be only on those canons in the 1917 Code that reflect the pre–Vatican II theological understanding.[12]

The first of these canons is 1012, which states, "Christ our Lord elevated the very contract of marriage between baptized persons to the dignity of a sacrament." The canon goes on to say that, therefore, "it is impossible for a valid contract of marriage between baptized persons to exist without being by that very fact a sacrament." In their commentary on this canon, Bouscaren and Ellis explain: "For this supernatural elevation to take place in any concrete instance, it is necessary and sufficient that *both parties* be validly baptized and validly married."[13]

Two canons especially reflect further the Code's theological understanding of marriage. "Matrimonial consent is an act of the will by which each party gives and accepts a perpetual and exclusive right over the body, for acts which are of themselves suitable for the generation of children" (canon 1081, no. 2). "The primary end of marriage is the procreation and education of children; its secondary end is mutual help and the allaying of concupiscence" (canon 1013, no. 1). "The essential properties of marriage are unity and indissolubility, which acquire a peculiar firmness in Christian marriage by reason of its sacramental character" (canon 1013, no. 2).

Based on these two canons, Bouscaren and Ellis frame the following definition: "Marriage is a lawful and exclusive contract by which a man and a woman mutually give and accept a right over their bodies for the purpose of acts which are in themselves suitable for the generation of children."[14] They go on to note that the Holy Office again stressed the primacy of procreation and education in a decree of April 1, 1944, and condemned the views of "certain writers" who deny either that "these constitute the primary end or hold that the secondary ends are equally principal and independent."[15] The authors further note that Pius XII in his allocution of October 29, 1951, accepted the responsibility for that declaration, and confirmed it.[16]

The Holy Office's condemnation of certain writers indicates that while the Tridentine and post-Tridentine view of marriage continued to be upheld by the Vatican, a few German philosophers and theologians in the 1920s and 1930s were proposing a new way of understanding the meaning of marriage. As Theodore Mackin points out, principal among these were Dietrich von Hildebrand and Heribert Doms. "Their thesis," Mackin states, "was in one sense a counter thesis to the accepted Catholic teaching about the natural end of marriage and of sexuality in marriage."[17] Mackin goes on to explain the thinking of these two authors:

> They did not counter-claim, as the Church's Congregation of the Holy Office protested when condemning their thesis in 1944, that procreation and nurture are not the primary end of marriage, but its secondary or even lesser end. Indeed, they accepted the traditional hierarchy of ends in marriage. What they did claim was that marriage is not to be understood primarily according to its ends, that its ends are not its first intelligible element. Marriage is not an instrument reality, they insisted. It is not for anyone or anything outside of itself.
>
> They insisted rather that marriage is primarily understandable in its meaning. This meaning is the becoming-one, the being-one and the growing in oneness of the two sexually complementary human beings. Therefore, too, their sexuality is not instrumental. It is not meant to realize some goal outside itself. Rather it is the territory, the conduct, in which specifically and most richly, the man and woman create their oneness and grow in it. As married persons, they come to their chosen fullness of personhood mainly in their sexual lovemaking.[18]

This kind of interpersonal thought would, some three decades later, influence the profound shift in the Catholic understanding of marriage realized at the Second Vatican Council.[19]

The Second Vatican Council

The bishops of the Second Vatican Council treat Christian marriage in chapter 1 of part II of the Pastoral Constitution on the Church in the Modern World, *Gaudium et spes*, issued December 7, 1965. This chapter, "The Dignity of Marriage and the Family," begins with a statement of purpose: "The council intends to present certain key points of the church's teaching in *a clearer light*; and it hopes to guide and encourage Christians and all others who are trying to preserve and to foster the dignity and supremely sacred value of the married state."[20]

This expressed intent immediately signals a stark contrast with Trent's treatment of marriage. While Trent's purpose was to refute and anathematize errors and reform practices regarding marriage, Vatican II is interested in shedding new theological light on the meaning of this sacrament. It explains this meaning first by referring to marriage as an intimate partnership of life and love, which is rooted in the couple's irrevocable personal consent, by which they "mutually surrender themselves to each other."[21] God, the bishops say, "is the author of marriage and has endowed it with various values and purposes: all of these have a very important bearing on the continuation of the human race, on the personal development and eternal destiny of every member of the family, on the dignity, stability, peace, and prosperity of the family and of the whole human race."[22] The institution of marriage and married love is ordered by its very nature to the procreation and education of the offspring and in them finds "its crowning glory." Thus, the couple "help and serve each other by their marriage partnership; they become conscious of their unity and experience it more deeply from day to day. The intimate union of marriage, as a mutual giving of two persons, and the good of the children demand total fidelity from the spouses and require an unbreakable union between them."[23]

Furthermore, the council describes some of the sacramental dimensions of Christian marriage. Christ has abundantly blessed marital love, "which is rich in its various features, coming as it does from the spring of divine love and modeled on Christ's own union with the church."[24] Christ abides with the married couple so that "by their mutual self-giving spouses will love each other with enduring fidelity, as he loved the church and delivered himself for it."[25] Genuine marital love, the bishops continue, "is caught up into divine love and is directed and enriched by the redemptive power of Christ."[26] As a result, spouses are led to God and helped in their parental role. Fulfilling their marital and family role "by virtue of this sacrament, spouses are penetrated with the spirit of Christ and their whole life is suffused with faith, hope and charity; thus they increasingly further their own perfection and their mutual sanctification, and together they render glory to God."[27]

Gaudium et spes further develops the meaning of married love. It is "an eminently human love because it is an affection between two persons rooted in the will and it embraces the good of the whole person; it can enrich the sentiments of the spirit and their physical expression with a unique dignity and ennoble them as the special features and manifestations of the friendship proper to marriage."[28] The sacramentality of this love brings together the human and the divine, and "leads the partners to a free and mutual self-giving, experienced in tenderness and action, and permeating their entire lives; this love is actually developed and increased by its generous exercise."[29]

The Council then speaks of marital sexual intimacy:

Married love is uniquely expressed and perfected by the exercise of the acts proper to marriage. Hence the acts in marriage by which the intimate and chaste union of the spouses takes place are noble and honorable; the truly human performance of these acts fosters

the self-giving they signify and enriches the spouses in joy and gratitude. Endorsed by mutual fidelity and, above all, consecrated by
Christ's sacrament, this love abides faithfully in mind and body in
prosperity and adversity and hence excludes both adultery and divorce. The unity of marriage, confirmed by Christ, is clearly apparent in the equal personal dignity that is accorded to man and wife in
mutual and unreserved affection. Outstanding virtue is required for
the constant fulfillment of this Christian calling. Married couples,
therefore, strengthened by grace for leading a holy life, will persever-
ingly practice and will pray for a love that is firm, generous, and
ready for sacrifice.[30]

The bishops reiterate that marriage and marital love are by nature ordered
to the procreation and education of children. "Without intending to underestimate the other ends of marriage, it must be said that true married love and
the family life that flows from it have this end in view: that the spouses would
cooperate generously with the love of the Creator and Savior, who through
them will in due time increase and enrich his family."[31]

In fulfilling the mission of procreation and education of children, the couple needs to take into consideration "their own well-being and the well-being
of their children already born or yet to come, being able to read the signs of
the times and assess their own situation on the material and spiritual level,
and, finally, an estimation of the good of the family, of society, and of the
Church. It is the married couple themselves who must, in the last analysis,
arrive at these judgments before God."[32] The bishops are careful, however, to
keep this mission of procreation and education of children in the context of
the total meaning of marriage:

But marriage was not instituted solely for the procreation of children: its nature as an indissoluble covenant between two people and
the good of the children demand that the mutual love of the partners be properly expressed, that it should grow and mature. Even in
cases where despite the intense desire of the spouses there are no
children, marriage still retains its character of being a whole manner and communion of life and preserves its value and indissolubility.[33]

If the family, which is, in a sense, "a school for human enrichment," is to
achieve "the full flowering of its life and mission, it requires an affectionate
sharing of souls between the married couple and their commitment to cooperation in the children's upbringing."[34] The Council concludes its treatment of
marriage and family in *Gaudium et spes* with this exhortation:

Let married people themselves, who are created in the image of the
living God and constituted in an authentic personal dignity, be

united together in equal affection, agreement of mind and mutual holiness. Thus, in the footsteps of Christ, the principle of life, they will bear witness by their faithful love in the joys and sacrifices of their calling, to that mystery of love which the Lord revealed to the world by his death and resurrection.[35]

One other important insight related to marriage, found in the Dogmatic Constitution on the Church, also goes beyond the pre–Vatican II thinking. In chapter 2, "The People of God," the bishops reflect briefly on each of the sacraments that are an integral part of the life of the Church. In speaking of the family that emerges from the sacrament of marriage, the bishops revive a notion found in the very early tradition of the Church (for example, Augustine in the West, Chrysostom in the East), but set quietly aside for centuries. They refer to the Christian family as a domestic church where "the parents are to be the first preachers of the faith for their children by word and example."[36]

Implications of the Theological Shift at Vatican II

In this section, I want to focus on six of the important theological changes in the Church's understanding of marriage that took place at Vatican II, as indicated above: first, marriage as a partnership; second, marriage as a covenant; third, the marital relationship and procreation placed on equal standing; fourth, the sacramentality of marriage; fifth, marriage as a call to holiness; and, finally, marriage creating a domestic church. I will briefly discuss the significance of each of these theological developments and some of the implications they have for Christian marriage today.

Marriage as a Partnership

Referring to marriage as a partnership breaks sharply with the millennia-old patriarchal view that perceived the husband not as his wife's partner but as her "head," and saw her as subservient to him.[37] This shift is even more telling in light of the fact that certain biblical texts had for centuries been interpreted in a way that gave "divine support" for the patriarchal structure of marriage.[38] This partnership the bishops speak of is not just a functional one, or a professional one, but an intimate partnership that incorporates the couple's life and love. It involves, in other words, their minds, their hearts, their souls, and their bodies. It extends not just to one aspect of their life, but to the totality of their living together.

This view places husband and wife on an equal plane in everything that pertains to their marital union. This does away with all the gender stereotypes that for centuries have been applied to marriage and survive in many cultures today. Wife and husband as coauthors of the marriage and co-heads of the household replace the male as "master" of the home. Obedience of the woman to the man gives way to mutual decision-making, leadership, and cooperation. No longer are tasks assigned on the basis of gender; rather, they are shared through mutual agreement and in a spirit of fairness, sensitivity, and service. Both have equal responsibility for the health of the marriage as well as equal rights and privileges. Both deserve the same respect for their personal dignity and well-being. In the area of sexual intimacy, a uniquely integral part of marriage, neither mate has advantage over the other. They are equal partners in the giving and receiving of their bodies. The sexual needs, desires, and comforts of the wife are as important and deserving of the same communication and response as those of the husband.[39]

The experience of daily growing in an authentic partnership of life and love with one's spouse brings about a gradual conversion of mind, heart, and soul. It empowers one to die gradually to the dark pockets of sexism that continue to reside in the human bloodstream, and to come to new respect for the opposite gender. It enables one to conquer slowly that need to control and possess another and, rather, become sensitive to what God is calling the other to be. It helps people to overcome the proclivity toward self-centeredness and self-importance, and to appreciate the complementarity of the gifts of wisdom, personal insight, and balance that this other of the opposite gender can bestow.[40] Undergoing this conversion in the intimacy of marriage can carry over to all opposite-gender relationships in the wider arena of life.

Marriage as a Covenant

Vatican II's view of marriage as a covenant is in sharp contrast with the 1917 Code's perception of marriage as a contract. The notion "contract" is a legal one. It spells out in specific, measurable terms the obligations and compensations of the agreement relating, for example, to employment, a business partnership, an investment, or the sale and purchase of property. As previously considered, the 1917 Code speaks of the marriage contract in the limited and measurable terms of the mutual exchange of one's body for acts suitable for procreation (canon 1081, no. 2).

On the contrary, the word "covenant" is a biblical one. It immediately brings to mind God's covenant of unlimited faithful love, kindness, and compassionate concern for the Israelite people. This covenant between God and humans is renewed in a most visible way by the incarnation, life, death, and resurrection of Jesus. He poured out his blood, his mortal life, for all on the cross, in order to take up his life again in a new way and be with his Church forever, bringing the very Spirit of God, whereby Christ unites the community to himself and to the one he calls "Father."

As God shares the divine life in an unbounded way, so the married couple, on a human level, are images of God's covenant by giving of themselves to one another in open-endedness. Though there are contractual elements in a marriage, the marital union is transcontractual, going beyond any limits imposed by a contract. The couple give themselves to one another without reserve.

Marital fidelity in this covenantal context is much more than not committing adultery or "sticking it out under the same roof" until death intervenes. It means accepting the other in the deepest identity of his or her being. It is to nurture, support, and guide one another in the journey and struggle of becoming what God is calling each person to be as a unique individual. Marital fidelity is being constantly true to the commitment of growing in a personal, caring presence to and for one another in all the affairs of married life. It involves persistently pursuing deeper dimensions of mutual love that point toward a fulfillment that will be perfectly achieved only eschatologically.

The Marital Relationship and Procreation

The pre–Vatican II position, as seen above, was very clear: the primary end of marriage is the procreation and education of children, while the secondary end is the couple's mutual help and the "allaying of concupiscence." Marriage was primarily defined in terms of its ends. The bishops at Vatican II not only dropped hierarchical terminology in regard to the purpose or goals of marriage; they also moved far beyond the negative perception of sexual intimacy that had reduced it to allaying concupiscence. Instead of defining marriage primarily by its goals, the purpose of marriage is perceived in the context of its existential meaning, "an intimate partnership of life and love."

This thinking, of course, reflects the reality. What comes first chronologically is obviously the relationship between the couple. This has its beginnings in their first meeting, their dating, and their growing in personal intimacy. Their commitment to one another becomes more binding when they become formally engaged, and as they pursue the premarital journey toward the wedding day. They marry in order to grow in a unique way in mind, heart, soul, and body through the mutual sharing of their lives. Children may or may not flow from their marital union. The depth and holiness of their marriage depends primarily on how generously they give of themselves to one another in all the dimensions of their being, not on whether or not children emerge from their union. This may well be a matter beyond their control.

Even when a marriage is blessed with children, the first focus must continue to be nurturing the quality of the marital relationship. The greatest gift the couple can give their children is their own sacramental, loving marriage. This provides for them a safe environment in which they can feel secure now and tomorrow. The loving marriage becomes for them the school in which they can learn what true love means, and discover the genuine meaning of sexuality. Living in the context of the love of their parents for one another and for them, they can learn how to grow as loving human beings, even in the midst of the inevitable struggles and conflicts of life.

This focus on the meaning of the marital relationship and the shift away from perceiving procreation as the primary purpose of marriage have profound implications for perceiving the significance of marital intercourse, and for understanding what are the essential elements that constitute a truly human, not to mention Christian, approach to this area of married life. It is precisely this kind of shift in understanding that has led so many Catholic moral theologians, such as Charles E. Curran, Lisa Sowle Cahill, and the late Richard A. McCormick, to develop the tradition on this topic in new ways.[41] It would be far beyond the scope of this chapter to reflect on these developments. Be it enough to say here that once one accepts the meaning of marriage as an intimate partnership of life and love, procreation gives way to the quality of the marital and sexual relationship as the primary principle that is needed to guide individuals in determining what is truly human, constructive, and moral in their sexual encounters, versus what can be humanly destructive and, hence, immoral.

The Sacramentality of Marriage

From Trent to Vatican II, Catholic thought emphasized four important elements of the sacrament of matrimony. The human reality of marriage was "elevated" by Christ to a sacrament. This sacrament provided graces for the couple to meet the challenges and fulfill the responsibilities inherent in their marriage. The administering and "receiving" of this sacrament was identified with the wedding ceremony. The valid marriage of any baptized couple was ipso facto a sacrament.

While there are some important lasting truths in these pre–Vatican II formulas, there are also certain inadequacies. Contemporary theologies of marriage provide a more personalistic understanding. It was never really explained how Christ "elevated" marriage to a sacrament other than the fact that, because of Christ, this "natural reality" now also became a "supernatural" reality and gives us grace. This "elevation" seemed somewhat automatic or magical, and grace was perceived mostly in terms of divine aids that were somehow bestowed on the couple, so that their marital obligations could be fulfilled.

A renewed understanding of the meaning of grace as God's self-gift through the ongoing presence of the risen Christ by the power of the Holy Spirit has revealed a much more profound understanding of the sacramentality of marriage. To those with a living faith, the Trinitarian God is present in their loving, committed marital union. God's faithful and caring love is experienced in their mutual fidelity and loving service to one another. Their gift of their personal presence to one another is an effective sign of God's gift of his personal presence to them and through them. The mutual gift of their body-persons in all the shared moments of their married life, celebrated visibly in their sexual lovemaking, sacramentalizes Christ's eucharistic self-gift: "This is my body given for you; this is the cup of my blood, my life, poured out for you."[42]

Understood in this light, the sacrament of marriage cannot be confined to the church wedding ceremony. All of married life is called to be sacramental. The married couple does not minister this sacrament to one another merely when they exchange their marriage vows, but as they live them in the totality of their marriage. Indeed, they become sacrament to one another.

It is also clear that this perception of the sacramentality of marriage raises serious theological difficulties with the traditional Church assumption that the valid marriage of two baptized persons is automatically a sacrament. A Christian marriage is sacramental only to the degree that it signifies to the couple the love of God in Christ. This requires the manifestation of love to one another, and faith in the God of Jesus Christ.[43]

Marriage as a Call to Holiness

Two elements in recent theological development now interpret marriage as a call to holiness. The first is that marriage is a *call*, that it is a divine vocation, a call from God. Many pre–Vatican II Catholics may recall vocation talks that often gave the impression that all young people who had sufficient physical and mental health and moral values were called to be a priest or a member of a religious community. If one was not "generous enough" to respond to that call, then one stayed "out in the world" and married, almost by default. The idea that God was actually calling one to marriage and that this was God's "preferential" will for that person was foreign to a Church that made clear in many ways that celibacy was the "higher state."

The second aspect is that marriage is a call to *holiness*. The commonplace mind-set of the hierarchical Church and, consequently, that of the faithful at large was that priests and members of religious communities were called to holiness and the rest were called to "save their souls." One of the important roles of the former was to help the latter do just that. Chapter 5 of *Lumen gentium*, "The Universal Call to Holiness," presents a complete reversal of this prior thinking. It states that all in the Church, whether they belong to the hierarchy or are cared for by it, are called to holiness, according to St. Paul's saying: "For this is the will of God your sanctification" (1 Thess. 4:3; see Ephesians 1:4).[44] Jesus, the document continues, "preached holiness of life, which he both initiates and brings to perfection, to each and every one of his disciples *no matter what their condition of life*: 'You, therefore, must be perfect as your heavenly Father is perfect'" (Matt. 5:48).[45] This point is reiterated further on:

"It is therefore quite clear that all Christians *in whatever state or walk in life* are called to the fullness of Christian life and to the perfection of charity."[46]

In light of this position of the bishops at Vatican II, it is clear that the call to the fullness of holiness cannot be attached to a particular state or walk in life. It is rooted in Christians' baptismal call to share in the death and resurrection of Jesus, to die increasingly to their sinfulness, and to put on ever more fully Jesus Christ (see Rom. 6:1–11). All the baptized are called to have fulfilled in them the prayer of the Pauline author of the Letter to the Ephesians:

> I kneel before the Father, from whom every family in heaven and on earth is named, that he may grant you in accord with the riches of his glory to be strengthened with power through his Spirit in the inner self, and that Christ may dwell in your hearts through faith; that you, rooted and grounded in love, may have strength to comprehend with all the holy ones what is the breadth and length and height and depth, and to know the love of Christ that surpasses knowledge, so that you may be filled with all the fullness of God. (3:14–19, NAB translation)

Marriage and the Church of the Home

In their pastoral message "Follow the Way of Love," the United States bishops further develop the notion of domestic Church that was reintroduced by Vatican II. They refer to the family as "church of the home." "We give the name *church* to the people whom the Lord gathers, who strive to follow his way of love, and through whose lives his saving presence is made known."[47] The family is the first community, "and the most basic way the Lord gathers us, forms us, and acts in the world."[48] Later, the bishops explain that Christian families "not only belong to the Church," but their daily life "is a true expression of the Church."[49] If the notion of the Christian family as a church is taken seriously, it means that families do not merely belong to a parish with the obligation to support it; rather, they constitute the parish. The parish, in other words, is best understood as a community of churches of the home.

The challenge to families is that they increasingly become a church by living out their baptismal commitment to share in the ongoing prophetic, priestly, and kingly mission of Christ. The U.S. bishops demonstrate this when they explain that the family carries out the mission of the church of the home when they educate, evangelize, pray together, forgive and seek reconciliation, serve one another, act justly, welcome the stranger, and celebrate and affirm life.[50] If the family is truly the church of the home or domestic church, then its relationship with the wider Church goes two ways. While the family learns from the broader Church, the latter must learn from the truly Christian family.

A Future Agenda

Thus far, we have traced some of the major theological developments that are rooted in Vatican II's treatment of marriage and, for the most part, have become a part of official Church teaching. This view of marriage, however, raises further theological questions that have yet to be officially addressed by the college of bishops in union with the Pope.[51] In this concluding section, I would like to point out a few of these.

The Marital Bond

In present Church teaching, the bond in a valid, consummated marriage between two baptized persons can never be broken except by death, even if the marriage is irreversibly irreconcilable. But if marriage is, as Vatican II insists, an intimate partnership of life and love, what bond remains when the wife and husband have become emotionally estranged, physically separated, or even divorced; when their love has turned to apathy or even hatred; or when their relationship has become destructive rather than life-giving? If Christian marriage is a covenant of unlimited self-giving, reflective of God's infinite self-giving, what bond remains when that covenant has been irreversibly broken or abandoned by one or both parties? If an essential meaning of marriage between two baptized Christians is that it is a sacrament, a sign of Christ's love that is effectively grace-giving, what bond remains when the marital relationship no longer can reflect the grace-giving, life-giving love of Jesus Christ?

If the official Church continues to teach, as Pope Paul VI did, that the marital bond remains even when all love has gone from the marriage, and hence precludes a second valid marriage, it must explain what this bond is that exists apart from and independent of the quality of the personal relationship between the couple. At the present time, this teaching continues to be an unintelligible puzzle to an increasing majority of committed, believing Catholics.

Sexual Intimacy and Procreation

As already seen, one of the most significant shifts the bishops of Vatican II made in regard to the theology of marriage and sexual intimacy was removing procreation as the primary goal and placing the personal relationship of the couple at least on an equal level of importance. In light of my treatment of this shift above, I believe the official hierarchy needs to grapple with three further issues.

First, since in the human experience of marriage, it is the couple's relationship that draws them to the decision to marry, and the primary energy they must put into the marriage is to nurture for the rest of their lives the quality of that communion they already enjoy, ought it not be clearly stated that the *primary* purpose of their marriage, and hence of their sexual intimacy, is to grow in this sacramental union? The having of children is subordinate to the relationship, and the quality of the parenting is in so many ways dependent on the strength of their marital love.

Second, and flowing from this, is the need for the hierarchy to reevaluate the present teaching of the Catholic Church, reiterated in *Humanae vitae* and many times by John Paul II, "that each and every marriage . . . must remain open to the transmission of life."[52] Besides the fact that in reality the vast majority of acts of sexual intercourse are by nature not open to procreation, certainly the new theological emphasis on the equality, if not the primacy, of the personal relationship calls for an official reconsideration of this topic, so vital to the vast majority of human beings. While the unitive and procreative meanings of marital intercourse cannot be denied, where there is a conflict between the two, ought not the latter give way to the former?[53]

Third, in line with this, is the question of whether or not there is a need for a reevaluation of the thinking behind canon 1101 in the 1983 Code of Canon Law, which views a marriage as invalid if a couple "through a positive act of the will" excludes from their marriage vows the intent ever to have children.[54] Perhaps theology can learn from the reality of many married couples who contract a valid marriage even though they know that because of age, infertility, or some other physical disability they will never able to have children. While such couples do not come under this canon, their situation reveals that the validity of marriage stands independent of the ability to have children. Thus, the question emerges of whether there are situations where for serious reasons a couple can be validly married even if they intentionally exclude the having of children. What, for example, of a couple who are called to marriage but do not feel called to be parents? Two examples come to mind: What of the couple who just know that, considering their temperamental and psychological structures, they would not be good parents, but believe they would have a marriage that is fruitful and life-giving in many other ways? Or a couple who are both in the medical field and feel called to dedicate their lives working together with AIDS patients in Africa, but see this as incompatible with rearing a family?

Marriage and Priesthood

Questioning about the law in the Latin rite of the Roman Catholic Church that excludes married persons from ordained priestly ministry is almost always argued from an understanding of the sacrament of orders and from pastoral concerns.[55] Such an approach is, of course, significant and valid. However, it is equally important, I believe, to approach this question from the opposite direction, namely, from a consideration of the theological meaning of the sacrament of marriage.

The basic question is this: What is there about the sacrament of Christian marriage that is contradictory to the exercise of priestly ordained ministry? This question becomes more critical in light of the recent disclosures of pedophilia and ephebophilia sexual abuse cases among Catholic priests. A quick glance at the period since the mid-1960s reveals the stark contrast between the Church's handling of such cases and their actions toward priests who wanted to marry. Priests guilty of sexual abuse were given treatment, usually paid for by the diocese, and then transferred to other parishes and dioceses. On the other hand, any priest who "attempted" marriage was automatically suspended.[56] Those who were granted permission by the Pope to marry had to immediately cease any ordinary exercise of priestly function. What was the *operative* theology of marriage that led Church leaders to see the marital state as more incompatible with priestly ministry and less tolerable than the sexual abuse of minors?

If we really believe that married couples are signs of Christ and sacraments of Christ's love—not despite, but precisely because of—their intimate sexual relationship, then what is the theological incompatibility between marriage and the sacrament of orders? If the married couple is called through their baptism to share in the priestly, prophetic, and kingly mission of Christ—not despite, but precisely in terms of, their marital state—then what is the theological incompatibility between their marital ministry and priestly ministry? If the married couple is called through their baptism to the fullness of holiness, the perfection of love—not despite, but precisely in terms of, their marriage—then what is the theological incompatibility between the holiness required in marriage and what is required in ordained priesthood? Such questions as these demand, I believe, serious theological inquiry on the part of the magisterium that should take precedence over the pastoral aspects of the issue, as important as the latter may be.

In concluding this chapter, I can only trust that the same Spirit, who has guided the Church in the developments in the theological understanding of marriage over the past four and a half centuries from Trent to Vatican II and beyond, will continue to be with the community as it questions the issues that require further critical analysis.

NOTES

1. My principal sources for this first section of this chapter are *The Church Teaches: Documents of the Church in English Translation* (St. Louis, Mo.: Herder, 1955), 335–338, nos. 855–868 (direct quotations of Trent's treatment of marriage will be taken from the translation in this volume, and references will be made to the section

numbers); Theodore Mackin, *The Marital Sacrament* (New York: Paulist Press, 1989), 426–434; Paolo Sarpi, *The History of the Council of Trent*, trans. Nathanael Brent (London: J. Macock, 1676), see esp. 620, 698–699, 705–707, 730–737; Rev. J. Waterworth, ed. and trans., *The Canons and Decrees of the Sacred and Oecumenical Council of Trent* (London: Dolman, 1848), 192–204. Through the courtesy of the Hanover Historical Texts Project, these pages from Waterworth can be found on the Internet at http://history.hanover.edu/texts/trent/ct24.html.

2. *The Church Teaches*, no. 855.

3. Ibid.

4. Ibid.

5. Ibid.

6. Ibid.

7. Ibid., no. 856.

8. Ibid., nos. 857–868.

9. Ibid., no. 866.

10. Waterworth, *Canons and Decrees*, 196–198.

11. Ibid., 199–204.

12. All quotations in this section are taken from T. Lincoln Bouscaren and Adam C. Ellis, *Canon Law: A Text and Commentary* (Milwaukee, Wis.: Bruce, 1957).

13. Ibid., 446. Italics in original.

14. Ibid., 447.

15. Ibid., 448. This condemnation is published in *Acta apostolici sedis* [*AAS*], vol. 36, 103.

16. Ibid. Pius XII's allocution is published in *AAS*, vol. 43, 835.

17. Ibid., 598. See also 624 for corresponding footnote.

18. Ibid., 598.

19. For a detailed summary and critical analysis of the development of the Catholic theology of marriage since the nineteenth century, see Mackin, *The Marital Sacrament*, chs. 12–14.

20. *Gaudium et spes*, 47; emphasis added. All quotations from this Council are taken from Austin Flannery, ed., *Vatican Council II: The Basic Sixteen Documents* (Northport, N.Y.: Costello, 1996).

21. Ibid., 48.

22. Ibid.

23. Ibid.

24. Ibid.

25. Ibid.

26. Ibid.

27. Ibid.

28. Ibid., 49.

29. Ibid.

30. Ibid.

31. Ibid., 50.

32. Ibid.

33. Ibid.

34. Ibid., 52.

35. Ibid.

36. *Lumen gentium*, 11. For a brief summary of the history of the early usage of the notion "domestic church," see Joann Heaney-Hunter, "A Domestic Church: Guiding Beliefs and Daily Practices," in *Christian Marriage and Family: Contemporary Theological and Pastoral Perspectives*, ed. Michael G. Lawler and William P. Roberts (Collegeville, Minn.: Liturgical Press, 1996), 62–63 and accompanying endnotes.

37. For fuller treatment of marriage as partnership, see Challon O'Hearn Roberts and William P. Roberts, *Partners in Intimacy: Living Christian Marriage Today* (New York: Paulist Press, 1988), ch. 1, "Marriage as Partnership," 3–16; and William P. Roberts, "Toward a Post–Vatican II Spirituality of Marriage," in Lawler and Roberts, *Christian Marriage and Family*, 125–129.

38. Three of the key biblical texts that have been thus interpreted are Genesis 2: 7, 18–25; Genesis 3:16; and Ephesians 5:21–33. For an alternative way of interpreting these texts, see Raymond E. Brown, Joseph A. Fitzmyer, and Roland E. Murphy, eds., *The New Jerome Biblical Commentary* (Englewood Cliffs, N.J.: Prentice-Hall, 1990), 12 and 890.

39. This is in sharp contrast to the appalling view of the old moral manuals that stressed the wife's duty "to render the debt."

40. I am well aware that introducing the word "complementarity" here may offend some feminists. Some rightly reject that word because of the patriarchal way it has often been misused in the past. ("This is man's God-given place in the world, this is woman's God-given place in the home." "These are male prerogatives, these are female responsibilities," etc.) I hope that it is obvious from the context that I, too, reject such misuse of the word. But this misinterpretation ought not obfuscate the need each gender has for the other, and the authentic ways in which each can complement the other.

41. For a good summary of the Catholic tradition and contemporary approaches to this topic, as well as a lengthy bibliography, see Vincent J. Genovesi, *In Pursuit of Love: Catholic Morality and Human Sexuality*, 2nd ed. (Collegeville, Minn.: Liturgical Press, 1996), esp. chs. 4–6. A summary and analysis of Charles E. Curran's work on this topic over a forty-year period can be found in the volume published in his honor: James J. Walter, Timothy E. O'Connell, and Thomas A. Shannon, eds., *A Call to Fidelity: On the Moral Theology of Charles E. Curran* (Washington, D.C.: Georgetown University Press, 2002). Part Two of the volume is dedicated to "Sexual and Medical Ethics." See esp. ch. 6, "Sexual Ethics," by Lisa Sowle Cahill.

42. I am using the term "body-person" in its holistic sense of the inspirited body, the embodied spirit. What I speak of here is the gift of the whole person, including the physical, emotional, psychosexual, and spiritual dimensions that constitute the totality of one's being.

43. The need for active faith for the sacrament of marriage has been stressed by several authors. See, for example, Michael G. Lawler, "Faith, Contract, and Sacrament in Christian Marriage: A Theological Approach," in Lawler and Roberts, *Christian Marriage and Family*, 38–58. Also in the same volume, Joann Heaney-Hunter, "Living the Baptismal Commitment in Sacramental Marriage," 106–124. See also the treatment of this theme in William P. Roberts, *Marriage: Sacrament of Hope and Challenge* (Cincinnati, Ohio: St. Anthony Messenger Press, 1988), 32–38, and in "Marriage and

Divorce: Twenty-five Years After Vatican II," in *The Church in the Nineties: Its Legacy, Its Future*, ed. Pierre M. Hegy (Collegeville, Minn.: Liturgical Press, 1993), 173–174.

44. *Lumen gentium*, 39.

45. Ibid., 40. Emphasis added.

46. Ibid. Emphasis added.

47. *Follow the Way of Love: A Pastoral Message of the U.S. Catholic Bishops to Families* (Washington, D.C.: United States Catholic Bishops Conference, 1994), 8.

48. Ibid.

49. Ibid.

50. Ibid., 9–10.

51. A number of these issues are discussed at greater length in some of the volumes already mentioned in this chapter, as well as in, among others: Ladislas Orsy, *Marriage in Canon Law* (Wilmington, Del.: Michael Glazier, 1986), esp. "Problem Areas and Disputed Questions," 260–294; William P. Roberts, ed., *Commitment to Partnership: Explorations of the Theology of Marriage* (New York: Paulist Press, 1987); William P. Roberts, ed., *Divorce and Remarriage: Religious and Psychological Perspectives* (Kansas City, Mo.: Sheed and Ward, 1990); and William P. Roberts, *Thorny Issues: Theological and Pastoral Reflections* (Huntington, N.Y.: Nova Science Publishers, 2000). Because of the confines of this chapter, the scope must be much narrower and the treatment briefer.

52. Pope Paul VI, *Of Human Life* (Boston: Pauline Books and Media, 1968), 11; see also 12.

53. I have discussed the topic of birth control in more detail in *Thorny Issues*, 20–23.

54. Section 2 of this canon states: "But if either or both parties through a positive act of the will should exclude marriage itself, some essential element or an essential property of marriage, it is invalidly contracted." See James A. Coriden, Thomas J. Green, and Donald E. Heintschel, eds., *The Code of Canon Law: A Text and Commentary* (New York: Paulist Press, 1985), 784–787, for a rather detailed commentary on this canon. Two brief quotes must suffice here. "Foremost among the essential elements of marriage is its ordination to the good of children" (785). "The relationship between the conjugal community and the openness to procreation is fundamental. The obligation to accept children is essential to the marriage covenant. Those who consent to marriage with a firm purpose of avoiding all children or restricting their number consent invalidly" (786).

55. The topic of marriage and priesthood has been treated at some length in *Thorny Issues*, 59–80.

56. 1983 Code of Canon Law, canon 1394, 1.

13

Religious Life for Women: From Enclosure to Immersion

Doris Gottemoeller

The theme of religious life as a gift to the whole People of God figures prominently in recent Church statements: "The consecrated life
is not something isolated and marginal, but a reality which affects
the whole Church . . . it is a precious and necessary gift for the present and the future of the People of God, since it is an intimate part
of her life, her holiness, and her mission."[1] Thus, a way of life embraced by only a small minority of Christians is intended to have
significance far beyond its size, and any renewal of the Church must
include a renewal among the members of religious institutes. Contrasting the approach to reform and renewal in the sixteenth and
twentieth centuries is an interesting illustration of this phenomenon.

The Council of Trent's mandate to women religious consisted
of an insistence on the rules of enclosure. The Second Vatican
Council, in turn, mandated religious to examine every aspect of
their lives in order to discard outmoded customs and practices in
light of the needs of their times. In other words, religious women
were to become more available to ministries that addressed the
forms of human suffering today. One age called for a separation
from the world; the other, for immersion in the cares of the
world. Highlighting the contrast in this way, however, does not do
justice to the complexities of the two movements for renewal nor
to the results of each. In the following pages, we will examine
each, focusing on the situations prior to the councils, the conciliar
mandates, their implementation, and their short- and long-term
effects. The comparison will allow us to make some observations

about the gift of consecrated life to the Church and, especially, about the role and contribution of women religious.

The focus in this chapter is on the experience of women religious, rather than on religious life of women and men, for two reasons. The majority of male religious are ordained, or belong to orders which include both the ordained and nonordained. This introduces questions of clerical status and vocation that require a separate analysis. Second, women religious have been in the vanguard of those introducing a feminist consciousness into the Church, a contribution that deserves special mention.

Sixteenth-Century Reform Efforts

By the beginning of the sixteenth century, women's religious life in Europe consisted largely of the traditional monastic forms and "second orders" of the mendicant communities founded by men beginning in the thirteenth century. The commitment of women to the apostolic mobility characteristic of mendicants was circumscribed, however, by the Church's insistence on enclosure. In 1298, Boniface VIII had decreed strict cloister for women religious in his bull *Periculoso*.[2] No doubt, this legislation encouraged the growth of semireligious or noncanonical groups in the fourteenth century—Beguines in Germany and the Netherlands, *beatas* in Spain—who lived in community without religious vows, devoting their lives to prayer and work.[3] The Sisters of the Common Life, founded by Gerard Groote in 1379 as an expression of the new *devotio moderna*, was another example of a quasi-monastic order.[4] The Sisters differed from the Beguines by holding all property in common.

Religious orders were frequent targets of criticism in the late Middle Ages. In the case of women's orders, one author describes convents as "refined dumping grounds for the unmarried daughters of European elites."[5] Though that was not universally true, convent life did offer a refuge for the unmarried and unmarriageable. Some girls were consigned to a convent for care and schooling at very young ages, and then never had an opportunity to leave—or to make a free and mature choice of religious life. Further, some convents reproduced the social classes of their entrants: the wealthy who brought large endowments lived in comfort and considered those from poorer families little more than servants.

The literature from this period contains many allegations of sexual improprieties; whether they were based on fact or on the pornographic fantasies of the writers is hard to determine.[6] What is true is that women's groups experienced an essential dependence on men's orders or on the secular clergy for sacramental ministry and guidance. Monasteries and bishops often resented their responsibility for the *cura mulierum* and exercised it indifferently or grudgingly. Instances of pseudo-mystical behavior and bizarre practices were not unknown. Further, women's monasteries were subject to the vagaries of wealthy patronage, armed conflict, weather, and commerce; agricultural lands could be confiscated in wartime or fail to produce in bad times, reducing the nuns to penury.

There were frequent efforts to introduce reform into religious life during the sixteenth century, either by recovering the primitive rigor of existing orders or by founding new groups adapted to new pastoral needs. The renewal of existing groups sometimes led to their division. For example, the Franciscans split into the Conventual and the Observant orders in 1517, and the Capuchins branched off in 1528. The female Capuchins were founded in 1538. Teresa of Avila began the reform of the Spanish Carmelites in 1562. Over the years, their original discipline had deteriorated into a life of luxury bordering on the scandalous. Within twenty years, Teresa founded seventeen convents of Discalced nuns and fifteen communities of men.

Examples of new groups were the Ursulines and the Institute of the Blessed Virgin Mary or the English Ladies, as they were popularly known. Angela Merici founded the Ursulines at Brescia in northern Italy in 1535. The original group of twenty-eight pious women formed a religious society to lead frugal lives and to carry out social works of charity, including service in hospitals, orphanages, hostels for prostitutes, and, especially, teaching religion to girls. Brescia's bishop gave the sisterhood approval and a chaplain in 1536. Within four years, there were 150 members, living in community or remaining within families. Often likened to the Jesuits, whose organization they consciously modeled, they became the most numerous of the female orders.[7] Mary Ward founded her Institute at St. Omer in 1612 as a group of uncloistered nuns without any distinctive habit, bound together by their vows and their rule, available for assignment by a superior general, and committed to apostolic work such as the management of free schools for girls.[8] Despite these efforts at self-reform, the reform commission set up by Paul III in 1537 argued that all the conventual orders had become so deformed that they should be done away with by prohibiting the admission of novices. Other cardinals urged the amalgamation of the existing orders into a few basic types.

The Council of Trent waited until its last session, in December 1563, to address religious life in twenty-two chapters titled "Concerning Regulars and Nuns." The text affirms the contribution of the way of life when well ordered: "How great a splendor and usefulness accrues to the Church of God from monasteries properly regulated." It affirms the efforts of many orders to return to the purity of their original rules, including the practice of poverty, the common life, precautions to safeguard the freedom of action in making profession, fixity of place for monks, and enclosure for nuns. Three years later, Pius V ruled that the law of enclosure applied to all professed nuns, even to members of third orders who lived in the world and had made only vows of chastity. Those who had not taken solemn vows were instructed to do so or have their communities closed, and women who were not nuns were forbidden to form communities.[9] The implementation of these instructions was difficult and uneven. Families were not necessarily eager to have their daughters return to the world and claim their inheritances or to remain strictly enclosed within a cloister. Groups that failed to practice strict enclosure suffered repeated attempts to suppress them. The Ursulines had been given a rule and episcopal approval by Charles Borromeo, who championed their cause with other Italian bishops who, in turn, welcomed them into their dioceses. However, as the Ursulines expanded into France, the practice of living in community became more common, and their digression from the policies of Trent more obvious. In 1612, the Paris community accepted monastic enclosure, followed in time by the other French houses. "This was the result partly of pressure from the French hierarchy, who had set out to bring all women's congregations into line with the Roman policy, partly of pressure from French society which hesitated to accept uncloistered single women living outside the home, but also partly of the desire of the women themselves who at this time of religious revival in France and the introduction of the Discalced Carmelites saw a greater value in the strict cloistered life."[10] At the same time, the community was able to secure papal approval of its mission of educating young women, thus ensuring the continuation of an active ministry.

As Mary Ward's Institute spread through Germany and Italy, it came under increasing attack: in 1629, the Congregation of the Propaganda suppressed these "Jesuitesses." "Publication of the decree to the various nuncios was neither simultaneous nor clear, and Mary's attempt to steady the confidence of her sisters was considered rebellion. She was imprisoned for a short time in the Anger convent in Munich but was released after a personal appeal to the Pope."[11] The Institute was definitively suppressed in 1631, but survived in the form of some sisters living in community under private vows and continuing their educational mission. Interestingly, it received papal approbation only in 1877, although most modern congregations developed along similar lines.

The Daughters of Charity, first recognized as a confraternity by the Archbishop of Paris in 1646, circumvented the requirement of enclosure by taking private vows of poverty, chastity, obedience, and service of the poor, renewed annually. Thus, they were not religious, canonically speaking. Their numbers grew so rapidly that they soon became the largest community of women in the world.

Overall, in the decades after Trent most congregations reverted to a semi-contemplative monastic lifestyle. But eventually, with social change and vigorous episcopal support from some quarters, active female religious congregations with only limited enclosure came to be tolerated by Rome—even though they were not, strictly speaking, religious orders. Full papal ecclesiastical recognition of noncloistered women with simple vows and active apostolates was finally given in 1900 in the apostolic constitution *Conditae a Christo* of Pope Leo XIII.[12]

Two tendencies struggled against one another in the development of women's congregations in the sixteenth and early seventeenth centuries: one toward a monastic, enclosed way of life and the other toward an active, apostolic way of life. In 1586, Sixtus V established the first Vatican organ to deal explicitly with the affairs of religious; it became the Congregation for Religious after the reorganization of the Roman curia two years later. "Generally the Vatican fostered centralization within orders and congregations and a generic concept of 'religious' that tended to downplay the distinctive features of orders and congregations and to favour the monastic vision of religious, especially in the case of women religious."[13] At the same time increasing pastoral needs arising from the growth of urban populations caused bishops to welcome women religious who could teach the young, care for the sick and poor, shelter and rehabilitate prostitutes, and visit the imprisoned—work that required a degree of mobility and freedom from cloister.

The preference for enclosure for women was fed in part by a patronizing attitude toward women, the belief that they were the weaker sex, more liable than men to be harmed by contact with the world or led astray by false teaching, and in need of protection by husbands or churchmen. One author describes the condemnation of Mary Ward's Institute as "a project destroyed by little more than unreasoning ecclesiastical anti-feminism and prejudice: typical of charges against her and her colleagues was that: 'They are idle and talkative. They boast of their freedom from enclosure. They do not conform to feminine modesty.'"[14]

As the decades passed, pastoral need and feminine zeal and creativity outweighed masculine reservations, and women's congregations expanded enormously in number and size. By the eighteenth and, especially, the nineteenth and twentieth centuries, women's congregations had moved beyond Europe to Africa, Australia, and the Americas in response to new needs. Assessing the impact of Trent on women's religious life, we can say that the effects of its specific legislation were negligible, since renewal efforts were well under way before the Council, and many subsequent efforts were in tension with its specific mandates. But effects of the broader conciliar event and of ongoing world events were tremendous. I will discuss this in more detail later.

Renewal in the Twentieth Century

Picking up the story at the end of the first third of the twentieth century, we find women's religious life again in need of renewal, but from an altogether different perspective. By now, apostolic women's religious life, as defined in the 1917 revision of the Code of Canon Law, was the dominant form throughout the Western world. Women religious worldwide numbered in the hundreds of thousands, a number that was to increase until it reached a peak in the 1960s. They staffed schools and colleges, hospitals, orphanages, homes for the aged and handicapped, retreat houses, and social agencies of many kinds. They resided in motherhouses or in convents associated with one of their institutions or a parish. They were immediately recognizable by their habits and universally respected for the good that they did, even by those who did not share their religious beliefs or who would not want their daughter to choose this life.

Under this picture of ministerial zeal and public approval, however, lay the need for change. Sisters were often inadequately prepared for ministry, taking twenty years of summer school to earn a bachelor's degree or professional qualification in teaching, nursing, or social work. Furthermore, selection of new candidates was often not discriminating and their religious formation minimal, the latter depending on mentoring by older religious as much as on formal teaching. The lifestyle itself included practices that were anachronistic if not downright psychologically harmful.

By mid-century, efforts at renewal started to emanate from Church leaders and from women religious themselves. Beginning in 1947 with the publication of *Provida mater*, the charter of secular institutes, Pius XII issued a series of instructions calling for the adaptation of the forms of religious life. Modification of the habit, professional preparation for nursing and teaching, the founding of the Regina Mundi Institute in Rome in 1954 for the advanced education of sisters, modification of the enclosure for contemplatives, the use of motor bikes (!) to reach distant apostolates: these were some of the topics treated in papal allocutions and letters. In 1950, Pius XII convoked the first international meeting of heads of religious communities (male and female) in order to urge a renewal in religious life, including "theological education and professional credentials for those teaching and doing other professional work" and "the elimination of outdated customs and clothing that estranged them from those they served."[15]

In the United States, preconciliar renewal was promoted by the Sister Formation Movement, developed initially under the umbrella of the National Catholic Education Association and then spun off into the Sister Formation Conference (SFC) in 1954. Its aims were to educate sisters to the bachelor's degree level before ministry, in a setting apart from seculars, with a heavy emphasis on the humanities and liberal arts and on personal and religious integration. These aims were embodied in the so-called Everett curriculum and in the founding of special sisters' colleges. Though strongly opposed in many instances by bishops and clergy who resented the fact that young religious were being held back from active ministry, most major superiors embraced the aims of the Movement beginning in the early 1950s and gave their new members the opportunity for education and religious formation. Through its meetings and publications, the SFC was very influential in the life of religious congregations in the United States and, by implication, on the quality of ministry they performed. It was significant that the period during which the Movement was a strong agent for change coincided with the period of theological, ecumenical, and liturgical innovation just before the Council.

In 1956, the Conference of Major Superiors of Women (later renamed the Leadership Conference of Women Religious) was founded in response to a Vatican directive.[16] Its annual conventions and regional meetings became important forums for intercongregational collaboration and for the dissemination of new ideas and programs from that time on. Later, delegates from around the world formed the International Union of Superiors General, headquartered in Rome, to further similar aims on a worldwide scale. The combination of all of these organizational and educational efforts created a body of women uniquely poised to respond to the message of the Second Vatican Council.

The Council produced two principal texts dealing with religious life: chapter 6 of the Dogmatic Constitution on the Church (*Lumen gentium*) and the Decree on the Appropriate Renewal of the Religious Life (*Perfectae caritatis*). The former contains doctrinal principles about religious life in the context of the whole Church, and the latter gives the call to renewal and guidelines for its achievement.

Chapter 6 is an instance where the medium is at least part of the message, in that its placement within the overall text was of extraordinary importance. The original draft constitution described "states" in the Church in the traditional order: hierarchy, religious, and laity. This was changed by the Coordinating Commission to hierarchy, laity, and religious. The chapter on religious, originally titled "The State of Evangelical Perfection to Be Acquired," was changed to "Of Those Who Bind Themselves to the Evangelical Councils," and finally evolved into a chapter called simply "Religious," following the chapter on the call to holiness. It consists of five rather brief sections dealing with the definition of religious life, its origin in the word and example of Christ, its orientation to mission based on baptismal consecration, its sign value, and its relationship to Church authority.

Perfectae caritatis, adopted in October 1965, had a similar bumpy path through the Council. It began life as a set of about 200 articles developed prior to the Council by the Preparatory Commission. Between the first two sessions, it was abbreviated by the secretary of the Commission for Religious and a few *periti*, and subsequently by a plenary session of the Commission. Then it was passed on to the Coordinating Commission of the Council, which objected to numerous points. After several more additions and deletions, it was finally sent to the Council fathers. At this point, it consisted of fifty-one articles in nine chapters. Written comments from Council members ranged from unqualified praise to extreme criticism. During this time the Commission on

Religious Life was preoccupied with the fourth (ultimately the fifth) chapter of *Lumen gentium*, and the draft that was to become *Perfectae caritatis* never made its way to the Council floor.

At this point, the Coordinating Commission requested that the text be cut even more, and it was reduced to nineteen articles running to scarcely four pages. A year and a half and several versions later, it emerged in its present form of twenty-five paragraphs dealing in a rather straightforward fashion with principles and procedures for renewal; various forms of religious life (i.e., contemplative life, apostolic life, monasticism, lay or nonclerical religious, and secular institutes); the vows; community life; and specifics to be adapted, such as the cloister, habit, and formation processes. It also mentioned the suppression and union of congregations, conferences of major superiors, and vocations.

With all this effort, what had been accomplished? The Council affirmed a deeper theological and spiritual understanding of religious life rooted in the universal call to holiness. Religious are persons who have responded to their baptismal vocation by dedicating themselves to the lifelong following of the evangelical counsels. What distinguishes their following of Christ from that of others is the choice of a stable lifestyle formally approved by the Church. *Lumen gentium* made clear that the religious life is not part of the hierarchical structure of the Church; it is not an intermediate state between clergy and laity. However, by its approval the Church confers on religious life the dignity of public canonical status. The theological and ecclesiological bases of this definition are a departure from the former juridical emphasis on vows or from a strictly ascetical interpretation of the counsels. Instead, it emphasizes the centrality of the following of Christ under the inspiration of the Spirit within the community of the Church.

The unambiguous call to change, to renew, and to adapt was probably the most powerful contribution of the Council to religious life. The renewal was to be based on a twofold movement: a continuous return to the sources of all Christian life and to the original inspiration behind a given community, and an adjustment of the community to the changed condition of the times.[17] In order to effect the latter, "communities should promote among their members a suitable awareness of contemporary human conditions and of the needs of the Church. For if their members can combine the burning zeal of an apostle with wise judgments, made in the light of faith, concerning the circumstances of the modern world, they will be able to come to the aid of humankind more effectively."[18] The scope of change was laid out in the next section: "The manner of living, praying, and working should be suitably adapted to the physical and psychological conditions of today's religious and also, to the extent required by the nature of each community, to the needs of the apostolate, the requirements of a given culture, the social and economic circumstances anywhere, but especially in missionary countries. The way in which communities are governed should also be examined in light of these same standards." The text also asserts that constitutions, directories, custom books, books of prayers and ceremonies, and similar compilations are to be suitably revised, including the suppression of any outmoded regulations. Finally, the text emphasizes that successful renewal and proper adaptation cannot be achieved unless every member of a community cooperates.

The *Norms for the Implementation of Perfectae Caritatis,* published in 1966, called for a period of experimentation in every congregation. Special chapters of renewal were to be held in each congregation and current constitutions set aside. The period of experimentation would come to an end approximately twelve years later, depending on the timing of subsequent chapters, with the adoption of new constitutions and their submission to the Congregation for Religious for approval.

Before proceeding to assess the implementation of the Council's call for renewal, a few thoughts about the conciliar message are in order. First, the assertion of the fundamental equality of all Christians and of the universal call to holiness eliminated any elitist interpretation of the religious state. Similarly, the fact that the call to mission is shared by all Christians means that it is not the prerogative of religious. As ennobling as this affirmation is, it did relativize the commitment of religious, especially the nonordained, in a way that some found disconcerting. In a more positive vein, there were a number of other concepts significant to religious life which were part of the overall focus and pastoral character of the Council, but which have specific implications for religious life. Most notable are the concepts of participation, of collegiality, and of authority as service. There are also phrases and ideas scattered throughout chapter 6 of *Lumen gentium* and of *Perfectae caritatis* that, while not developed extensively, are pregnant with meaning. Examples are "active and responsible obedience" (*Perfectae caritatis,* 14), "genuine development of the human person" (*Lumen gentium,* 46), and "living and thinking with the Church" (*Perfectae caritatis,* 6).

It can safely be said that no group within the Church took the admonitions of the Council more seriously or implemented its decrees with more sincerity than women religious. Coming on the heels of the Sister Formation Movement, the Council inaugurated a period of enormous activity within women's congregations. Special renewal chapters were followed by experiments in community living, dress, governance, and prayer forms. New ministries designed to address contemporary human conditions blossomed everywhere. All of this activity was animated and guided by innumerable workshops, charism retreats, study days, consultations, questionnaires, and constitutional drafts. Not surprisingly, these efforts produced a measure of internal dissension and external criticism. Some members felt that changes were being made too quickly; others complained that the pace lagged. Some observers felt that women religious had lost their way or betrayed their call—especially when their numbers in traditional ministries such as parish schools declined.

There were two notions promoted by the Council that proved to have ambiguous results: the concepts of experimentation and of the retrieval of charism. The notion of experimentation connotes a scientific objectivity that was completely unrealistic in dealing with persons' lives. An experiment, once embraced, inevitably changed the participants in ways that barred them from dispassionate evaluations and from returning to the earlier status quo. Since everyone was mandated to participate in the new "experimental" ways of living and acting, there was no control group with which to compare the results after several years' experience with new ways of living.

The Council drew on the biblical notion of differing gifts, that is, charisms or manifestations of the Spirit, in its description of the universal call to holiness; all persons should walk according to their own personal gifts: bishops, clerics, deacons, religious, married couples, parents, laborers, and so on (*Lumen gentium*, 41). With respect to religious, it asserted that the evangelical counsels are a divine gift and that the religious state is a particular gift in the life of the Church. *Perfectae caritatis* accounted for the diversity of religious congregations in terms of the different gifts or graces given them. This concept of the unique gift of each congregation and, originally, of its founder had a very liberating and positive effect on congregations as they began renewal. It encouraged return to the spirit of the founder and a creative interpretation of that spirit in the present.

Gradually, however, the usefulness of the concept began to wane. First, the historical search did not always reward the investigator. Some founders had established more than one congregation—what was his or her charism? Some congregations had to admit that their founders were clearly eccentric or not particularly original, AWOL from another congregation, or simply bishops looking for a dedicated workforce; some had later left the congregations they had founded "under a cloud." Some founders were rehabilitated in this process, but overall, it was not guaranteed to produce clarity as to what the Spirit might have in mind for the congregation today. Second, the charisms of the founder could not be equated with those of the congregation. The former had the inspiration from God and the requisite gifts to found something—an essentially nonrepeatable act. Those gifts needed to persevere, change, and develop might be something else indeed. Thus, the rediscovery of an early charism might inhibit needed change today. This was especially true if the founder or members of the first generation were still alive! Third, it had to be admitted after a while that differentiating and concretizing charisms among various communities is an elusive task. For example, Sisters of Mercy might *feel* different from Sisters of Divine Providence, but translating that difference in tangible terms to nonmembers or new members, and for insertion into congregational documents, was very difficult. It can be likened to family identity—it is real and powerful, but almost impossible to analyze.

The most dramatic change in women's religious life since the Council is the significant decline in membership. In 1965, there were 179,954 religious sisters in the United States; in 2003, the number was 73, 316.[19] Similar figures could be given for western Europe; but there are modest increases in eastern Europe and larger increases in some African, Asian, and Latin American nations.[20] While the phenomenon is not completely understood, a number of causes can be identified for the decline. In the early decades after the Council, members left in large numbers, dissatisfied with the pace of change, whether too fast or too slow. Others seem to have concluded that if religious life is not a better or more perfect option, then the sacrifices inherent in the vows are not warranted. Furthermore, the new attention given to psychological maturity opened some to what was lacking in their own motivation for entering a congregation in the first place, and they left. Most who departed, for whatever reason, had the benefit of an education which made it easier for them to find professional opportunities than it would have been prior to the 1960s. In recent decades, congregations have failed to attract new members in numbers sufficient to replace those who have died or departed. Here again, reasons are various: the small size of families today; opportunities open to women in the business world and professions; opportunities for Church ministry which do not require the commitment of religious life; and the diminished visibility of religious life as an option. In fact, an unintended consequence of the annual bishops' collection for retired religious is to reinforce a public image of religious as elderly, frail, and dependent—a phenomenon of the past rather than of the future.

Reflections on Two Experiences of Renewal

The period since the Second Vatican Council does not provide the same perspective on that experience that we can have on the Council of Trent. Nevertheless, a few reflections are in order. A common thesis about religious life, from a social science perspective, is that it is cyclical, flourishing in one epoch and declining in another.[21] We have seen that both councils were preceded by periods of reform, both self-initiated and promoted by the Pope and bishops. Both were followed by intense activities on the part of women's congregations. However, each council addressed the reality at a different point on the bell curve of change. In the sixteenth century, women's congregations were approaching a period of enormous growth, as they responded to the needs arising from urbanization and global expansion. In the twentieth century, women's congregations peaked in size during the Council or shortly thereafter, and began a precipitous decline in numbers which is still unabated. This observation points to another, namely, that change within women's religious life has been promoted more by the general impetus of the two councils and by factors external to them rather than by specific mandates to women religious.

The emphasis at Trent on education and sound doctrine advanced the growth of an active teaching apostolate for women. The responsibility of bishops for promoting reform reinforced their desire for active apostolic women's congregations within their dioceses. The dawn of the modern age, with the growth of cities and the colonization of the New World, led to a rapid expansion of new and existing orders. The first women's congregations to come to America started schools, hospitals, and orphanages, and congregations founded here in succeeding years responded to similar needs. The rules of enclosure survived in terms of a medieval dress and some customs (such as a curfew and the practice of traveling in pairs) that created a kind of quasi-separation from the surrounding world. But as the work that congregations embraced required more interaction with parents and professional peers, the separation became less and less tenable.

The emphasis at Vatican II on embracing the concerns of the modern world led women religious into ministries of social change beyond the classroom setting. The turbulent 1960s invited involvement in antiwar protests, civil rights marches, and the war on poverty. Further change in religious life was encouraged by the changing social status and roles of women. The feminist movement found many adherents within religious congregations and led to support for a larger role in Church leadership, including, in some cases, a desire for ordination. A related phenomenon of the Church today is the percentage of women religious serving in administrative and service roles in parishes and dioceses. Some commentators have pointed out that this parochialization of religious life diminishes the prophetic character of religious congregations.[22] Similarly, the consideration of ordination as an option for women religious could lead to a clericalization of their congregations.[23]

In 1994, Pope John Paul II convened a monthlong synod on consecrated life, and the subsequent papal apostolic exhortation, *Vita consecrata*, was published in 1996. A survey of the years since the Second Vatican Council shows the document to be sympathetic and positive. The period of renewal has been "full of hopes, new experiments and proposals aimed at giving fresh vigor to the profession of the evangelical counsels, but it has also been a time of tension and struggle, in which well-meaning endeavors have not always met with positive results." Nevertheless, the difficulties must not lead to discouragement, but to fresh enthusiasm, "for the Church needs the spiritual and apostolic contribution of a renewed and revitalized consecrated life" (*Vita consecrata*, 13).[24]

One way in which the struggle is sometimes framed is in terms of a tension between consecration and mission. Is the meaning of religious life to be found primarily in terms of *being* or of *doing*, of the witness of a particular vowed lifestyle or of apostolic activity? The synod integrates the two aspects in terms of the consistency between proclamation and life (*Vita consecrata*, 85). "Consecrated persons are 'in mission' by virtue of their very consecration by which they bear witness in accordance with the ideal of their Institute" (*Vita consecrata*, 72). Religious are called on not only to continue their many ministries that are still needed and effective, but also to devise "new answers to new problems" (*Vita consecrata*, 73). At the same time, this apostolic activity will be fruitful only if it is understood to flow from a life that is totally dedicated to the love of God and God's people. The challenge of religious life, then, is to forge a new integration of consecration and mission in every age and culture, a witness that is transparent to the divine and in touch with the needs of suffering humanity. This is the gift that women's religious life seeks to bring to the Church and the world today.

NOTES

1. John Paul II, *Apostolic Exhortation Vita Consecrata* (1996), no. 3. Similar thoughts are expressed in the Dogmatic Constitution on the Church (1964), VI, 43, and in *The Relationship of Bishops and Religious Orders*, published by the Congregation for Bishops and the Congregation for Religious and Secular Institutes (1978), no. 3.

2. Elizabeth McDonough, *Religious in the 1983 Code: New Approaches to the New Law* (Chicago: Franciscan Herald Press, 1985), 76.

3. Hubert Jedin and John Dolan, eds., *History of the Church*, vol. 4, *From the High Middle Ages to the Eve of the Reformation,* by Hans-Georg Beck et al. (New York: Crossroad, 1982), 244–246.

4. Ibid., 426–432.

5. Michael A. Mullett, *The Catholic Reformation* (London: Routledge, 1999), 107.

6. For a discussion of this issue, see Jo Ann Kay McNamara, *Sisters in Arms: Catholic Nuns Through Two Millennia* (Cambridge, Mass.: Harvard University Press, 1996), 353–382.

7. Mullett, 106; Robert Bireley, *The Refashioning of Catholicism, 1450–1700* (Washington, D.C.: Catholic University of America Press, 1999), 38ff.

8. "Mary Ward," in *New Catholic Encyclopedia* (New York: McGraw-Hill, 1967), vol. 14, 808–809.

9. Bireley, *The Refashioning of Catholicism*, 38.

10. Ibid., 40.

11. "Mary Ward," 809.

12. McDonough, *Religious in the 1983 Code,* 79.

13. Bireley, *The Refashioning of Catholicism*, 43.

14. Mullett, *The Catholic Reformation*, 110.

15. Marjorie Noterman Beane, *From Framework to Freedom* (Lanham, Md.: University Press of America, 1993), 2. This is the definitive history of the Sister Formation Conference.

16. For a history of the Leadership Conference of Women Religious, see Lora Ann Quinoñez and Mary Daniel Turner, *The Transformation of American Catholic Sisters* (Philadelphia: Temple University Press, 1992).

17. *Perfectae caritatis*, C, 2.

18. Ibid.

19. *The Cara Report* (Georgetown University, Center for Applied Research in the Apostolate) 9, 1 (Summer 2003): 6.

20. Helen Rose Ebaugh summarizes the worldwide changes between 1975 and 1985 in "The Growth and Decline of Catholic Religious Orders of Women Worldwide: The Impact of Women's Opportunity Structures," *Journal for the Scientific Study of Religion* 32, no. 1 (1993): 68–75. African nations and Asian nations (excluding Japan and the oil-rich Mideastern nations) grew 13.1 percent and 24.9 percent, respectively. Her thesis is that growth is inversely proportional to GNP.

21. See, for example, Patricia Wittberg, *The Rise and Fall of Catholic Religious Orders: A Social Movement Perspective* (Albany: State University of New York Press, 1994).

22. David J. Nygren and Mirian D. Ukeritis, "Religious Life Futures Project: Executive Summary" (Chicago: De Paul University, Center for Applied Social Research, 1992).

23. Doris Gottemoeller, "The Priesthood: Implications in Consecrated Life for Women," in *A Concert of Charisms: Ordained Ministry in Religious Life*, ed. Paul K. Hennessy (New York: Paulist Press, 1997).

24. More recently, the Congregation for Institutes of Consecrated Life and Societies of Apostolic Life repeated this hopeful message in an instruction commemorating the fifth anniversary of *Vita consecrata:* "Starting Afresh in Christ," *Origins*, July 4, 2002.

14

From Confession to Reconciliation and Back: Sacramental Penance

W. David Myers

Sacramental penance in recent decades appears to be in crisis. Since the 1950s, reception of the sacrament has dropped markedly.[1] Catholic commentators both in America and abroad have lamented the decline in the practice of frequent reception—an observance that has been personally championed by a number of Popes, most recently John Paul II in a 2004 speech to participants in a course on the "internal forum" organized by the Tribunal of the Apostolic Penitentiary.[2] In an excellent recent book surveying the current state of Catholicism in America, Peter Steinfels does not mention confession even once.[3] Troubling though this situation might seem to Catholics steeped in the religious practices and expectations of the twentieth century, it does not mark the end of penance or even of confession. Despite an increased communal and ecclesiological dimension incorporated since Vatican Council II, the Pope and numerous bishops have repeatedly emphasized the central features of Tridentine practice. They have warned Catholics not to mistake the many communal forms of penance now available for the actual sacrament itself, which requires specific confession to, and individual absolution from, a priest. Sacramental penance, however, has changed greatly since the first century. As this chapter will demonstrate, the form of confession prevalent today is in fact a product of the High Middle Ages and most particularly the religious reforms of the Council of Trent. Furthermore, modern devotion to the sacrament signaled by frequent reception is a relatively recent phenomenon that has varied greatly since the Council of Trent.

Definitions and First Impressions

Both the Council of Trent and the Second Vatican Council place the specific sacrament of penance within a larger context of the history of justification and salvation. The differences between the two treatments, though, their purposes and their goals, are apparent from the very beginning. The decrees and canons of the fourteenth session at Trent, issued on November 25, 1551, consist of nine separate chapters on doctrine and fifteen canons anathematizing the errors of Protestants and others. In the documents of Vatican II, references to sacramental penance appear only twice, with one sentence in chapter 11 of *Lumen gentium*, The Constitution on the Church, and another in chapter 72 of *Sacrosanctum concilium*, The Constitution on the Sacred Liturgy. This second reference merely states enigmatically, "The rite and formulas for the sacrament of penance are to be revised so that they more clearly express both the nature and effect of the sacrament."[4] The result of this was the promulgation of the new *Ordo paenitentiae* in 1973.

Although both treatments stress divine mercy, the great disparity in the amount of space dedicated to penance indicates very different historical situations. Trent was the first council to give a comprehensive treatment of the sacrament. In extremely difficult circumstances, Trent laid out the terms under which the sacrament would henceforth be understood and with which Vatican II must reckon. Trent defined a particular Roman Catholic position that would simultaneously include the traditions of the Church yet exclude the beliefs of the new Protestant churches. Even at its broadest, the language of Trent has a slightly technical caste: "But because God, rich in mercy, knows our frame, *He hath bestowed a remedy of life even on those who may, after baptism, have delivered themselves up to the servitude of sin and the power of the devil,—the sacrament to wit of Penance, by which the benefit of the death of Christ is applied to those who have fallen after baptism.*"[5] Martin Luther had argued that Christ's merits were not a treasury from which the Church could draw later, but were applied once and for all, for the justified. In response, Trent presented the sacrament as an element of justification, crucial to the economy of salvation.

In contrast, Vatican II felt less need to define and protect doctrine from outside threats than to reengage the world in a sympathetic fashion. According to *Lumen gentium*, through sacramental penance, Christians ". . . obtain pardon from the mercy of God for offenses committed against him, and are, at the same time, reconciled with the Church which they have wounded by their sins and which by charity, by example, and by prayer labors for their conversion" (*Lumen gentium*, 11). *Lumen gentium* deemphasizes technical language and stresses a more pastoral approach. Most significantly, it refers to the goal of reconciliation with the Church as well as the hope of divine pardon. If the formulations of Trent appear narrow and constraining, however, the broad statements of Vatican II are unsatisfyingly vague. They extol the purpose of sacramental penance but neglect its contents. This again reflects historical circumstances.

Late Medieval and Reformation Contexts for the Council of Trent

The decisions of Trent distilled a long and confused medieval evolution of both practice and theology that increasingly focused attention on the individual encounter between priest and penitent. The core document of this development was the decree *Omnis utriusque sexus,* promulgated at the Fourth Lateran Council in 1215: "All the faithful of both sexes, after they have reached the age of discretion, shall faithfully confess all their sins at least once a year to their own priest and perform to the best of their ability the penance imposed, receiving reverently at least at Easter the sacrament of the Eucharist."[6] The decree includes two specific demands with serious consequences. First, the faithful were to confess all sins to their own priest at least once every year, thus enabling priests to safeguard against heresy and better oversee and guide the morals of lay Catholics. While scholastic theologians generally emphasized the need to confess only "grave" offenses, the decree of the Lateran Council does not distinguish "mortal" and "venial" sins—that would happen later, at Trent. Indeed, though scholastic authors distinguished generically between "mortal" and "venial," they had a difficult time in practice weeding out which was which, and recommended confessing all misdeeds as the safer method. Whether or not the Council intended confession to become a means of "social control," pastors theoretically had in their hands a powerful disciplinary tool.[7]

The second demand is that Christians receive the Eucharist annually, at Eastertide, with confession as the preparation, which ultimately strengthened the already traditional connection between the two sacraments. Although the decree allows for more frequent confession, the Council was actually reducing the number of receptions demanded and bowing to the realities on the ground.[8] Henceforth, the Church expected all Christians to confess during the penitential season of Lent and to receive Communion with renewed purity during Eastertide.

By the time of the Reformation, this demand was being met but not exceeded. "Frequent" Communion in that period meant perhaps four times per annum.[9] There was little incentive to confess more frequently. Great efforts were made to guarantee the presence of confessors during Lent, especially Holy Week, less so at other times. Confession also took place without a specific physical space in the church dedicated to its reception. No confessional yet existed to set the sacrament apart. Church law stipulated only that penance must take place in the church, in a public place, for the sake of dignity and to preclude scandal with women penitents. Secret though confessions may have been, they were still a public affair. In addition, because they typically took place during Holy Week around Holy Thursday, confessions were likely to be witnessed by others.[10]

A practice occurring only annually, with no fixed place within the church for its reception, sacramental penance was nonetheless critical to religious life. Late medieval piety was devoted to "the penitential cycle, which drew its meaning and motivation from the sacrament of penance, the place at which the power of the keys touched laypeople most directly."[11] Other rituals and penitential practices revolved around the central act of confessing.[12] One must keep these realities of medieval penance in mind when considering the late twentieth-century "crisis." Mere annual confession was actually the center of a vital penitential cycle that involved entire congregations, not isolated individuals. It offered in practice an "unofficial" (though nonsacramental) communal dimension.

Through Lateran IV's *focus* on practice and discipline, the sacrament of penance became synonymous with individual confession. Theology followed suit. By 1500, four elements came into play: on one side stood three actions by the penitent, which were then "formed" by the confessor's absolution. The penitent must *confess*: "a detailed self-accusation of all sinful acts, their frequency, and their circumstances."[13] The penitent must also agree to make *satisfaction*: "remitting through spiritual, physical, or material punishment the debt still owed even after eternal guilt had been absolved in the sacrament."

The third act of the penitent was the most important and also the most complex. The penitent must show *contrition*: "a sorrow of the soul and a *destestation* of sin committed, with a determination of not sinning in the future."[14] Contrition could be defined as a perfect sorrow, sufficient for forgiveness even without actual confession, in contrast to *attrition*, which was imperfect and insufficient. Contrition indicated the presence of grace, while attrition did not.[15] For Thomas Aquinas, the two were continuous, but not identical, and grace might transform attrition to contrition by infusing the love of God into the soul. Duns Scotus, however, distinguished them entirely on the basis of whether grace had been infused. Subjectively, contrition and attrition were indistinguishable, and so it was possible in theory to possess attrition so intense that God would transform it even without the sacrament. Duns Scotus recommended confession as safer and surer.[16] Fourteenth-century theologians compounded the complexities by arguing that the crucial distinction between contrition and attrition was entirely subjective, depending on either the sinner's sense of love for God (contrition) or fear of punishment (attrition). By the sixteenth century, most confessors anticipated that penitents would approach them in a state of attrition, but a number of theologians important for their influence on Martin Luther, Gabriel Biel chief among them, argued that only contrition, now defined subjectively as love of God, could suffice for absolution.[17]

The final element was *absolution,* pronounced by the confessor in order to bring into play the "power of the keys." Once contrition became the decisive element in determining forgiveness, what was the purpose of the absolution? Further, defining contrition subjectively made the sacrament a psychological matter. An "inverse relationship" developed between the sinner's sorrow and the power of the priestly absolution. Theologians who demanded a "perfect" contrition downplayed or denied the priest's power to forgive, while, as a rule, those who championed the sacramental absolution minimized the intensity of sorrow required to obtain forgiveness.[18] By the Reformation, the latter group was ascendant, though not dominant. And even the "contritionist" group acknowledged that most penitents would come to the sacrament attrite. The question for everyone was how to distinguish the levels of acceptable and unacceptable sorrow for the absolution to work. By 1500, the sacrament had narrowed theologically to an individual encounter between the penitent's psyche and the priest's power to absolve.

It was just this relationship that was at the heart of Protestant criticism of the sacrament. Martin Luther believed that assessing "sufficient sorrow" was a waste of time. Luther began as a strict contritionist and, paradoxically, remained one all his life. He agreed that only perfect contrition could satisfy God's justice. That was exactly the problem, since no human being could ever achieve such a state or be certain he/she had done so: "Rather, you should be assured of this, that after all your efforts your contrition is not sufficient."[19] Luther resolved this problem in confession by emphasizing not the power of the priest but of the absolution itself, understood as God's freely given, undeserved grant of mercy.[20] Luther thus rendered the medieval apparatus pointless.

As to complete confession, Luther argued that it was humanly impossible, and the true Christian would always admit failure. To demand detailed confession smacked of Law rather than Gospel—the other great Reformation criticism of Luther and Calvin of medieval sacramental penance. Both denied categorically that secret confession and absolution were mandated by God or practiced in the early Church, and they suggested that the practices were an invention of Lateran IV. By demanding of humans what God has not commanded them to do, the Roman Church violated the most basic principles of the Gospel.

Council of Trent

The Council of Trent was both end and beginning: the culmination of medieval developments and the start of a new culture of confession that lasted until the late twentieth century. Doctrinally, this meant *clarifying* scattered medieval teachings by using Thomistic terminology. As to discipline, Trent emphasized the *judicial* character of penance as a forensic decree pronounced by a judge possessing the authority and the jurisdiction to absolve bindingly in the name of God. Pastorally, Trent produced a new and extensive system of practices designed to make confession easier, surer, and more effective at both controlling the behavior of sinners and consoling the consciences of Christians.

Trent took up the issue of penance in a world that in less than fifty years had changed rapidly. The dynamic new churches challenging Roman hegemony in Europe had either dramatically diminished confession or abolished it outright. In each case, the ostensible grounds were a return *ad fontes*, either to Scripture itself or to patristic sources favored by humanists such as Erasmus. The medieval tradition had to come to grips with the patristic evidence and understandings advanced by Protestants and humanists. In short, how could the late medieval development of individual confession be made consistent with the earlier, more communal forms that the Reformers were exploring and advancing? Furthermore, the cacophony of different theological and pastoral voices even within the Roman communion must somehow be reconciled into a single doctrine. It was this confusion, many thought, that had led to the outbreak of Protestantism in the first place. Having received scant attention from previous councils, the doctrine of penance needed defining.

A second set of problems that Trent had to address concerned pastoral theology and practice. Among the stinging charges brought by Luther and others was that the Church had taken an overly juridical approach to confession, evident in the demand for specifics and the concern to distinguish "mortal" from "venial" sins, which placed more emphasis on Law than on Gospel, and on judgment rather than consolation. This Protestant criticism found an echo in humanists and ecclesiastics who remained Catholic. Erasmus, for example, outlined just such an approach in his *Exomologesis, sive modus confitendi*.[21] How could the Church simultaneously defend the imagery of confessor as judge while providing the consolations of the merciful God?

Third, Trent must incorporate changes and developments already occurring pastorally but not yet reflected in official doctrine or practice. Among these were the beginnings of a move toward greater and more frequent reception of Communion, of which the Church had traditionally been wary. In early sixteenth-century Spain and elsewhere, however, preachers and Catholic spiritual reformers were advocating an intensive cultivation of the sacraments among the laity. Ignatius Loyola and the early Society of Jesus confronted a Church quite suspicious of this attitude. Frequent confession would guarantee that frequent Communion was not a sign of heresy.[22] For Ignatius, though, frequent confession was a positive spiritual end on its own terms. The *Spiritual Exercises* involved multiple ways of confessing and examining the conscience in an assault on sin. Was it advisable to try to transmit this piety to the population at large?

The fathers of the Council recognized the significance of the task, incorporating sacramental penance in the decree on justification in the sixth session. Religious upheaval made further consideration imperative: "So great is in our days the number of errors relative to this sacrament, that it will be of no little general benefit to give to it a more exact and complete definition. . . ."[23] Accordingly, the decree on penance in the fourteenth session employs the language of scholastic theology. The absolution is the *form* of the sacrament, "in which its efficacy chiefly consists," while "the acts of the penitent himself, namely, contrition, confession and satisfaction, constitute the *matter* of this sacrament."[24]

The decree begins with *contrition*, which implies conversion, "not only an abstention from sin and the resolution and beginning of a new life, but also a hatred of the old."[25] Though it is technically possible for a perfect contrition to effect forgiveness before receiving the sacrament, true contrition always entails desire to confess. The decree steers carefully between the leading theologies of the late medieval period but clearly reduces the authority of earlier contritionists. It also defines attrition as "imperfect contrition," concentrating on the acts necessary for absolution. Attrition alone is insufficient, but it does "dispose him [the sinner] to obtain the grace of God in the sacrament of penance." Left unspecified in this careful formulation is whether attrition must become contrition through the sacrament for absolution to work, or whether the attrite sinner remains attrite, but forgiven. In the seventeenth century, as will be seen below, this ambiguity would help fuel the great Jansenist controversies.

Confession receives the greatest attention in the decree: "All mortal sins of which they have knowledge after a diligent self-examination, must be enumerated by the penitents in confession. . . ."[26] Contrary to Protestant assertions, specific confession is a matter of divine law from the inception of the Church and the commandment of Christ.[27] Furthermore, the divine institution also specifies priests as "rulers and judges, to whom all the mortal sins into which the faithful of Christ may have fallen should be brought. . . ." The priestly absolution is no mere declaration dispensing Gospel bounty, but is a judicial act, "by which sentence is pronounced by him as by a judge."[28] This judicial mentality of the decree also appears as grounds for demanding complete and detailed accounting of sins by penitents. How can the wise confessor bind, loose, or assess the proper penalty without full knowledge? The only sacramental practice clearly established by Christ was the demand for secret confession to a priest.[29]

Satisfaction is the final act making up the *matter* of penance. Although less significant in the theology of penance (because absolution was now granted in advance of the satisfaction, and on the basis of contrition and confession), satisfaction played a great role in Reformation theological disputes about merit and the sufficiency of Christ's atonement. The decree counters that the penalties to be imposed by confessors are not simply to encourage new life, but are "for the atonement and punishment of past sins." Here again, the judicial character of the Tridentine sacrament emerges, for "the early Fathers also believed and taught that the keys of the priests were bestowed not to loose only but also to bind."[30] Satisfaction is also prominent as a source of discipline: "These satisfactions greatly restrain from sin, check as it were with a bit, and make penitents more cautious and vigilant in the future; they also remove remnants of sin, and by acts of the opposite virtues destroy habits acquired by evil living."[31]

The canons accompanying the decree summarize well the crucial points. Anathema is pronounced on anyone who denies the divine institution of sacramental confession or claims that secret confession is "at variance with the institution and command of Christ" (canon 6); denies the need for confessing each and all mortal sins recalled "after a due and diligent examination" (canon 7); or rejects the priestly absolution as a judicial act rather than a mere pronouncing of forgiveness (canon 9).[32] In the final analysis, then, the decree affirms that sacramental penance means individual confession and absolution, and modern Catholicism would now be defined in part by this peculiar institution.

The pastoral issues were perhaps even more important for the future than doctrinal theology, in which Trent was careful but not innovative. The Council of Trent advocated great changes in pastoral care for which confession, especially frequent confession, seemed to be the ideal vehicle. In the minds of Catholic reformers, confession would be the tie that bound the official Church to its lay subjects. Catholic reformers concerned with the souls of Christians and the morality of the people also recognized the potential usefulness of confession as a means of disciplining the population generally. The *Roman Catechism* of 1566 is quite specific: "Another advantage of confession, which should not be overlooked, is that it contributes powerfully to the preservation of social order. Abolish sacramental confession, and that moment you deluge society with all sorts of secret and heinous crimes—crimes too, and others of still greater enormity, which men, once they have been depraved by vicious habits, will not dread to commit in open day. The salutary shame that attends confession restrains licentiousness, bridles desire and checks wickedness."[33] The sanctified Catholic of the early modern world was an obedient soul in a chastened body.

Post-Tridentine Developments

Two interrelated developments associated with Trent actually took place after the Council itself. The first was the formalization of ritual, and especially the absolution, so that a uniform practice would be in place throughout Catholic Europe. The second was the development of the confessional booth in the second half of the sixteenth century. Each would have a profound impact on the way the sacrament was performed and perceived, and each had the effect of strengthening the individual cast of mind so prominent at the Council.

Although the Council of Trent fixed with great precision the elements of sacramental penance and other celebrations, the fathers left the ritual to be worked out later. The need for a uniform way of performing confession was evident in northern Europe, where the proliferation of new sects and churches made for a confusing tangle in which authentic Catholic practices were occasionally hard to separate from Protestant forms. This was especially true in German-speaking lands, where the relatively conservative Lutheran Reformation continued to practice a form of individual absolution.[34] The Catholic Church had to distinguish itself from competitors by adopting unmistakably Catholic rituals. At the same time, from a pastoral standpoint, Catholic churchmen were concerned about invalid confessions even among devout Catholic confessors; to them, the salvation of souls was at stake along with ecclesiastical discipline.

Thus, in the second half of the sixteenth century, Catholic reformers made a sustained effort to replace local rituals with a uniform, visibly Catholic form of the sacrament. Among the measures undertaken, confessors were to vest themselves properly for confession. More important, the rituals to be employed, in particular the absolution, were to be as simple, clear, and direct as possible, and they were to conform to the rituals established by Rome. In terms of the absolution, this meant paring down the number of different formulas in use to a single and universally applied wording, first set down at the Council of Florence (1439) and later fixed by the *Rituale romanum* (1614).[35]

The second crucial development after the Council of Trent was the confessional booth, associated primarily with Charles Borromeo, Archbishop of Milan following Trent.[36] Italian reforming bishops had toyed with a device intended to separate confessor from penitent, including the use of a panel with a perforated grille. The First Provincial Council in Milan (1565) mandated the essential structure, followed by Borromeo's treatise on Church architecture, *Instructionum fabricate et supellectilis ecclesiasticae* (Milan, 1577). The Borromean confessional proved hard to resist, at least as far as Church authorities were concerned. It also helped to establish a kind of etiquette in conducting the sacrament and served, through its visibility, to make confession part of the mental furniture of the Church.

Historians view the appearance of the confessional in a number of ways. Did the confessional create a sphere of anonymous revelation and spiritual reflection, furthering the tendency toward a psychological and personal understanding of the sacrament? Did it emphasize the power of the confessor and the jurisdiction of the Catholic Church over the soul of the individual

penitent? Whatever the ultimate impact, the confessional was originally intended to serve a traditional end: separating confessor from female penitents
so that no hint of scandal could arise.[37] Anyone looking at the Borromean
confessional immediately sees that it was particularly suited to segregating
penitent from confessor—as described by Borromeo or Jacob Müller (*Kir-
chengeschmuck*, 1591)—while the open front would keep the process in view
of the public. These were not the fully enclosed structures that Catholics
would see in the twentieth century, with curtains hung to screen both participants from those outside. Early confessionals and the synods that recommended them also intended that the device keep the public somewhat at
a distance, maintaining decorum appropriate to the solemn event. The presence of a permanent structure—a tabernacle for the sacrament, as it were—
served as a constant reminder of the possibilities open to the sinner, as well
as his/her responsibility.

The idea that confession may have fostered privacy in matters of conscience by enforcing a sphere of anonymous and individual spiritual counsel
carries force, but did not do so in the sixteenth century, and probably not until
the eighteenth at the earliest. First, the confessional did not spread throughout
Catholic Europe before the middle or end of the seventeenth century.[38] When
it appeared in France, congregations refused to enter—the confessional
seemed automatically to confer guilt upon the person who entered.[39] Second,
the design of the confessional, as noted above, was not intended or suited for
anonymous, individual counsel and judgment, but was open to the public's
view. Only when the confessional became fully enclosed, shutting off both
penitent and confessor from the public and from one another, could the experience become fully anonymous, private, and individual. When this in fact
happened remains a matter of conjecture.[40]

The different factors—doctrine, design, and ritual—did combine to diminish the communal possibilities in the sacrament. Yet all of these factors
and reformers' aims for the sacrament also depended on the success of the
Church in inculcating its understanding of confession among the Christian
population. How well did the Church succeed at this task? A number of recent
studies have examined the implementation of Tridentine reforms among the
populations of Italy, Germany, and France. Before turning to their findings, a
brief examination of the main theological controversies sparked by the Council
of Trent is essential.

Doctrinal Controversy

Conciliar emphasis on individual confession and absolution formalized in doctrinal terms the theological speculation of the Middle Ages. With the options
for sacramental penance narrowed to a juridical transaction between penitent

and priest, and with disciplinary goals at the center, it is no surprise that the greatest controversies of the post-Trent era involved the conditions for individual absolution and the moral theology to be applied. The debate over contrition versus attrition continued until the eighteenth century. It was closely involved with controversy over the logic by which the conscience should judge acts and the relative clemency of the confessor in accommodating the weaknesses of individual penitents—should the casuistry of the Church follow a "laxist" or "rigorist" path?

The Council of Trent defined attrition as imperfect contrition arising either from the consideration of the heinousness of sin or from the fear of hell and of punishment. If this sorrow "renounces the desire to sin and hopes for pardon, it not only does not make one a hypocrite and a greater sinner, but is even a gift of God and an impulse of the Holy Ghost, not indeed as already dwelling in the penitent, but only moving him, with which assistance the penitent prepares a way for himself unto justice."[41] The decree then stipulates, "And though without the sacrament of penance it cannot *per se* lead the sinner to justification, it does, however, dispose him to obtain the grace of God in the sacrament of penance."[42] Clear though this formulation might seem on the surface, the question arose whether at some point the penitent seeking absolution (and therefore justification) must demonstrate at least an incipient love of God rather than mere fear of the consequences of his/her sin. The Jansenists, with their belief in a twofold love—either love of God or of the world, either charity or cupidity—"flatly rejected sorrow motivated by fear as immoral."[43] Jansenist criticism, particularly of Jesuit confessors, was most famously expressed by Pascal in the *Provincial Letters*: "When you say that 'attrition motivated solely by fear of punishment' is enough with the sacrament to justify sinners, does it not follow that one could expiate sins in this way all one's life, and so be saved without ever in one's life having loved God?"[44] The *Letters* conclude sarcastically, "Thus those who have never loved God all their lives are by you made worthy to enjoy him throughout eternity."[45] Despite being condemned by Clement XI in 1713, the rejection of "servile fear" remained a Jansenist theme until the end of the eighteenth century.[46]

The extreme positions of the Jansenists should not obscure the existence of a more mainstream version of post-Tridentine "contritionism," which did not reject attrition as an honest and salutary act, but denied that it was a sufficient disposition for worthy reception of the sacrament.[47] These contritionists also appealed to the Council of Trent, but instead of seeking confirmation in the decree on the sacrament of penance, they turned to the decree on justification formulated at the sixth session. There, one finds the statement "When, understanding themselves to be sinners, they, by turning themselves, from the fear of divine justice whereby they are profitably agitated, to consider the mercy of God, are raised unto hope, confiding that God will be propitious to them for Christ's sake; and *they begin to love Him* [italics mine] as the fountain of all justice; and are therefore moved against sins by a certain hatred and detestation, to wit, by that penitence which must be performed before baptism."[48] If justification demands an incipient love of God, then how can the sacrament that enacts and reenacts the process not include it?

In strictly doctrinal terms, the controversy between attritionists and contritionists was never resolved. So charged was the debate, however, that in 1667 Alexander VII prohibited each side from censuring the other until the Holy See could decide—and this never happened.[49] Even then, Alexander acknowledged that attritionism was the more common opinion. Some attritionist theologians abstained entirely from using the term "love." Others, in their own defense, argued that the "incipient love" demanded by the decree on justification could be found in the "hope of pardon" mentioned in the decree on penance.[50] This hope is implicitly present in every penitential act. Fear of God is the beginning of wisdom—perhaps it is also the beginning of charity.[51] This was indeed the view of Alphonsus Liguori and, through his influence, it emerged as the predominant opinion throughout the nineteenth and even twentieth centuries.

The controversies over "laxism" and "rigorism" were resolved in a similar way. "Probabiliorism," which stipulates that in moral questions one must obey the side of law unless the position of the conscience is much more certain, corresponded well to demands for discipline and obedience. This rigorous morality, associated frequently with the Jansenists, contrasts with "probabilism," a line of moral thinking permitting the individual to choose in favor of liberty, if law and conscience are equally probable. Associated with the extensive pastoral work of the Jesuits, "probabilism" not only allowed for some choice in matters of conscience but also eased the path to absolution by lessening the demand for absolute obedience. It was this concern over access to the sacraments that finally swayed Alphonsus Liguori to favor a *via media*, "equiprobabilism," which allowed for freedom of conscience in cases of doubt concerning the existence of a law but ruled for law in cases in which the only question was whether an acknowledged law remained in force or had been fulfilled. For Liguori, the excessive rigor of "probabiliorism" as applied to sin and absolution had the effect of driving Catholics away from the sacrament. It was the moderate and lighter approach of Liguori, favoring both "attritionism" and "equiprobabilism," that prevailed in Catholic pastoral and penitential theology of the modern era.

Discipline and Reform

Catholic reformers viewed sacramental confession as a grand opportunity to bind Christians to the Church and to inculcate the spiritual and moral values associated with the Catholic Reformation. This was the revolution in pastoral care initiated by Trent. As recent scholarship indicates, it operated on two fronts. The religious orders, in particular the Society of Jesus, have traditionally been credited with leading the drive for renewed practice in which penance was the cornerstone of the individual Catholic's relationship to the Church. Their efforts began before the Council of Trent but intensified in its aftermath. Working outside the established parish structure, the Jesuits and others employed missions, schools, and confraternities as the settings for spiritual counsel and development. Trent, however, focused much attention on the renewal of the episcopacy and secular clergy as a focal point for reform. As Wietse de Boer demonstrates, episcopal influence was as significant as the regular clergy.[52] In the end, though, the efforts of the secular and the regular clergy cannot be separated clearly.

At the diocesan and parish levels, Trent spurred notable reform efforts among Catholics, in which confession played an important role. First, compliance with the traditional command to confess and to receive Communion at least once a year became a sign of obedience to the Church, especially in contested lands. In the Habsburg Empire, officials demanded that subjects in suspect regions demonstrate their allegiance by receiving the sacraments, with fines and possibly expulsion as the penalty for refusal. Imperial commissions, complete with troops, went into the countryside accompanied by preachers and confessors to guarantee fulfillment of the new religious duties.[53] In these lands, as well as in Bavaria, officials demanded that subjects procure certificates (Beichtzettel) demonstrating that they had fulfilled their Easter duties. Pastors handing out Communion to Catholics who had confessed outside the parish also could demand a Beichtzettel, and a lively trade in false certificates arose. Since this was the minimum requirement, spiritual writers of the late sixteenth and seventeenth centuries scorned those Christians whose devotion went no further than mere compliance.

In Milan, considered by many scholars to be a "laboratory" for the implementation of Tridentine ideals, the same pattern occurred. The diocese was located in a religious "border zone," dangerously close to Calvinist Geneva.[54] One of the first tasks of the estimable Archbishop Charles Borromeo was to monitor his flock in order to guarantee compliance with Church commandments, most visibly the obligation to confess annually. As described by Wietse de Boer, the result was a "capillary system" spread throughout the parishes of the diocese.[55] Penitents must obtain a certificate from their confessor and present it to their parish priest as a prerequisite to receiving Easter Communion. The pastor could then check the parish register and note those who had not confessed. In Milan, as in Austria and Bavaria, fraud accompanied this bureaucratic structure.[56]

Charles Borromeo also hoped that penance would be a means to rejecting the past and beginning a new life, as Trent had intended.[57] That process of conversion and redemption should take place under the watchful eyes of the clergy and hierarchy.[58] The clergy, at first, were not up to the task. Borromeo installed an elaborate, centralized system for training confessors. Clergy were to report to district vicars, who reported to regional visitors, who reported to the curia, who reported to the diocesan penitentiary and ultimately to Borromeo himself. This allowed the episcopal authorities to supervise confessors and at the same time to use them to transmit instructions and exhortations to the dioceses. By attempting to strengthen the use of "reserved cases," the bishop could inform penitents which sins were most significant in the eyes of the diocese, but the penitentiary could also learn something about the behavior of the diocese's subjects.[59]

Among the religious orders, the Society of Jesus early on manifested a strong devotion to frequent confession and Communion. Regular participation enabled the penitent to remember and enumerate sins more easily, guaranteeing a complete confession. It was not only a simple matter of frequent reception, but also one of development of an inner world of constant self-reflection and constraint, a moral compass pointed always toward Rome as its true north. The Jesuit approach focused on the examination of conscience not simply to monitor the number of sins, but also to foster a sense of true sorrow for sin. The use of vivid imagery so integral to the *Spiritual Exercises* (and also in catechisms and preaching) first raised the penitent's awareness of the dangers that confronted him or her, then awakened sorrow based on grateful love for Christ's sacrifice. The Jesuits quite literally *engraved* a sense of contrition in the hearts of the pious. Their plans corresponded to the Tridentine understanding that attrition and contrition are distinguished psychologically. As such, attrition might lead to contrition as the motive for sorrow changed, a task accomplished through intensive introspection and frequent confession. In the confessional itself, attrition might also be transformed through the absolving power of the priest.

The Society of Jesus used various means to instill its piety in laypeople. Catechisms and handbooks recommended that all individuals confess at regular times during the year, and children should be encouraged or required to confess more frequently still, as often as once a week. As Jesuit schools and colleges multiplied in Europe (and throughout the world) in the centuries after Trent, the order had the opportunity to inculcate its values amid a worldwide network of students, many of them members of the secular elite. Jesuit confraternities also required particular attention to confession and Communion. While dioceses required *Beichtzettel* to demonstrate minimum compliance, the confraternities rewarded members with certificates proclaiming their greater and deeper devotion.[60]

As if to summarize the success of the Jesuits' drive, the poet Jeremias Drexel wrote in 1625:

It occurs to me, and I think, not without heartfelt sighs, how it was in the world a hundred years ago in Luther's time. Oh unworthy age!! Then one could distinguish Catholic from heretic only with difficulty. A person made his confession only once a year and quite reluctantly, without any zeal. . . . Now, however, through the kind watchfulness of God, the times have changed, so that I may truthfully say that whoever in our time makes only one confession in the entire year, gives himself away and demonstrates to everyone that they should not consider him to be anything other than a completely cold, half-hearted Christian who, were he not held to it by the commandment [of the Church], would not even once purify his conscience through confession, but would remain jolly with his sins and vices.[61]

Certainly the Society of Jesus and other orders witnessed, or at least claimed to produce, a vast outpouring of fervor for the sacrament of penance.

Not everyone would agree, then or now. The success of these drives toward intense sacramental devotion remains a matter of dispute. It may seem odd to judge the sacrament by the frequency of its reception, but the Council of Trent and Church authorities understood confession to be not simply a matter of consolation for sin, but also a discipline and a sign of orthodoxy. A record of compliance, therefore, signaled the success of the Tridentine doctrine of sacramental penance. At the parish and diocesan levels, evidence from northern Europe suggests that lay reception may have increased in frequency from yearly confession to perhaps five times a year, spread throughout great feasts of the liturgical calendar. In Spain, efforts to make the sacrament a center of the Catholic Reformation showed dramatic spiritual results by the final quarter of the sixteenth century.[62] As in Bavaria, mere annual compliance became a matter of scorn among devout Catholics. In other northern areas, especially in the countryside, the success of the Tridentine reforms is less clear. Not only was attendance limited, but congregations continued to crowd the confessional (where there was one) at the last minute, and suitable etiquette was predictably lacking. One would be hard pressed to claim that a new style of piety prevailed everywhere.

Even in Milan, the results among the laity were disappointing, at least in the short run. As Wietse de Boer notes, "While Carlo Borromeo advocated frequent confession as part of his program of lay devotion, it is unclear if the practice took off in any significant and lasting way beyond limited circles of the devout and beyond (or even in) the colleges and confraternities in which whey were institutionalized."[63] De Boer also notes that the drive for greater frequency or at least greater compliance in Lent and at Eastertide may have been counterproductive, since it increased the burden on an already stretched clergy. As the quantity of confessions increased, their quality may well have decreased.[64] Milan may have resembled the crowded process in Bavaria in the late sixteenth century or in rural dioceses of the seventeenth, where perfunctory recitations and absolutions were repeated every few minutes, following desultory recounting of sins.[65] Even in Spain, new problems arose because the educated clergy needed to conduct the sacrament properly were, and remained, sorely lacking.[66]

In France, hotbed of rigorist penitential thinking and Jansenism, the overall results were similarly mixed. In Sennely-en-Sologne, where in the late seventeenth century the congregation had refused to enter the confessional,[67] the pastor held the sacrament elsewhere in the church, but people attempted to overhear. People came to confession unprepared, not knowing their sins, and on feast days they crowded noisily into the church.[68] In the mid-eighteenth century, the Bishop of Boulogne lamented the neglect of the sacrament of penance, owing, he thought, to the laziness and negligence of the confessors. In the face of lay recalcitrance, pastors were likely to make a separate peace with their parishioners.[69] The situation was hardly different on the eve of the French Revolution.[70]

In each of these cases, the attempt to impose intense discipline over a large Catholic population failed. The more disciplinary and rigorous the effort, the more it drove congregations away from penance. In French dioceses, where rigorist Jansenists made strict demands, attendance might fall 50 percent or more.[71] The greatest casuist of the age, Alphonsus Liguori, argued in the eighteenth century that increasing rigorism among confessors was driving ever greater numbers of sinners away from the sacrament. On the other hand, congregations were not indifferent to their religious obligations. It was simply that they understood sacramental confession as one part of a larger religious world of prayer and celebration, and in general refused to see absolution apart from norms to which the community at large subscribed. As part of a heightened cycle of reception that became a marker of increased participation in a devotional and liturgical life shaped by the official Church rather than by local custom, Tridentine confession entered the consciousness of most Catholics. As a spiritual practice subscribed to by an intensely devout and significant section of the laity, it was a splendid success. As a discipline to be imposed by external sources, however, confession was doomed by the end of the eighteenth century.

Modern Developments: From Discipline to Reconciliation

Following the French Revolution, and the secularization and the "de-Christianization" of European society, the ability of the Church to employ sacramental confession as a disciplinary tool diminished. Exhortations and incentives to frequent Communion and confession were part of a general attempt at spurring voluntary devotion, and the sacrament increasingly became a means for intensifying spiritual life and improving morals. Patterns of reception are incompletely understood, but it is possible that easing absolution, as advocated by Alphonsus Liguori, was a key to increasing reception.[72] The disciplinary demand to confess annually remained in force for all Catholics, as is evident in the Code of Canon Law of 1917. During the twentieth century, the Church and the Popes—among them Pius XII, John XXIII, and John Paul II— increasingly advocated confession as a devotional practice among the devout, even as parish practice leveled off or declined.

At the same time, historical studies of the early Church by both Protestants and Catholics presented a much different picture of the penitential practices of early Christianity. The more scholars examined the penitential processes of the ancient Church, the clearer it became that private, individual, auricular confession was not the original form of ecclesiastical penance.[73] Dissenting Catholic and non-Catholic scholars questioned whether the authenticity of auricular confession could be proved from patristic sources. In response, Pius X condemned any reconsideration of the origins, authenticity, or practice of sacramental penance in his general denunciation of modernism, the decree *Lamentabili* (July 3, 1907).[74]

Only following World War I did neoscholastic theologians begin successfully to incorporate an ecclesiological element in defining sacramental penance without denying the significance of interior remorse and individual, secret confession. Maurice de la Taille, Bartholomé María Xiberta, and Karl Rahner explored the ways in which the repentant sinner reconciles with God through the experience of reconciling with the Church.[75] On the basis of these reflections, grounded both in scholastic theology and in early Church history, theological attention shifted from the issue of the penitent's disposition (contrition or attrition?) to the question of reconciliation with the Church as the center of the sacrament.[76]

The significance of this shift and its implications for Vatican II were great. From 1215, but most significantly from the Council of Trent, theological speculation had emphasized, and ecclesiastical practice had demanded, an ever narrower focus on the sinner's individual conscience and secret dialogue with the absolving priest. Even the limited public dimension retained by Trent and the early Catholic Reformation gave way to the sacrament as a private encounter. Now, however, that long development came to a close.

Vatican II and After

Vatican II makes slim reference to the sacrament. *Lumen gentium* refers to penance in a general discussion of the sacraments as the expressions of the "sacred nature and organic structure of the priestly community." In this framework, "Those who approach the sacrament of Penance obtain pardon from the mercy of God for the offence committed against Him and are at the same time reconciled with the Church, which they have wounded by their sins, and which by charity, example, and prayer seeks their conversion."⁷⁷ *Sacrosanctum concilium* seems to adopt a generally more corporate form of worship wherever possible.⁷⁸ Yet, concerning penance itself, *Sacrosanctum concilium* states only, "The rite and formulas for the sacrament of penance are to be revised so that they more clearly express both the nature and effect of the sacrament."⁷⁹ The revisions so tantalizingly promised finally appeared in 1973, with the official appearance of the new *Ordo paenitentiae*. The ten years that separated *Sacrosanctum concilium* and the new *Ordo* were fateful, however, with two developments that would condition the new rituals. First, during the 1960s, the practice of individual confession, whether for discipline or for devotion, collapsed along with other supporting elements of the sacrament. The astonishing and immediate decline of priestly vocations was part of this change. The moral controversies that occupied the Church during that period, especially the decision on contraception (*Humanae vitae*), may also have contributed to the unwillingness of individuals to avail themselves of the sacramental option.

Accompanying the rapid decline in individual confessions was the proliferation of other forms of reconciliation, official and unofficial, as substitutes. Informal and experimental use of general absolution without specific recounting of sins, unacceptable in Roman Catholic practice since the Council of Trent, raised alarms in the Church. In 1972, the Sacred Congregation for the Doctrine of the Faith declared:

A number of local Ordinaries have been disturbed at the difficulty for their faithful to go to confession individually because of the shortage of priests in some regions. They have also been troubled at certain erroneous theories about the doctrine of the Sacrament of Penance and the growing tendency to introduce the improper practice of granting general sacramental absolution to people who have made only a generic confession. They have therefore asked the Holy See to recall to the Christian people, in accordance with the true nature of the Sacrament of Penance, the conditions needed for the right use of this sacrament and to issue norms in the present circumstances.

The norms were a stinging rejection of communal or general absolution and a ringing return to the precepts of the Council of Trent:

The teaching of the Council of Trent must be firmly held and faithfully put into practice. This implies a reprobation of the recent custom which has sprung up in places by which there is a presumption to satisfy the precept of sacramentally confessing mortal sins for the purpose of obtaining absolution by confession made only generally or through what is called a community celebration of Penance. This reprobation is demanded not only by divine precept as declared by the Council of Trent, but also by the very great good of souls deriving, according to centuries-long experience, from individual confession and absolution rightly administered. Individual and integral confession and absolution remain the only ordinary way for the faithful to be reconciled to God and the Church unless physical or moral impossibility excuses from such confession.

The danger of death is one exception. Yet the document also allows general absolution when "in view of the number of penitents there are not enough confessors at hand to hear properly the confessions of each within an appropriate time, with the result that the penitents through no fault of their own would be forced to do without sacramental grace or Holy Communion for a long time. This can happen especially in mission lands but in places also and within groups where it is clear that this need exists."[80] These cautions and restrictions were later incorporated into the revised Code of Canon Law (1983).[81] Some analysts have argued that these statutes represent a "retrenchment from a more flexible pastoral approach" following Vatican II.[82] If this is so, retreat began within a decade of the Council.

The *Ordo paenitentiae* accordingly lays out three rites, the first of which is the private ritual reminiscent of Tridentine practice; now, however this individual event is part of a larger communal process in which the priest represents the community as well as the juridical authority of the Church. Rite I also shifts the place of penance from the traditional confessional booth to a more comfortable venue, if congenial to the penitent. These "reconciliation spaces" are perhaps the most visible signal of a changed goal in confession, from discipline to consultation and reconciliation. In practice, they take a wide variety of forms, but as the 1983 Code of Canon Law stipulates, the traditional confessional with grate separating priest and penitent is to be available. Rite II provides a communal frame, including a homily and public prayer, surrounding the individual confessions and absolutions. Finally, Rite III outlines a fully congregational celebration, with a general confession and communal absolution, to be employed only in emergencies, and where the number of penitents is too large for the number of priests present, which would result in denial of the sacrament to the faithful. Here, too, the 1983 Code of Canon Law follows the instructions of 1972, severely limiting the validity of Rite III.

The *Ordo paenitentiae* of 1973, along with the restrictions introduced in 1972 and codified in Canon Law in 1983, suggests the continuing influence of Trent on the parties responsible for interpreting Vatican II. Despite the greater ecclesiological dimension set out in the conciliar constitutions, individual private confession as laid out at the Council of Trent remains very much the norm. Indeed, from the moment the new rites appeared, the papacy and curia have increasingly tried to strengthen the Tridentine understanding of the sacrament and in particular to interpret the communal perspective within the customary framework of individual and specific confession. Pope John Paul II, in his exhortation following the 1984 synod Reconciliation and Penance, made this very clear:

> The first form—reconciliation of individual penitents—is the only normal and ordinary way of celebrating the sacrament, and it cannot and must not be allowed to fall into disuse or be neglected. The second form—reconciliation of a number of penitents with individual confession and absolution—even though in the preparatory acts it helps to give greater emphasis to the community aspects of the sacrament, is the same as the first form in the culminating sacramental act, namely individual confession and individual absolution of sins. It can thus be regarded as equal to the first form as regards the normality of the rite. The third form, however—reconciliation of a number of penitents with general confession and absolution—is exceptional in character. It is therefore not left to free choice but is regulated by a special discipline.[83]

Even the more accepted communal rite receives its special validity from individual confession. A separate section of the document details the restrictions that encumber Rite III. The same concern for preserving and enhancing the norm of individual, specific confession appears in a circular on penance from the Congregation for Divine Worship during the Jubilee year 2000.

It is clear, then, that Trent remains very much in the forefront of Roman Catholic thinking. Vatican II offered a different perspective rather than a radical new direction. The period since the mid-1980s has witnessed more of an attempted revival of Tridentine customary practices, such as frequent confession and confession of venial sins (which John Paul II recommended as recently as 2004), than of an exploration of the possibilities latent in the documents of Vatican II or the *Ordo paenitentiae*. The problem is that since the 1960s, the relation of the laity to sacramental penance has changed dramatically.[84] For whatever reason, a large percentage of the Catholic population worldwide has simply ceased to confess more than (or even) annually. Furthermore, any hope for a return to the frequent confession so sentimentally remembered founders with the collapse of the Catholic clergy in Europe and the United States. The emergency may lie not in the paucity of penitents but in the lack of confessors, which may soon be the standard condition of the Church. Without confessors, the majority of Catholics cannot confess, and the only penitential rites they will experience will be communal celebrations, valid or not. The opportunities for frequent devotional confession will simply not exist, except for the fortunate few.

Before lamenting this situation, however, it is well to remember that frequent recourse to confession is a relatively recent event as measured by the long history of Catholic Christianity. Before Trent, annual confession during Lent was the norm, and it anchored other penitential practices throughout the year. Even at the height of Catholic power in the Tridentine era, as noted earlier, the Church's ability to compel compliance was not guaranteed. To be sure, by the 1960s, confession was already perched for a decline. In America, the drop in numbers of students attending Catholic schools meant that a convenient venue for enforced regular confession was less and less available. CCD classes did not provide a substitute. And a generally more permissive and individual society in both America and Europe refused to submit to the mores of the Church. These developments, though, must be understood within a larger historical context. Laypeople have always proved quite capable of resisting the strictures and commandments of the Church, whether in the Middle Ages or in the Catholic Reformation. In the final analysis, the Church's ability to exercise discipline depends on lay complicity. That was true in 1215 and in 1565, and it remains true today. In all ages, laypeople have translated their unwillingness into recalcitrance. The individual confessor has generally been forced to go it alone; he also has a decision to make about his congregation and his standing in the community.

What is happening today may be the historical norm for Catholics rather than an anomaly produced by modern decline. After Trent, as now, the grand schemes of pastoral care were undermined by the inability of the Church to provide adequately trained clergy in sufficient numbers. The late medieval pattern of annual or intermittent confession anchoring a variety of other penitential practices in the appropriate liturgical season may very well prove to be the future of penance, at least in the short term. The decline in confession may well be seen as a return to normal. In the very long term of Church history, the Council of Trent may prove to have been less influential than has been imagined.

NOTES

1. Konrad Baumgartner, "Bußsakrament VII. Praktisch-theologisch," in *Lexikon für Theologie und Kirche*, ed. Walter and Konrad Baumgartner (Freiburg: Herder, 1994), vol. 2, 854–855. Groupe de la Bussière, *Pratiques de la confession: Dès pères du désert à Vatican II* (Paris: Cerf, 1983), describes a "crise contemporaine" in the sacrament.

2. "Address of John Paul II to the Participants in the Course on the Internal Forum Organized by the Tribunal of the Apostolic Penitentiary (March 27, 2004)," http://www.vatican.va/holy_father/john_paul_ii/speeches/2004/march/documents/hf _jp-ii_spe_20040327_apostolic-penitentiary_en.html.

262 FROM TRENT TO VATICAN II

3. Peter Steinfels, *A People Adrift: The Crisis of the Roman Catholic Church in America* (New York: Simon and Schuster, 2003).

4. Constitution on the Sacred Liturgy Solemnly Promulgated by His Holiness Paul VI on December 4, 1963 (*Sacrosanctum concilium*), 72, http://www.vatican.va/archive/hist_councils/ii_vatican_council/documents/vat-ii_const_19631204
_sacrosanctum-concilium_en.html.

5. H. J. Schroeder, ed. and trans., *The Canons and Decrees of the Council of Trent* (St. Louis, Mo.: Herder, 1941), sess. 14, ch. 1, 88.

6. H. J. Schroeder, ed. and trans., *Disciplinary Decrees of the General Councils* (St. Louis, Mo.: Herder, 1937), 259.

7. Thomas Tentler, *Sin and Confession on the Eve of the Reformation* (Princeton, N.J.: Princeton University Press, 1977), 345–347.

8. On the requirement to confess, see Martin Ohst, *Pflichtbeichte* (Tübingen: Mohr, 1995). On the relationship between confession and Communion and the annual duty, see Peter Browe, *Pflichtkommunion im Mittelalter* (Münster: Regensbergische Verlagsbuchhandlung, 1940), and "Die Pflichtbeichte im Mittelalter," *Zeitschrift für katholische Theologie* (1933): 335–383.

9. Peter Browe, *Die häufige Kommunion im Mittelalter* (Münster: Regensbergische Verlagsbuchhandlung, 1938), 28–29.

10. See W. David Myers, *"Poor, Sinning Folk": Confession and Conscience in Counter-Reformation Germany* (Ithaca, N.Y.: Cornell University Press, 1996), 33–46.

11. A general discussion of the penitential cycle is in Euan Cameron, *The European Reformation* (Oxford: Oxford University Press, 1991), 14. For a fine account of confession in late medieval and Reformation Nuremberg, see Ronald Rittgers, *The Reformation of the Keys: Confession, Conscience, and Authority in Sixteenth-Century Germany* (Cambridge, Mass.: Harvard University Press, 2004), 25.

12. Myers, *"Poor, Sinning Folk,"* 60.

13. Ibid., 16.

14. Schroeder, *Canons and Decrees*, sess. 14, ch. 4, 91. See also P. De Letter, "Contrition," in *New Catholic Encyclopedia*, 2nd ed., vol. 4, 278–282, http://find
.galegroup.com/gvrl/infomark.do?&type=retrieve&tabID=T001&prodId=GVRL&docId=CX3407702769&source=gale&userGroupName=fordham_main&version
=1.0>.

15. Aquinas understood contrition as a freely willed sorrow occurring simultaneously with the divine implanting of grace in the soul to forgive the penitent, so that it was both a human act and a result of God's love. Attrition, in contrast, was an incomplete or unformed repentance normally preceding and preparing for the infusion of grace. Pierre Adnes, "Pénitence," in *Dictionnaire de spiritualité, ascétique et mystique*, (Paris: Beauchesne, 1984), vol. 12, 972; and Gordon Spykman, *Attrition and Contrition at the Council of Trent* (Kampen: Kok, 1955), 59–60.

16. Ibid., 73–79; Valens Heynck, "Attritio sufficiens," *Franziskanische Studien* 31 (1949): 93–100.

17. For an intriguing examination of the role of contritionism and attritionism in late medieval religion, see Anne T. Thayer, *Penitence, Preaching, and the Coming of the Reformation* (Aldershot, U.K.: Ashgate, 2002).

18. Myers, *"Poor, Sinning Folk,"* 19.

19. Martin Luther, "A Sermon on the Sacrament of Penance," in *Luther's Works*, ed. Jaroslav Pelikan and H. T. Lehmann, 55 vols. (St. Louis, Mo.: Concordia, 1955–1986), vol. 35, 15.

20. ". . . cast yourself upon the grace of God, hear his sufficiently sure word in the sacrament, accept it in free and joyful faith, and never doubt that you have come to grace—not by your own merits or contrition but by his gracious and divine mercy." Luther, "A Sermon on the Sacrament of Penance," 15.

21. *Exomologesis, sive modus confitendi* (Basel, 1524).

22. John O'Malley, *The First Jesuits* (Cambridge, Mass.: Harvard University Press, 1993), 136–137, 152–157.

23. Schroeder, *Canons and Decrees*, sess. 14, Introduction, 88.

24. Ibid., ch. 3, 90.

25. Ibid., ch. 4, 91.

26. Ibid., ch. 5, 93.

27. "From the institution of the sacrament of penance as already explained, the universal Church has always understood that the complete confession of sins was also instituted by the Lord and is by divine law necessary for all who have fallen after baptism." Schroeder, *Trent*, sess. 14, ch. 5, 92. The decree also argued that Lateran IV referred only to the precept of annual confession, lauding the customary practice of confessing during Lent. Ibid., 94.

28. Ibid., ch. 6, 95.

29. While individuals might expiate their sins by revealing them publicly, "this is not commanded by divine precept; nor would it be very prudent to enjoin by human law that offenses, especially secret ones, should be divulged by a public confession." Ibid.

30. Ibid., ch. 8, 98.

31. Ibid., 97.

32. Ibid., canons 102–103.

33. *Catechism of the Council of Trent for Parish Priests*, trans. John A. McHugh and Charles J. Callan (London: Herder, 1923), 283.

34. Ernst Tomek, *Kirchengeschichte Österreichs* (Innsbruck: Tyrolia-Verlag, 1949), vol. 2, 356–389.

35. On the formula of absolution, see the illuminating discussion by Josef Jungmann, *Die lateinischen Bußriten in ihrer geschichtlichen Entwicklung* (Innsbruck: Rauch, 1932), 223–234. Despite this achievement, however, some diversity of rituals persisted into the twentieth century. Jungmann, 236–237.

36. Numerous texts have discussed the development of the confessional, but the most thoughtful approach is that of Wietse de Boer, who focuses on Milan. See Wietse de Boer, *The Conquest of the Soul: Confession, Discipline, and Public Order in Counter-Reformation Milan* (Leiden: E. J. Brill, 2001), 84–125. For developments north of the Alps, see Myers, *"Poor, Sinning Folk,"* 131–143. Both authors agree that the original impetus behind the development was traditional in nature.

37. De Boer's *The Conquest of the Soul* strongly emphasizes this traditional function as Borromeo's intention (90–96). Myers makes a similar point, but stresses the

innovative elements of Borromeo's design. Both historians see a determination to enforce appropriately decorous behavior as important to the creation and use of confessionals.

38. Myers, *"Poor, Sinning Folk,"* 137–142.

39. Robin Briggs, "Sins of the People," in his *Communities of Belief* (Oxford: Oxford University Press), 323.

40. On this subject, see Myers, *"Poor, Sinning Folk,"* 139–140.

41. Schroeder, *Trent*, sess. 14, ch. 4, 92.

42. Ibid.

43. Bernhard Poschmann, *Penance and the Anointing of the Sick*, trans. and rev. Francis Courtney (New York: Herder and Herder, 1964), 204. Poschmann notes that this insistence led to continued papal censure of Jansenist propositions.

44. Blaise Pascal, *Provincial Letters*, trans. A. J. Krailsheimer (Baltimore: Penguin, 1967), 158–159.

45. Ibid., 162.

46. Among the propositions of Pasquier Quesnel (d. 1719) condemned by Clement XI in 1713 is the claim that "Fear restrains nothing but the hand, but the heart is addicted to the sin as long as it is not guided by a love of justice." Henricus Denzinger, *Enchiridion symbolorum*, translated by Roy Deferrari as *The Sources of Catholic Dogma* (St. Louis, Mo.: Herder, 1957), no. 1411, 351. See also Paul F. Palmer, "Attrition and Attritionism," in *New Catholic Encyclopedia*, 2nd ed., vol. 1, 1032–1033. In 1786, the decree of the Reform Synod of Pistoia, 94, demanded that even within the sacrament of penance, the "fervor of charity" must be evident. Herbert Vorgrimler, *Buße und Krankensalbung* (Freiburg: Herder, 1978), 190.

47. Vorgrimler, *Buße und Krankensalbung*, 190–191.

48. Schroeder, *Trent*, sess. 14, ch. 6, 32.

49. Deferrari, *Sources of Catholic Dogma*, no. 1146, 322–323; Poschmann, *Penance and Anointing*, 207.

50. Poschmann, *Penance and Anointing*, 206.

51. Ibid., 207.

52. De Boer, *Conquest of the Soul*, 43–45.

53. Johann Loserth, *Akten und Korrespondenzen zur Geschichte der Gegenreformation in Innerosterreich unter Karl II und Ferdinand II*, 2 vols. (1898–1907), vol. 1, 616–617. See also Myers, *"Poor, Sinning Folk,"* 122; and Robert Bireley, *Religion and Politics in the Age of the Counterreformation: Emperor Ferdinand II, William Lamormaini, S.J., and the Formation of Imperial Policy* (Chapel Hill: University of North Carolina Press, 1981), 37.

54. Wietse de Boer, "Confession in Counter-Reformation Milan," in *Penitence in the Age of Reformations*, ed. Katharine Lualdi and Anne Thayer (Aldershot, U.K.: Ashgate, 2000), 123.

55. De Boer, *Conquest of the Soul*, 185–188.

56. De Boer, "Confession in Counter-Reformation Milan," 123–124.

57. Ibid., 122. This corresponded to the purpose of penance as described by the Council of Trent.

58. Ibid.

59. Ibid., 122–123.

60. See Myers, *"Poor, Sinning Folk,"* 159–160, 187–188. See also Louis Châtellier, *The Europe of the Devout: The Catholic Reformation and the Formation of a New Society,* trans. Jean Birrell (Cambridge: Cambridge University Press, 1989).

61. Jeremias Drexel, *Nicetas* (Munich, 1625).

62. Stephen Haliczer, *Sexuality in the Confessional: A Sacrament Profaned* (Oxford: Oxford University Press, 1996), 22–41.

63. De Boer, *Conquest of the Soul,* 328.

64. Ibid.

65. Myers, *"Poor, Sinning Folk,"* 96, 188–189.

66. Halizcer, *Sexuality in the Confessional,* 40.

67. See note 39 above.

68. Briggs, "Sins of the People," 325–326.

69. "The peasantry successfully resisted Borromeo's moral vision along with his confessional, asserting their own pragmatic styles of life and worship. What might in theory have been the greatest repressive movement in European history disintegrated before their largely mute tenacity." Briggs, "Sins of the People," 338.

70. John McManners, *Church and Society in Eighteenth-Century France,* vol. 2, *The Religion of the People and the Politics of Religion* (Oxford: Clarendon Press, 1998), 254–262.

71. Ibid., 253.

72. On Liguori, see the fascinating treatment by Jean Delumeau, *L'Aveu et le pardon: Les Difficultés de la confession XIII–XVIII siècle* (Paris: Fayard, 1990), 151–167.

73. Vorgrimler, *Buße und Krankensalbung,* 193.

74. Specifically, *Lamentabili* rejected the following assertions: "In the primitive Church the concept of the Christian sinner reconciled by the authority of the Church did not exist. Only very slowly did the Church accustom herself to this concept. As a matter of fact, even after Penance was recognized as an institution of the Church, it was not called a Sacrament since it would be held as a disgraceful Sacrament. The words of the Lord, 'Receive the Holy Spirit; whose sins you shall forgive, they are forgiven them; and whose sins you shall retain, they are retained' (John 20: 22–23), in no way refer to the Sacrament of Penance, in spite of how it pleased the Fathers of Trent to say." *Syllabus Condemning the Errors of the Modernists* (July 3, 1907), nos. 46, 47, http://www.papalencyclicals.net/Pius10/p10lamen.htm. See also Vorgrimler, *Buße und Krankensalbung,* 193.

75. For Rahner, "paenitentia interior" includes willingness to be reconciled to the Church (a traditional position, to be sure, in the sense that all true repentance entailed willingness to receive the sacrament, but in this formulation the sacrament also means reconciliation with the Church). For a succinct summary of Rahner's views on the subject, see Karl Rahner, "Penance," in *Sacramentum Mundi: An Encyclopedia of Theology,* ed. Karl Rahner et al. (New York: Herder and Herder, 1979), vol. 4, 385–399.

76. This follows the felicitous formulation in J. Dallen, "Contrition," in *New Catholic Encyclopedia,* 2nd ed., vol. 2, 71.

77. *Lumen gentium,* 11.

78. *Sacrosanctum concilium,* 27.

79. Ibid., 72.

80. Sacred Congregation for the Doctrine of the Faith, *Pastoral Norms Concern-*

ing the Administration of General Sacramental Absolution (1972), http://www
.papalencyclicals.net/Paul06/p6pastor.htm.

81. Code of Canon Law (1983), nos. 961–963, http://www.vatican.va/archive/
ENG1104/__P3F.HTM.

82. Regis A. Duffy, "Reconciliation," in The New Dictionary of Theology, ed. Joseph A. Komonchak, Mary Collins, and Dermot Lane (Wilmington, Del.: Michael
Glazer, 1987), 831.

83. Reconciliation and Penance. Post Synodal Apostolic Exhortation of John Paul II
on Reconciliation and Penance in the Mission of the Church Today (1984), part III, ch.
2.32.193, http://www.vatican.va/holy_father/john_paul_ii/apost_exhortations/
documents/hf_jp-ii_exh_02121984_reconciliatio-et-paenitentia_en.html.

84. Duffy, "Reconciliation," 831. For decline since 1950 in Germany, see note 1
above.

15

Responding to Religious Difference: Conciliar Perspectives

Jeannine Hill Fletcher

On the seventeenth day of June 1546, in their fifth session, the bishops at the Council of Trent declared, "Unless one is born again of water and of the Holy Spirit, he cannot enter into the kingdom of God." They affirmed that "there is no other name [than the name of Jesus Christ] under heaven given among people by which we must be saved," and asserted the contours of the Catholic faith, "without which it is impossible to please God."[1] Citing Scripture for each case, these statements narrowly construe the path to salvation. From the writings of Trent, it is easy to conclude that the Catholic response to religious difference was simply "extra ecclesiam nulla salus." Outside the Church, there is no salvation.

Nearly 420 years later and grounded in the same scriptural sources, the bishops who gathered at the Second Vatican Council voiced the matter differently. In the lines of their dogmatic constitutions they declared, "There are those who without any fault do not know anything about Christ or his church . . . these too can obtain eternal salvation."[2] And their pastoral constitutions affirmed that "Since Christ died for everyone, and since the ultimate calling of each of us comes from God and is therefore a universal one, we are obliged to hold that the Holy Spirit offers everyone the possibility of sharing in this paschal mystery in a manner known to God."[3] A measure of inclusiveness had leavened the bishops' presentation, for they were able to assert that the mystery of Jesus' salvation extends beyond the boundaries of the Catholic Church.

In looking at these excerpts from the two councils, it is clear that a shift occurred in the articulation of a Catholic position on religious differences. But why? What factors were in place that contributed to this change? A closer look at the specifics of each gathering will provide a background for considering these questions.

The Profession of Faith at Trent: *Extra Ecclesiam Nulla Salus*

While there are no formal documents on religious pluralism among the declarations of the Council of Trent, this does not mean that religious differences were not part of the horizon of understanding among Christians at the time. In fact, when the bishops of the Catholic Church gathered at Trent to defend the faith, Islam was a living presence in many parts of Europe. When the papal bull that convoked the council describes the encroachment of the "infidels" as punishment from God, it is this reality that the statement reflects. Pope Paul III wrote:

> Whilst we desired the commonwealth to be safe and protected
> against the arms and insidious designs of the infidels, yet, because
> of our transgressions and the guilt of us all, indeed, because of the
> wrath of God hanging over us by reason of our sins, Rhodes had
> been lost, Hungary ravaged, war by land and sea intended and
> planned against Italy, and against Austria and Illyria, since the Turk,
> our godless and ruthless enemy, was never at rest and looked upon
> our mutual enmities and dissensions as his fitting opportunity to
> carry out his designs with great success.[4]

The negative tone of the bull reflects the reality that responding to religious difference was also bound up with political concerns. Yet, the portrait of religious others as the "godless and ruthless enemy" makes it seem as though all Christians were necessarily distanced and antagonistic toward people of other faiths. Paul glosses over the more varied relationships that might have been the case. For example, centuries earlier Spanish Christians under Muslim rule participated in a vibrant society where they were allowed the freedom to practice their faith in contact and conversation with the traditions of Islam and Judaism. Furthermore, many key theological themes taken up in the treatises of Thomas Aquinas had been presented in direct conversation with the thought of Muslim intellectuals. Clearly, the faith perspectives of Judaism and Islam were within the theological constellations of Christians in the sixteenth century even though they were not the topic of discussion at Trent. Furthermore, it was very likely that not only the religions of Abraham may have been known to Christians in this time period. The explorations around the globe and systems of trade with the East meant that Buddhism, Hinduism, and Confucianism could also have been familiar to many Europeans of the day. Letters and logs of tradespersons and missionaries, like those of Francis Xavier, who followed the routes of Portuguese merchants, relayed commentaries on these diverse forms of faith for Christian Europe. Even the so-called discovery of the New World, although recent in time, had brought the awareness of diverse indigenous faiths into religious and political consciousness. Lawmakers such as Bartolomé de Las Casas urged Popes and princes to consider the dignity of the native peoples and defend their human rights.

Evidence that "New World" encounters with peoples of native faiths had reached the halls of the Vatican is available through writings such as *Sublimis Deus*. In this decree, the same Pope who convokes Trent defends the rights, liberty, and humanity of native peoples, "outside the faith though they be."[5] At the Council of Trent, the spirit of the times certainly included an awareness of the diversity of religions. It is clear, however, that religious differences outside the Christian faith were not the primary concern. The issue with religious difference was much closer to home. Yet, while defending the position of Roman Catholicism against intra-Christian disagreements of the Reformers, the bishops simultaneously outlined statements that could be taken as assessments of other faiths. As Francis Sullivan describes the situation: "Pope Pius VI, in his bull *Iniunctum Nobis*, also known as the Profession of Faith of the Council of Trent (1564), required Catholics to profess and hold 'this true Catholic faith, outside of which no one can be saved. . . . '"[6] Reading this statement in light of the diversity of religions, it appears that the response to religious difference at Trent was to reserve salvation for Catholic Christians exclusively.

Inclusivist Reflections at the Second Vatican Council

When the bishops of the Catholic Church gathered in 1962 to define the faith, they did so in a very different world. The trade systems of colonization had expanded to the patterns of globalization and the world had seemingly become a single place. There was an interconnected network not only of politics and economics, but also of communications and culture that brought religious difference into even greater awareness. The documents of Vatican II often reflect a self-conscious recognition of this reality. For example, the Declaration on the Church's Relation to Non-Christian Religions opens with the assertion, "In our age, when the human race is being daily brought closer together and contacts between the various nations are becoming more frequent, the church is giving closer attention to what is its relation to non-Christian religions."[7] The world since Trent had changed. The Church, too, had changed. Once the representative of European colonial presence in many parts of the world, Catholicism had become an indigenous reality in those same places. So, when the bishops gathered at Vatican II, they brought with them an increasing awareness of, and concern for, people of other faiths. Unlike the texts of Trent, the response to non-Christian religions was a central focus of conciliar pronouncements. Two documents stand out as significant attempts to respond to this reality of religious difference: the Declaration on the Church's Relation to Non-Christian Religions, *Nostra Aetate*, and the Declaration on Religious Freedom, *Dignitatis Humanae*.

The Declaration on the Church's Relation to Non-Christian Religions encourages a positive relationship with persons of the many faith traditions throughout the world, recognizing all people as members of a single human community. It describes the way in which all persons seek truth and meaning, and "expect from the different religions an answer to the obscure riddles of the human condition which today also, as in the past, profoundly disturb their hearts."[8] Hinduism, Buddhism, Islam, and Judaism, as well as indigenous faiths throughout the world, are directly addressed. The document boldly proclaims, "The Catholic Church rejects nothing of those things which are true and holy in these religions."[9] Taking a decidedly theological approach, the Declaration on the Church's Relation to Non-Christian Religions emphasizes the one God as creator of all humanity despite religious differences. Nevertheless, Council fathers also recognized the need for practical, even political, strategies that would enable the different traditions to coexist in the world. Again underscoring that this pressing need arises from a global interconnectedness, The Declaration on Religious Freedom lays the foundation for coexistence in religious freedom as a basic human right:

> For quite clearly all nations are daily becoming more united, people of different culture and religious belief are bound together by closer ties, and there is a growing awareness of the responsibility of each. To the end, therefore, that relations of peace and harmony may be established and deepened in the human race, it is essential that religious freedom be given adequate legal protection throughout the world, and that the supreme duties and rights of people in regard to the freedom of their religious life in society should be upheld.[10]

While these two documents stand out as direct addresses to the reality of religious pluralism, woven throughout the documents of Vatican II are additional references that reveal this concern for people of other faiths. The Dogmatic Constitution on Divine Revelation encourages the sharing of sacred Scripture with non-Christians; the Decree on the Apostolate of the Laity outlines the cooperation and collaboration between Christians and persons of other faiths; and section 16 of the Dogmatic Constitution on the Church describes how persons of other faiths can experience salvation.

Recognizing this wide concern for, and acceptance of, people of other faiths, it is clear that a shift had taken place between Trent and Vatican II. In contemporary terminology, the shift from exclusivism, in which persons of other faiths are excluded from salvation because salvation is an exclusively Christian reality, to inclusivism, where persons of other faiths are included in the saving work of Jesus Christ, is evident in comparing these conciliar statements. But the question remains: Why this shift? If we take a step back and look at history in its broad strokes, we might hypothesize an answer. This essay will argue five theses to explain the conditions that precipitated this change:

Thesis I: The discovery of the so-called New World
Thesis II: The development of a global Church
Thesis III: The turn to the subject
Thesis IV: A Church engaged in the world
Thesis V: The relationship between ecumenical and interreligious statements.

Thesis I: Discovery of the So-Called New World: From Colonization to Globalization

In his comprehensive study, *Salvation Outside the Church?: Tracing the History of the Catholic Response*, Francis Sullivan marks the discovery of the "New World" as a pivotal moment in the Christian response to religious difference. He writes:

> The conviction of medieval theologians that no one lacking Christian faith and baptism could be saved was conditioned by the fact that their world was practically coextensive with Christian Europe. Given the limits of their horizon, it is understandable that they could have presumed that anyone who was not Christian had heard enough about the faith to be guilty of having rejected it. . . . The medieval worldview was drastically altered with the discoveries of the fifteenth and sixteenth centuries. . . . Christian thinkers began to revise their understanding of the possibility of salvation for people "outside the church" in the light of this newly acquired knowledge.[11]

The moment in time was indeed an important one. Religious encounters like those of Las Casas and his companions shaped theological thinking of the Church; but this trajectory to the Americas was not the only site of encounter. The continued missions to the East, following the path of Xavier, forced a deepened theological reflection on the particulars of other faiths. For when missionaries such as Matteo Ricci and Roberto DiNobili had successes in planting the Gospel on Eastern soil, the interaction between Christianity and native religions raised questions that needed to be addressed by authorities back home. For example, when the rites controversy arose in Ricci's China, Vatican officials had to think theologically about whether or not the veneration of Confucius and one's ancestors constituted a threat to the Catholic faith for Chinese Christians. At this point in time, the response from Rome was still shaped by a Eurocentric understanding of the faith, and respect for these religious practices could not be fostered. Discovery and encounter in non-Christian lands did not fully affect the Church's thinking.

Yet, as missionary and colonial expansions increased in the eighteenth and nineteenth centuries, the information that flooded back to Europe from the far reaches of the globe developed into the study of non-Christian religions at universities. This brought an understanding of religious differences into easier reach, in a sense, allowing Europeans back home to discover the new worlds of religious difference for themselves. In the twentieth century, when world networks of globalization advanced the flow of immigrants to the West, accounting for religious differences became more than an intellectual activity. It was a lived reality. And so the "discovery of the New World" of the Americas was compounded by the discovery of the new worlds of other religions in scholarly writings and in real-life encounters. Such discoveries necessitated new theological reflections, and they were expressed at Vatican II.

Thesis II: The Becoming of a Global Church—The Third World and American Bishops

The shift indicated in this second thesis is a corollary to thesis I: with the discovery of the so-called New World the reality of the globe shifted from a universe bounded by the continents of Europe, Africa, and Asia to one that had more far-reaching boundaries. As the Church itself developed from colonization to globalization, its self-understanding as universal was also transformed.

The Eurocentrism of Trent is evident in the opening pages of its history as Pope Paul III's convocation is defined by the concerns of Europe. Even the selection of location, while situated especially with German Christians in mind, gives evidence of the limits of the catholicity, that is, universality, of the church: "Accordingly, we have chosen the city of Trent as that in which the ecumenical council is to be held . . . selecting that place as a convenient one in which the bishops and prelates from Germany and from the nations bordering Germany can assemble very easily and those from France, Spain and other more remote provinces without difficulty."[12] When Paul III sent out the invitation to Trent, he envisioned a central site that all Christendom could access. In calling together representatives from Christian nations, Paul was not concerned with the newly converted peoples of the Far East and the Americas. The issues on the table were decidedly rooted in Europe.

Pope John XXIII issued his call to a very different Church. The representative Catholic presence at the edge of Christendom in the days of Trent had grown into full-fledged Catholic communities by Vatican II. The global nature of the Church in the 1960s was embodied in the 2,600 delegates who came to the Council from diverse nations and cultures. These Council fathers came from 134 countries not only in Europe, but also in Africa, Asia, Central America, South America, Oceania, and North America as well. John XXIII announced, "The coming council by virtue of the number and variety of those who will participate in its meetings evidently will be the greatest of the councils held by the Church so far."[13] Two important shifts in the demographics make up Thesis II: the presence of non-European bishops and the large number of representatives from North America.

The concerns of Catholics represented by the bishops from non-Western countries were a significant part of the collective response to religious difference voiced at Vatican II. The distinctiveness of these concerns is rooted in the reality that these Christians lived not only in non-Western cultures, but in non-Christian ones as well. For these Catholics, what it meant to be "church" was to be engaged in a living dialogue with people of native faiths. The theological response to religious diversity was not only a theoretical and doctrinal issue, but a practical one as well.

The bishops of North America also created the response to religious difference from out of a practical and living context. With the second largest percentage of Council fathers (241 representatives, second to Italy's 430), these delegates drew on experiences parallel to those of Christians in non-Christian lands in their own type of minority experience. Guided by the insights of the American Jesuit John Courtney Murray, these bishops distinctly influenced the Declaration on Religious Freedom. While the Council's defense of individual religious freedom and the requisite social and political conditions grew out of the experience of American Catholics as a religious minority, it would have repercussions for non-Christian minorities in predominantly Christian lands. The experience of being the "religious other" shaped the Catholic response to religious others at Vatican II.

The Church at Vatican II was influenced by the experiences of Catholics from all parts of the globe, notably those Catholics in multireligious contexts outside of Europe. This is not to say, however, that the traditions of Europe did not continue to inform the response to religious difference. In one distinctive way, the tradition of Continental philosophy had a significant impact. The "turn-to-the-subject" that had come to dominate European philosophy and theology must be counted among the significant factors that shaped Vatican II's response to religious difference. This turn is the subject of thesis III.

Thesis III: The Turn to the Subject: Historical Consciousness and Religious Freedom

Simply put, the "turn-to-the-subject" is the outgrowth of the Enlightenment emphasis on individual reason and responsibility. By the time of Vatican II, mainstream theology had embraced philosophy's emphasis on the role of the human subject in understanding the world, and had extended this insight to recognize the human starting point for theology. As the Pastoral Constitution on the Church in the World of Today concurs, "Believers and unbelievers are almost at one in considering that everything on earth is to be referred to humanity as its centre and culmination."[14] Importantly, the principles articulated in the turn-to-the-subject were seen in harmony with the theological anthropology rooted in Christian Scripture. That is, humans had been endowed by God with free will and reason, and while created to use them to know God, they could not be coerced into doing so. This attention to the human subject carried with it a new recognition of the dynamic development of persons in new and changing historical situations. Thus, the turn-to-the-subject had an impact on the issue of religious pluralism in two distinct ways: by fostering the sense of the dignity of each human person and by underscoring his or her historical situation.

On the first point, it is evident that Vatican II embraced this concept of the dignity of the human person. In document after document, this idea is explicitly articulated and, with respect to different religions, even the Decree on Missionary Activity, *Ad Gentes*, sees mission work among non-Christians to be aimed at "fostering their dignity."[15] The humane recognition of individual dignity is understood theologically when the Pastoral Constitution on the Church in the Modern World asserts that "The outstanding feature of human dignity is that human beings have been called to communion with God."[16] It is this same firm defense of the dignity of each human person that undergirds the response to religious diversity in the Declaration on Religious Freedom. The document reads:

> It is in accordance with their dignity as persons, equipped with reason and free will and endowed with personal responsibility, all are impelled by their own nature and are bound by a moral obligation to seek truth, above all religious truth. They are further bound to hold to the truth once it is known and to regulate their whole lives by its demands. But people are able to meet this obligation only in ways that accord with their own nature, if they enjoy both psychological freedom and immunity from external coercion. Thus, the right to religious freedom is based on human nature itself, not on any merely personal attitude of mind.[17]

When the consistent ethic of human dignity intersects with historical consciousness, an awareness of how persons are distinctively shaped by their cultural and religious traditions further develops the positive response to diverse faiths. Recognizing that religions are associated with distinctive civilizations, the language of the Declaration on the Church's Relation to Non-Christian Religions brings to the foreground the reality that religious pursuits are not engaged in isolation, but influenced by societies into which persons are born.[18] Commitment to the dignity of the human person and recognition of historical consciousness support the document's defense of the individual's search for ultimate meaning, even when it is conditioned by a distinctive culture and its attendant religious tradition.

Thesis IV: A Church Engaged in the World

Embracing historical consciousness, the Church at Vatican II also embraced its particular historical moment by committing itself to engagement in the world. The self-understanding of the Church was not merely as a "depository for salvation," as Gustavo Gutierrez remarks, but as an active agent for the betterment of the world. Put succinctly, the church had a dual function: to develop citizens both of this world and of the world to come. In the words of John XXIII, "Our mortal life is to be ordered in such a way as to fulfill our duties as citizens of earth and of heaven. . . ."[19] Far from distancing itself from the lived situation of Christians and presenting itself on a higher plane than the world, the Catholic Church at Vatican II decisively committed itself to participation in the world. The Pastoral Constitution on the Church in the Modern World, *Gaudium et Spes*, announced with great clarity and unanimity the Church's concern for the world. The text opens, "The joys and hopes and the sorrows and anxieties of people today, especially those who are poor and afflicted, are also the joys and hopes, sorrows and anxieties of the disciples of Christ, and there is nothing truly human which does not also affect them."[20] And it continues, "Today particularly there is a pressing obligation on us to be a neighbour to every single individual and to take steps to serve each individual whom we encounter. . . ."[21]

If the Church at Vatican II decisively affirmed the obligation to "every single individual" and if those individuals encountered were increasingly of diverse religions, then dialogue and cooperation with persons of different faiths had to be understood as part of the Church's commitment to engagement in the world. Yet, the thesis here consists in more than merely seeing religious differences as a reality that Christians might encounter as an engaged Church. Rooting the Church in the transformation of the world also transformed the concept of "salvation." As Gutierrez underscores, documents such as the Pastoral Constitution on the Church in the World of Today (*Gaudium et Spes*) reflect a shift from salvation as primarily an otherworldly concern for Christians to recognizing the establishment of a world of justice as part of the salvific process. Gutierrez identifies the term "integral" as marking this shift. He writes, "*Integral vocation* (for example in *Gaudium et Spes*, n. 57; see also 10, 11, 59, 61, 64, 75, 91, and *Ad Gentes*, 8) and *integral development* (*Populorum Progressio*, 14) are expressions which tend to stress the unity of the call to salvation."[22] If the teachings of Vatican II lean toward understanding the salvific process as rooted in the transformation of the world, then salvation itself, in a sense, has been broadened beyond the boundaries of the Church. While not identical with the workings of the world, salvation is integrally rooted in them. As *Gaudium et Spes* articulates:

> Although earthly progress must be carefully distinguished from the growth of Christ's kingdom, nevertheless its capacity to contribute to a better ordering of human society makes it highly relevant to the kingdom of God. For the values of human dignity, of fellowship and of freedom, those valuable fruits of nature and of our own energy which we shall have produced here on earth in the Spirit of the Lord and in obedience to God's command, will all be cleansed from all disfigurement and be shining and transformed, to be regained by us when Christ hands over to the Father an eternal and universal kingdom. . . . Here on earth that kingdom is already mysteriously present; at the Lord's coming it will be consummated.[23]

As salvation becomes a process rooted in the world, it becomes one not limited to orthodox confession and Church membership, but encompasses the orthopraxis of right human relations. By the Church's extending itself to incorporate the world, its understanding of salvation is also expanded to include the orthopraxis of non-Christians.

Thesis V: Intra-Christian Concerns Impact Interreligious Statements

In the preceding four theses, there is a certain interrelation and logic. The Church first discovers a new world, becomes part of that new world, and takes a positive stance toward the world and individuals within it. My series of theses, however, is not yet complete, and the most obvious factor has yet been overlooked. That is, in the statements of Trent, the hard line toward differences within Christianity left little room for appreciating differences outside. By the writings of Vatican II, the rebuilding of ties with non-Catholic Christians provided the space for developing ties with people of non-Christian faiths.

The bishops of the Council of Trent needed to strictly pronounce the requirements for salvation vis-à-vis the emerging Protestant explanations. Strong statements narrowly defined the conditions for salvation through the vehicle of the Catholic Church. Reading these statements with the question of non-Christian religions in mind, all non-Catholics appear to be excluded from salvation. This pattern of using statements on intra-Christian diversity as a gauge for considering the non-Christian religions is an interpretive pattern that dates to the early centuries of the Church. Indeed, the statement *extra ecclesiam nulla salus* was itself originally intended as a pronouncement against groups within Christianity. Warning so-called schismatics and heretics of the dangers of defying centralized authorities, Cyprian, the third-century Bishop of Carthage, writes, "Let them not think that the way of salvation exists for them, if they have refused to obey the bishops and priests. . . . The proud and insolent are killed with the sword of the Spirit, when they are cast out from the Church. For they cannot live outside, since there is only one house of God, and there can be no salvation for anyone except in the Church."[24]

While Cyprian directed his charge against other Christians and not toward persons of other faiths, it became a central teaching more widely applied to anyone not associated with the Christian Church. With the documents of Trent, the pattern is repeated. Once the narrowness of salvation had been defined defensively against non-Catholic Christians (and the path had been further delineated through the specificity of the sacraments), it is difficult not to read these also as statements about the status of non-Christians.

If Trent attempted to define clearly the authoritative position of the Roman Catholic Church in order to create clear and distinct differences from the opinions of the Reformers, we might see the bishops of Vatican II as concerned with underscoring the similarities to repair the differences that had grown since 1542. As the Decree on Ecumenism articulates, "The restoration of unity among all Christians is one of the principal concerns of the second Vatican synod."[25] The efforts of reconciliation and unity among Christians might carry over to the relationship toward non-Christian faiths. John XXIII articulates a vision that encompasses such a broad range of unity:

> Indeed, if one considers well this same unity which Christ implored for His Church, it seems to shine, as it were, with a triple ray of beneficent supernal light: namely, the unity of Catholics among themselves, which must always be kept exemplary and most firm; the unity of prayers and ardent desires with which those Christians separated from this Apostolic See aspire to be united with us; and the unity in esteem and respect for the Catholic Church which animates those who follow non-Christian religions.[26]

That the unity of humankind was among the aims of Vatican II is clear. That the positive efforts toward that unity among Christians influenced an openness toward people of other faiths is a distinct possibility. The argument for this crossover effect is supported by the fact that the statement on non-Christian religions originated under the auspices of the Committee on Ecumenism. In its earliest form, the Declaration on the Church's Relation to Non-Christian Religions was developed as a section devoted to Jewish–Christian relations within the Decree on Ecumenism. When the committee decided to expand this section, the document was moved and later developed to include statements on the diversity of religions. Thus, the positive spirit of the Decree on Ecumenism may have infused the statement on Jewish–Christian relations and carried over into the Declaration on Non-Christian Religions. Whether or not this direct influence can be demonstrated, the absence of a hard line toward differences among Christians—in distinction to Trent—created one of the conditions for a positive stance toward differences among the religions.

Trent and the Seeds of Change

These five conditions, and arguably many others, came together to justify a shift in theological expression between Trent and Vatican II. Yet, while the articulations of the two councils appear quite distinctive and the contrast between exclusivism and inclusivism can be identified, the positive possibilities of Vatican II might also be recognized in germinal form at the time of Trent. This can be seen in three specific areas: the definition of Church, the possibilities for baptism, and the importance of works.

While Trent asserted the necessity of the Church for salvation, theologians of the day were also offering interpretations of "Church" itself that opened up a more inclusivist position. For example, Cardinal Robert Bellarmine identified the "body" of the Church as visible Christians (in attendance at Mass, for example). Yet, he argued for a distinction between this "body" and its "soul." For Bellarmine, the soul of the Church consisted in those who demonstrated the spiritual gifts that enliven the community. His distinction was made in order to insist that, while the collective group of baptized Christians could be identified as the Church, this was not necessarily identical or concurrent with being a member of its vivifying soul. What Bellarmine articulated near the time of Trent developed over the centuries as a way for theologians to explain salvation outside the Church. If the soul includes faith, hope, charity, grace, and the gifts of the Holy Spirit, then, Cardinal Gousset argued in 1848, "one can belong to the body [of the Church] without belonging to the soul; just as one can belong to the soul without belonging to the body of the Church."[27] Even as it restricted the door to salvation through the Catholic Church, the era of Trent provided windows to open more inclusive avenues of thought.

That the redefinition of the church took place outside the context of Trent does not mean that this was entirely at odds with the conditions of possibility for salvation defined at Trent. In fact, even in the documents of Trent there is evidence that salvation might be achieved by persons outside the Church. This evidence is found in the decrees on baptism and its use of a concept from Thomas Aquinas. In the *Summa Theologica*, Aquinas allows for the possibility of baptism to be effected not only by the direct participation in the sacrament, but also in anticipation of participation for those who desire it. He writes:

> The sacrament of baptism may be wanting to someone in reality but
> not in desire: For instance, when someone wishes to be baptized,
> but by some ill chance is overtaken by death before receiving bap-
> tism, such a person can obtain salvation without being actually bap-

tized, on account of the person's desire for baptism. This desire is
the outcome of faith that works through charity, whereby God,
whose power is not tied to visible sacraments, sanctifies a person in-
wardly (*ST* III, q. 68, a. 2).[28]

The distinction presented in the *Summa* develops into a tradition of recognizing persons as being part of the Church through baptism *in re* (in reality)
or *in voto* (in desire). As Jacques Dupuis explains, Aquinas also extended the
idea of baptism by desire to persons "who had not heard Christ announced to
them but whose desire to conform to the will of God afforded them the faith
and charity which justify."[29] In the statements at Trent, even while salvation is
being defined narrowly via the sacraments, the *in re–in voto* distinction is invoked. That is, canon 5 in the Decree on Baptism clearly states, "If anyone says
that baptism is optional, namely that it is not necessary for salvation: let him
be anathema."[30] Yet, the Decree on Justification expresses the idea that transition to the state of grace "cannot take place without the waters of rebirth *or
the desire for them*."[31] By using this language, Trent incorporates into the tradition the possibility of salvation for persons outside the faith. Dupuis concludes, "It is this doctrine of implicit *votum baptismi* [articulated by Aquinas]
that, in the new circumstances created by the discovery of the New World, later
theologians would develop on a broad scale . . . it would also be followed by
the Council of Trent, and through it would become received doctrine."[32] While
articulated in the era of "no salvation outside the Church," even the documents
of Trent allow for salvific possibilities outside the Church.

A third concept from Trent that flowers in the documents of Vatican II
and its response to religious differences is in the idea of orthopraxis indicated
earlier. This seed comes from the heart of the disagreement with Martin Luther.
While Luther insisted that faith alone justifies the sinner, Trent saw faith and
works as cooperating in human justification and salvation. In defense of works,
the Council declared: "Thus, to those who work well right to the end and keep
their trust in God, eternal life should be held out, both as a grace promised in
his mercy through Jesus Christ to the children of God, and as a reward to be
faithfully bestowed, on the promise of God himself, for their good works and
merits."[33] In arguing so vocally in defense of works as a mode toward salvation,
Council fathers laid the groundwork for the notion of salvation that emerges
more clearly at Vatican II. The emphasis on works shifts salvation from assent
to an external source of beliefs to the internal dictates of conscience that become manifest in actions. The flowering of the seed planted at Trent comes at
Vatican II in statements such as:

> There are those who without any fault do not know anything about
> Christ or his church, yet who search for God with a sincere heart
> and, under the influence of grace, try to put into effect the will of
> God as known to them through the dictate of conscience: these too

can obtain eternal salvation. Nor does divine Providence deny the helps that are necessary for salvation to those who, through no fault of their own, have not yet attained to the express recognition of God yet who strive, not without divine grace, to lead an upright life.[34]

The striving to "put into effect the will of God" and "to lead an upright life" develops the idea of works so clearly present at Trent. Orthopraxis opens salvation to all those of goodwill.

As Vatican II responds with a vivid openness to the diverse religious traditions of the world, it represents a change from the presentation at Trent. But at the same time, the councils stand in continuity. Both councils share the same scriptural sources—a site of undeniable continuity. But each interprets those sources with a different emphasis in light of changed conditions. Even beyond the interpretive continuity and change, Vatican II builds on the foundations laid more than 400 years before. At the social level, missionary explorations at the time of Trent serve as the foundation for the global Church that emerges at Vatican II. On the theological level, interpretive emphases at Trent open into the positive response to religious difference at Vatican II. Thus, although the response to religious difference is voiced in different language and communicated with distinct emphases, the position of Vatican II nevertheless stands in continuity with seeds of the faith planted at the time of Trent.

NOTES

1. "Decree Concerning Original Sin," in Norman P. Tanner, ed., *Decrees of the Ecumenical Councils*, vol. 2 (Washington, D.C.: Georgetown University Press, 1990), 667, 666, and 665.

2. "Dogmatic Constitution on the Church," 16, in ibid., 861.

3. "Pastoral Constitution on the Church in the Modern World," 22, in ibid., 1082.

4. "Bull of the Convocation of the Holy Ecumenical Council of Trent," in *The Canons and Decrees of the Council of Trent*, trans. H. J. Schroeder (Rockford, Ill.: Tan Books, 1978), 1.

5. Paul III, *Sublimis Deus*, as quoted in Bartolomé de las Casas, *The Only Way*, ed. Helen Rand Parish, trans. Francis Patrick Sullivan (New York: Paulist Press, 1991), 115.

6. Francis A. Sullivan, *Salvation Outside the Church? Tracing the History of the Catholic Response* (New York: Paulist Press, 1992), 6.

7. "Declaration on the Church's Relation to Non-Christian Religions," 1, in Tanner, *Decrees*, 968.

8. Ibid.

9. Ibid., 2, in Tanner, *Decrees*, 969.

10. "Declaration on Religious Freedom," 1, in ibid., 1010.

11. Sullivan, *Salvation Outside the Church?*, 63.

12. Bull of Convocation, Pope Paul III, in Schroeder, *Canons and Decrees of Trent*, 7.

13. Pope John XXIII as cited in *Council Daybook*, vol. 1, ed. Floyd Anderson (Washington: National Catholic Welfare Conference, 1965), 21.

14. "Pastoral Constitution on the Church in the World of Today," 12, in Tanner, *Decrees*, 1075.

15. "Decree on the Missionary Activity of the Church," 12, in ibid., 1021.

16. "Pastoral Constitution on the Church in the World of Today," 19, in ibid., 1079.

17. "Declaration on Religious Freedom," 2, in ibid., 1003.

18. "Declaration on the Church's Relation to Non-Christian Religions," 2, in ibid., 969.

19. Pope John's Opening Speech, in *The Documents of Vatican II*, ed. Walter M. Abbott, trans. Joseph Gallagher (New York: Guild Press, 1966), 714.

20. "Pastoral Constitution on the Church in the World of Today," 1, in Tanner, *Decrees*, 1069.

21. Ibid., 27, in Tanner, *Decrees*, 1085.

22. Gustavo Gutierrez, *A Theology of Liberation: History, Politics, and Salvation*, rev. ed., ed. and trans. Caridad Inda and John Eagleton (Maryknoll, N.Y.: Orbis, 1988), 45.

23. "Pastoral Constitution on the Church in the World of Today," 39, in Tanner, *Decrees*, 1093.

24. Cyprian of Carthage, *Epistle 4*, 4, in *Corpus Scriptorum Ecclesiasticorum Latinorum*, cited in Jacques Dupuis, *Toward a Christian Theology of Religious Pluralism* (Maryknoll, N.Y.: Orbis, 1997), 88.

25. "Decree on Ecumenism," 1, in Tanner, *Decrees*, 908.

26. Pope John's Opening Speech, in Abbott, *Documents of Vatican II*, 717.

27. Cardinal Gousset, *Théologie Dogmatique* (Paris, 1848), 497, as quoted in John J. King, *The Necessity of the Church for Salvation in Selected Theological Writings of the Past Century* (Washington, D.C.: Catholic University of America Press, 1960), 5.

28. Thomas Aquinas, *Summa Theologica*, as quoted in Dupuis, *Toward a Christian Theology*, 115–116.

29. Dupuis, *Toward a Christian Theology*, 116.

30. "First Decree [On the sacraments]," in Tanner, *Decrees*, 685.

31. "Decree on Justification," ch. 4, in Tanner, *Decrees*, 672. *Emphasis mine.*

32. Dupuis, *Toward a Christian Theology*, 116.

33. "Decree on Justification," ch. 16, in Tanner, *Decrees*, 678.

34. "Dogmatic Constitution on the Church," 16, in ibid., 861.

16

"Beset on Every Side": Reimagining the Ideology of the *Roman Catechism* (1566)

Robert J. Brancatelli

The catechism as a written genre dates back to the emergence of private confession in Europe during the early Middle Ages, when monks began composing lists of sins and their corresponding penances to help penitents in confession. By the eighth century, these lists were expanded to include basic Christian teachings such as the Apostles' Creed, the Ten Commandments, and the Lord's Prayer. During this time, the practice of yearly confession with a priest became the norm in England and France, and a spirituality of self-examination and individual piety developed throughout Europe.[1] With the invention of the printing press in the West in 1445, "catechisms" became available to the laity in a variety of forms, from prayer books and devotional guides to manuals on how to live a moral life and prepare for confession. By 1480, concern for the "perfect confession" can be found in the first printed German catechism, Dietrich Kolde's *A Fruitful Mirror* or *Small Handbook for Christians*, which showed "how one should live according to the will and the commandments of God" by renouncing "rotten, vile, stinking sins."[2]

Beyond concern for confession and personal morality, catechisms have been used to instruct the faithful and the clergy, and to systematize the ways in which the faith is handed on to the next generation. As early as 1357, *The Lay Folks' Catechism* attempted to raise the level of education among the clergy in England by instructing them in the Apostles' Creed, the Ten Commandments, the sacraments, the seven works of mercy, the seven virtues, and the seven deadly sins (i.e., the medieval *septenaria*).[3] In the preface to his small catechism of 1529, Martin Luther excoriated the "deplorable conditions" he found among the villagers of Saxony, who had "no knowledge whatever of Christian teaching" and lived "as if they were pigs and irrational beasts."[4] Reflecting Luther's law-gospel theology, *Der Kleine Katechismus* begins with the Ten Commandments and then presents the Apostles' Creed in three articles, the seven petitions of the Lord's Prayer, baptism, confession, and the "Sacrament of the Altar in the plain form in which the head of the family shall teach it to his household."[5] In 1566, three years after the final session of the Council of Trent, Pius V published the *Catechismus ex Decreto Concilii Tridentini ad Parochos*, or *Roman Catechism*, to stem abuses in preaching, liturgy, and catechesis on the part of the clergy and to help educate the laity.[6] It was also used to counter the influence of Protestant catechisms, particularly those of Luther and John Calvin, which by then were in widespread circulation.

A less obvious but perhaps more revealing use of catechisms can be found in a hermeneutical analysis of their texts in light of Paul Ricoeur's interpretive theory. By applying his concepts of ideology, distanciation, and appropriation, catechisms may be seen as ideological statements that reflect their authors' views not just of the *depositum fidei,* but also of the nature of the Church and the Church's relationship to the larger society. As ideological statements, they portray a world in which the Church's primary role is to defend itself from dissolution and attack. Historically, catechisms have been used in just this way to defend the Church against two specific threats: threats to its survival from without and threats to its structure from within. Thus, they often appear during periods when the Church feels besieged by forces bent on its destruction or the compromise of revealed truth. As the *Roman Catechism* reminded those who could read it, without "that great promise of our Savior, 'You are Peter and on this rock I will build my Church, and the powers of death shall not prevail against it' (Mt. 16:18), we would be filled with fear lest the Church of God should fall in these days beneath their efforts. For she is beset on every side."[7]

This chapter will examine the *Roman Catechism,* which is the Church's first universal *catechismus major,* or catechism designed for professional use rather than for those being catechized, as a response to these threats. First, it will review the historical development of the catechism and critique portions of its text according to Ricoeur's understanding of ideology and distanciation. Second, it will show how the catechism conveys an ideology in which the Church's primary role is to defend itself against threats to its survival and internal structure. Finally, it will suggest possibilities for appropriating or reimagining the catechism's defensive posture of Tridentinism in the context of the contemporary Church. It begins with an introduction to ideology and distanciation.

Ideology and Distanciation

Ricoeur's hermeneutic theory differs from Romanticism's quest for intelligibility as well as from Hans-Georg Gadamer's concept of a "historically effected consciousness" in which the reader dialogues with the text concerning its truth claims.[8] According to Gadamer, the reader suspends disbelief and engages the text without losing sight of his or her existential situation.[9] Ricoeur takes the opposite approach by freeing the text from the author's intention, the historical conditions surrounding it, and the audience for which it was written, so that the reader may appropriate it in ways that make sense to postmodern sensibilities. Rejecting structuralism, Ricoeur is not interested in meanings hidden "behind" the text, but in the possibilities that lie "in front of" it; that is, in a new "mode of being" beyond the text's explicit message and content, particularly when the content contains ideological distortions.[10]

Ricoeur views ideological distortions as the inevitable result of the two major functions of ideology, which are to interpret and to justify systems of authority among social groups. Within the interpretive function, an ideology emerges in "the distance that separates the social memory from an inaugural event which must nevertheless be repeated. Its role is not only to diffuse the conviction beyond the circle of founding fathers, so as to make it the creed of the entire group; its role is also to perpetuate the initial energy beyond the period of effervescence."[11] Whether the event is an actual occurrence, spoken discourse, or written text, memories of the event evolve, change, and adapt, eventually becoming the norm by which the event exists. Thus, an ideology creates a reality and then objectifies that reality through a symbol system that regulates thinking and behavior. It functions as "a grid or code for giving an overall view, not only of the group, but also of history and, ultimately, of the world."[12] Ideologies tend to be neither critical nor reflective, since they must justify their existence through the truth claims of their own interpretive codes.

The justificatory function of ideology is related to the need for legitimacy on the part of those who regulate the interpretive code.[13] An ideology must be perceived not merely as one interpretive code among many, but as the only legitimate way of being in the world. Accordingly, an ideology becomes "something *in which* men live and think, rather than a conception *that* they pose. In other words, an ideology is operative and not thematic. It operates behind our backs, rather than appearing as a theme before our eyes. We think from it rather than about it."[14] An ideology justifies existing systems of authority and the interests of hegemonic groups in society through the projection of a form of consciousness to which subordinate groups submit. Anything that does not fit into this consciousness is not only inconceivable but also nonexistent. This domination of one form of consciousness over all others constitutes *dissimu-*

lation, which is perhaps most apparent when a historical community is denied the capacity to make decisions and thus become a political reality.[15]

Despite Ricoeur's understanding of ideology as the temporal distance between an event and its recollection, he is more concerned with the distance created when an event, whether physical action or spoken discourse, is recorded as part of the effort to transmit its memory to future generations. This distance may be considerable, since "writing renders the text autonomous with respect to the intention of the author. What the text signifies no longer coincides with what the author meant; henceforth, textual meaning and psychological meaning have different destinies."[16] When oral discourse is written down, the world of the author and the world of the text split apart, and the text is freed from the inaugural event so that the reader may interpret it in a number of ways, which Ricoeur refers to as the text's "surplus of meaning."[17] Once free of the author's world, the text can be recontextualized in the reader's world in such a way that it is given new life, new meaning, and new possibilities for appropriation.[18]

Distanciation allows the reader to transcend the text by entering an alternative reality that, although based on the original text and context, "explodes" the meaning of both.[19] The reader discovers "another level, more fundamental than that attained by the descriptive, constative, didactic discourse which we call ordinary language."[20] However, engaging the "first-order reference" of a text (i.e., its language, content, and structure) is still necessary for arriving at this "second-order reference, which reaches the world not only at the level of manipulable objects, but at the level that Husserl designated by the expression *Lebenswelt* [life-world] and Heidegger by the expression 'being-in-the-world.' "[21] Thus, the possible worlds *projected* by the text and the text's actual language, content, and structure are not identical, and may even be in conflict when experienced by a new generation of readers. An example from the *Roman Catechism* will help illustrate this.

Despite the influence of reform-minded delegates at the Council of Trent who argued for "nothing less than a revolution in theological studies under the banner of humanism,"[22] the *Roman Catechism* maintains a scholastic approach to sacraments, emphasizing the correct matter, form, intention, minister, and effects of each sacrament, and, in the case of "Holy Orders," the distinction between jurisdiction and order. In Holy Orders, the text's first-order reference reflects a feudal view of church and civil society in which the laity occupies the lowest level of a hierarchical pyramid. This is clear in its portrayal of bishops and priests as "interpreters and messengers of God, commissioned in his name to teach men the divine law. They act in this world as the very person of God. It is evident that no office greater than theirs can be imagined. Rightly have they been called angels (Mal. 2:7), even gods (Ex. 22:28), holding as they do among us the very name and power of the living God."[23]

However, in addition to this sacerdotal or "external priesthood," the catechism describes an "internal priesthood" consisting of "all the baptized, and more particularly those in the state of sanctifying grace. These are all 'priests' in the sense that they are anointed by the Spirit of God, and are made living members of the High Priest, Christ Jesus. Through faith made alive by charity (Gal. 5:6), they offer spiritual sacrifices to God on the altar of their hearts. . . ."[24] Although "spiritual sacrifices" are not liturgical acts (Thomas Aquinas used the phrase to describe the "passive power" of the laity as opposed to the "active power" of the clergy), and the internal priesthood mimics the external one (baptism derives from the priesthood of Christ),[25] this text offers a new way of imagining the Church that explodes the world of Tridentinism. Its description of a "twofold priesthood" conveys a sense of equality that, for many postmodern readers, cannot be suppressed through dissimulation or an appeal to ecclesial authority. Interestingly, in the Second Vatican Council's Dogmatic Constitution on the Church, *Lumen Gentium* (1964), the faithful are referred to as a "priestly people" and a "royal priesthood" that participates with the priest in offering the Eucharist.[26] "Though they differ essentially and not only in degree, the common priesthood of the faithful and the ministerial or hierarchical priesthood are none the less ordered one to another; each in its own proper way shares in the one priesthood of Christ."[27] However, John Paul II's letter *Dominicae Cenae* (1980) returns to the Thomistic distinction between the sacramental offering of the priest *in persona Christi* and the "spiritual" offering of the assembly.[28]

Ricoeur's distanciation compensates for ideological distortions so that the text assumes a new mode of being, but in doing so, it substitutes one set of ideological, psychological, and cultural realities for another. For instance, applied to the *Roman Catechism*, distanciation replaces the worldview of Thomistic metaphysics and divinely instituted sacraments with ritual practice, community, and ecumenism, particularly when read from an American lay perspective. Nevertheless, such a substitution is legitimate only when it does not stray beyond the bounds of the first-order reference; that is, the text is not open to *any* interpretation but only to those that fall within its language, content, and structure.[29] "So while a text may allow several interpretations, it does not follow that all of these interpretations are of equal status; and the elimination of inferior interpretations is not an empirical matter of verification and proof, but a rational process of argumentation and debate."[30] Before the catechism can be appropriated in a new way, it is necessary to examine the ideological distortions of its first-order reference, which may be done by reviewing text and context.

Trent and the *Roman Catechism*

Although it was not until November 11, 1563, during the twenty-fourth session
of the Council of Trent, that the delegates approved a *catechismus major* in the
canon *Ut Fidelis*, interest in such an undertaking existed as early as the winter
of 1546.[31] At that time, a commission charged with investigating dogmatic and
disciplinary abuses of Scripture identified the poor quality of instruction being
given in cathedral churches, public schools, monasteries, and convents as a
major problem that needed to be addressed.[32] Among the proposed solutions
was a *methodus ad sacras litteras*, or a compendium of Catholic doctrine for
clergy, designed to be a "correct and organic exposition of Christian faith and
morality" and a resource for preaching.[33] The purpose of the *methodus* was to
deepen the theological formation of the secular clergy, which was often inferior
to that of the religious orders, thereby improving instruction of the laity.[34] In
addition to poor training, the Council had to deal with the fact that the quality
of preaching had been deteriorating for centuries as a result of changes in the
liturgy. By the fifth century, the transformation of the eucharistic liturgy from
a ritual meal of thanksgiving into a propitiatory sacrifice was nearly complete,
and the role of the presbyter had become purely cultic. By the Gregorian reform
of the eleventh century, "the majority of priests simply ceased to exercise the
ministry of the word at all—in general they would not have been capable of
doing so—and further they seemed to have almost no awareness of any responsibility to evangelize."[35]

As grave as this situation had become, there was another area of abuse
even more troubling. By April 1547, after the Council had moved temporarily
from Trent to Bologna because of the Smalcaldic War and an outbreak of ty-
phus, the debate had shifted to include sacraments, particularly baptism and
confirmation.[36] The delegates realized that any reform of preaching had to
include sacraments, because it was during the liturgy that most preaching and
instruction took place. In Bologna, they considered a catechism for pastors,
eventually rejecting proposals for the *methodus*, a *homilarium*, and a *catechismus
pro pueris et adultis indoctis erudiendis*, or a catechism for youth and uneducated
adults.[37] The delegates believed that existing works such as Aquinas's *Compendium*, Peter Lombard's *Sententiae*, and Desiderius Erasmus' *Enchiridion* already
provided the necessary resources for preaching and instruction.[38] However, it
was not until late 1563 that they proposed a catechism for clergy in order to
address abuses in the administration of sacraments and the doctrinal confusion that they felt had worsened since the early days of the Council. They
wanted a systematic presentation of doctrine that would set the standard for
liturgy, preaching, and catechetical instruction, to be written by the Council *ex
novo*.[39]

Nevertheless, the commission charged with writing the catechism did not have time to finish its work, but provided a draft to a postconciliar commission headed by Cardinal Guglielmo Sirleto, who was appointed by Pius V.[40] Several members of the earlier commission also worked on the new missal, the breviary, and the *Index Librorum Prohibitorum*, with the Dominican theologian Francisco Foreiro serving as secretary to the commission on the *Index*.[41] Despite such apparent orthodoxy, however, these men were Christian humanists and reformers in their own right. For instance, Leonardo Marini served as papal nuncio to Charles V and Phillip II of Spain between the second and third periods of the council; and Egidio Foscarari had attempted to explain Catholic doctrine by using empirical methods, and was imprisoned for heresy by the Inquisition in 1558.[42] These scholars had written a catechism that, although based on the language and conceptual categories of scholasticism, reflected Erasmian humanism and that movement's use of Scripture and the writings of the Church fathers.[43]

The catechism's ideology can be seen clearly in the first-order reference of the preface and of part two, on the sacraments, *De Sacramentis*. The preface notes that the purpose of the catechism is to instruct pastors in the care of souls, and that catechesis should remind the faithful that eternal life consists of knowing God and Jesus Christ.[44] "The next principle, closely connected with the preceding, is to urge upon them that their lives are not to be wasted in ease and indolence," and that they should guard against ignorance of Christian doctrine and the attacks of heretics.[45] Regarding the latter, the catechism leaves no doubt as to their danger:

> Those who desire to corrupt the minds of the faithful have been aware that they cannot contact each one personally to pour into their ears their erroneous doctrines. They have therefore adopted a different approach that disseminates unsound teaching more readily and extensively. They have composed heavy books to subvert the Catholic faith. But, since they contain open heresy, it is perhaps not so difficult to be on guard against them. The great danger comes from their innumerable smaller writings that disguise their errors under the appearance of piety. These deceive the simple and incautious with incredible ease.[46]

These "smaller writings" included the catechisms of Bucer (1534), Calvin (1536), the Church of England (1549), and Bern (1552), and the *Heidelberg Catechism* of the Dutch Reformed Church (1563). The preface explains that to refute these writings, pastors and catechists should hand on the *depositum fidei* in a way that emphasizes Scripture and tradition, considers the "cultural background and particular circumstances" of the faithful, and follows the ancient sequence of creed, sacraments, Decalogue, and Lord's Prayer.[47] These were believed to constitute the "four principal doctrinal headings" of the Christian faith given directly to the apostles by Jesus.[48] The catechism's authors hoped to show that this more authentic order gave the catechism an authority unrivaled by Protestant catechisms, which often began with the law and focused on humanity's "wretchedness."[49] According to the current edition, the *Roman Catechism* "rises above the Sixteenth Century to that level above time where witness of the Catholic Church to the Lordship of Jesus stands. This is the secret of its abiding relevance to catechesis, for this authentic and positive witness shares in the fact that 'Jesus Christ is the same today as he was yesterday and as he will be forever (Heb. 13:8)."[50]

This interpretation of the catechism as transcending history to arrive at doctrinal certitude over the "pestilence of erroneous teaching" constitutes a distortion within the interpretive and justificatory functions of ideology.[51] For example, the preface creates a reality in which the church is besieged by a "great and harmful evil" in the form of heretics who are "practiced in all the arts of Satan" and undermine the faith with their "ungodly" views of justification, sacraments, grace, and priesthood.[52] In response, the catechism demands a return to the authentic magisterium of the Church, justifying this demand by claiming the divine origin of Church teaching. Such justification is evident in *De Sacramentis*, which treats the sacraments as sacred realities instituted by Christ that "have their origin directly from God."[53] Throughout this section, divine institution serves as a way not only of situating the sacraments theologically but also of justifying the claim that Protestants "have gone astray from the path of the truth."[54] This appeal to divinity legitimizes the Church's worldview so that anything that does not conform to it is judged heretical. Thus, Protestant challenges to key doctrinal issues fall outside the boundaries of orthodox Christianity. How far outside is evident in Bartolomé Carranza's celebrated *Comentarios sobre el Catechismo Cristiano* (1558), in which the Archbishop of Toledo attributes Protestant teachings to the "spirit of darkness," the devil, who has called upon his subjects to spread false doctrine.[55]

These ideological distortions are embedded in the precise terminology, unambiguous definitions, and absolute logic of scholasticism. They also reflect what might be called "sacramental wretchedness," or unworthiness, in contrast to the ontological wretchedness of most Protestant catechisms. *De Sacramentis* encourages pastors to provide "frequent instruction in the sacraments" so that "the faithful will be able to approach these sacred realities more worthily and profitably, and priests will not break the divine injunction: 'Do not give dogs what is holy; and do not throw your pearls before swine' (Mt. 7:6)."[56] The text is clear about the need for the Church to defend itself against the threats of heresy from without and of dissipation from within, but dissimulation occurs as this approach becomes the sole way of interpreting historical events and Church teaching even as that teaching is refined through conciliar debate:

> For as the end held up to man as his final happiness is far above the
> reach of the human understanding, it was necessary that human

persons should receive knowledge of it from God himself. This knowledge is nothing else than the faith by which we give our unhesitating assent to whatever the authority of our Holy Mother the Church teaches us as revealed by Almighty God. For no person of faith can have doubt about those things which have God, who is truth itself, as their author (see Jn. 14:6).[57]

By handing on the *depositum fidei* in this way, the catechism also hands on, wittingly or not, these distortions, resulting in a rejection not only of the distortions but of the entire catechism and its teachings by many contemporary readers. In appropriating the catechism for the current Church, the task becomes one of discovering what Sandra Schneiders has called the "real referent of the text," while conveying the deposit of faith and attending to the "particular circumstances" of the faithful.[58]

"Appropriating" the *Roman Catechism*

Given the tone of the catechism in general and the language of the preface and *De Sacramentis* in particular, discovering the real referent might seem problematic, but the example cited earlier offers some insight. The text on Holy Orders was interpreted in a way that exploded its first-order reference and resonated with the more current view of the priesthood as expressed in Vatican Council II documents such as *Lumen Gentium*. As this occurred, the meaning of priesthood changed for the reader, and this change, presumably, transformed the reader's understanding of Church and self. According to Ricoeur, in genuine interpretation the reader breaks free of ideological distortions to create new meaning based on the real referent, while the referent, in turn, influences the reader and the reader's worldview. In the encounter between reader and referent, the reader undergoes a *metanoia* in which the false consciousness of the old self gives way to a new consciousness.[59] Not only does the meaning of the text change, but the "meaning" of the reader changes as well. For Ricoeur, appropriating a text is not simply a matter of applying the referent to one's immediate situation. Rather, it "is to receive an enlarged self from the apprehension of proposed worlds which are the genuine object of interpretation."[60] The self matures through discourse with the text's real meaning as the reader moves from explanation to understanding. The entire process may be said to consist of identifying distortions through first-order textual analysis, discovering the real referent, and appropriating the referent in a way that empowers the reader to overcome personal distortions.[61]

The catechism's real referent, which is found throughout the text, emerges with particular clarity in the section of *De sacramentis* on the propitiatory sacrifice of the Mass, which was a major point of contention between the Church and the Reformers. There, the Mass is described as

> not just a sacrifice of praise and thanksgiving; nor again is it mere commemoration of the Sacrifice of the Cross. Rather, it is also a sacrifice of propitiation, by which God is appeased and rendered propitious. This is the express teaching of the Council of Trent. If, therefore, with faith, purity and contrition, we offer in sacrifice this most holy victim, we shall undoubtedly "receive mercy [from God] and find grace to help in time of need" (Heb. 4:16). So acceptable to God is the sweet odor of this sacrifice that because of it he pardons our sins and gives us his grace. For thus the Church solemnly prays: "As often as the commemoration of this victim is celebrated, so often is effected the work of our salvation." Indeed, the infinite merits of the Cross are ours to be gained through this unbloody Sacrifice of the Mass.[62]

This description, based on the *Canones de Sacrificio Missae* (session 22), reflects a theology of atonement in which the faithful share in the remission of sins won for them by Christ on Calvary. The unique sacrifice of the cross (Heb. 9:24–28) is made available sacramentally (Matt. 26:26–29) to Christians through the priest's action in the Mass (*representatio*). In re-presenting the sacrifice of the cross, the Mass does not repeat the original sacrifice, but makes that inaugural event present to all Christians, living and dead, through the words of consecration. Modern scholarship has noted the relationship of this Tridentine doctrine, which is based on the medieval understanding of *sacramentum tantum–res et sacramentum–res tantum,* to a theology of symbol in which the reality symbolized becomes present in its outward expression. The Reformers objected to this concept of sacrifice, believing it undermined Christ's Passion and death on the cross and referring to it as an abomination (*Smalcaldian Articles*) and an accursed idolatry (*Heidelberg Catechism*).[63]

Following the interpretive process outlined above, it is obvious that in first identifying ideological distortions, the text proposes an understanding of the Mass as a propitiatory sacrifice in which the sins of humanity are pardoned through the sacrifice of the cross. It connects the sacrifice of the Mass to the sacrifice of the cross through the action of the priest, so that it cannot be said that the Mass is merely a *commemoratio* and not an efficacious symbol of Christ's Passion. To drive home the point, the canon upon which the text is derived declares anyone who teaches otherwise to be "anathema."[64] As a form of ideology, the doctrine of propitiatory sacrifice moves the inaugural event of crucifixion beyond the "circle of founding fathers" so that it becomes the "creed of the entire group," perpetuating its memory "beyond the period of effervescence."[65] Distortions occur as this doctrine becomes the only way of imagining the Mass as sacrifice.

Second, discovering the real referent of the text requires a closer examination of the final two lines. The "infinite merits" of the inaugural event are made available to Christians through an act of distanciation in which the Crucifixion projects an alternative reality outside of time and space. The original bloody sacrifice does not end with the death and resurrection of Christ; it assumes eschatological significance through the distanced, unbloody sacrifice of the Mass as described in the text. And this projected world of salvation becomes available to Christians every time the Mass is celebrated. "As often as the commemoration of this victim is celebrated, so often is effected the work of our salvation."

Third, by demonstrating the need for a perpetual oblation for the forgiveness of sins, the catechism shows the Mass to be a symbolic discourse in which the Crucifixion is distanced and then appropriated by contemporary Christians, who are transformed in the process. By pointing out the dynamic nature of the Mass, the real referent also shows the dynamic nature of faith in its written expression in the catechism. Through appropriation, the reader encounters a projected world of love and forgiveness in which neither sin nor death has the last word, and faith becomes a living, dynamic reality. In effect, the text breaks through the limitations of its own language and projects a reality that is closer than the scholastic world of the catechism to the *depositum fidei*. Ironically, in transcending language, content, and structure, this projected world fulfills the original purpose of the catechism, which was to bring Christians into communion with Christ. The self and community become enlarged by the experience of this communion, and both are transformed.

It is interesting to note that the catechism's treatment of propitiatory sacrifice makes use of *anamnesis* without explicitly mentioning it, even though one of the Council's aims was to provide a scriptural and patristic basis for Church doctrine. *Anamnesis* calls to mind the supper narratives of the New Testament, in which the Church connects cross and covenant through sacramental action.[66] It is a memorial that is not restricted to the inaugural event, since the event takes on a life of its own in the minds of those who remember. In this sense, *anamnesis* resembles appropriation, and it can be used to reimagine the *Roman Catechism* for the contemporary Church. Used in this way, the catechism's ideological distortions are overcome through the interpretive process and an understanding of *anamnesis* as the Church making present the risen Christ. Thus, the doctrine of propitiatory sacrifice serves as an example of how the rest of the catechism may be appropriated, and exemplifies in a unique way Ricoeur's interpretive theory.

Finally, discovering the real referent of a text—whether the text is considered sacred or merely historically valuable—may provide an answer to the question of how the faith can be conveyed while attending to the particular circumstances of the faithful. Ricoeur's appropriation has the potential to distill Church teaching in the context of the Christian community through the active engagement of its members. Thus, reimagining the *Roman Catechism* amounts to retrieving its claim to eternal truth, but for this community in this time.

Conclusion

This chapter has reviewed the historical development of the *Roman Catechism*, analyzing portions of its text according to Ricoeur's interpretive theory. It then demonstrated how the catechism conveys an ideology in which the Church's primary role is to defend itself against threats to its survival and internal structure. Finally, it proposed a way of reimagining the catechism based on a process of identifying its distortions, discovering the real referent, and then appropriating that referent for current readers. A possibility for further study and analysis consists in examining Church texts to see whether the *Roman Catechism* already exists in an appropriated form. Is there a document or text that actually reflects an appropriated version of the original 1566 catechism, and, if so, which one?

Interestingly, an examination of the only other *catechesimus major* for the Universal Church, the *Catechism of the Catholic Church* (1992), reveals the ideology of the *Roman Catechism*. This new catechism creates a world in which Catholics practice their faith and the norms by which that faith is sustained and justified. However, while the new catechism reflects the ideology of the old one, it is not an appropriated ideology but one that contains many of the ideological distortions of the sixteenth-century text. In introducing the catechism, John Paul II reminds readers that the duty of the Church "is to dedicate ourselves with an earnest will and without fear to the work which our era demands of us, thus pursuing the path which the Church has followed for 20 centuries."[67] It is not clear whether this path leads to something similar to Ricoeur's interpretive process, or the perpetuation of an inaugural event without its real meaning. Judging from the amount of commentary on the "old and the new" that appears in the catechism, the answer appears to be "both."[68]

An appropriated version of the *Roman Catechism* may exist in the documents of Vatican Council II, which Paul VI called "the great catechism of modern times."[69] These texts are able to convey the *depositum fidei* in a way that resonates with the hopes and aspirations of postmodern Christians, who face extraordinary challenges unlike those of the sixteenth century. It is this appropriated expression of faith that has allowed adults to live a mature relationship with Christ in an increasingly ecumenical, interreligious, and agnostic world. Rather than look for a catechism in the traditional sense of a text with "four principal doctrinal headings," the documents of Vatican II present an adult view of faith with all of the intellectual and cultural challenges that this implies. It is, in the end, an appropriated catechism that merits appreciation and further study.

NOTES

1. Josef Andreas Jungmann, *Handing on the Faith: A Manual of Catechetics* (New York: Herder and Herder, 1959), 14. Jungmann notes that a significant way "to promote religious training of the faithful during the whole of the Middle Ages was the Sacrament of Penance."

2. Denis Janz, *Three Reformation Catechisms: Catholic, Anabaptist, Lutheran*, Texts and Studies in Religion, 13 (New York: Edwin Mellen, 1982), 99.

3. Berard Marthaler, *The Catechism Yesterday and Today: The Evolution of a Genre* (Collegeville, Minn.: Liturgical Press, 1995), 13. Despite its title, "*The Lay Folks' Catechism* was not written primarily for the laity, but for the clergy. Parish priests were to instruct the faithful who in turn were to teach their children 'if thai any haue' (line 64)."

4. "Martin Luther's *Small Catechism* (1529)," in *Confessions and Catechisms of the Reformation*, ed. Mark Noll (Grand Rapids, Mich.: Baker Book House, 1991), 61–62.

5. Ibid., 75. Luther retained the classic catechesis derived from Augustine but changed its order to accommodate his view of justification (*Gebot–Glaube–Gebet*). See Janz, *Three Reformation Catechisms*, 18. For Luther, "Code must come first, and this reflects his view of the primary function of the law as that which heightens man's consciousness of his own sinfulness and the impossibility of fulfilling the law: the law, according to Luther, 'drives man to Christ.' This is followed by what Luther calls the 'remedy' for man once he has recognized his sinfulness, namely faith (i.e., creed), the center of which is Christ. Finally, Luther follows this with the means by which man appropriates the remedy offered in Christ, namely prayer and sacraments (i.e., cult)."

6. The official title is *Catechismus ex Decreto Concilii Tridentini ad Parochos, Pii V Pont. Max. Jussu Editus*. All quotes and references are from *The Roman Catechism, Translated and Annotated in Accord with Vatican II and Post-Conciliar Documents and the New Code of Canon Law*, trans. Robert Bradley and Eugene Kevane (Boston: St. Paul Editions, 1985). Hereafter *Roman Catechism*.

7. Ibid., 5.

8. See Sandra M. Schneiders, "Feminist Ideology Criticism and Biblical Hermeneutics," *Biblical Theology Bulletin* 19 (1989): 6. Ricoeur translates Gadamer's *wirkungsgeschichtliches Bewußtsein* as "consciousness exposed to the effects of history," in his *Hermeneutics and the Human Sciences: Essays on Language, Action, and Interpretation*, ed. and trans. John B. Thompson (New York: Cambridge University Press, 1981), 70. Hereafter *Hermeneutics and the Human Sciences*.

9. Hans-Georg Gadamer, *Truth and Method*, rev. ed., trans. Joel Weinsheimer and Donald Marshall (New York: Continuum, 1995), 305.

10. *Hermeneutics and the Human Sciences*, 93. For Ricoeur, "The most decisive break with Romantic hermeneutics is here; what is sought is no longer an intention hidden behind the text, but a world unfolded in front of it. The power of the text to open a dimension of reality implies in principle a recourse against any given reality and thereby the possibility of a critique of the real."

11. Ibid., 225.

12. Ibid., 226.

13. Ibid., 228. "To explain this phenomenon, I shall refer again to the well-known analyses of Max Weber concerning authority and domination. All authority, he observes, seeks to legitimate itself, and political systems are distinguished according to their type of legitimation. . . . I see therein an irreducible phenomenon of surplus-value, if by that we understand the excess of the demand for legitimation in relation to the offer of belief. Perhaps this is the real surplus-value: all authority demands more than our belief can bear in the double sense of supplying and supporting. Ideology asserts itself as the transmitter of surplus-value and, at the same time, as the justificatory system of domination."

14. Ibid., 227. Italics in original.

15. Ibid., 229.

16. Ibid., 139.

17. See Schneiders, "Feminist Ideology," 7.

18. *Hermeneutics and the Human Sciences*, 139.

19. Ibid. For Ricoeur's "forms" of distanciation, see John B. Thompson, *Critical Hermeneutics: A Study in the Thought of Paul Ricoeur and Jürgen Habermas* (Cambridge: Cambridge University Press, 1981), 52–53.

20. *Hermeneutics and the Human Sciences*, 141.

21. Ibid.

22. Hubert Jedin, *A History of the Council of Trent*, vol. 2, *The First Sessions at Trent 1545–47*, trans. Ernest Graf (St. Louis, Mo.: Herder, 1961), 104.

23. *Roman Catechism*, 308. "The power to consecrate and offer the Body and Blood of our Lord and the power to forgive sins—which is the power of their priesthood—is beyond all human comprehension. Nothing on earth can be compared with it."

24. Ibid., 319.

25. P. M. Gy, "Évangélisation au Moyen Âge," in *Humanisme et Foi Chrétienne*, ed. Charles Kannengiesser and Yves Marchasson (Paris: Beauchesne, 1976), 572, quoted in Louis-Marie Chauvet, *Symbol and Sacrament: A Sacramental Reinterpretation of Christian Existence*, trans. Patrick Madigan and Madeleine Beaumont (Collegeville, Minn.: Liturgical Press, 1995), 309, n. 34. Chauvet does "not deny that this kind of theology has something important to say about the difference between the baptismal priesthood and the 'ministerial priesthood.' But it says it in a way that mirrors, *justifies*, and reinforces the progressive nibbling away at the assembly's liturgical activity in favor of the clergy's, which the history of Eucharistic practices abundantly illustrates." Italics added.

26. *Lumen Gentium, AAS* 57 (1965): 14–15. For the English translation, see *Vatican Council II*, vol. 1, *The Conciliar and Post Conciliar Documents*, rev. ed., ed. Austin Flannery (Northport, N.Y.: Costello; Dublin: Dominican Publications, 1998), 361.

27. Ibid.

28. David Power, *The Sacrifice We Offer: The Tridentine Dogma and Its Reinterpretation* (New York: Crossroad, 1987), 21–26. Power believes that "the pope uses a distinction which is found in the Tridentine decree on the mass in a way that may go beyond the Council's usage."

29. Thompson, *Critical Hermeneutics*, 53.

30. Ibid.

31. Pedro Rodríguez and Raúl Lanzetti, *El Catecismo Romano: Fuentes e Historia del Texto y de la Redacción. Bases Críticas para el Estudio Teológico del Catecismo del Concilio de Trento 1566* (Pamplona: Ediciones Universidad de Navarra, 1982), 71. Hereafter *Catecismo Romano.* For more on the catechism, see Gerhard Bellinger, *Der Catechismus Romanus und die Reformation: Die Katechetische Antwort des Trienter Konzils auf die Haupt-Katechismen der Reformatoren* (Paderborn: Bonifacius, 1970); and Maurice Simon, *Un Catéchisme Universel pour l'Église Catholique du Concile de Trente à Nos Jours* (Leuven: Leuven University Press, 1992).

32. Simon, *Un Catéchisme Universel*, 11. "Le premier de ces nouveaux abus dénoncés concerne la manière dont se fait l'enseignement de la doctrine (*lectio sacrae scripturae*) dans les églises cathédrales, les collèges publics, les monastères et les couvents; il y a une telle négligence que le peuple chrétien n'est moins instruit dans aucune autre doctrine que dans la doctrine chrétienne, et que les enfants ne peuvent être instruits ni par leurs parents ni par leurs maîtres des réalités de la vie chrétienne qu'ils ont professées au baptême." See also Jedin, *History of the Council of Trent*, 99–124.

33. *Catecismo Romano*, 33. Translation by author.

34. Ibid., n. 14. See Jedin, *History of the Council of Trent*, 100–101.

35. Chauvet, *Symbol and Sacrament*, 309.

36. Jedin, *History of the Council of Trent*, 396–443.

37. *Catecismo Romano*, 34–38.

38. Ibid., 35.

39. Ibid., 126–128. See also *Roman Catechism*, 6, which states that there should be "one standard and prescribed rule for handing on the faith and for instructing the Christian people in all duties of the Catholic religion."

40. *Catecismo Romano*, 131, 117–118.

41. Ibid., 90.

42. Ibid., 95–100.

43. Ibid., 33. "Una gran preocupación de los redactors del Catecismo de Trento fué . . . la de exponer la doctrina de la Escritura según la interpretación de los Padres: sobre todo, en los puntos de controversia con los protestantes se observa una llamativa abundancia de citaciones patrísticas. Ya se comprende que la parte *de sacramentis* tiene que destacar a este respecto: se trataba ahí especialmente de demostrar la *antiquitas* de la doctrina católica, quedando descartada por ese solo hecho la innovación de los 'novatores' " (ibid., 199).

44. *Roman Catechism*, 7.

45. Ibid.

46. Ibid., 5–6.

47. Ibid., 8–10.

48. Ibid., 11. See *Catecismo Romano*, 128: "El Sínodo Tridentino vió con particular claridad lo que quería que fuese su Catecismo. . . . sobre todo, se tiene un diseño claro de la estructura general del Catecismo, configurada en torno a las cuatro piezas clásicas de la catequética de entonces. . . ."

49. "The Heidelberg Catechism (1563)," in Noll, *Confessions and Catechisms of the Reformation*, 137.

50. *Roman Catechism*, v, n. 7. For more on this view, see Bellinger, *Der Catechis-*

mus Romanus und Die Reformation, 16–19, 74; and Robert Bradley, *The Roman Catechism in the Catechetical Tradition of the Church: The Structure of the Roman Catechism as Illustrative of the "Classic Catechesis"* (Lanham, Md.: University Press of America, 1990).

51. *Roman Catechism*, 5: "There is no region however remote, no place however securely guarded, no corner of Christendom, which is secure from the infiltration of this pestilence of erroneous teaching."

52. Ibid., 5–6.

53. Ibid., 149.

54. Ibid., 5.

55. Bartolomé Carranza de Miranda, *Comentarios sobre el Catechismo Christiano*, vol. 1, ed. José Ignacio Tellechea Idígoras (Madrid: Biblioteca de Autores Cristianos, 1972), 119–120. "Pero agora el espíritu de la tinieblas, que es el diablo, ha levantado tantos ministros y siervos que destruyan toda la obra que hicieren los ministros de Cristo, que si todos los que somos de su bandera, cada uno en su lugar y oficio, no nos ponemos en la defensa y en resistir a estos enemigos de nuestra religión, veremos a mayores males y daños de los que antes padecía el pueblo por ignorancia: porque son tantos los herejes que se han levantado y cada día se levantan enseñando falsas doctrinas, que ya es menester salir todos a la defensa."

56. *Roman Catechism*, 145. A similar concern was expressed regarding the use of the vernacular in the liturgy. See Power, *The Sacrifice We Offer*, 97.

57. *Roman Catechism*, 15. Compare with the current *Catechism of the Catholic Church* (Washington, D.C.: United States Catholic Conference, 1994), nos. 84–87, in which the faithful are described as receiving "with docility the teachings and directives that their pastors give them in different forms" (no. 87).

58. Schneiders, "Feminist Ideology," 8. The real referent is "the truth claim of the text, what the text finally says about reality, what the text is actually about."

59. Ibid.

60. *Hermeneutics and the Human Sciences*, 182–183.

61. This process will be developed in detail elsewhere as part of the author's theory of transformative catechesis.

62. *Roman Catechism*, 253. Compare with Bellinger, *Der Katechismus Romanus und Die Reformation*, 200–201.

63. *The Church's Confession of Faith: A Catholic Catechism for Adults*, trans. Stephen Wentworth Arndt, ed. Mark Jordan (San Francisco: Ignatius Press, 1987), 290.

64. Power, *The Sacrifice We Offer*, 191: "Si quis dixerit, in missa non esse sacrificium nec oblationem pro peccatis, sed tantum commemorationem sacrificii in cruce peracti, aut vocari translato nomine sacrificium, et vere et proprie non esse: anathema sit."

65. *Hermeneutics and the Human Sciences*, 225.

66. Power, *The Sacrifice We Offer*, 7.

67. John XXIII, Discourse at the Opening of the Second Vatican Ecumenical Council (October 11, 1962), *AAS* 54 (1962), 788–791, quoted in John Paul II, Apostolic Constitution, *Fidei Depositum* (October 11, 1992), *AAS* 86 (1994), 113.

68. See Berard Marthaler, ed., *Introducing the Catechism of the Catholic Church: Traditional Themes and Contemporary Issues* (New York: Paulist Press, 1994); Thomas

Reese, ed., *The Universal Catechism Reader: Reflections and Responses* (San Francisco: HarperCollins, 1990); and Michael Walsh, ed., *Commentary on the Catechism of the Catholic Church* (Collegeville, Minn.: Liturgical Press, 1994). As an example of appropriation, the new catechism treats liturgy as something more than a nonessential ritual. "Liturgy is not a pious corollary to the actual work of the Church. Rather, it is one of the principal ways in which she accomplishes that work, for all liturgy effectively symbolizes in an incipient way the reign of God." Regis Duffy, "The Sacramental Economy (Paragraphs 1066–1209)," in Walsh, *Commentary on the Catechism of the Catholic Church*, 236.

69. Berard Marthaler, "The Catechism Seen as a Whole," in Reese, *The Universal Catechism Reader*, 16.

17

Trent and Vatican II: Two Styles of Church

John W. O'Malley

The points of continuity and discontinuity between the Council of Trent and Vatican II are so numerous as almost to defy counting. If we are to understand the two councils, we need to lay out those points as copiously and carefully as we have tried to do in this volume. In the process, however, we must not allow ourselves to get lost amid the trees of the two forests and fail to keep in view the quite distinctive contours of the forests themselves. Trent and Vatican II dealt not only with different issues in quite dissimilar historical circumstances, or dealt with and/or avoided the same issues in the same or different ways. They were different cultural entities. In this regard, Vatican II was not only unlike Trent but unlike any council that preceded it.

We are dealing, in other words, with two significantly different models of council. True, within Catholicism the continuities almost always outweigh the discontinuities. But Trent and Vatican II, when viewed in the large, are emblematic of two fundamental, interrelated, but notably different traditions of the Western Church. Those traditions are the juridical or legislative-judicial and the poetic-rhetorical. They both have their origins in the Greco-Roman world of antiquity and antedate the advent of Christianity. Very early, however, they worked their way into the Christian fabric, and they have continued to color it into the present.[1]

The traditions express themselves most manifestly in distinctive styles of discourse. In so doing, they express and promote two styles of being Christian; two styles, therefore, of spirituality; and, thus, two styles of church. The poetic-rhetorical tradition provided the principles and the models that shaped the preaching and scriptural exegesis of the Fathers of the Church and, thereby, shaped the scope and ethos of Christian theology/spirituality down to the twelfth century, when it achieved another great flowering in such brilliant Cistercian abbots as St. Bernard and St. Ailred of Rielvaulx. It was then eclipsed by the scholastic tradition but was revived in the Renaissance by Erasmus and other humanists. Although still influential, it suffered another eclipse with the scholastic revival of the late sixteenth and seventeenth centuries. It again began to revive in the nineteenth, with Migne's monumental *Patrologia Graeca* and *Patrologia Latina* being the revival's most obvious and lasting monument. Forced again to the sidelines by Leo XIII's promotion of Thomism, it began again, as an aspect of the *nouvelle théologie*, to be cultivated by a few hardy souls. It emerged from the shadows at Vatican II, when, for the first time, a council adopted in a consistent and comprehensive way the poetic-rhetorical mode of discourse for its enactments.

The implications are great, but until now they have been little commented upon or appreciated. *The History of Vatican II*, edited by Giuseppe Alberigo, is as authoritative and comprehensive as we will probably ever have. It is a remarkable achievement. Yet, in the volumes published thus far, none of the authors comments on the style and literary genre of the documents, although those are the most immediately obvious ways Vatican II differs from previous councils. It is as if *Formgeschichte* and Form Criticism were hermeneutical instruments of use only to biblical scholars and were in no way pertinent to the interpretation of ecclesiastical documents.

Through the centuries, councils have made use of a range of literary genres. Practically all those genres, however, evince characteristics derived from the legislative-judicial traditions of discourse developed in the Roman Empire. These genres in large measure were or closely resembled laws or judicial sentences. It is perhaps not too far off the mark to postulate that the implicit model for the early synods and councils of the Church was the Roman Senate. Although that body had lost much of its authority by the time Constantine assumed a leadership role in the Church, it continued to legislate both in Rome and in its counterpart in Constantinople, where Constantine presided over it.

When Constantine convoked the Council of Nicaea, he held it there in his palace. He acted as a kind of honorary president of the assembly and intervened from time to time in the deliberations. A pattern was set. All the councils up through Nicaea II (787) were convoked by the Emperor or Empress. While assuring correct belief in the Church and appropriate behavior, especially of the clergy, were of course the fundamental concerns of the councils, these aims were not, and could not be, separated from the achievement of proper order in society.

The fundamental assumption governing councils from their very inception, therefore, was that they were legislative bodies that issued ordinances regarding doctrinal formulations and public behavior—regarding, that is, *fides et mores*. Such ordinances, meant primarily for the good of the Church, were, when appropriate, to be enforced by the secular authorities. To these ordinances were often attached penalties for those who failed to obey them. The very first canon of Nicaea imposed suspension on any cleric who castrated himself, and the second imposed the same penalty on any cleric convicted through the testimony of two or three witnesses of "some sin of sensuality."[2] The first canon of the next council, First Constantinople, anathematized all heresies, "in particular that of the Eunomians or Anomoeans, that of the Arians or Eudoxians, that of the Semi-Arians or Pneumatomachi, that of the Sabellians, that of the Marcellians, that of the Photinians and that of the Apollinarians."[3]

The Tridentine Style

Among the literary forms that councils would employ through the centuries were confessions of faith, historical narratives, bulls and letters, judicial sentences against ecclesiastical criminals, constitutions, and various kinds of "decrees." The principal form employed by Nicaea and by many subsequent councils, however, was the canon, usually a relatively short ordinance that often entailed punishment for failure to comply. It is a form that clearly manifests the assumption that a council is a legislative-judicial body. Although Trent indeed used other literary forms, especially the "chapters," which, for doctrinal issues, complemented the canons, its most characteristic genre was without doubt the latter.

"Canon" had multiple meanings in antiquity and in early Christianity, indicating, for instance, an authoritative list—as with the canon of Scripture. In its legal meaning, it referred to behavior, to exterior acts that conformed to or violated a norm. In ecclesiastical usage, the term implied that observance of the canons provided a sure criterion for behaving in accord with the way to salvation. According to some interpreters, Christians adopted this term to distinguish their laws from both the Mosaic and, especially, the civil law.[4]

"Canons," then, were in the first instance those enactments that looked to public discipline within the Church rather than to orthodoxy of belief. But usage in the councils was far from consistent, as is already clear from the example I cited from First Constantinople. Enactments concerning belief were often called "decrees" to distinguish them from canons, but "decree" was also applied to disciplinary decisions. In Trent, the disciplinary enactments were sometimes termed "decrees," sometimes "canons." But all the doctrinal condemnations were called canons. Trent issued some 130 doctrinal canons, an extraordinarily large number, and they all employed the same formula: "If anyone should . . . let him be anathema."

We need to note that even these dogmatic canons do not strike directly at what a person might believe or think, but at what he or she may "say" or "deny," thus at something that is observable, at something in the realm of behavior. Trent's many enactments concerning "reform" (*de reformatione*)—that is, concerning ecclesiastical discipline, whether called chapters or canons—did not follow the same formulaic wording as the doctrinal canons, but the same intent prevailed. That is, the chapters/canons either forbade certain practices and threatened with penalties, often financial, those who persisted in them, or they required a certain action to be performed and threatened with penalties those who did not comply. Like any good law, canons and their equivalents, whether dealing with doctrine or discipline, were formulated to be as unambiguous as possible. They draw clear lines. They speak a language that unmistakably distinguishes "who's in" and "who's out," which often entails not only meting out punishment for the latter but even considering them enemies.

As has often been noted since Vatican II, most councils were convoked because of some "clear and present danger" to the Church. There were exceptions, such as Lateran IV (1215) and, of course, Vatican II. For most of the time, councils were responding to a crisis, with the almost inevitable assumption that enemies were responsible for the dangerous situation in which the Church found itself. The language of the councils, of which the canon in a generally milder way would be emblematic, was sometimes vehement in its depiction of those who subverted the good of the Church, whether by bad belief or bad "customs." The language is agonistic, the language of battle against the foe. Julius II's decree at Fifth Lateran against the cardinals who attempted to depose him minced no words: "We condemn, reject and detest, with the approval of this same council, each and every thing done by those sons of perdition."[5] Paul III in his letter of May 22, 1542, convoking the Council of Trent, had surprisingly little to say about the "Lutherans" but kept recurring to the threat posed by the Turks, "our godless and ruthless enemy" and "our cruel and everlasting foe." The final result he hoped for from the Council was the strengthening of Christendom so that a successful war could be launched against the "attacks of barbarians and infidels whereby they seek the overthrow of all Christendom."[6]

At Trent, the call for a crusade against the Turks never made its way into the decrees, nor did it affect the deliberations in any significant way. Nonetheless, awareness of living in calamitous times appears at Trent in particularly intensified form.[7] For doctrinal questions, the enemies were of course the heretics, whose errors were disposed of in the canons. Those who held heretical or erroneous opinions were declared "out," *anathema*. If they wanted back "in," they had to renounce their error. The pronouncement against them was final, not open to discussion. As the Council stated on its very last day, December 4, 1563:

This has been a time of such disaster, and the malice of heretics so obdurate, that there is nothing they have not infected with error at the instigation of the enemy of the human race, even in what was clearest in our profession of faith or most certainly defined. Hence the holy council has mainly been concerned to condemn and anathematize the chief errors of the heretics of our age, and to hand on and teach the true catholic doctrine, according as it has now condemned, anathematized and taught.[8]

The doctrinal "chapters" were a somewhat different matter, for they were intended to provide material that could be used by preachers and teachers in a positive way.[9] Like the canons, they assiduously avoided taking sides in any dispute in which "Catholics" disagreed, that is, in disputes between theological schools such as Thomists and Scotists, Realists and Nominalists. The chapters on justification, hammered out during the first period of the Council, are different from subsequent ones in that for the most part they avoid the technical terms and categories of medieval scholasticism. They strive to express their points, insofar as possible, in scriptural language and are not without warmth or eloquence. In this regard, they manifest some characteristics of the poetic-rhetorical culture that in this early phase of the Council exerted more influence than it would later.[10]

The chapters and canons on the sacraments, which form the largest single body of the doctrinal decrees of Trent, derived more directly from scholastic speculation on sacraments from the thirteenth century forward, a framework that Protestants of almost all stripes had rejected and that would have to be much simplified and patiently explained to make it intelligible to persons in the pews of the churches. They also show another characteristic of the juridical tradition and of scholasticism: minimal awareness of the historical conditioning of norms, axioms, principles, and authoritative statements. This characteristic appears in intensified form at the Council of Trent because of Luther's claim that much of what the Church did and taught was the result of unwarranted accretions through the centuries and, in particular, that at least four of the seven sacraments fell into this category.

The Council felt compelled, therefore, to assert the unbroken and unchanged continuity of its teaching with the teaching of Christ and the apostles. Although Trent sometimes softened its language, as when it referred to the origins of indulgences and the practice of venerating saints, on questions of doctrine and sacramental practice it insisted, more forcefully than any previous council had, on the identity of the present with the apostolic age and on the unchanging nature of the intervening tradition. Thus the Council gave great impetus to the Catholic persuasion, which was taking on more considered shape in the sixteenth century, that the Church and its teaching sailed through the sea of history, buffeted by many storms but unchanged by the experience.[11]

Besides enemies of true doctrine, the Council had to deal with the prospect of enemies of "reform." These potential enemies were the papacy, the bishops themselves, and all those charged with the *cura animarum* who, it was feared, would resist the efforts of the Council to make them conform to the norms of law. Even today, historians continue to debate about how bad (or good) the religious situation was on the eve of the Reformation. More and more evidence is emerging to challenge the older view that the situation was almost uniformly rotten. In one area, however, it is clear that, if we take the canonical tradition as our norm, the situation was abusive. That area was the systemic disregard for the traditional provisions of canon law meant to assure effective pastoral practice on the part of bishops and others with the *cura animarum*.

Many bishops had obtained dispensations from residing in their dioceses, and sometimes dispensations that allowed them to collect the benefices from more than one diocese.[12] Pastors of parishes and others with the *cura animarum* often had similar dispensations, which were not obtainable except through some form of financial outlay. The situation was made possible through a network of dispensations from the canons that reached all the way back to the papacy itself. It was at this situation that the Council took aim. As Jedin maintains, the ultimate goal was to transform the bishops (and others) from collectors of benefices to shepherds of souls.[13]

The bishops at the Council found themselves unable to reform the papacy, but they could, despite the fear and resistance many of them felt, reform themselves. This meant reforming themselves where it hurt most—in their bank accounts. In this regard, the two most fundamental reforms were requiring residence and forbidding the holding more than one bishopric at a time. It is difficult for us to realize the dramatic redefinition of episcopal lifestyle that such decrees were perceived to entail and how deeply they were seen as cutting into the pocketbooks of many bishops. If there was a "moral miracle" at Trent, this was it. The Council then provided an agenda for bishops once they were back in their dioceses—holding regular synods with their clergy, visiting the parishes of the diocese, preaching on Sundays and feast days, and so forth. These elements were for the most part traditional, but they were now expressed in what, in retrospect, we can call a formal program. It was a program that looked to pastoral effectiveness.

Trent must therefore be considered a pastoral council. Its reform, or disciplinary, decrees, which make up about half of its enactments, were for the most part intended to promote better pastoral practices and looked directly to "the good of souls." To distinguish Trent from Vatican II as a doctrinal council from a pastoral one is to do an injustice to both of them. Both are doctrinal and both are pastoral, but they are doctrinal and pastoral in notably different modes or styles.

No realistic person at Trent believed that exhortation would make its ambitious pastoral program work. The patterns were too deeply embedded; the stakes, too high. To try to ensure compliance with its provisions, the Council had to put teeth into them through heavy sanctions, many of which were, as stated, monetary. This means that much of the so-called reform legislation of Trent reads almost like a penal code. Trent made no statement about inquisitions, but "surveillance and punishment," as Michel Foucault's famous title has it, seems to have been a leitmotif of the Council: "Do this or else!" In trying to replace one time-honored way of behaving with another presumed to be more pastorally apposite, the Council could hardly have proceeded otherwise. It had to "make them behave."

The enactments of Trent, then, both doctrinal and pastoral, when taken as a whole amount to a highly detailed code of conduct. That code looked to public order within the Church regarding both what one might say or deny and how one might behave. Who was to enforce it? The Council reminded bishops of their traditional rights and resources in that regard—suspension, excommunication, and so forth. But in its decree "Reception and Observance of the Council's Decrees" (December 4, 1563), it called upon secular rulers to do their duty by cooperating in the enforcement of the Council's enactments: "It now only remains [on this last day of the Council] to charge all princes in the Lord, as it now does, to give their help and not allow the decrees here made to be abused or violated by heretics, but to see that they are devoutly received and faithfully observed by them and by all."[14] We know that, in the "confessional age" after the Council, secular authorities did their part in enforcing the Tridentine decrees, especially when it was to their advantage to do so.[15] They needed the Church to shore up their authority, just as the Church needed them to shore up its authority.

Did the Council succeed in its reforming efforts? Not immediately, but in the long run the ideal of resident bishops and pastors imbued with the ideal of fulfilling their traditional duties prevailed, due in large measure to what the Council enacted and to what both ecclesiastical and secular authorities were able to enforce.[16] In this regard, we are today much indebted to Trent and to the sanctions it imposed. Trent succeeded where other efforts, especially from the time of the Council of Constance forward, had failed. The "hard rhetoric" of the Council, a rhetoric or style of discourse intent on closing loopholes and on enforcing conformity to the law, was the instrument that ultimately brought to pass at least part of what the Council hoped to achieve.

Trent, therefore, had a style of discourse. That style comprised two basic elements. The first was a literary genre—the canon or its equivalent. The second element was the vocabulary typical of the genre and appropriate to it. Every doctrinal canon ended with the word "anathema," a word of exclusion. Every doctrinal canon began with "If anyone should [dare] . . . ," a word of threat and intimidation. The disciplinary decrees/canons manifest similar characteristics, though not in such a formulaic way. All the canons and decrees, moreover, utilized language that avoided metaphor in order to avoid ambiguity. The canons looked to the enforcement of external behavior, and hence they did not employ words designed to win internal assent. Their wording implied a superior speaking to inferiors, for the canons are top-down pronouncements. They often assume that they are directed equivalently to an enemy.

This all sounds grim. It might also sound devoid of even the slightest concern for the spirit, a good case of the "letter killing." Even if, as I have argued, the bishops at Trent had no real alternative to intimidation in their reform decrees, the enactments still seem devoid of any spiritual dimension. I believe, however, that we must give the bishops, as well as this whole mode of discourse in the Council, a more generous assessment. The bishops, beyond being determined to assure proper order in the Church and better pastoral practice, surely hoped that bishops and priests, by behaving more in accord with the requirements of their office, would develop the inner sentiments appropriate to shepherds of souls. By forbidding people to say or deny certain things, they surely hoped that external conformity would express or lead to inner acceptance of proper belief. The enactments deal with the exterior but, insofar as they are inspired by Christian principles, they must be presumed to have some relationship to conversion of heart. They are intended, as Trent often explicitly reiterated, to lead to salvation.

Nevertheless, Trent's style of discourse expressed and promoted procedures in accord with a certain style. That means it expressed and promoted a certain style of how the Church itself "behaves." Despite the great achievements of the Council, inconceivable without the "language game" the council adopted, in the long run the Tridentine procedures reinforced "social disciplining" as an ecclesiastical style and promoted the image of the Church as a stern, exigent, and suspicious parent, concerned with the observance of predetermined patterns of behavior. The language projected the image, and the image promoted the reality and helped it to self-fulfill.

From Trent to Vatican II

In the nineteenth century, that reality expressed itself with increased insistence and prominence at the highest level in the style of papal pronouncements, such as Gregory XVI's *Mirari vos* (1832), Pius IX's *Syllabus of Errors* (1864), and, in the early twentieth century, Pius X's *Lamentabili* and *Pascendi* (1907). The language of these documents is the language of adversarial relationships. "We would have drowned," said Gregory, "as a result of the terrible conspiracy of impious men," so that we had "to restrain the great obstinacy of these men with the rod." The times are evil and threatening: "Depravity exults; science is impudent; liberty dissolute. The holiness of the sacred is despised . . . and errors of all kinds spread boldly."[17]

Errors Gregory especially denounced were freedom of the press, liberty of conscience, separation of church and state, and rebellion against monarchs. These are errors that were peculiarly "modern" since they derived most immediately from the Enlightenment and received their most effective expression in the battle cry of the French Revolution—"Liberty, Equality, Fraternity." The battle cry overthrew the old order. As monarchies toppled, so did their spouse, the Church. Convents were sacked, churches were desecrated, and the blood of priests and nuns ran in the streets. In the aftermath, the Church's battle against a new enemy, "the modern world," was thus launched. It was launched with a battle of words, with the development, employment, and deployment of a certain ecclesiastical style of discourse that revealed and promoted a particular style of thinking, feeling, and behaving—a style of being church.

When Vatican II opened, that style was in certain quarters still considered normative, at least for certain kinds of ecclesiastical statements. As is well known, the first serious clash at the Council between the so-called conservatives and liberals took place beginning on November 14, 1962, when Cardinal Alfredo Ottaviani and Monsignor Salvatore Garofalo introduced the schema then called "On the Sources of Revelation." The document, besides other traits of the legislative-judicial style, contained expressions such as "Let no one dare . . ." and "The church utterly condemns. . . ."

In their presentations of the schema, Ottaviani and Garofalo anticipated criticism and tried to forestall it. In this regard, it is significant that they felt compelled at such an early stage in the Council to address the question of style. Ottaviani said:

> I have heard that some are criticizing the schema because it is not
> written in the spirit and style of discourse of the new theology (nou-
> velle théologie) that has been in vogue among some theologians for
> thirty years. An Ecumenical Council, however, must make use of the
> spirit and style of discourse that the church has used through the
> centuries. . . . You need to be aware that the style of councils is con-
> cise, clear, brief, and is not the same as for sermons, or for some
> bishop's pastoral letter, or even for the encyclicals of the Supreme
> Pontiff. The style proper to a council is the style that has been sanc-
> tioned by the practice of the ages.

Garofalo made the same points in almost the same words, but added, "Nor can an Ecumenical Council surrender its duty and obligation to condemn errors, no matter what form such condemnation might take."[18]

The Council adopted, however, precisely the style that the two prelates considered inappropriate. As Ottaviani and Garofalo would quite correctly have seen it, the Council thus defied "the practice of the ages." It adopted the poetic-rhetorical tradition of discourse and virtually abandoned the legislative-judicial. This meant, negatively stated, that it put aside the literary form of the canon, which in turn meant that it abandoned the condemnatory tone of the schema cited above. Positively stated, this meant that the Council formulated its enactments in a different literary form, a form that in a generic way replicated the homilies of the patristic period, which in turn meant that it put its enactments into a vocabulary appropriate to the aim and ethos of the new form. As the form was new to councils, so was the vocabulary. The literary form and the vocabulary were the constitutive elements of the distinctive style of discourse of Vatican II.

The style of Vatican II, as is always the case, influenced content, just as the content of some of the decrees of Vatican II influenced the form. *Verba* and *res*—style and message—are inextricable in discourse. Style, sometimes misunderstood as merely an ornament of speech, an outer garment enclosing thought, is, rather, the ultimate conveyer of meaning. This is obviously true for poetry and great novels, but just as true for the texts we are considering. If we are to get at their deep reality, we must recognize their style as constitutive of them. For the councils as for individuals, style is the manifestation of their personalities. It is not merely the shell encasing their message. It is indistinguishable from the message, indistinguishable from the "teaching," from the "doctrine."

The Dramatic Shift in Style at Vatican II

The poetic-rhetorical tradition that took shape in fifth-century Athens was soon codified into an educational program that became normative in the ancient world. That program was fundamentally literary in the sense that poetry, drama, history, and rhetoric were its fundamentals. It claimed to educate men for an active life devoted to the good of their city and its citizens. Rhetoric, understood as the art of winning consensus and of uniting people to work for the common good, became the culminating discipline in the program. This was, then, an education to train leaders in society who could appeal to the goodwill of others to sacrifice themselves in a worthy cause. The leaders were concerned with contingencies—Is war required of us *now*? What are its possible outcomes? They had to argue, therefore, from probabilities to attain a solution not certain but more likely of success than its alternatives. Such leaders had to engage in dialogue, for they could not shun the negotiating table.

Everything rested, of course, on the power of such leaders to reach the hearts and souls of the persons they hoped to influence. This is one reason that poetry remained such a fundamental component in the program. In poetry, the reasons of the heart prevail, and those reasons are conveyed especially through image and metaphor. The ambiguity of image induces an appreciation for rich layers of meaning and the inexhaustible depth, reach, and even mystery of the poet's subject. This is a quality extraordinarily appropriate when the subject is a mystery such as God or the Church.

This was the *paideia* that formed the Fathers of the Church and that provided them with the principles and the models for their discourse.[19] The rhetoric, the "style," of Vatican II, fits into this tradition, a tradition venerable in the Church but never before adopted in such a consistent way for the enactments of a council. The Council took place, however, at a particular time and place, so that its adaptation of the style had quite specific characteristics.

From its origin in ancient Greece, the tradition had a noteworthy irenic bias because it had to smooth over differences to get people to work together. But sometimes this meant getting them to work together against an enemy. It could therefore be vehement against the foe. That is an aspect of the tradition almost entirely missing from Vatican II. This phenomenon opens up complex issues, but two factors certainly help explain it. The first is the actions of Pope John XXIII, especially his welcoming "the separated brethren" as observers at the Council and then the conciliatory message he delivered in his opening allocution. On the day he delivered it, October 11, the allocution seemingly did not have a big impact on the members of the Council, but that changed as the Council developed.[20] The key sentences are now familiar:

> Nowadays, however, the spouse of Christ prefers to make use of the medicine of mercy rather than that of severity. She considers that she meets the needs of the present day by demonstrating the validity of her teaching rather than by condemnations . . . [she] desires to show herself to be the loving mother of all, benign, patient, full of mercy and goodness toward the children separated from her.[21]

This gentle urging to avoid condemnations seemed almost to wag a finger at the many condemnations that the Holy See itself had issued, especially since the beginning of the nineteenth century, most of which were in some way or other directed against "modernity" in all its forms and guises. The relationship of the Church to "modernity" was thus intimately tied up with the "medicine of severity" and a rhetoric of reproach. The great cultural shift of the Council was in its replacing the hostile attitude toward "the modern world" with a more neutral one that was not afraid even to show appreciation. In this regard, too, the Council amplified upon hints dropped by John XXIII in his allocution, as when he praised "the marvelous progress of the discoveries of human genius" and his dismissal of "prophets of doom."

The Church in the middle of the twentieth century had enemies, among which, in the eyes of most people, Communism certainly held pride of place. The more pervasive and seditious enemy in eyes of certain churchmen, however, was modernity, which was a code word for the decline of civilization into irreligion and immorality that had been under way for centuries. In those eyes, Vatican II, like previous councils, yet contrary to what is usually said about it, faced a "clear and present danger."

A second factor helping to explain the irenic rhetoric, therefore, was the Council's reluctance openly to criticize earlier papal denunciations of the modern world. Its strategy was to reject them silently, as if they had never happened. This strategy was widely at work in the Council, for the issue of modernity is almost omnipresent in the documents, not simply in *Gaudium et Spes*. It is implied, in fact, in the very word *aggiornamento*. The strategy favored a new style of discourse, a "soft rhetoric," and the new style of discourse was appropriate to the strategy.[22]

Through these and other factors, the stage was set for a "new" style. That style was present in an inchoate form even in the first draft of the constitution on the liturgy, which in the earliest days of the Council was criticized for being too verbose and too "poetical and ascetical."[23] An important turning point, however, was on November 19, during the ongoing debate on "The Sources of Revelation." Bishop Émile Josef de Smedt of Bruges, an eloquent speaker, made an important intervention in which he directly challenged what Ottaviani and Garofalo maintained. He said that if the Church were to be effective in the modern world, and especially to communicate with those outside it, it would have to find a new way of communicating. Scholasticism would not do. The Church needed to speak in a new voice if it were to be heard. "What is needed is a biblical and patristic way of teaching."[24] Pope John XXIII's intervention two days later, withdrawing the original schema and ordering it to be revised by a mixed commission, can be seen in retrospect as another step setting the Council on the way to a different form of discourse. De Smedt spoke on behalf of the Secretariat for Promoting Christian Unity and advocated the style favored by the Secretariat, which now joined the Theological Commission for the revision of the decree.

Two weeks later, discussion on the schema on the Church began, and lasted for a week. During it, several bishops criticized its juridical language, but on the opening day, Bishop de Smedt again made a particularly powerful impression. He criticized the schema not only for being triumphalistic and too clerical but also for being too juridical.[25]

By this point, the Council seemed almost committed to adopting a new style of discourse. We are ill informed, however, about the precise steps that made that commitment firm and operative. In any case, models for a new style were at hand. It can hardly be coincidence that the chapter titles of Henri de Lubac's *Méditation sur l'Église* correlate in part with those into which *Lumen gentium* was divided. The *Méditation*, a product of *la nouvelle théologie*, was written in the poetic-rhetorical style of the Church Fathers. (The title of the English-language edition is *The Splendour of the Church*.)

No matter how little or how much de Lubac's book influenced the development of *Lumen Gentium*, the splendor of the Church could be taken almost as the leitmotif of the Council, a motif utterly appropriate for the specific literary genre within the poetic-rhetorical tradition that the Council adopted. The Council raised up before our eyes the Church—as well as Christ, God, and human dignity—to excite us to admiration and wonder. It thus engaged in a rhetoric of praise and congratulation. It engaged in panegyric, the "art of praise," a rhetorical genre well known and systematically analyzed from classical antiquity all the way up almost to the present.[26] The technical name of the genre is epideictic or demonstrative rhetoric, or oratory.

The purpose of the genre is to heighten appreciation for a person, an event, or an institution, and to excite to emulation of an ideal. Lincoln's Gettysburg Address is a secular example of the genre at its best.[27] In that speech Lincoln did not reproach the Confederates for their actions, nor did he try to prove that the war was just. He tried simply to raise appreciation for what was at stake and, at least by implication, to praise it as noble and worthy of the great cost. He wanted to touch the affect of the members of his audience by holding up for admiration high ideals, whose attractiveness would motivate them to strive to achieve them. He employed a rhetoric of invitation.

The documents of Vatican II fit into this mold. That is their "style." They hold up ideals or images for admiration. They then draw conclusions from them and spell out consequences, as with the decree on bishops, in which bishops' responsibilities are laid out clearly. The responsibilities are laid out, however, not as a code of conduct to be enforced but as ideals to be striven for, with the understanding that they are to be adapted to times and circumstances. A specific type within the epideictic genre was the "mirror" literature, that is, a delineation of idealized types, as in Erasmus's treatise "On the Christian Prince." *Christus Dominus* is a "mirror," a portrait of the ideal bishop. It holds up for admiration and emulation a noble and attractive ideal. Embedded and implicit in the Tridentine decrees concerning bishops was an ideal, of course, but the medium in which it was expressed was largely negative.

The epideictic genre as part of the rhetorical tradition is a form of the art of persuasion, and thus of reconciliation. While its primary purpose is to raise appreciation, it creates or fosters among those it addresses a realization that they all share—or should share—the same ideals, and need to work together to achieve them. This genre reminds people of what they have in common rather than of what might divide them, and the reminder motivates them to cooperate on enterprises more important than their divisions.

To engage in persuasion is to some extent to put oneself on the same level as those being persuaded. Persuaders do not command from on high. Otherwise, they would not be persuading but forcing. Persuasion works from the inside out. In order to persuade, moreover, persuaders need to establish an identity between themselves and their audience, and to make the latter understand that they share the same concerns—the same hopes and fears.

Those are some of the traits of the genre, and they characterize the discourse of Vatican II. The Council was about persuading and inviting. To attain that end, it used principally the epideictic genre. Of course, I am not saying that the bishops and theologians at Vatican II self-consciously adopted a specific genre of classical rhetoric, but I am saying that the documents of the Council, for whatever reason, fit that pattern and, therefore, need to be interpreted accordingly.

The most concrete manifestation of the character of the genre, and therefore the key to interpreting its import, is the vocabulary that it fosters and utilizes. Nowhere is that vocabulary more significant than in Vatican II, nowhere more a contrast with Trent, and nowhere more indicative of what the genre stands for and, therefore, of the style of church the Council promoted by means of it.

We must look, therefore, at words. What kinds of words, first of all, are absent? Notably missing are words of alienation, words of exclusion, words of enmity, words of threat or intimidation, words of surveillance and punishment. There are no verdicts of "guilty as charged." "Anathema," in use from Nicaea all the way up to and including Vatican I, does not appear a single time. Although the hierarchical character of the Church is sometimes stressed and the prerogatives of the Supreme Pontiff reiterated almost obsessively, the members of the Church are never described as subjects.

What kinds of words are present? Words new to council vocabulary. Some of them, of course, have occurred in previous councils because they are so central to the Christian tradition. But others are altogether new, and even the traditional ones had not occurred in the systemic way they occur in Vatican II. None of these words can be considered casual asides or mere window dressing. They are used far too insistently and characteristically for that. They do not occur as isolated instances here and there, but are an across-the-board phenomenon, appearing in all or almost all the documents of the Council. If one wishes to get at "the spirit" of Vatican II, they are the best indicators of what that "spirit" is. They make it possible for us to escape from the trap of proof-texting and to see patterns and overall orientation. They provide us with that much sought-after "horizon of interpretation."

I will analyze the words into categories, but the categories are imperfectly distinct from each other. They overlap and complement each other. They criss-cross back and forth, making the same or related points. Largely, therefore, they simply represent different perspectives on the same reality. They are all, moreover, consonant with the ethos and aim of the epideictic genre and with the wider poetic-rhetorical tradition, the tradition of the "art of persuasion." Genre and vocabulary taken together constitute and manifest a style of discourse, which almost by definition manifests the mentality, the approach, and the "heart" of the person thus speaking. In this instance, the person speaking is the Church.

One large category of the Council's vocabulary is made up of horizontal words—words such as "brothers and sisters" that stress and give color to the wide range of horizontal relationships characterizing the Church. They contrast with the vertical or from-the-top-down words typical of former councils and especially of the nineteenth-century papacy. The most widely invoked of such horizontal words after the Council and the one that remains best-known, despite its somewhat problematic implications, is "people of God." While top-down words are certainly not absent from Vatican II, so notable in chapter 3 of *Lumen Gentium*, they are balanced by the others or occasionally almost subordinated to the others, as in that same document, where chapter 2, on the "people," by deliberate design precedes chapter 3, on the hierarchy.

"People of God" also provides a good illustration of the intrinsic relationship between thought or content and "teaching" and style. "People of God" answers a "what question"—*What* is the Church? But at the same time, and especially in the context of the Council's genre, it answers a "how question"— *How* is the church, or, in other words, how is the Church's style? The answer is that its style (within certain limits, of course) is the style of equals dealing with equals or at least with persons in reciprocally beneficial relationships.

Among the horizontal words of the Council are, therefore, reciprocity words, such as "cooperation," "partnership," and "collaboration." The Council did more, however, than encourage an attitude of reciprocity. It promoted institutions of reciprocity, such as parish councils and bishops' synods. Perhaps most extraordinary in this regard are the bald statements in *Gaudium et Spes* (40, 44) that just as the world needs to learn from the Church, so the Church learns from the world—in this case, from the *modern* world!

In the horizontal-reciprocity category, the two most significant words, obviously, are "dialogue" and "collegiality." It sometimes seems that there is hardly a page in the Council documents on which "dialogue" or its equivalent does not occur. After the Council, the word was invoked so often as the solution to problems that one became almost ashamed to use it. That does not affect, however, its crucial role in the documents of Vatican II, a radical shift from the prophetic "I-say-unto-you" style that earlier prevailed. The Council's promotion of dialogue with Protestants, and thus Catholic participation in the ecumenical movement, marked a radical about-face from Pius XI's abhorrence at the suggestion that the Church might lower itself to deal with Protestants as "equals with an equal."[28]

"Collegiality," as we know, did not find its way into the Council's vocabulary without a fierce battle.[29] It cannot be dismissed, therefore, as a slip of the pen or a momentary aberration. Although it referred primarily to the relationship between the Pope and the bishops, it had wider repercussions as an expression of the general style of all relationships in the Church and of all the Church's relationships to those outside it. Collegiality is the corporate or institutional expression of dialogue.

Closely related to words of reciprocity are the friendship words. Most striking among these is the all-inclusive "human family" to whom *Gaudium et Spes* is addressed. Similarly related to reciprocity are the humility words, beginning with the description of the Church as "pilgrim." Among the redefinitions the Council effected, few are more striking than what it did with the triad of prophet, priest, and king. In some passages, prophet became partner in dialogue, priesthood was extended to all believers, and king was defined as servant.

The Church itself, *Gaudium et Spes* tells us, is in service to the world (3, 93). But the redefinition of the triad, which is adapted to bishops, priests, and laity in the documents respectively addressed to them, represents a crucial shift from a vocabulary of control words to a vocabulary of service words. The pastoral implications are immense. To serve effectively means to be in touch with the needs of those being served, not supplying them with prefabricated solutions and especially not supplying them with prefabricated solutions to problems they do not have.

The servant model is not, however, the model of inferior obeying superior. While final responsibility for decisions rests with the hierarchy, the Council does not envisage the servant-Christian as a passive implementer of orders from on high, but as an active participant in the great enterprise to which he or she was committed at baptism. The active participation of the whole congregation was the fundamental and explicit aim of the reform of the liturgy. If the way we pray is a norm for the way we believe, here we can take our style of prayer as a norm for the way we behave. Active engagement of everybody becomes constitutive of the style of the Church.

Even though the word "change" occurs in the first paragraph of *Sacrosanctum concilium*, the first document approved by the Council, the well-known Catholic allergy to it prevails elsewhere. A remarkable feature of the vocabulary of the Council, nonetheless, is its employment of words that in fact indicate change. I refer to words such as "developments," "progress," and "evolution." "Pilgrim church" and similar expressions can be included here. This is a break with the static framework of presentation of doctrine, discipline, and style of being of previous councils, especially of the Council of Trent. When John Courtney Murray said that "development of doctrine was *the* issue underlying all issues" at Vatican II, he put his finger on a great cultural shift that took place within the Council: its awareness that the "modern world" thinks historically and its realization that the Council somehow had to think and speak in a historically conscious style.[30] The classic posing of the development issue came of course from Newman, who not coincidentally had been trained in the poetic-rhetorical tradition.

The most familiar change word associated with Vatican II is the innocent-sounding *aggiornamento*. No doubt the word can be interpreted in a minimal and traditional sense, but when it is framed within the full context of the Council, it becomes one more indicator of a more historical, and therefore more relativized and open-ended, approach to issues and problems. What the approach implies is the inevitability of further change in the future, and it even suggests that the Council itself must be interpreted in an open-ended way. The Council, therefore, cannot be interpreted and implemented as if it said "thus far and no further."

The final category to which I will call attention is interiority words. "Joy and hope, grief and anguish"—these are the famous words opening the Constitution on the Church in the Modern World. The document goes on: for disciples of Christ, nothing that is human fails to find echo in their hearts. In their hearts? Yes, in their hearts. Joy, hope, grief, anguish—this is the language of the heart, not the language of the lawmaker or judge. It is language consonant with the poetic-rhetorical tradition, which is intent on persuasion, on winning inner consent and commitment. The whole sweep of the epideictic genre and of its vocabulary is directed to this goal, to a change of heart and mind or at least to a firmer commitment of heart and mind. In the Christian terms of the Council, as *Gaudium et Spes* (11) reminds us, this change of heart and mind, this firmer commitment, is done "under the impulse of the Holy Spirit."

Vatican II was about interiority. It was about holiness in a way and in a style different from previous councils. Perhaps the most remarkable aspect of *Lumen Gentium* is chapter 5, "The Call to Holiness." Holiness is what the Church is all about. An old truth, this, but no previous council had ever asserted it so forcefully and certainly had never developed it at such length. This is a call to something more than external conformity to enforceable codes of conduct. It is a call [*vocatio*] which, though it may have an external form, is related, as the document describes it, more immediately to the outpouring of the Spirit into the hearts of the faithful and to their free and willing commitment to service of others in the world.

In this regard *Dignitatis Humanae* and *Gaudium et Spes* are of critical importance with their emphasis on conscience as the ultimate factor in moral choice:

> Deep within their conscience individuals discover a law which they
> do not make for themselves but which they are bound to obey,
> whose voice, ever summoning them to love and do what is good and
> avoid what is evil, rings in their hearts when necessary with the
> command: Do this, keep away from that. For inscribed in their
> hearts by God human beings have a law whose observance is their
> dignity and in accordance with which they are to be judged.[31]

While Christians must take full and serious account of Church teachings and guidance, they must ultimately be guided by the inner law. This is another old truth, but the fact that its implications, as spelled out in *Dignitatis Humanae*, aroused such hostility in the Council indicates that it was a truth badly eclipsed and in need of restoration. Conscience is a preeminently interiority word. It provides an example, therefore, of how "teaching" and style are inseparable.

Was Trent not about holiness? It was. Its pastoral decrees looked to the spiritual good of those who fell within their scope. The same can be said of the other councils. They tried to create the situations "out there" that would allow the salvation and sanctification of Catholics to take place. Vatican II tried to do the same, but its most distinctive feature was its moving the primary point of reference from the exterior to the interior. Its "teachings" and its style of discourse convey the same message: of a style of being Christian, and therefore of a style of church that reflects that point of reference.

Perhaps that style can be summarized by a simple litany that indicates some of the elements in the change in style of the Church indicated by the Council's vocabulary: from commands to ideals, from passivity to activity, from ruling to serving, from vertical to horizontal, from exclusion to inclusion, from hostility to friendship, from static to changing, from prescriptive to principled, from retrospective to forward-looking, from definitive to open-ended, from threat to invitation, from behavior modification to conversion of heart, from the dictates of law to the dictates of conscience, from external conformity to the joyful pursuit of holiness. Every one of those phrases needs a thousand qualifications, but the litany as a whole conveys the sweep of the change in the style of church held up for our contemplation and actualization by the Second Vatican Council. This is the substantive teaching or doctrine of Vatican II. It is not an insignificant teaching or a merely "pastoral" recommendation. My style, after all, expresses what I am in my truest and deepest self.

In adopting a new style of discourse for its enactments, the Council thus effected a shift of momentous import, a few of whose ramifications I have tried to suggest. It is perhaps fitting to conclude with one the most radical of those ramifications. Vatican II was, indeed, unlike any council that preceded it. In fact, by adopting the style of discourse that it did, the Council in effect redefined what a council is. Vatican II did not take the Roman Senate as its implicit model. I find it difficult to pinpoint just what the implicit model was, but it was much closer to guide, partner, and friend than it was to lawmaker and judge.

NOTES

1. I describe this phenomenon in some detail in John W. O'Malley, *Four Cultures of the West* (Cambridge, Mass.: Harvard University Press, 2004). I explicitly treat Trent at 103–115, and Vatican II at 174–177.

2. See Norman P. Tanner, ed., *Decrees of the Ecumenical Councils*, 2 vols. (Washington, D.C.: Georgetown University Press, 1990), vol. 1, 6.

3. Ibid., 31.

4. See M. Lalmont, "Canon," in *Dictionnaire de Droit Canonique*, 7 vols. (Paris: Librairie Letouzey et Ané, 1935–1965), vol. 2, 1283–1288.

5. Tanner, *Decrees*, vol. 1, 597.

6. *The Canons and Decrees of the Council of Trent*, trans. H. J. Schroeder (Rockford, Ill.: Tan Books, 1978), 1, 2, 9.

7. See John W. O'Malley, "Reform, Historical Consciousness, and Vatican II's Aggiornamento," *Theological Studies* 32 (1971): 573–601, esp. 581. See also O'Malley, "Historical Thought and the Reform Crisis of the Early Sixteenth Century," *Theological Studies* 28 (1967): 531–548.

8. Tanner, *Decrees*, vol. 2, 798.

9. See Hubert Jedin, *A History of the Council of Trent*, trans. Ernest Graf, 2 vols. (London: Thomas Nelson and Sons, 1957–1961), vol. 2, 310.

10. See ibid., 104, 122–124.

11. See O'Malley, "Reform, Historical Consciousness," 581–583.

12. See, e.g., Barbara McClung Hallman, *Italian Cardinals, Reform, and the Church as Property* (Berkeley: University of California Press, 1985).

13. See, e.g., Hubert Jedin and Giuseppe Alberigo, *Il tipo ideale di vescovo secondo la Riforma Cattolica* (Brescia: Morcelliana, 1985).

14. Tanner, *Decrees*, vol. 2, 798.

15. This is a theme of the growing literature on "confessionalization." See, e.g., Wolfgang Reinhard, "Reformation, Counter-Reformation, and the Early Modern State: A Reassessment," *Catholic Historical Review* 75 (1989): 383–404. For an analysis of the category, see John W. O'Malley, *Trent and All That: Renaming Catholicism in the Early Modern Era* (Cambridge, Mass.: Harvard University Press, 2000), 106–117.

16. See, e.g., Joseph Bergin, *The Making of the French Episcopate, 1589–1661* (New Haven, Conn.: Yale University Press, 1996).

17. Gregory XVI, *Mirari Vos*, in *The Papal Encyclicals*, ed. Claudia Carlen, 5 vols. (Wilmington, N.C.: McGrath, 1981), vol. 1, 236.

18. For the condemnatory passages in the original document, see "Schema constitutionis dogmaticae de fontibus revelationis," in *Acta Synodalis Sacrosancti Concilii Oecumenici Vaticani Secundi* (Vatican City: Typis Polyglottis Vaticani, 1971), vol. 1, part 3:16, 17, 22, 25. For Ottaviani and Garofalo, see ibid., 27–32. The translations are mine.

19. See O'Malley, *Four Cultures of the West*, 127–149, as well as his "Erasmus and Vatican II: Interpreting the Council," in *Cristianesimo nella Storia: Saggi in onore di Giuseppe Alberigo*, ed. Alberto Meloni et al. (Bologna: Il Mulino, 1996), 195–211.

20. See Andrea Riccardi, "The Tumultuous Opening Days of the Council," in *History of Vatican II*, ed. Giuseppe Alberigo, 5 vols. (Maryknoll, N.Y.: Orbis, 1995–2005), vol. 2, 1–67, esp. 14–19.

21. Pope John XXIII, "Gaudet Mater Ecclesia," in *Council Daybook, Vatican II, Session 1–4*, ed. Floyd Anderson (Washington, D.C.: National Catholic Welfare Conference, 1965–1966), 25–29. For the Latin original, see "Summi pontificis allocutio," in *Acta . . . Vaticani Secundi* (1970), vol. 1, part 1: 166–175.

22. On the "soft" quality of the rhetoric, see John W. O'Malley, "Developments, Reforms, and Two Great Reformations: Towards a Historical Assessment of Vatican II," *Theological Studies*, 44 (1983): 373–406, esp. 395–398.

23. See Mathus Lamberights, "The Liturgy Debate," in Alberigo, *History*, vol. 2, 116.

24. This sentence is from Yves Congar's report on the speech, as quoted by Giuseppe Ruggieri, "The First Doctrinal Clash," in ibid., 259.

25. See Giuseppe Ruggieri, "Beyond an Ecclesiology of Polemics: The Debate on the Church," in ibid., 337.

26. See John W. O'Malley, *Praise and Blame in Renaissance Rome: Rhetoric, Doctrine, and Reform in the Sacred Orators of the Papal Court, c. 1450–1521* (Durham, N.C.: Duke University Press, 1979), for an analysis of the genre and case studies of the interrelationship between content and form.

27. The epideictic character of the speech is analyzed by Garry Wills, *Lincoln at Gettysburg: The Words that Remade America* (New York: Simon and Schuster, 1992).

28. Pius XI, *Mortalium Animos* (7), in Carlen, *Papal Encyclicals*, vol. 3, 315.

29. It was an ongoing point of debate in the Council, but see, e.g., Joseph Famerée, "Bishops and Dioceses and the Communications Media," in Alberigo, *History*, vol. 3, 149–152.

30. John Courtney Murray, "This Matter of Religious Freedom," *America* (January 9, 1965): 43 (his italics). See also O'Malley, "Reform, Historical Consciousness."

31. *Gaudium et Spes*, 16, translation from Tanner, *Decrees*, vol. 2, 1077.

18

Conclusion: A Clash of Ecclesiologies

Frederick J. Parrella

Trent and Vatican II: The Evidence

Theology, as Piet Schoonenberg reminded us almost a half century ago, "stands in history, not in eternity. Theologians who thought that they wrote for all times show, through that very fact, that they were historically conditioned. They belong to that stage of history in which [people] were not at all or not sufficiently aware of [their] own historicity."[1] The collection of articles in this volume has provided convincing evidence that Schoonenberg's insight is true. The preceding chapters on the two most significant councils of the second millennium of Christianity help us to grasp and understand the Church not as an eternal community with unchangeable teachings and rituals but as a historical and dynamic reality with a rich and vibrant theological tradition.

The contributors have demonstrated the extent to which history is an essential dimension of theology. Even formal doctrinal statements must evolve in their interpretations as times and contexts change. Karl Rahner tells us that faith that "clings to forms once effective but are now ineffective and meaningless" is faith that "will involve itself in its destruction."[2] From Trent in the sixteenth century to the Second Vatican Council in the twentieth century, philosophy, politics, and the emergence of the social sciences have deeply affected and transformed the Catholic tradition. During this period, the Church evolved from an institution cloven by the Protestant Reformers, struggling to reform itself after centuries of failed efforts, to a "world church,"[3] striving to engage modern secular thought, the emergence of the technological era, and the new multicultural world that followed two world wars.

As these essays reveal, Vatican II often "followed in the footsteps" of Trent—or, to use Barth's phrase, moved "forward from the footsteps of those Councils." Joseph Komonchak makes it clear that the documents of Vatican II often cite Trent's decrees in support of their own positions; in many ways, Trent was indeed *at* Vatican II. Had traditionalists at Vatican II, such as Cardinal Ottaviani, won the day, Vatican II might have resembled Trent much more than it actually did. Both Trent and Vatican II responded to the urgent need for change in the Church: *reform* at Trent during a period of crisis, and *renewal* at Vatican II in a time of the Church's growing irrelevance in the modern world. (Kenan Osborne, in his chapter on priestly formation, suggests that "reform" was a treasured word after Trent and "renewal" a more comfortable term for Catholics after Vatican II.) Both councils, in very different ways, rescued the Church at major moments of *kairos* in its history.

Underlying both councils were two very different and distinct types of ecclesiology. The first, which hardened into a system called Tridentinism, understood the Church as a *societas perfecta*, an institution in possession of changeless, divine truth in its doctrinal and moral proclamations. This Church stood solidly for centuries in a defensive mode against the modern world; it was in constant battle against the errors of the Protestant Reformers and such threats as Gallicanism, rationalism, Darwinism, Modernism, Communism, and secularism. This understanding of the Church was exemplified at Vatican I, where ecclesiology was reduced to a "hierarchology" (in Congar's oft-quoted term) and the laity were uninvited. In contrast, the second ecclesiology restored a biblical and historical approach to theological research and broke with the neoscholastic era; it opened the doors of the Church and admonished it to scrutinize "the signs of the times." It understood the Church as "the people of God" and the "sacrament of the world's salvation," and proclaimed that all its members are called to holiness. Even before the Council itself, the Church was described as the "meeting place of all mysteries,"[4] and theology itself became an "ecclesial science."[5]

Further substantiating Schoonenberg's claim, the theology that emerged at both councils, as well as the ecclesiological and ecclesiastical reform and renewal that followed them, had their roots in the preceding centuries. Before Trent, as the Introduction makes clear, efforts at reform, such as those of the Dominican Antonino Pierozzi and Cardinal Nicholas of Cusa, prepared the way for the reform of Church life and discipline at Trent. Likewise, the roots of Vatican II's understanding of the Church go back as far as the theology of Johann Adam Möhler in the first half of the nineteenth century and, ironically, to the words of those very theologians who prepared the schema for the *De ecclesia* of Vatican I.[6] After World War I, the foundation of Vatican II's theology and ecclesiology began in the biblical and patristic movements and the revival of the liturgy and liturgical theology.[7] When Paul III convoked the Council of Trent and John XXIII summoned Vatican II, the roots of reform and renewal had been firmly established prior to the councils.

Similarly, in the aftermath of both Trent and Vatican II, a time of theological fruitfulness and change took place. After Trent, authentic reform of ecclesiastical abuses was firmly set in motion. The formation of priests, described by Kenan Osborne, was unified in a system of seminaries under the bishop, where the *cura animarum* became the principal focus. A system of discipline confined bishops to their diocese and their work as pastors became primary. The *Roman Catechism* was promulgated in 1566 and, as Robert Brancatelli points out, reflected "the nature of church and the church's relationship to the larger society." In addition, by 1570, a new missal and breviary also were published. Giuseppe Alberigo persuasively shows how the struggle to implement the reforms promulgated by Trent was a long and difficult one. By 1590, major institutional changes were launched, changes that basically established Tridentine ecclesiology and an understanding of the Church that pre–Vatican II Catholics largely accepted as universal and normative. These changes, supported by Bellarmine's ecclesiology, encouraged a much greater Roman centralization of the governance and discipline of the Church. By the end of the sixteenth century, the reforms of the Council of Trent had evolved into the system Alberigo calls "Tridentinism," and which Congar describes as "an all-embracing system of theology, ethics, Christian behavior, religious practices, liturgy, organization and Roman centralization brought about by the reforms of the Council of Trent."[8] Alberigo's distinction between the reforms of Trent and the post-Tridentine legislation is crucial for understanding later ecclesiological developments.

Similarly, in the wake of Vatican II, a renewal of theology emerged, which in different forms continues into this new century. Unlike Trent, which was concerned with responding to the challenges posed by the Reformers and reforming the structure of Catholic life, theology after Vatican II was concerned with updating itself and adapting itself to an ecumenical and multicultural world. This theology began with explication of the documents of the Council and the implications of the Council for the life of the Church. Once again, ecclesiology was the primary focus. Not long after, however, questions about the extent and the limits of change in the Church developed, creating a polarization between some who thought that the changes of Vatican II had gone far enough or too far, and others who pushed for even greater changes in Church life. Such turbulence occurred, according to John O'Malley, not only because of the abruptness with which conciliar reforms took place but also because "no paradigms of reform were operative which were appropriate to the reality [the Church] began to experience."[9] Amid this tension, theology expanded its focus from ecclesiology with its related questions of authority, the papacy, collegiality, and the local Church, to Christology, Scripture, and social and political issues.

The contributors to this revival in theology are well known: Rahner, Congar, de Lubac, Schillebeeckx, Küng, Dulles, and McBrien, among others (including some of the distinguished contributors to this volume).

Although the work of reform and renewal before and after both Trent and Vatican II shares some similar formal patterns, the style and content of theology, both at the councils themselves and in their aftermath, were very different. John O'Malley draws attention to the fundamental differences in rhetorical styles of the two councils: from the juridical or legislative-judicial style of Trent to the poetic-rhetorical approach of Vatican II. These dissimilarities, it must be noted, are as much between Tridentinism and Vatican II as between the two councils themselves. Many of our contributors point out these dissimilarities in style and substance between the councils. Kenan Osborne observes that the two councils "reflect different ages and dissimilar worldviews, as well as changing foci and diverse goals." James Boyce describes the significant changes in liturgical music during the course of four centuries and accurately draws attention to the kinds of ecclesial self-understanding that support these ongoing developments. William Roberts evaluates the profound change in the theological interpretation of marriage in four centuries. Gerard Sloyan describes, with some justifiable regret, the loss of unity in worship and theology since the demise of Latin after Vatican II. Doris Gottemoeller portrays the history of religious women as a movement from enclosure and separation from the world to immersion in the Church's apostolic work. David Myers, in his examination of penance/reconciliation, suggests that the decline in the sacrament may well represent "the historical norm for Catholics rather than an anomaly . . . and the late medieval pattern of annual or intermittent confession . . . may very well prove to be the future of penance." In his treatment of the laity, Paul Lakeland argues that the ontological change at baptism is the foundation of a common priesthood of both the clergy and the laity; as he says, the layperson, not the ordained, is the "default Christian."

In her examination of religious pluralism, Jeannine Hill Fletcher affirms that "the position of Vatican II stands in continuity with seeds of the faith planted at the time of Trent," but she also acknowledges the "vivid openness to the diverse religious traditions of the world" that characterized Vatican II. In comparing and contrasting the *Roman Catechism* after Trent and the *Catechism of the Catholic Church*, Robert Brancatelli argues that the documents of Vatican II are, in the words of Paul VI, "the great catechism of modern times." Robert Daly, in his explication of the Eucharist after Trent, considers "the embarrassing dichotomy between the teaching of the contemporary official Roman magisterium and that of most contemporary liturgical theologians." He suggests the cause lies in "the magisterium's continued acceptance of some of the shortcomings of post-Tridentine Catholic eucharistic theology." The same pattern appears to hold in moral theology as well. James Keenan considers the tension between the twentieth-century revisionists—those who progressively abandoned the fixed and settled judgments of Tridentine morality in favor of a more person-centered approach—and the restorationists (primarily among the hierarchy and their theologians) who in the wake of the Council began to develop a method that "bears some analogous resemblance to the case summaries after Trent." Thus, both Daly and Keenan suggest that the Tridentine mentality still flourishes in parts of the Church. Finally, following Jedin's conviction that "Trent was not revised, but it was expanded" at Vatican II, Komonchak contends that at the twentieth-century Council, "the tradition was no longer read in the light of Trent; Trent was read in the light of the tradition." Thus, Trent and Tridentinism became historical events in the life of the Church rather than the transhistorical norm of all Church life and theology itself.

The End of Tridentinism?

Historical reconstruction (or deconstruction) is inevitable as new hermeneutical principles or new historical data emerge. Just as the contemporary Church has reevaluated the thought of Pelagius and Nestorius in a more favorable light, so it must continue to evaluate both the Council of Trent and the Tridentine system that followed it. As the Church explores new directions for the Church of the twenty-first century, it is vital to assess the achievements of Vatican II correctly and to determine to what extent Vatican II has departed from Tridentinism.

Of course, not every aspect of the Church's life can be examined in a single volume. One area of study not considered in this book that requires careful analysis is canon law. How has the self-understanding of the Church from the Tridentine system to the documents of Vatican II affected canon law as well as the context in which the law operates? While the chapter "Trent and Vatican II" considered in brief fashion the crucial question of Scripture and Tradition, a much fuller consideration of this topic is necessary in light of the ecumenical dialogue begun in the twentieth century. Likewise, the papacy itself needs more theological scrutiny. It was due to the special efforts of the papacy that the reforms of Trent were fully implemented at the local level, but the Chair of Peter itself assiduously avoided any reform of its own structure, consistently separating the office from any individual holding it. Especially in view of Vatican I's *De Summo Pontifice*, which granted the Pope universal jurisdiction over every bishop and diocese within the Church, the papacy, like the whole *ecclesia*, must submit to the norm of *semper reformanda*.[10] At the diocesan level, the juridical reforms of Trent must be reevaluated in light of the ecclesiology of Vatican II so that the values of the Gospel may better infuse institutional structures and give them greater credibility, especially in the wake of the recent sex abuse scandals both in the United States and in other parts of the world. A final and significant area of further study is the spiritual life of the Church after both councils. While the term "spirituality" was unknown at Trent, the Council had an enormous impact on the Christian life, sacramental practice, and personal devotion of the faithful. In the wake of Vatican II, when the term "spirituality" has become popular both within and outside of the Church, further study of the impact of the conciliar documents and their implementation on the devotional life of the faithful would help illumine our present, often perplexing, religious situation.[11]

While these areas for further consideration are *ad intra*, the unique perspective of Vatican II was to turn the church *ad extra*. Here, the situations of Trent and Vatican II are very different. After Trent, the expansion of the Church to the "New World," described by Anthony Stevens-Arroyo, was still far from creating a World Church, transcending the boundaries of its European roots. By way of contrast, the Church today is both *catholic* and *ecumenical*, in the original meanings of both words; with this changed reality come unprecedented challenges as well as opportunities. In an age described as "la revanche de Dieu,"[12] filled with neofundamentalisms on one side, and solipsistic post-modernity on the another, the Catholic Church is uniquely positioned to bring the gospel of peace, truth, love, and toleration to a hopeful but fearful human family at the beginning of the new millennium. In its doctrines, its rituals, and its communal life, it offers a religious substance through which the transcendent is visible and transformative in the lives of people who hunger for meaning. If the Tridentine system was concerned about orthodoxy in doctrine and practice, the post–Vatican II pilgrim Church is challenged to unite orthodoxy and orthopraxis in the service of God's Kingdom.

Was Yves Congar correct about the demise of Tridentinism? As Giuseppe Alberigo points out, since the end of the sixteenth century, the papacy encouraged the Church to view Trent as the normative word in matters of faith and discipline. The reform decrees of Trent, written by the Council to respond to the historical challenges of the Reformers and to reform the abuses of Church life and structure, developed into an efficient but rigid system. The documents of Vatican II, designed to renew the Church and to bring *aggiornamento* to its self-understanding and its relationship to the world of today, have recently led the Church into a turbulent theological polarization among three groups, some adhering to the spirit of the conciliar documents, others wishing to push reforms beyond what they explicitly said, and still others—in many cases the official magisterium—who embody a restorationist, or what might be called a "neo-Tridentine," attitude. Whether this last attitude will result in a kind of post–Vatican II version of Tridentinism, ultimately more faithful to Sixtus V than to John XXIII, remains to be seen.

The contributors and the editors of this volume suggest that the exact relationship between Trent and Vatican II, as well as Tridentinism and the post–Vatican II era, needs further exploration. Continued research and reevaluation are essential. Understanding the relationship between these councils is a critical task of theology at the present time, as the Church continues its mission to preach Christ, the light of the nations, to the people of this new millennium. As Anthony Stevens-Arroyo aptly remarks: the Church must continually "learn how to anticipate [its] future by revisiting its past."

NOTES

1. Piet Schoonenberg, *Man and Sin: A Theological View,* trans. Joseph Donceel (Notre Dame, Ind.: University of Notre Dame Press, 1965), 192.

2. Karl Rahner, *Belief Today,* trans. M. H. Heelan et al. (New York: Sheed and Ward, 1976), 52.

3. Karl Rahner, *Theological Investigations,* vol. 20, *Concern for the Church,* trans. Edward Quinn (New York: Crossroad, 1981), ch. 8.

4. Henri de Lubac, *The Splendour of the Church,* trans. Michael Mason (New York: Deus Books, 1962), 14.

5. See M. D. Chenu, "Theology as an Ecclesial Science," *Concilium* 21 (1967): 95–106.

6. For example, Clement Schräder proposed to define the Church as the mystical body of Christ in the first chapter. In his *De Ecclesia Christi,* written as early as the 1850s, Charles Passaglia suggested a new method and point of departure for a theology of the Church in which theology was grounded not in the laws of human society and natural law, but instead in biblical images and spiritual ideas from the Fathers. See Edward J. Gratsch, *Where Peter Is: A Survey of Ecclesiology* (New York: Alba House, 1975), 164.

7. Suffice it to mention these familiar names from the end of World War I to Vatican II: Romano Guardini, Karl Adam, Dom Odo Casel, Emile Mersch, Yves Congar, Henri de Lubac, Yves de Montscheuil, Otto Semmelroth, Edward Schillebeeckx, and Karl Rahner, among many others. See Avery Dulles, "A Half Century of Ecclesiology," *Theological Studies* 50 (1989): 419–442.

8. Yves Congar, *Fifty Years of Catholic Theology,* ed. Bernard Lauret (Philadelphia: Fortress Press, 1988), 3–4.

9. John O'Malley, *Tradition and Transition: Historical Perspectives on Vatican II* (Wilmington, Del.: Michael Glazier, 1989), 44. The literature here is very large. Besides the writings of the contributors themselves, see, for example, three works written within a decade after Vatican II: Avery Dulles, *The Resilient Church: The Necessity and Limits of Adaptation.* (Garden City, N.Y.: Doubleday, 1977); and Richard McBrien, *Do We Need the Church?* (New York: Harper & Row, 1969) and *The Remaking of the Church: An Agenda for Reform* (New York: Harper & Row, 1973).

10. See *Lumen Gentium,* 8; in Norman P. Tanner, ed., *The Decrees of the Ecumenical Councils,* 2 vols. (Washington, D.C.: Georgetown University Press, 1990), vol. 2, 856.

Index